# THE LITURGY DOCUMENTS
## A PARISH RESOURCE

# THE LITURGY DOCUMENTS
## A PARISH RESOURCE

Volume I

*Third Edition*

**LTP**

LITURGY
TRAINING
PUBLICATIONS

Printed in the United States of America

05 04 03 02 01 00 99 98    9 8 7 6 5

This book was edited by Elizabeth Hoffman, with assistance from Theresa Pincich, Lorraine Schmidt, Joan Salazar and Victoria M. Tufano. The Index was compiled by Elizabeth Hoffman. Ana Aguilar-Islas designed the book and Mark Hollopeter set the type. Cover design by Barb Rohm. Cover art © 1997 Romare Bearden Foundation/Licensed by VAGA, New York, NY, *Farewell Eugene.*

ISBN 0-929650-46-8
LDOC/R

# CONTENTS

# UNITED STATES BISHOPS' DOCUMENTS

# ABBREVIATIONS

Many texts listed here appear in *Documents on the Liturgy, 1963–1979: Conciliar, Papal and Curial Texts* (DOL) (Collegeville MN: The Liturgical Press, 1982).

AAS    *Acta Apostolicae Sedis*

AG    *Ad gentes*, Vatican Council II, *Decree on the Missionary Activity of the Church.* (DOL 17)

AP    Congregation for Divine Worship, instruction *Actio pastoralis.* (DOL 275)

Baptism    *Rite of Baptism for Children.* (DOL 295)

BCL    Bishops' Committee on the Liturgy

BCLN    *Bishops' Committee on the Liturgy Newsletter: 1965–1975* (Washington DC: United States Catholic Conference, 1977)

CCL    Code of Canon Law, 1983

CDW    Congregation for Divine Worship

CR    Congregation of Rites

CSDW    Congregation for the Sacraments and Divine Worship

CSL    *Constitution on the Sacred Liturgy (Sacrosanctum Concilium)*, Vatican Council II. (DOL 1)

CTr    John Paul II, apostolic exhortation *Catechesi tradendae.* (DOL 76)

DC    John Paul II, epistle *Dominicae Cenae*, 24 Feb 1980: AAS 72 (1980)

DMC    *Directory for Masses with Children.* (DOL 276)

DV    *Dei Verbum*, Vatican Council II, *Dogmatic Constitution on Divine Revelation.* (DOL 14)

EAW    *Environment and Art in Catholic Worship*

EM    Congregation of Rites, *Eucharisticum mysterium* (on Worship of the Eucharist). (DOL 179)

EN    Paul VI, apostolic exhortation *Evangelii nuntiandi.* (DOL 236)

GCD    *General Catechetical Directory*

GI    *General Instruction of the Roman Missal.* (DOL 208)

GIapp    Appendix to the *General Instruction* for the Dioceses of the United States

GNLY    *General Norms for the Liturgical Year and the Calendar.* (DOL 442)

ID    Congregation for the Sacraments and Divine Worship, instruction *Inaestimabile Donum*, 3 April 1980: AAS 72 (1980)

IOe    Congregation of Rites, instruction *Inter Oecumenici.* (DOL 23)

LG    *Lumen Gentium*, Vatican Council II, *Dogmatic Constitution on the Church.* (DOL 4)

LI    Congregation for Divine Worship, instruction *Liturgicae instaurationes.* (DOL 52)

LMIn    *Lectionary for Mass: Introduction*, second *editio typica* (1981)

LMT    *Liturgical Music Today*

MCW    *Music in Catholic Worship*

MQ    Paul VI, motu proprio *Ministeria quaedam.* (DOL 340)

MS    Congregation of Rites, instruction *Musicam sacram.* (DOL 440)

| | |
|---|---|
| PG | *Patrologiae cursus completus: Series graeca* (ed. Migne) |
| PL | *Patrologiae cursus completus: Series latina* (ed. Migne) |
| PO | *Presbyterorum Ordinis,* Vatican Council II, *Decree on the Ministry and Life of Priests.* (DOL 18) |
| RCIA | *Rite of Christian Initiation of Adults* |
| RM | Roman Missal *(Missale Romanum)* |
| RR | Roman Ritual *(Rituale Romanum)* |

# GENERAL INTRODUCTION

John M. Huels, OSM

The purposes of this volume are at the same time modest and ambitious. Its modest aim is to provide an accessible collection of basic liturgical documents for pastoral ministers, students and worshipers at large. Its more ambitious, long-term aim is to promote good liturgical celebrations. The two goals are related. The starting point for good liturgy is the reading, studying and reading again of the basic official documents of the church on the sacred liturgy such as are assembled here. Effective liturgical celebration cannot come about merely by trying to copy what other worship assemblies do. Each assembly's gifts and talents are unique, and its styles of celebration differ, but all Catholic communities find a common ritual structure and shared norms and principles in the liturgy documents of the church. The documents provide the skeletal directions for the liturgy, which then must be enfleshed by the ideas and talents of the community and its leaders.

The success of the first two editions of *The Liturgy Documents: A Parish Resource* has demonstrated to Liturgy Training Publications the ongoing need for a "primer" of liturgical documents. This third edition contains all new introductions to each document authored by various liturgical experts. It also adds three new documents to those found in the second edition. The new selections are: 1. Excerpts from the 1984 *Ceremonial of Bishops*; 2. the 1985 *Directory for the Celebration and Reception of Communion under Both Kinds* of the National Conference of Catholic Bishops (NCCB) entitled "This Holy and Living Sacrifice"; and 3. *Fulfilled in Your Hearing: The Homily in the Sunday Assembly*, issued in 1982 by the NCCB's Committee on Priestly Life and Ministry.

The remainder of this general introduction is a canonical orientation to all the documents of this volume. It is intended to help the reader understand the varying levels of authority possessed by the documents and to identify the major literary forms of canonical writing contained in them. This background knowledge can assist ministers, students and others to interpret the documents intelligently and to apply them with greater pastoral benefit in the worship setting.

## THE CANONICAL WEIGHT OF THE DOCUMENTS

As in the previous two editions, the documents of this third edition focus on the celebration of the eucharist. The eucharist is the principal liturgical rite of the church and the one that involves the most people on an ongoing basis. Although this volume is unified by its focus on the eucharist, it is important to bear in mind that the documents that follow are not all of the same nature but rather possess varying degrees of canonical authority or weight.

Some of these documents pertain to the discipline of the universal Latin-rite Roman Catholic church, while others are intended only for the Latin-rite churches of the United States. The Eastern Catholic churches have their own long-standing liturgical traditions and are not affected by the liturgical laws of the Latin rite. The general theological and ritual considerations in the documents, however, especially the *Constitution on the Sacred Liturgy*, also are applicable to the Eastern ritual churches.

The documents pertaining to the universal Latin church are of three kinds: a conciliar constitution, liturgical laws from select liturgical books and a directory from a Roman congregation. The documents pertaining to the churches in the United States are of two kinds: norms approved by the NCCB, which are binding on all dioceses of the United States, and documents published by NCCB committees that serve as pastoral directives for the benefit of all persons interested in good worship.

1.    *The Constitution on the Sacred Liturgy (Sacrosanctum Concilium)* was promulgated by Pope Paul VI and the fathers of the Second Vatican Council on December 4, 1963. It is the "Magna Charta" for all the liturgical reforms instituted since the Council was held (1962–1965). It provides the basic doctrinal and disciplinary principles that inspired and guided all subsequent liturgical documents. Here is found the genesis of the great changes and reforms of the post-Tridentine liturgical books, such as the use of the vernacular instead of only Latin, the administration of holy communion under the forms of both bread and wine instead of the consecrated bread only, and the wider acceptance of the principle—taught by nearly all the popes of the twentieth century—that the faithful ought to participate actively in all liturgical celebrations, not only by means of their mental attentiveness to the celebration and their physical postures and gestures, but also by saying and singing aloud the prayers, acclamations and other parts of the liturgy proper to the assembly.

2.    The majority of the documents in this volume consist of liturgical laws found in the liturgical books. The principal liturgical books are: the *Roman Missal*, consisting of the lectionary, used by the readers and cantors at the ambo, and the sacramentary, used by the celebrant and deacon at the presidential chair and the altar; the *Roman Pontifical*, consisting of the rites at which a bishop presides; the *Roman Ritual*, consisting of the rites, published separately, at which a priest presides; the *Liturgy of the Hours*; the *Roman Calendar*; and the *Ceremonial of Bishops*. All of these books contain norms and/or rubrics that together constitute the major source of universal law governing the liturgy.

The *General Instruction of the Roman Missal* (GIRM), which serves as an introduction to the sacramentary, was first published in 1969 and underwent several revisions and corrections, most recently following the promulgation of the revised *Code of Canon Law* in 1983. The GIRM contains both doctrinal principles and disciplinary norms governing the celebration of the eucharist. It is complemented by the *Introduction to the Lectionary for Mass*, first published in 1969 and revised in 1981, which provides additional directives for the liturgy of the word.

The *General Norms for the Liturgical Year and the Calendar* applies to the liturgy of the hours and other liturgical celebrations as well as to the eucharist. It provides theological principles and disciplinary norms governing the church's liturgical year with its temporal and sanctoral cycles of celebrations.

These three documents—the *General Instruction of the Roman Missal*, the *Introduction to the Lectionary for Mass* and the *General Norms for the Liturgical Year and the Calendar*—comprise the most important sources of law governing the eucharist. Canonically, they have a higher legal authority or weight than the other documents in this collection. As universal laws, they enjoy the same authority as the canons of the *Code of Canon Law*.

The *Ceremonial of Bishops* is also universal liturgical law, but it is directed to a more restricted audience, namely to bishops, episcopal masters of ceremonies and others involved in the preparation and celebration of liturgies at which the bishop presides, especially in the cathedral church. Although traditionally called a liturgical book, the *Ceremonial of Bishops* is not used during the celebrations of the liturgy. Akin to the ancient Roman ordinals *(ordines Romani)*, it consists solely of directives guiding the various episcopal liturgies. Despite its limited scope, the *Ceremonial* contains principles and norms that also are valuable for nonepiscopal liturgical celebrations. In this regard, the *Ceremonial* looks on the liturgy of the bishop as a model for the whole diocese:

> Hence liturgical celebrations in which the bishop presides manifest the mystery of the church as that mystery involves Christ's presence; such celebrations, then, are not a mere display of ceremony.
>
> These celebrations should also serve as a model for the entire diocese and be shining examples of active participation by the people. The whole gathered community should thus take part through song, dialogue, prayerful silence, and attentiveness and by sharing in the sacraments. (no. 12)

The *Ceremonial*, a book of substantial size, consists of eight parts with a total of 1,210 articles. The excerpted passages in this volume refer chiefly to the celebration of the eucharist. It should be noted that the laws of the *Ceremonial* are not intended to be applied rigidly and uniformly, but are to be adapted in accord with the customs and practices of the local church. The reader, therefore, should treat the *Ceremonial* as a helpful resource, not as a burdensome body of restrictive legislation.

3.    In the third category of documents affecting the universal Latin-rite church is the *Directory for Masses with Children*. This directory was published by the Vatican Congregation for Divine Worship in 1973 in response to the Second Vatican Council's desire that the eucharist be adapted for various kinds of groups and cultures. The directory's aim is eminently pastoral—to provide assistance to parents, ministers and religious educators in fostering meaningful eucharistic celebrations for the children. A directory is not a legislative text but is executive, or administrative, in nature. Its norms are binding in much the same way as laws are, but they do not enjoy the same juridical weight as a legislative document does. For this reason, it must be classed in a category of its own.

4.    There are two documents in the category of normative particular law, the *Appendix to the General Instruction for the Dioceses of the United States* and the *Directory for the Celebration and Reception of Communion under Both Kinds*, entitled "This Holy and Living Sacrifice." Both contain policies of the NCCB applicable to the dioceses of the United States.

The first document contains adaptations of the Roman liturgy by the NCCB. In the *Constitution on the Sacred Liturgy*, no. 22, §2, Vatican II gave a role to the conferences of bishops in the regulation of the liturgy in the dioceses of a nation or region. The specific forms this regulation may take are determined in the law itself, chiefly in the liturgical books and in the *Code of Canon Law*. Other adaptations, not foreseen in the law, require prior authorization from the Holy See before a conference may approve them. For a decision of the bishops' conference to be binding on all dioceses, it must be accepted by a two-thirds vote of all members of the conference and be reviewed favorably by the Holy See.

The *Appendix to the General Instruction of the Roman Missal* contains policies regarding aspects of the eucharistic celebration that have been adopted by the bishops of the United States at various times since 1969 when the *General Instruction* was first published.

The *Directory for the Celebration and Reception of Communion under Both Kinds* was reviewed favorably by the Holy See in 1984. It is normative in the dioceses of the United States for all eucharistic celebrations in which communion is distributed under forms of both bread and wine.

5.    In the final category are four documents issued by committees of the NCCB. The first three were issued by the Bishops' Committee on the Liturgy: *Music in Catholic Worship, Liturgical Music Today* and *Environment and Art in Catholic Worship.* The final document, *Fulfilled in Your Hearing,* is authored by the Bishops' Committee on Priestly Life and Ministry. The first two deal with liturgical music; the third discusses the church building and furnishings and the gestures and movement of the liturgy; the fourth covers the liturgical homily in the Sunday assembly.

The documents in this category are not, strictly speaking, liturgical law, for they were not issued by a legislative authority but only by committees of the NCCB. This does not mean, however, that they are merely optional. They are the products of wide consultation among the American bishops and the liturgical experts who advise them, and their publication was approved by the Administrative Committee of the NCCB. Many times their content is based directly on other documents that are legally binding. Moreover, because the bishop is a true legislator for the liturgy in his diocese, any document in this category can become official policy within a diocese if the diocesan bishop so decrees.

## LITERARY FORMS

To understand and implement ecclesiastical documents such as those found in this volume, it is not sufficient only to know their classification by nature and weight. One also must attend to the literary forms found in them.

Anyone familiar with biblical scholarship knows that the sacred scriptures have a variety of literary forms. The same is true with the laws and canonical documents of the church. Usually, various styles or forms of writing exist within the same document or liturgical book. The literary forms of liturgical documents can be classified according to two broad categories—"theological principles" and "juridic norms."

Theological principles are quite easily recognizable. They appear, as a rule, at the beginning of a document and provide foundational information—scriptural, doctrinal, historical, ritual and the like. (The principles may appear at other places, however; for example, at the beginning of a new section of a document or in the same paragraph as juridic norms.) They serve as the theoretical underpinning for the normative material of the document and provide the rationale for the liturgical rite and its postconciliar revision. Theological principles are, moreover, the interpretative key for understanding and implementing the norms and rubrics of the rites. Those who understand the theology underlying the church's liturgy are much better positioned to plan and execute liturgical functions as provided in the official rites. Good liturgical practice does not result from mere slavish adherence to the juridic norms. Rather, the juridic norms always must be seen in light of the theological foundation on which they are based.

Some examples of theological principles are the *Constitution on the Sacred Liturgy*, nos. 5–10; the *General Instruction of the Roman Missal*, the Introduction and nos. 1–8; the *Introduction to the Lectionary for Mass*, nos. 1–10. Many other examples are found elsewhere in these and in the other documents of this collection.

Most of the norms in canonical documents and liturgical books are "juridic" in nature, that is, they are not theoretical principles but norms for action. They tell liturgical planners what is to be done in the celebration of a rite. They give general and specific rules for the external discipline of the liturgy and the actual execution of the rites. When they appear in legally binding documents such as the liturgical books, they are properly called "liturgical laws." They are part of canon law and bind in the same way as other church laws.

We already have seen that juridic norms can have differing degrees of external authority according to the nature and authorship of the document. They also can have differing degrees of *internal* weight. Some laws within the same document are more important, more binding, than others. Not all juridic norms have the same weight, the same preceptive force.

The key to identifying the weight of juridic norms is to examine the verbs that are used in them. Some statements are very strong and admit no exceptions. The lawgiver uses strong commanding verbs such as "must," "it is necessary to," and "is to," or negatively, "must not," "is not permitted to," "is not to" and the like. Often liturgical law simply uses the third-person present tense as a form of command. The minister or assembly is directed to do something in descriptive fashion, for example, in GIRM, no. 89: "After the opening prayer, the reader goes to the lectern for the first reading. All sit and listen and make the acclamation at the end." Although the text seems merely to be describing in the third person what takes place, in reality it has the effect of prescribing an action that must take place. When verbs like these are used, a preceptive rule is indicated, a law whose observance is obligatory.

Another form of juridic norm can be described as a "mild command." These laws describe *general* rather than specific modes of action. The lawgiver states what is pastorally and liturgically optimal and desirable as a general rule, without requiring that it always be performed exactly as specified in each and every case. The verbs used in these norms are considerably milder than in the strong commands, words such as "may," "should," "is preferable," "is desirable," "is fitting," "is optimal," "is proper" and so forth. Such language frequently is found in the introductions to liturgical books. The *Appendix to the GIRM for the Dioceses of the United States* is a good example of a document that frequently employs this kind of command. By using this language, the lawgiver intends that liturgy planners, ministers and assembly should strive for the liturgical ideals expressed in such norms, without being constricted by unbending rules that admit no exceptions in particular circumstances.

A third kind of juridic norm may be called an "option." Options direct the minister or liturgical planner to choose from among various scriptural texts, prayers, acclamations, admonitions, or sometimes even to use one's own words, to speak or sing "in these or similar words." A command is implicit in this literary form. The ministers *must* choose one option, but which one is left to their own discretion.

It is helpful to be able to identify these various literary forms. It brings to consciousness the fact that not every norm, even within the same document, is intended to have the same force. Some norms actually are statements of theological principles; some represent general values and ideal modes of action; some are precise rules for the conduct of the liturgy.

## CONCLUSION

Knowing something about the canonical weight of documents and the literary forms of their content is useful information to those who seek to understand and apply them. Some documents are not legally binding, but provide helpful guidelines. Even in properly legal documents, individual laws have different literary forms and varying degrees of preceptive force. Some laws are quite forceful commands that admit little or no exception. Others express more general values and are more susceptible to adaptation because of various needs and circumstances. All laws must be seen in light of the theology on which they are based.

Canon law, of which liturgical law is a part, frequently is viewed negatively by pastoral ministers, despite the fact that the law is intended to reflect the reforms of Vatican II and the postconciliar era. To a great extent, this reputation is not deserved. The law itself is seldom the problem; rather, it is the rigid way the law is applied. The mind-set of some people remains that of the prevailing legalism of pre–Vatican II days: They trivialize the purpose of law by a mindless literalism that elevates all laws and documents, no matter what their degree of authority, to the same level as doctrines of faith. In contrast, those who are able to identify the weight of canonical documents and the preceptive force of the juridical norms in them are better equipped to apply the law in a pastoral spirit proper to good canonical interpretation.

A study of liturgical law and liturgical documents does not, however, in itself assure good worship. That also requires the talents, creativity and, yes, the hard work of dedicated people. The word "liturgy" is derived from the Greek for the "work of the people." Any enterprise, whether artistic or scientific, academic or practical, for fun or for profit, requires work and effort if it is to be performed well and achieve good results. The same is true with the liturgy. The liturgy documents are the blueprint for the liturgical celebration: They are not the finished product. A careful study of these documents provides a solid foundation for the other work, prayer, planning and practice that are all part of what it takes to have more personally meaningful and community-building liturgical celebrations, liturgies that truly are the source and the summit of the Christian life.

# CONSTITUTION
## ON THE
# SACRED LITURGY

SACROSANCTUM CONCILIUM

# OVERVIEW OF THE *CONSTITUTION ON THE SACRED LITURGY*

Kathleen Hughes, RSCJ

The *Constitution on the Sacred Liturgy* (CSL) was approved virtually unanimously by "Paul, Bishop, Servant of the Servants of God, together with the Fathers of the Council" and duly promulgated on December 4, 1963. That the CSL was the first document of the Second Vatican Council was evidence of the maturity of the twentieth-century liturgical movement, the consensus that had built around major issues of reform and the pastoral and ecumenical stamp that the Council desired to give to all of its deliberations.

As the initial document of Vatican II, the CSL's theological foundations became the measure for subsequent conciliar reflections on such topics as ecclesiology and church order. The CSL also planted seeds of other redefinitions including the role of the laity, the authority of territorial conferences of bishops, and the relationship and tension between unity and catholicity in a multicultural church.

At the same time, the development of the CSL suffered the vicissitudes of any first effort: Insights had not yet crystallized, procedures of debate were not in place and the document itself is a curious amalgam of broad principles and minute details, the latter the result of inevitable compromises that were reached in the course of conciliar discussion. While some sections of the CSL now seem curiously anachronistic, the theological foundations have yet to be completely understood and appropriated. This remains a document to be studied in depth so that its spirit may permeate our lives.

The CSL is like a blueprint for liturgical reform. In its first chapter are theological and pastoral principles that anchor the reform of the liturgy in a particular vision of Christ and the church. Next, the CSL offers specific procedures of reform, steps to be taken in the development of a fully renewed liturgy. Finally, the CSL gets down to cases; the last six chapters mandate concrete reforms.

This introduction to the *Constitution on the Sacred Liturgy* will highlight the most significant of these *principles, procedures* and *reforms* and will conclude with an assessment of the work that remains to be done—our continuing liturgical agenda.

## THEOLOGICAL AND PASTORAL PRINCIPLES

The following principles articulated in the CSL provide a succinct summary of contemporary liturgical theology:

1. The heart of the liturgy is the celebration of the paschal mystery of Jesus Christ in whose life, death and rising the redemption of humankind was accomplished once for all, and through whose pascha the church was born (nos. 5, 61).

2. Every liturgy is an exercise of the priestly office of Jesus Christ, head and members, for the glory of God and the sanctification of humankind (no. 7). All members of the community, priestly people through baptism, are copresiders with Christ, the one and only high priest and leader of prayer.

3. In the liturgy, Christ is present in many ways (no. 7). To Christ's presence under the appearance of bread and wine—the traditional localization of the "real presence"—the CSL adds Christ's presence in the other sacraments, in the proclamation of the word of God, in the ministers of the liturgy and in the assembly gathered for prayer and praise.

4. The liturgy is the most perfect manifestation of the church. The mystery of Christ is made visible when God's holy people actively participate in the same eucharist, at a single altar, each according to his or her role (nos. 2, 26, 28, 41). "Church" is not an abstraction but a reality when a community gathers to be the sign of Christ's presence with one another.

5. The liturgy is thus the fount and summit of the Christian life (no. 10). Evangelization, conversion and faith find their ultimate expression in the liturgy, which, in turn, is the source of all holiness. At the same time, liturgical participation commits one to a life of faithful discipleship. Liturgical spirituality is rooted in this realization of the centrality of the liturgy in the Christian life. Other spiritual exercises, such as contemplation and popular devotions, will be oriented to the liturgy and derived from its true spirit (nos. 12–13).

6. Active participation in the liturgy is essential so that this primary and indispensable source of all holiness may achieve its end (no. 14). Active participation, the right and duty of all in the assembly by reason of their baptism, is both internal and external, including verbal participation, actions, gestures, bodily attitudes and silence (nos. 19, 30, 48–50, 113). While active participation often is expressed outwardly, it is primarily a habit of interior presence and assent.

7. Catechesis is fundamental if the community is to be fully aware of what it is doing, actively engaged in the rite and enriched by its effects (no. 11). The clergy, above all, must receive appropriate liturgical instruction so that they may live the liturgy themselves (nos. 14, 18) and teach their communities its spirit and power (nos. 14, 19).

PROCEDURES OF REFORM

The CSL specified broad procedures for the reform of the liturgy, including preliminary research and methods of revision, publication and implementation. Implied in the CSL are further procedures of experimentation and more radical adaptation after the community's initial experience of the rite has been assessed.

The first series of procedures have been completed:

1. Preliminary research included historical, theological and pastoral investigation of all the rites in order to recover their authentic spirit (no. 23), to separate immutable elements from those elements subject to change (no. 21) and to assure organic growth in any new form adopted (no. 23).

2. Among the methods of revision of rites and texts suggested by the CSL are: suppression (dropping useless repetitions), addition (adding options where pastorally appropriate), restoration (recovery of forms such as the catechumenate that were lost over the course of time), adaptation (particularly apparent in attempts to admit cultural elements into the initiation, marriage and funeral rites) and development (organic growth from forms already existing) (nos. 21, 23, 34, 37–40, 47 and passim).

3. The CSL anticipated the publication of new liturgical books after the collaboration of experts and with the consultation of bishops from various parts of the world (no. 25), a work virtually complete with the publication of the *Book of Blessings* in 1988.

Several features of the revised books stand out:

a. the presence of more, varied and suitable readings from sacred scripture (nos. 24, 35);

b. the possibility for extensive use of the vernacular, together with provision for appropriate translation (no. 36);

c. a style that is both simple and clear (nos. 21, 34); and

d. the presence of variants and options to suit particular situations (no. 68).

4. The CSL also anticipated that each new ritual book would require implementation. To this end, the *Constitution* proposed the establishment of national liturgical centers and diocesan liturgical commissions through which experts in liturgy, music and the arts would collaborate to promote the liturgical life of the territory or diocese (nos. 43–46). Furthermore, the CSL recognized that continued serious and thoughtful implementation depends on a liturgically literate clergy and so specified that liturgy should have a preeminent place in the seminary, both in theoretical courses and in celebration (nos. 15–17).

Regrettably, implementation has been curtailed for several reasons. Some have equated the publication of new rites with the completion of the reform. In fact, a new liturgical library signals only the beginning of implementation. At the same time, diocesan offices are being closed or cut back and liturgy is yet to be given pride of place in seminary curricula. Thus pastors are ill-equipped at the parochial level to assume leadership in the continuing process of renewal and, in many cases, they do not have the support of diocesan resources.

The reform procedure still to be carried out is that of adapting the liturgy to the cultures and traditions of peoples (nos. 37–40). The CSL proposes that the church, respecting the genius and talents of peoples (no. 37), will admit legitimate variations and adaptations of the rites while preserving the substantial unity (no longer "uniformity") of the Roman rite (no. 38). Territorial ecclesiastical authority will guide the process of adaptation (no. 39), determine the need for more radical cultural adaptation and oversee appropriate experimentation with the advice and consent of the Apostolic See (no. 40). Since the promulgation of the CSL, some ritual experimentation has been approved, notably, in Zaire, India and the Philippines. More recently, the Apostolic See appears more skittish about experimentation and cultural adaptation and only minimal, extrinsic changes in the rites currently are being approved.

## CONCRETE REFORMS (NOS. 47–130)

Theological principles and concrete procedures of revision are followed in the CSL by specific directives for the reform of particular rites. In six chapters, the bishops of the Council gave precise instructions to postconciliar working groups regarding the eucharist, other sacraments and sacramentals, the liturgy of the hours, the liturgical year, music and art.

Because these reforms are now so familiar, it is possible to overlook how extraordinary were the mandates contained in the CSL that produced: a new lectionary; the restoration of the adult catechumenate and the integrity of the sacraments of initiation; recovery of pastoral care of the sick alongside the church's ministry to the dying; revision of the rites for Christian burial; development of three rites of reconciliation; recovery of the centrality of Sunday and the major feasts and seasons of the liturgical year; some simplification of the liturgy of the hours with emphasis on the sanctification of the day; and, in the celebration of the eucharist, the restoration of the homily, the prayers of the faithful, communion under two species and the possibility of concelebration—this last discovered in hindsight to be of dubious merit and even more dubious ritual form. Less inspired and still in need of reform are the rituals for orders and marriage. The spare directives regarding music and the arts of the CSL have been augmented for the church in the United States in *Music in Catholic Worship, Liturgical Music Today* and *Environment and Art in Catholic Worship.*

CONTINUING AGENDA

The renewal of the liturgy envisioned by the CSL is well begun. In fact, historical distance will teach us how swift, profound and unparalleled has been the reform of the church's worship in our day. Among the areas still in need of our attention, four stand out:

1. Because of the rapidity of reform, new rites often were introduced without serious catechetical preparation. Perhaps many even assumed that vernacular translations would obviate the need for catechesis, but understanding words does not guarantee understanding the deeper meaning of the ritual event. A new catechetical effort might well include: study of the theological and pastoral principles that undergird the reform; careful reading of the major documents on the liturgy, most of them collected in this volume; and examination of the structure and content of the rites to allow the liturgy itself to be the primary way that Christians learn the habits of prayer and praise.

2. New catechetical efforts naturally will promote full, conscious and active participation, a second area in need of continuing attention. Active participation depends on catechesis because it is rooted in a profound understanding of the liturgy. A community that is participating internally as well as externally is fully aware of what it is doing, actively engaged in the rite and enriched by the rite's effects.

3. Active participation involves justice commitments, and this is an area sadly underdeveloped by the CSL, perhaps because it was the first document of the Council. If the CSL had come toward the end of Vatican II, it is conceivable that "the joy and hope, the grief and anguish of the men and women of our time, especially of those who are poor or afflicted in any way" *(Pastoral Constitution on the Church in the Modern World)* would have found its way with some insistence into the vision of liturgy in the CSL. One could even paraphrase the next line of the *Pastoral Constitution* and suggest that "nothing that is genuinely human would fail to find an echo in our liturgy." Despite only oblique reference to justice themes in the CSL, active participation logically leads to commitment to that world of equality and justice that is mirrored when the body of Christ gathers at table.

4. The continuing liturgical agenda includes, lastly, a serious reappraisal of the relationship between culture and liturgical expression, an issue not confined to so-called "mission countries." Is it possible that what has been called the "substantial unity of the Roman rite" prevents the incarnation of the gospel and its celebration in certain cultures? To this end, theological content and ritual form must be analyzed: The former belongs to that category called "immutable," the latter may well represent "elements subject to change." Such decisions belong appropriately at the level of national or territorial conferences of bishops.

Promotion of liturgical catechesis, active participation, a life of justice and celebrations adapted to the cultural experience of peoples is an arduous agenda. Fortunately, the reader will find in the *Constitution on the Sacred Liturgy* fresh inspiration for the effort required to renew the church's worship.

# OUTLINE

# CONSTITUTION ON THE SACRED LITURGY

1.   This Sacred Council has several aims in view: it desires to impart an ever increasing vigor to the Christian life of the faithful; to adapt more suitably to the needs of our own times those institutions that are subject to change; to foster whatever can promote union among all who believe in Christ; to strengthen whatever can help to call the whole of humanity into the household of the Church. The Council therefore sees particularly cogent reasons for undertaking the reform and promotion of the liturgy.

2.   For the liturgy, "making the work of our redemption a present actuality,"[1] most of all in the divine sacrifice of the eucharist, is the outstanding means whereby the faithful may express in their lives and manifest to others the mystery of Christ and the real nature of the true Church. It is of the essence of the Church to be both human and divine, visible yet endowed with invisible resources, eager to act yet intent on contemplation, present in this world yet not at home in it; and the Church is all these things in such wise that in it the human is directed and subordinated to the divine, the visible likewise to the invisible, action to contemplation, and this present world to that city yet to come which we seek.[2] While the liturgy daily builds up those who are within into a holy temple of the Lord, into a dwelling place for God in the Spirit,[3] to the mature measure of the fullness of Christ,[4] at the same time it marvelously strengthens their power to preach Christ and thus shows forth the Church to those who are outside as a sign lifted up among the nations,[5] under which the scattered children of God may be gathered together,[6] until there is one sheepfold and one shepherd.[7]

3.   Wherefore the Council judges that the following principles concerning the promotion and reform of the liturgy should be called to mind and practical norms established.

Among these principles and norms there are some that can and should be applied both to the Roman Rite and also to all the other rites. The practical norms that follow, however, should be taken as applying only to the Roman Rite, except for those that, in the very nature of things, affect other rites as well.

4.   Lastly, in faithful obedience to tradition, the Council declares that the Church holds all lawfully acknowledged rites to be of equal right and dignity and wishes to preserve them in the future and to foster them in every way. The Council also desires that, where necessary, the rites be revised carefully in the light of sound tradition and that they be given new vigor to meet the circumstances and needs of modern times.

# CHAPTER I
## GENERAL PRINCIPLES FOR THE REFORM AND PROMOTION OF THE SACRED LITURGY
### I. NATURE OF THE LITURGY AND ITS IMPORTANCE IN THE CHURCH'S LIFE

5.   God who "wills that all be saved and come to the knowledge of the truth" (1 Tm 2:4), "who in many and various ways spoke in times past to the fathers by the prophets" (Heb 1:1), when the fullness of time had come sent his Son, the Word made flesh, anointed by the Holy Spirit, to preach the Gospel to the poor, to heal the contrite of heart;[1] he is "the physician, being both flesh and of the Spirit,"[2] the mediator between God and us.[3] For his humanity, united with the person of the Word, was the instrument of our salvation. Therefore in Christ "the perfect achievement of our reconciliation came forth and the fullness of divine worship was given to us.[4]

The wonderful works of God among the people of the Old Testament were a prelude to the work of Christ the Lord. He achieved his task of redeeming humanity and giving perfect glory to God, principally by the paschal mystery of his blessed passion, resurrection from the dead, and glorious ascension, whereby "dying, he destroyed our death and, rising, he restored our life."[5] For it was from the side of Christ as he slept the sleep of death upon the cross that there came forth the sublime sacrament of the whole Church.[6]

6.   As Christ was sent by the Father, he himself also sent the apostles, filled with the Holy Spirit. Their mission was, first, by preaching the Gospel to every creature,[7] to proclaim that by his death and resurrection Christ has freed us from Satan's grip[8] and brought us into the Father's kingdom. But the work they preached they were also to bring into effect through the sacrifice and the sacraments, the center of the whole liturgical life. Thus by baptism all are plunged into the paschal mystery of Christ: they die with him, are buried with him, and rise with him;[9] they receive the spirit of adoption as children "in which we cry: Abba, Father" (Rom 8:15), and thus become true adorers whom the Father seeks.[10] In like manner, as often as they eat the supper of the Lord they proclaim the death of the Lord until he comes.[11] For that reason, on the very day of Pentecost when the Church appeared before the world, "those who received the word" of Peter "were baptized." And "they continued steadfastly in the teaching of the apostles and in the communion of the breaking of bread and in prayers . . . praising God and being in favor with all the people" (Acts 2:41–47). From that time onward the Church has never failed to come together to celebrate the paschal mystery: reading those things "which were in all the Scriptures concerning him" (Lk 24:27); celebrating the eucharist, in which "the victory and triumph of his death are again made present";[12] and at the same time giving thanks "to God for his inexpressible gift" (2 Cor 9:15) in Christ Jesus, "in praise of his glory" (Eph 1:12), through the power of the Holy Spirit.

7.   To accomplish so great a work, Christ is always present in his Church, especially in its liturgical celebrations. He is present in the sacrifice of the Mass, not only in the person of his minister, "the same now offering, through the

ministry of priests, who formerly offered himself on the cross,"[13] but especially under the eucharistic elements. By his power he is present in the sacraments, so that when a man baptizes it is really Christ himself who baptizes.[14] He is present in his word, since it is he himself who speaks when the holy Scriptures are read in the Church. He is present, lastly, when the Church prays and sings, for he promised: "Where two or three are gathered together in my name, there am I in the midst of them" (Mt 18:20).

Christ always truly associates the Church with himself in this great work wherein God is perfectly glorified and the recipients made holy. The Church is the Lord's beloved Bride who calls to him and through him offers worship to the eternal Father.

Rightly, then, the liturgy is considered as an exercise of the priestly office of Jesus Christ. In the liturgy, by means of signs perceptible to the senses, human sanctification is signified and brought about in ways proper to each of these signs; in the liturgy the whole public worship is performed by the Mystical Body of Jesus Christ, that is, by the Head and his members.

From this it follows that every liturgical celebration, because it is an action of Christ the Priest and of his Body which is the Church, is a sacred action surpassing all others; no other action of the Church can equal its effectiveness by the same title and to the same degree.

8.    In the earthly liturgy we take part in a foretaste of that heavenly liturgy celebrated in the holy city of Jerusalem toward which we journey as pilgrims, where Christ is sitting at the right hand of God, a minister of the holies and of the true tabernacle;[15] we sing a hymn to the Lord's glory with the whole company of heaven; venerating the memory of the saints, we hope for some part and fellowship with them; we eagerly await the Savior, our Lord Jesus Christ, until he, our life, shall appear and we too will appear with him in glory.[16]

9.    The liturgy does not exhaust the entire activity of the Church. Before people can come to the liturgy they must be called to faith and to conversion: "How then are they to call upon him in whom they have not yet believed? But how are they to believe him whom they have not heard? And how are they to hear if no one preaches? And how are men to preach unless they be sent?" (Rom 10:14–15).

Therefore the Church announces the good tidings of salvation to those who do not believe, so that all may know the true God and Jesus Christ whom he has sent and may be converted from their ways, doing penance.[17] To believers, also, the Church must ever preach faith and penance, prepare them for the sacraments, teach them to observe all that Christ has commanded,[18] and invite them to all the works of charity, worship, and the apostolate. For all these works make it clear that Christ's faithful, though not of this world, are to be the light of the world and to glorify the Father in the eyes of all.

10.    Still, the liturgy is the summit toward which the activity of the Church is directed; at the same time it is the fount from which all the Church's power flows. For the aim and object of apostolic works is that all who are made children of God

by faith and baptism should come together to praise God in the midst of his Church, to take part in the sacrifice, and to eat the Lord's Supper.

The liturgy in its turn moves the faithful, filled with "the paschal sacraments," to be "one in holiness";[19] it prays that "they may hold fast in their lives to what they have grasped by their faith";[20] the renewal in the eucharist of the covenant between the Lord and his people draws the faithful into the compelling love of Christ and sets them on fire. From the liturgy, therefore, particularly the eucharist, grace is poured forth upon us as from a fountain; the liturgy is the source for achieving in the most effective way possible human sanctification and God's glorification, the end to which all the Church's other activities are directed.

11.    But in order that the liturgy may possess its full effectiveness, it is necessary that the faithful come to it with proper dispositions, that their minds be attuned to their voices, and that they cooperate with divine grace, lest they receive it in vain.[21] Pastors must therefore realize that when the liturgy is celebrated something more is required than the mere observance of the laws governing valid and lawful celebration; it is also their duty to ensure that the faithful take part fully aware of what they are doing, actively engaged in the rite, and enriched by its effects.

12.    The spiritual life, however, is not limited solely to participation in the liturgy. Christians are indeed called to pray in union with each other, but they must also enter into their chamber to pray to the Father in secret;[22] further, according to the teaching of the Apostle, they should pray without ceasing.[23] We learn from the same Apostle that we must always bear about in our body the dying of Jesus, so that the life also of Jesus may be made manifest in our bodily frame.[24] This is why we ask the Lord in the sacrifice of the Mass that "receiving the offering of the spiritual victim," he may fashion us for himself "as an eternal gift."[25]

13.    Popular devotions of the Christian people are to be highly endorsed, provided they accord with the laws and norms of the Church, above all when they are ordered by the Apostolic See.

Devotions proper to particular Churches also have a special dignity if they are undertaken by mandate of the bishops according to customs or books lawfully approved.

But these devotions should be so fashioned that they harmonize with the liturgical seasons, accord with the sacred liturgy, are in some way derived from it, and lead the people to it, since, in fact, the liturgy, by its very nature far surpasses any of them.

## II. PROMOTION OF LITURGICAL INSTRUCTION AND ACTIVE PARTICIPATION

14.    The Church earnestly desires that all the faithful be led to that full, conscious, and active participation in liturgical celebrations called for by the very nature of the liturgy. Such participation by the Christian people as "a chosen race, a royal priesthood, a holy nation, God's own people" (1 Pt 2:9; see 2:4–5) is their right and duty by reason of their baptism.

In the reform and promotion of the liturgy, this full and active participation by all the people is the aim to be considered before all else. For it is the primary and indispensable source from which the faithful are to derive the true Christian spirit and therefore pastors must zealously strive in all their pastoral work to achieve such participation by means of the necessary instruction.

Yet it would be futile to entertain any hopes of realizing this unless, in the first place, the pastors themselves become thoroughly imbued with the spirit and power of the liturgy and make themselves its teachers. A prime need, therefore, is that attention be directed, first of all, to the liturgical formation of the clergy. Wherefore the Council has decided to enact what follows.

15. Professors appointed to teach liturgy in seminaries, religious houses of study, and theological faculties must be thoroughly trained for their work in institutes specializing in this subject.

16. The study of liturgy is to be ranked among the compulsory and major courses in seminaries and religious houses of studies; in theological faculties it is to rank among the principal courses. It is to be taught under its theological, historical, spiritual, pastoral, and canonical aspects. Moreover, other professors, while striving to expound the mystery of Christ and the history of salvation from the angle proper to each of their own subjects, must nevertheless do so in a way that will clearly bring out the connection between their subjects and the liturgy, as also the underlying unity of all priestly training. This consideration is especially important for professors of dogmatic, spiritual, and pastoral theology and for professors of holy Scripture.

17. In seminaries and houses of religious, clerics shall be given a liturgical formation in their spiritual life. The means for this are: proper guidance so that they may be able to understand the sacred rites and take part in them wholeheartedly; the actual celebration of the sacred mysteries and of other, popular devotions imbued with the spirit of the liturgy. In addition they must learn how to observe the liturgical laws, so that life in seminaries and houses of religious may be thoroughly permeated by the spirit of the liturgy.

18. Priests, both secular and religious, who are already working in the Lord's vineyard are to be helped by every suitable means to understand ever more fully what it is they are doing in their liturgical functions; they are to be aided to live the liturgical life and to share it with the faithful entrusted to their care.

19. With zeal and patience pastors must promote the liturgical instruction of the faithful and also their active participation in the liturgy both internally and externally, taking into account their age and condition, their way of life, and their stage of religious development. By doing so, pastors will be fulfilling one of their chief duties as faithful stewards of the mysteries of God; and in this matter they must lead their flock not only by word but also by example.

20. Radio and television broadcasts of sacred rites must be marked by discretion and dignity, under the leadership and direction of a competent person appointed

for this office by the bishops. This is especially important when the service to be broadcast is the Mass.

## III. THE REFORM OF THE SACRED LITURGY

21. In order that the Christian people may more surely derive an abundance of graces from the liturgy, the Church desires to undertake with great care a general reform of the liturgy itself. For the liturgy is made up of immutable elements, divinely instituted, and of elements subject to change. These not only may but ought to be changed with the passage of time if they have suffered from the intrusion of anything out of harmony with the inner nature of the liturgy or have become pointless.

In this reform both texts and rites should be so drawn up that they express more clearly the holy things they signify and that the Christian people, as far as possible, are able to understand them with ease and to take part in the rites fully, actively, and as befits a community.

Wherefore the Council establishes tbe general norms that follow.

### A. General Norms

22. § 1. Regulation of the liturgy depends solely on the authority of the Church, that is, on the Apostolic See and, accordingly as the law determines, on the bishop.

§ 2. In virtue of power conceded by the law, the regulation of the liturgy within certain defined limits belongs also to various kinds of competent territorial bodies of bishops lawfully established.

§ 3. Therefore, no other person, not even if he is a priest, may on his own add, remove, or change anything in the liturgy.

23. That sound tradition may be retained and yet the way remain open to legitimate progress, a careful investigation is always to be made into each part of the liturgy to be revised. This investigation should be theological, historical, and pastoral. Also the general laws governing the structure and meaning of the liturgy must be studied in conjunction with the experience derived from recent liturgical reforms and from the indults conceded to various places. Finally, there must be no innovations unless the good of the Church genuinely and certainly requires them; care must be taken that any new forms adopted should in some way grow organically from forms already existing.

As far as possible, marked differences between the rites used in neighboring regions must be carefully avoided.

24. Sacred Scripture is of the greatest importance in the celebration of the liturgy. For it is from Scripture that the readings are given and explained in the homily and that psalms are sung; the prayers, collects, and liturgical songs are scriptural in their inspiration; it is from the Scriptures that actions and signs derive their meaning. Thus to achieve the reform, progress, and adaptation of the

liturgy, it is essential to promote that warm and living love for Scripture to which the venerable tradition of both Eastern and Western rites gives testimony.

25.    The liturgical books are to be revised as soon as possible; experts are to be employed in this task and bishops from various parts of the world are to be consulted.

### B. Norms Drawn from the Hierarchic and Communal Nature of the Liturgy

26.    Liturgical services are not private functions, but are celebrations belonging to the Church, which is the "sacrament of unity," namely, the holy people united and ordered under their bishops.[26]

Therefore liturgical services involve the whole Body of the Church; they manifest it and have effects upon it; but they also concern the individual members of the Church in different ways, according to their different orders, offices, and actual participation.

27.    Whenever rites, according to their specific nature, make provision for communal celebration involving the presence and active participation of the faithful, it is to be stressed that this way of celebrating them is to be preferred, as far as possible, to a celebration that is individual and, so to speak, private.

This applies with special force to the celebration of Mass and the administration of the sacraments, even though every Mass has of itself a public and social character.

28.    In liturgical celebrations each one, minister or layperson, who has an office to perform, should do all of, but only, those parts which pertain to that office by the nature of the rite and the principles of liturgy.

29.    Servers, readers, commentators, and members of the choir also exercise a genuine liturgical function. They ought to discharge their office, therefore, with the sincere devotion and decorum demanded by so exalted a ministry and rightly expected of them by God's people.

Consequently, they must all be deeply imbued with the spirit of the liturgy, in the measure proper to each one, and they must be trained to perform their functions in a correct and orderly manner.

30.    To promote active participation, the people should be encouraged to take part by means of acclamations, responses, psalmody, antiphons, and songs, as well as by actions, gestures, and bearing. And at the proper times all should observe a reverent silence.

31.    The revision of the liturgical books must ensure that the rubrics make provision for the parts belonging to the people.

32.    The liturgy makes distinctions between persons according to their liturgical function and sacred orders and there are liturgical laws providing for due honors to be given to civil authorities. Apart from these instances, no special honors are to

be paid in the liturgy to any private persons or classes of persons, whether in the ceremonies or by external display.

### C. Norms Based on the Teaching and Pastoral Character of the Liturgy

33.   Although the liturgy is above all things the worship of the divine majesty, it likewise contains rich instruction for the faithful.[27] For in the liturgy God is speaking to his people and Christ is still proclaiming his gospel. And the people are responding to God by both song and prayer.

Moreover, the prayers addressed to God by the priest, who presides over the assembly in the person of Christ, are said in the name of the entire holy people and of all present. And the visible signs used by the liturgy to signify invisible divine realities have been chosen by Christ or the Church. Thus not only when things are read "that were written for our instruction" (Rom 15:4), but also when the Church prays or sings or acts, the faith of those taking part is nourished and their minds are raised to God, so that they may offer him their worship as intelligent beings and receive his grace more abundantly.

In the reform of the liturgy, therefore, the following general norms are to be observed.

34.   The rites should be marked by a noble simplicity; they should be short, clear, and unencumbered by useless repetitions; they should be within the people's powers of comprehension and as a rule not require much explanation.

35.   That the intimate connection between words and rites may stand out clearly in the liturgy:

1.   In sacred celebrations there is to be more reading from holy Scripture and it is to be more varied and apposite.

2.   Because the spoken word is part of the liturgical service, the best place for it, consistent with the nature of the rite, is to be indicated even in the rubrics; the ministry of preaching is to be fulfilled with exactitude and fidelity. Preaching should draw its content mainly from scriptural and liturgical sources, being a proclamation of God's wonderful works in the history of salvation, the mystery of Christ, ever present and active within us, especially in the celebration of the liturgy.

3.   A more explicitly liturgical catechesis should also be given in a variety of ways. Within the rites themselves provision is to be made for brief comments, when needed, by the priest or a qualified minister; they should occur only at the more suitable moments and use a set formula or something similar.

4.   Bible services should be encouraged, especially on the vigils of the more solemn feasts, on some weekdays in Advent and Lent, and on Sundays and holy days. They are particularly to be recommended in places where no priest is available; when this is the case, a deacon or some other person authorized by the bishop is to preside over the celebration.

36.  § 1. Particular law remaining in force, the use of the Latin language is to be preserved in the Latin rites.

§ 2. But since the use of the mother tongue, whether in the Mass, the administration of the sacraments, or other parts of the liturgy, frequently may be of great advantage to the people, the limits of its use may be extended. This will apply in the first place to the readings and instructions and to some prayers and chants, according to the regulations on this matter to be laid down for each case in subsequent chapters.

§ 3. Respecting such norms and also, where applicable, consulting the bishops of nearby territories of the same language, the competent, territorial ecclesiastical authority mentioned in art. 22, §2 is empowered to decide whether and to what extent the vernacular is to be used. The enactments of the competent authority are to be approved, that is, confirmed by the Holy See.

§ 4. Translations from the Latin text into the mother tongue intended for use in the liturgy must be approved by the competent, territorial ecclesiastical authority already mentioned.

### D. Norms for Adapting the Liturgy to the Culture and Traditions of Peoples

37.  Even in the liturgy the Church has no wish to impose a rigid uniformity in matters that do not affect the faith or the good of the whole community; rather, the Church respects and fosters the genius and talents of the various races and peoples. The Church considers with sympathy and, if possible, preserves intact the elements in these peoples' way of life that are not indissolubly bound up with superstition and error. Sometimes in fact the Church admits such elements into the liturgy itself, provided they are in keeping with the true and authentic spirit of the liturgy.

38.  Provisions shall also be made, even in the revision of liturgical books, for legitimate variations and adaptations to different groups, regions, and peoples, especially in mission lands, provided the substantial unity of the Roman Rite is preserved; this should be borne in mind when rites are drawn up and rubrics devised.

39.  Within the limits set by the *editio typica* of the liturgical books, it shall be for the competent, territorial ecclesiastical authority mentioned in art. 22, §2 to specify adaptations, especially in the case of the administration of the sacraments, the sacramentals, processions, liturgical language, sacred music, and the arts. This, however, is to be done in accord with the fundamental norms laid down in this Constitution.

40.  In some places and circumstances, however, an even more radical adaptation of the liturgy is needed and this entails greater difficulties. Wherefore:

1. The competent, territorial ecclesiastical authority mentioned in art. 22, §2, must, in this matter, carefully and prudently weigh what elements from the traditions and culture of individual peoples may be appropriately admitted into

divine worship. They are to propose to the Apostolic See adaptations considered useful or necessary that will be introduced with its consent.

2. To ensure that adaptations are made with all the circumspection they demand, the Apostolic See will grant power to this same territorial ecclesiastical authority to permit and to direct, as the case requires, the necessary preliminary experiments within certain groups suited for the purpose and for a fixed time.

3. Because liturgical laws often involve special difficulties with respect to adaptation, particularly in mission lands, experts in these matters must be employed to formulate them.

## IV. PROMOTION OF LITURGICAL LIFE IN DIOCESE AND PARISH

41.   The bishop is to be looked on as the high priest of his flock, the faithful's life in Christ in some way deriving from and depending on him.

Therefore all should hold in great esteem the liturgical life of the diocese centered around the bishop, especially in his cathedral church; they must be convinced that the preeminent manifestation of the Church is present in the full, active participation of all God's holy people in these liturgical celebrations, especially in the same eucharist, in a single prayer, at one altar at which the bishop presides, surrounded by his college of priests and by his ministers.[28]

42.   But because it is impossible for the bishop always and everywhere to preside over the whole flock in his Church, he cannot do otherwise than establish lesser groupings of the faithful. Among these the parishes, set up locally under a pastor taking the place of the bishop, are the most important: in some manner they represent the visible Church established throughout the world.

And therefore both in attitude and in practice the liturgical life of the parish and its relationship to the bishop must be fostered among the faithful and clergy; efforts must also be made toward a lively sense of community within the parish, above all in the shared celebration of the Sunday Mass.

## V. PROMOTION OF PASTORAL-LITURGICAL ACTION

43.   Zeal for the promotion and restoration of the liturgy is rightly held to be a sign of the providential dispositions of God in our time, a movement of the Holy Spirit in his Church. Today it is a distinguishing mark of the Church's life, indeed of the whole tenor of contemporary religious thought and action.

So that this pastoral-liturgical action may become even more vigorous in the Church, the Council decrees what follows.

44.   It is advisable that the competent, territorial ecclesiastical authority mentioned in art. 22, §2 set up a liturgical commission, to be assisted by experts in liturgical science, music, art, and pastoral practice. As far as possible the commission should be aided by some kind of institute for pastoral liturgy, consisting of persons eminent in these matters and including the laity as circumstances suggest. Under the direction of the aforementioned territorial ecclesiastical

authority, the commission is to regulate pastoral-liturgical action throughout the territory and to promote studies and necessary experiments whenever there is question of adaptations to be proposed to the Apostolic See.

45.    For the same reason every diocese is to have a commission on the liturgy, under the direction of the bishop, for promoting the liturgical apostolate.

Sometimes it may be advisable for several dioceses to form among themselves one single commission, in order to promote the liturgy by means of shared consultation.

46.    Besides the commission on the liturgy, every diocese, as far as possible, should have commissions for music and art.

These three commissions must work in closest collaboration; indeed it will often be best to fuse the three of them into one single commission.

## CHAPTER II
## THE MOST SACRED MYSTERY OF THE EUCHARIST

47.    At the Last Supper, on the night when he was betrayed, our Savior instituted the eucharistic sacrifice of his body and blood. He did this in order to perpetuate the sacrifice of the cross throughout the centuries until he should come again and in this way to entrust to his beloved Bride, the Church, a memorial of his death and resurrection: a sacrament of love, a sign of unity, a bond of charity,[1] a paschal banquet "in which Christ is eaten, the heart is filled with grace, and a pledge of future glory given to us."[2]

48.    The Church, therefore, earnestly desires that Christ's faithful, when present at this mystery of faith, should not be there as strangers or silent spectators; on the contrary, through a good understanding of the rites and prayers they should take part in the sacred service conscious of what they are doing, with devotion and full involvement. They should be instructed by God's word and be nourished at the table of the Lord's body; they should give thanks to God; by offering the immaculate Victim, not only through the hands of the priest, but also with him, they should learn to offer themselves as well; through Christ the Mediator,[3] they should be formed day by day into an ever more perfect unity with God and with each other, so that finally God may be all in all.

49.    Thus, mindful of those Masses celebrated with the assistance of the faithful, especially on Sundays and holy days of obligation, the Council makes the following decrees in order that the sacrifice of the Mass, even in its ritual forms, may become pastorally effective to the utmost degree.

50.    The Order of Mass is to be revised in a way that will bring out more clearly the intrinsic nature and purpose of its several parts, as also the connection between them, and will more readily achieve the devout, active participation of the faithful.

For this purpose the rites are to be simplified, due care being taken to preserve their substance; elements that, with the passage of time, came to be duplicated or were added with but little advantage are now to be discarded; other elements that have suffered injury through accident of history are now, as may seem useful or necessary, to be restored to the vigor they had in the traditions of the Fathers.

51.    The treasures of the Bible are to be opened up more lavishly, so that a richer share in God's word may be provided for the faithful. In this way a more representative portion of holy Scripture will be read to the people in the course of a prescribed number of years.

52.    By means of the homily the mysteries of the faith and the guiding principles of the Christian life are expounded from the sacred text during the course of the liturgical year; as part of the liturgy itself therefore, the homily is strongly recommended; in fact, at Masses celebrated with the assistance of the people on Sundays and holy days of obligation it is not to be omitted except for a serious reason.

53.    Especially on Sundays and holy days of obligation there is to be restored, after the gospel and the homily, "the universal prayer" or "the prayer of the faithful." By this prayer, in which the people are to take part, intercession shall be made for holy Church, for the civil authorities, for those oppressed by various needs, for all people, and for the salvation of the entire world.[4]

54.    With art. 36 of this Constitution as the norm, in Masses celebrated with the people a suitable place may be allotted to their mother tongue. This is to apply in the first place to the readings and "the universal prayer," but also, as local conditions may warrant, to those parts belonging to the people.

Nevertheless steps should be taken enabling the faithful to say or to sing together in Latin those parts of the Ordinary of the Mass belonging to them.

Wherever a more extended use of the mother tongue within the Mass appears desirable, the regulation laid down in art. 40 of this Constitution is to be observed.

55.    That more complete form of participation in the Mass by which the faithful, after the priest's communion, receive the Lord's body from the sacrifice, is strongly endorsed.

The dogmatic principles laid down by the Council of Trent remain intact.[5] In instances to be specified by the Apostolic See, however, communion under both kinds may be granted both to clerics and religious and to the laity at the discretion of the bishops, for example, to the ordained at the Mass of their ordination, to the professed at the Mass of their religious profession, to the newly baptized at the Mass following their baptism.

56.    The two parts that, in a certain sense, go to make up the Mass, namely, the liturgy of the word and the liturgy of the eucharist, are so closely connected with each other that they form but one single act of worship. Accordingly this Council

strongly urges pastors that in their catechesis they insistently teach the faithful to take part in the entire Mass, especially on Sundays and holy days of obligation.

57.    § 1. Concelebration, which aptly expresses the unity of the priesthood, has continued to this day as a practice in the Church of both East and West. For this reason it has seemed good to the Council to extend permission for concelebration to the following cases:

    1.  a.  on Holy Thursday, both the chrism Mass and the evening Mass;

        b.  Masses during councils, bishops' conferences, and synods;

        c.  the Mass at the blessing of an abbot.

    2.  Also, with permission of the Ordinary, who is the one to decide whether concelebration is opportune, to:

        a.  the conventual Mass and the principal Mass in churches, when the needs of the faithful do not require that all the priests on hand celebrate individually;

        b.  Masses celebrated at any kind of meeting of priests, whether secular or religious.

    § 2. 1. The regulation, however, of the discipline of concelebration in the diocese pertains to the bishop.

    2. This, however, does not take away the option of every priest to celebrate Mass individually, not, however, at the same time and in the same church as a concelebrated Mass or on Holy Thursday.

58.    A new rite for concelebration is to be drawn up and inserted into the Roman Pontifical and Roman Missal.

# CHAPTER III
# THE OTHER SACRAMENTS AND THE SACRAMENTALS

59.    The purpose of the sacraments is to make people holy, to build up the Body of Christ, and, finally, to give worship to God; but being signs they also have a teaching function. They not only presuppose faith, but by words and objects they also nourish, strengthen, and express it; that is why they are called "sacraments of faith." They do indeed impart grace, but, in addition, the very act of celebrating them disposes the faithful most effectively to receive this grace in a fruitful manner, to worship God rightly, and to practice charity.

    It is therefore of the highest importance that the faithful should readily understand the sacramental signs and should with great eagerness frequent those sacraments that were instituted to nourish the Christian life.

60.    The Church has, in addition, instituted sacramentals. These are sacred signs bearing a kind of resemblance to the sacraments: they signify effects, particularly of a spiritual kind, that are obtained through the Church's intercession. They dispose people to receive the chief effect of the sacraments and they make holy various occasions in human life.

61.   Thus, for well-disposed members of the faithful, the effect of the liturgy of the sacraments and sacramentals is that almost every event in their lives is made holy by divine grace that flows from the paschal mystery of Christ's passion, death, and resurrection, the fount from which all sacraments and sacramentals draw their power. The liturgy means also that there is hardly any proper use of material things that cannot thus be directed toward human sanctification and the praise of God.

62.   With the passage of time, however, certain features have crept into the rites of the sacraments and sacramentals that have made their nature and purpose less clear to the people of today; hence some changes have become necessary as adaptations to the needs of our own times. For this reason the Council decrees what follows concerning the revision of these rites.

63.   Because the use of the mother tongue in the administration of the sacraments and sacramentals can often be of considerable help for the people, this use is to be extended according to the following norms:

     a.  With art. 36 as the norm, the vernacular may be used in administering the sacraments and sacramentals.

     b.  Particular rituals in harmony with the new edition of the Roman Ritual shall be prepared without delay by the competent, territorial ecclesiastical authority mentioned in art. 22, §2 of this Constitution. These rituals are to be adapted, even in regard to the language employed, to the needs of the different regions. Once they have been reviewed by the Apostolic See, they are to be used in the regions for which they have been prepared. But those who draw up these rituals or particular collections of rites must not leave out the prefatory instructions for the individual rites in the Roman Ritual, whether the instructions are pastoral and rubrical or have some special social bearing.

64.   The catechumenate for adults, divided into several stages, is to be restored and put into use at the discretion of the local Ordinary. By this means the time of the catechumenate, which is intended as a period of well-suited instruction, may be sanctified by sacred rites to be celebrated at successive intervals of time.

65.   With art. 37–40 of this Constitution as the norm, it is lawful in mission lands to allow, besides what is part of Christian tradition, those initiation elements in use among individual peoples, to the extent that such elements are compatible with the Christian rite of initiation.

66.   Both of the rites for the baptism of adults are to be revised: not only the simpler rite, but also the more solemn one, with proper attention to the restored catechumenate. A special Mass "On the Occasion of a Baptism" is to be incorporated into the Roman Missal.

67.   The rite for the baptism of infants is to be revised and it should be suited to the fact that those to be baptized are infants. The roles as well as the obligations of parents and godparents should be brought out more clearly in the rite itself.

68.   The baptismal rite should contain alternatives, to be used at the discretion of the local Ordinary, for occasions when a very large number are to be baptized together. Moreover, a shorter rite is to be drawn up, especially in mission lands, for use by catechists, but also by the faithful in general, when there is danger of death and neither a priest nor a deacon is available.

69.   In place of the rite called the "Order of Supplying What Was Omitted in the Baptism of an Infant," a new rite is to be drawn up. This should manifest more clearly and fittingly that an infant who was baptized by the short rite has already been received into the Church.

Similarly, a new rite is to be drawn up for converts who have already been validly baptized; it should express that they are being received into the communion of the Church.

70.   Except during the Easter season, baptismal water may be blessed within the rite of baptism itself by use of an approved, shorter formulary.

71.   The rite of confirmation is also to be revised in order that the intimate connection of this sacrament with the whole of Christian initiation may stand out more clearly; for this reason it is fitting for candidates to renew their baptismal promises just before they are confirmed.

Confirmation may be conferred within Mass when convenient; as for the rite outside Mass, a formulary is to be composed for use as an introduction.

72.   The rite and formularies for the sacrament of penance are to be revised so that they more clearly express both the nature and effect of the sacrament.

73.   "Extreme unction," which may also and more properly be called "anointing of the sick," is not a sacrament for those only who are at the point of death. Hence, as soon as any one of the faithful begins to be in danger of death from sickness or old age, the fitting time for that person to receive this sacrament has certainly already arrived.

74.   In addition to the separate rites for anointing of the sick and for viaticum, a continuous rite shall be drawn up, structured so that the sick person is anointed after confessing and before receiving viaticum.

75.   The number of the anointings is to be adapted to the circumstances; the prayers that belong to the rite of anointing are to be so revised that they correspond to the varying conditions of the sick who receive the sacrament.

76.   Both the ceremonies and texts of the ordination rites are to be revised. The address given by the bishop at the beginning of each ordination or consecration may be in the vernacular.

When a bishop is consecrated, all the bishops present may take part in the laying on of hands.

77. The marriage rite now found in the Roman Ritual is to be revised and enriched in such a way that it more clearly signifies the grace of the sacrament and imparts a knowledge of the obligations of spouses.

"If any regions follow other praiseworthy customs and ceremonies when celebrating the sacrament of marriage, the Council earnestly desires that by all means these be retained."[1]

Moreover, the competent, territorial ecclesiastical authority mentioned in art. 22, §2 of this Constitution is free to draw up, in accord with art. 63, its own rite, suited to the usages of place and people. But the rite must always conform to the law that the priest assisting at the marriage must ask for and obtain the consent of the contracting parties.

78. Marriage is normally to be celebrated within Mass, after the reading of the gospel and the homily and before "the prayer of the faithful." The prayer for the bride, duly emended to remind both spouses of their equal obligation to remain faithful to each other, may be said in the vernacular.

But if the sacrament of marriage is celebrated apart from Mass, the epistle and gospel from the nuptial Mass are to be read at the beginning of the rite and the blessing is always to be given to the spouses.

79. The sacramentals are to be reviewed in the light of the primary criterion that the faithful participate intelligently, actively, and easily; the conditions of our own days must also be considered. When rituals are revised, in accord with art. 63, new sacramentals may also be added as the need for them becomes apparent.

Reserved blessings shall be very few; reservations shall be in favor only of bishops and Ordinaries.

Let provision be made that some sacramentals, at least in special circumstances and at the discretion of the Ordinary, may be administered by qualified laypersons.

80. The rite for the consecration to a life of virginity as it exists in the Roman Pontifical is to be revised.

A rite of religious profession and renewal of vows shall be drawn up with a view to achieving greater unity, simplicity, and dignity. Apart from exceptions in particular law, this rite should be adopted by those who make their profession or renewal of vows within Mass.

Religious profession should preferably be made within Mass.

81. The rite of funerals should express more clearly the paschal character of Christian death and should correspond more closely to the circumstances and traditions of various regions. This applies also to the liturgical color to be used.

82. The rite for the burial of infants is to be revised and a special Mass for the occasion provided.

# CHAPTER IV
## DIVINE OFFICE

83.   Christ Jesus, High Priest of the new and eternal covenant, taking human nature, introduced into this earthly exile the hymn that is sung throughout all ages in the halls of heaven. He joins the entire human community to himself, associating it with his own singing of this canticle of divine praise.

For he continues his priestly work through the agency of his Church, which is unceasingly engaged in praising the Lord and interceding for the salvation of the whole world. The Church does this not only by celebrating the eucharist, but also in other ways, especially by praying the divine office.

84.   By tradition going back to early Christian times, the divine office is so arranged that the whole course of the day and night is made holy by the praises of God. Therefore, when this wonderful song of praise is rightly performed by priests and others who are deputed for this purpose by the Church's ordinance or by the faithful praying together with the priest in the approved form, then it is truly the voice of a bride addressing her bridegroom; it is the very prayer that Christ himself, together with his Body, addresses to the Father.

85.   Hence all who render this service are not only fulfilling a duty of the Church, but also are sharing in the greatest honor of Christ's Bride, for by offering these praises to God they are standing before God's throne in the name of the Church, their Mother.

86.   Priests engaged in the sacred pastoral ministry will offer the praises of the hours with greater fervor the more vividly they realize that they must heed St. Paul's exhortation: "Pray without ceasing" (1 Thes 5:17). For the work in which they labor will effect nothing and bring forth no fruit except by the power of the Lord who said: "Without me you can do nothing" (Jn 15:5). That is why the apostles, instituting deacons, said: "We will devote ourselves to prayer and to the ministry of the word" (Acts 6:4).

87.   In order that the divine office may be better and more completely carried out in existing circumstances, whether by priests or by other members of the Church, the Council, carrying further the restoration already so happily begun by the Apostolic See, has seen fit to decree what follows concerning the office of the Roman Rite.

88.   Because the purpose of the office is to sanctify the day, the traditional sequence of the hours is to be restored so that once again they may be genuinely related to the hour of the day when they are prayed, as far as it is possible. Moreover, it will be necessary to take into account the modern conditions in which daily life has to be lived, especially by those who are called to labor in apostolic works.

89. Therefore, when the office is revised, these norms are to be observed:

a. By the venerable tradition of the universal Church, lauds as morning prayer and vespers as evening prayer are the two hinges on which the daily office turns; hence they are to be considered as the chief hours and celebrated as such.

b. Compline is to be so composed that it will be a suitable prayer for the end of the day.

c. The hour known as matins, although it should retain the character of nocturnal praise when celebrated in choir, shall be adapted so that it may be recited at any hour of the day; it shall be made up of fewer psalms and longer readings.

d. The hour of prime is to be suppressed.

e. In choir the minor hours of terce, sext, and none are to be observed. But outside choir it will be lawful to choose whichever of the three best suits the hour of the day.

90. The divine office, because it is the public prayer of the Church, is a source of devotion and nourishment also for personal prayer. Therefore priests and all others who take part in the divine office are earnestly exhorted in the Lord to attune their minds to their voices when praying it. The better to achieve this, let them take steps to improve their understanding of the liturgy and of the Bible, especially the psalms.

In revising the Roman office, its ancient and venerable treasures are to be so adapted that all those to whom they are handed on may more fully and readily draw profit from them.

91. So that it may really be possible in practice to observe the course of the hours proposed in art. 89, the psalms are no longer to be distributed over just one week, but over some longer period of time.

The work of revising the psalter, already happily begun, is to be finished as soon as possible and is to take into account the style of Christian Latin, the liturgical use of psalms, including their being sung, and the entire tradition of the Latin Church.

92. As regards the readings, the following shall be observed:

a. Readings from sacred Scripture shall be arranged so that the riches of God's word may be easily accessible in more abundant measure.

b. Readings excerpted from the works of the Fathers, doctors, and ecclesiastical writers shall be better selected.

c. The accounts of the martyrdom or lives of the saints are to be made to accord with the historical facts.

93. To whatever extent may seem advisable, the hymns are to be restored to their original form and any allusion to mythology or anything that conflicts with

Christian piety is to be dropped or changed. Also, as occasion arises, let other selections from the treasury of hymns be incorporated.

94. That the day may be truly sanctified and the hours themselves recited with spiritual advantage, it is best that each of them be prayed at a time most closely corresponding to the true time of each canonical hour.

95. In addition to the conventual Mass, communities obliged to choral office are bound to celebrate the office in choir every day. In particular:

a. Orders of canons, of monks and of nuns, and of other regulars bound by law or constitutions to choral office must celebrate the entire office.

b. Cathedral or collegiate chapters are bound to recite those parts of the office imposed on them by general or particular law.

c. All members of the above communities who are in major orders or are solemnly professed, except for lay brothers, are bound individually to recite those canonical hours which they do not pray in choir.

96. Clerics not bound to office in choir, if they are in major orders, are bound to pray the entire office every day, either in common or individually, following the norms in art. 89.

97. Appropriate instances are to be defined by the rubrics in which a liturgical service may be substituted for the divine office.

In particular cases and for a just reason Ordinaries may dispense their subjects wholly or in part from the obligation of reciting the divine office or may commute it.

98. Members of any institute dedicated to acquiring perfection who, according to their constitutions, are to recite any parts of the divine office are thereby performing the public prayer of the Church.

They too perform the public prayer of the Church who, in virtue of their constitutions, recite any little office, provided this has been drawn up after the pattern of the divine office and duly approved.

99. Since the divine office is the voice of the Church, that is, of the whole Mystical Body publicly praising God, those clerics who are not obliged to office in choir, especially priests who live together or who meet together for any purpose, are urged to pray at least some part of the divine office in common.

All who pray the divine office, whether in choir or in common, should fulfill the task entrusted to them as perfectly as possible: this refers not only to the internal devotion of their minds but also to their external manner of celebration.

It is advantageous, moreover, that the office in choir and in common be sung when there is an opportunity to do so.

100. Pastors should see to it that the chief hours, especially vespers, are celebrated in common in church on Sundays and the more solemn feasts. The laity,

too, are encouraged to recite the divine office either with the priests, or among themselves, or even individually.

101. § 1. In accordance with the centuries-old tradition of the Latin rite, clerics are to retain the Latin language in the divine office. But in individual cases the Ordinary has the power of granting the use of a vernacular translation, prepared in accord with art. 36, to those clerics for whom the use of Latin constitutes a grave obstacle to their praying the office properly.

§ 2. The competent superior has the power to grant the use of the vernacular in the celebration of the divine office, even in choir, to nuns and to members of institutes dedicated to acquiring perfection, both men who are not clerics and women. The version, however, must be one that has been approved.

§ 3. Any cleric bound to the divine office fulfills his obligation if he prays the office in the vernacular together with a group of the faithful or with those mentioned in §2, provided the text of the translation has been approved.

## CHAPTER V
## THE LITURGICAL YEAR

102. The Church is conscious that it must celebrate the saving work of the divine Bridegroom by devoutly recalling it on certain days throughout the course of the year. Every week, on the day which the Church has called the Lord's Day, it keeps the memory of the Lord's resurrection, which it also celebrates once in the year, together with his blessed passion, in the most solemn festival of Easter.

Within the cycle of a year, moreover, the Church unfolds the whole mystery of Christ, from his incarnation and birth until his ascension, the day of Pentecost, and the expectation of blessed hope and of the Lord's return.

Recalling thus the mysteries of redemption, the Church opens to the faithful the riches of the Lord's powers and merits, so that these are in some way made present in every age in order that the faithful may lay hold on them and be filled with saving grace.

103. In celebrating this annual cycle of Christ's mysteries, the Church honors with special love Mary, the Mother of God, who is joined by an inseparable bond to the saving work of her Son. In her the Church holds up and admires the most excellent effect of the redemption and joyfully contemplates, as in a flawless image, that which the Church itself desires and hopes wholly to be.

104. The Church has also included in the annual cycle days devoted to the memory of the martyrs and the other saints. Raised up to perfection by the manifold grace of God and already in possession of eternal salvation, they sing God's perfect praise in heaven and offer prayers for us. By celebrating their passage from earth to heaven the Church proclaims the paschal mystery achieved in the saints, who have suffered and been glorified with Christ; it proposes them to the faithful as examples drawing all to the Father through Christ and pleads through their merits for God's favors.

105. Finally, in the various seasons of the year and according to its traditional discipline, the Church completes the formation of the faithful by means of devout practices for soul and body, by instruction, prayer, and works of penance and of mercy.

Accordingly the sacred Council has seen fit to decree what follows.

106. By a tradition handed down from the apostles and having its origin from the very day of Christ's resurrection, the Church celebrates the paschal mystery every eighth day, which, with good reason, bears the name of the Lord's Day or Sunday. For on this day Christ's faithful must gather together so that, by hearing the word of God and taking part in the eucharist, they may call to mind the passion, the resurrection, and the glorification of the Lord Jesus and may thank God, who "has begotten them again unto a living hope through the resurrection of Jesus Christ from the dead" (1 Pt 1:3). Hence the Lord's Day is the first holy day of all and should be proposed to the devotion of the faithful and taught to them in such a way that it may become in fact a day of joy and of freedom from work. Other celebrations, unless they be truly of greatest importance, shall not have precedence over the Sunday, the foundation and core of the whole liturgical year.

107. The liturgical year is to be so revised that the traditional customs and usages of the sacred seasons are preserved or restored to suit the conditions of modern times; their specific character is to be retained, so that they duly nourish the devotion of the faithful who celebrate the mysteries of Christian redemption and above all the paschal mystery. If certain adaptations are considered necessary on account of local conditions, they are to be made in accordance with the provisions of art. 39 and 40.

108. The minds of the faithful must be directed primarily toward those feasts of the Lord on which the mysteries of salvation are celebrated in the course of the year. Therefore, the Proper of Seasons shall be given the precedence due to it over the feasts of the saints, in order that the entire cycle of the mysteries of salvation may be celebrated in the measure due to them.

109. Lent is marked by two themes, the baptismal and the penitential. By recalling or preparing for baptism and by repentance, this season disposes the faithful, as they more diligently listen to the word of God and devote themselves to prayer, to celebrate the paschal mystery. The baptismal and penitential aspects of Lent are to be given greater prominence in both the liturgy and liturgical catechesis. Hence:

a. More use is to be made of the baptismal features proper to the Lenten liturgy; some of those from an earlier era are to be restored as may seem advisable.

b. The same is to apply to the penitential elements. As regards catechesis, it is important to impress on the minds of the faithful not only the social consequences of sin but also the essence of the virtue of penance, namely, detestation of sin as an offense against God; the role of the Church in penitential practices is not to be neglected and the people are to be exhorted to pray for sinners.

110.   During Lent penance should be not only inward and individual, but also outward and social. The practice of penance should be fostered, however, in ways that are possible in our own times and in different regions and according to the circumstances of the faithful; it should be encouraged by the authorities mentioned in art. 22.

Nevertheless, let the paschal fast be kept sacred. Let it be observed everywhere on Good Friday and, where possible, prolonged throughout Holy Saturday, as a way of coming to the joys of the Sunday of the resurrection with uplifted and welcoming heart.

111.   The saints have been traditionally honored in the Church and their authentic relics and images held in veneration. For the feasts of the saints proclaim the wonderful works of Christ in his servants and display to the faithful fitting examples for their imitation.

Lest the feasts of the saints take precedence over the feasts commemorating the very mysteries of salvation, many of them should be left to be celebrated by a particular Church or nation or religious family; those only should be extended to the universal Church that commemorate saints of truly universal significance.

# CHAPTER VI
## SACRED MUSIC

112.   The musical tradition of the universal Church is a treasure of inestimable value, greater even than that of any other art. The main reason for this preeminence is that, as sacred song closely bound to the text, it forms a necessary or integral part of the solemn liturgy.

Holy Scripture itself has bestowed praise upon sacred song[1] and the same may be said of the Fathers of the Church and of the Roman pontiffs, who in recent times, led by St. Pius X, have explained more precisely the ministerial function supplied by sacred music in the service of the Lord.

Therefore sacred music will be the more holy the more closely it is joined to the liturgical rite, whether by adding delight to prayer, fostering oneness of spirit, or investing the rites with greater solemnity. But the Church approves of all forms of genuine art possessing the qualities required and admits them into divine worship.

Accordingly, the Council, keeping the norms and precepts of ecclesiastical tradition and discipline and having regard to the purpose of sacred music, which is the glory of God and the sanctification of the faithful, decrees what follows.

113.   A liturgical service takes on a nobler aspect when the rites are celebrated with singing, the sacred ministers take their parts in them, and the faithful actively participate.

As regards the language to be used, the provisions of art. 36 are to be observed; for the Mass, those of art. 54; for the sacraments, those of art. 63; for the divine office, those of art. 101.

114. The treasure of sacred music is to be preserved and fostered with great care. Choirs must be diligently developed, especially in cathedral churches; but bishops and other pastors of souls must be at pains to ensure that whenever a liturgical service is to be celebrated with song, the whole assembly of the faithful is enabled, in keeping with art. 28 and 30, to contribute the active participation that rightly belongs to it.

115. Great importance is to be attached to the teaching and practice of music in seminaries, in the novitiates and houses of study of religious of both sexes, and also in other Catholic institutions and schools. To impart this instruction, those in charge of teaching sacred music are to receive thorough training.

It is recommended also that higher institutes of sacred music be established whenever possible.

Musicians and singers, especially young boys, must also be given a genuine liturgical training.

116. The Church acknowledges Gregorian chant as distinctive of the Roman liturgy; therefore, other things being equal, it should be given pride of place in liturgical services.

But other kinds of sacred music, especially polyphony, are by no means excluded from liturgical celebrations, provided they accord with the spirit of the liturgical service, in the way laid down in art. 30.

117. The *editio typica* of the books of Gregorian chant is to be completed and a more critical edition is to be prepared of those books already published since the reform of St. Pius x.

It is desirable also that an edition be prepared containing the simpler melodies for use in small churches.

118. The people's own religious songs are to be encouraged with care so that in sacred devotions as well as during services of the liturgy itself, in keeping with rubrical norms and requirements, the faithful may raise their voices in song.

119. In certain parts of the world, especially mission lands, people have their own musical traditions and these play a great part in their religious and social life. Thus, in keeping with art. 39 and 40, due importance is to be attached to their music and a suitable place given to it, not only in forming their attitude toward religion, but also in adapting worship to their native genius.

Therefore, when missionaries are being given training in music, every effort should be made to see that they become competent in promoting the traditional music of the people, both in schools and in sacred services, as far as may be practicable.

120. In the Latin Church the pipe organ is to be held in high esteem, for it is the traditional musical instrument that adds a wonderful splendor to the Church's ceremonies and powerfully lifts up the spirit to God and to higher things.

But other instruments also may be admitted for use in divine worship, with the knowledge and consent of the competent territorial authority and in conformity with art. 22, §2, art. 37 and art. 40. This applies, however, only on condition that the instruments are suitable, or can be made suitable, for sacred use, are in accord with the dignity of the place of worship, and truly contribute to the uplifting of the faithful.

121. Composers, filled with the Christian spirit, should feel that their vocation is to develop sacred music and to increase its store of treasures.

Let them produce compositions having the qualities proper to genuine sacred music, not confining themselves to works that can be sung only by large choirs, but providing also for the needs of small choirs and for the active participation of the entire assembly of the faithful.

The texts intended to be sung must always be consistent with Catholic teaching; indeed they should be drawn chiefly from holy Scripture and from liturgical sources.

# CHAPTER VII
## SACRED ART AND SACRED FURNISHINGS

122. The fine arts are deservedly ranked among the noblest activities of human genius and this applies especially to religious art and to its highest achievement, sacred art. These arts, by their very nature, are oriented toward the infinite beauty of God, which they attempt in some way to portray by the work of human hands. They are dedicated to advancing God's praise and glory to the degree that they center on the single aim of turning the human spirit devoutly toward God.

The Church has therefore always been the friend of the fine arts, has ever sought their noble help, and has trained artists with the special aim that all things set apart for use in divine worship are truly worthy, becoming, and beautiful, signs and symbols of the supernatural world. The Church has always regarded itself as the rightful arbiter of the arts, deciding which of the works of artists are in accordance with faith, with reverence, and with honored traditional laws and are thereby suited for sacred use.

The Church has been particularly careful to see that sacred furnishings worthily and beautifully serve the dignity of worship and has admitted changes in materials, design, or ornamentation prompted by the progress of the technical arts with the passage of time.

Wherefore it has pleased the Fathers to issue the following decrees on these matters.

123. The Church has not adopted any particular style of art as its very own but has admitted styles from every period, according to the proper genius and circumstances of peoples and the requirements of the many different rites in the Church. Thus, in the course of the centuries, the Church has brought into being a treasury of art that must be very carefully preserved. The art of our own days, coming from every race and region, shall also be given free scope in the Church, on

condition that it serves the places of worship and sacred rites with the reverence and honor due to them. In this way contemporary art can add its own voice to that wonderful chorus of praise sung by the great masters of past ages of Catholic faith.

124. In encouraging and favoring art that is truly sacred, Ordinaries should strive after noble beauty rather than mere sumptuous display. This principle is to apply also in the matter of sacred vestments and appointments.

Let bishops carefully remove from the house of God and from other places of worship those works of artists that are repugnant to faith and morals and to Christian devotion and that offend true religious sense either by their grotesqueness or by the deficiency, mediocrity, or sham in their artistic quality.

When churches are to be built, let great care be taken that they are well suited to celebrating liturgical services and to bringing about the active participation of the faithful.

125. The practice of placing sacred images in churches so that they may be venerated by the faithful is to be maintained. Nevertheless there is to be restraint regarding their number and prominence so that they do not create confusion among the Christian people or foster religious practices of doubtful orthodoxy.

126. When deciding on works of art, local Ordinaries shall give hearing to the diocesan commission on sacred art, and if need be, to others who are especially expert, as well as to the commissions referred to in art. 44, 45, and 46. Ordinaries must be very careful to see that sacred furnishings and valuable works of art are not disposed of or damaged, for they are the adornment of the house of God.

127. Bishops should have a special concern for artists, so as to imbue them with the spirit of sacred art and liturgy. This they may do in person or through competent priests who are gifted with a knowledge and love of art.

It is also recommended that schools or academies of sacred art to train artists be founded in those parts of the world where they seem useful.

All artists who, prompted by their talents, desire to serve God's glory in holy Church, should ever bear in mind that they are engaged in a kind of sacred imitation of God the Creator and are concerned with works intended to be used in Catholic worship, to uplift the faithful, and to foster their devotion and religious formation.

128. Along with the revision of the liturgical books, as laid down in art. 25, there is to be an early revision of the canons and ecclesiastical statutes regulating the supplying of material things involved in sacred worship. This applies in particular to the worthy and well-planned construction of places of worship, the design and construction of altars, the nobility, placement, and security of the eucharistic tabernacle, the practicality and dignity of the baptistry, the appropriate arrangement of sacred images and church decorations and appointments. Laws that seem less suited to the reformed liturgy are to be brought into harmony with it or else abolished; laws that are helpful are to be retained if already in use or introduced where they are lacking.

With art. 22 of this Constitution as the norm, the territorial bodies of bishops are empowered to make adaptations to the needs and customs of their different regions; this applies especially to the material and design of sacred furnishings and vestments.

129. During their philosophical and theological studies, clerics are to be taught about the history and development of sacred art and about the sound principles on which the production of its works must be grounded. In consequence they will be able to appreciate and preserve the Church's treasured monuments and be in a position to offer good advice to artists who are engaged in producing works of art.

130. It is fitting that the use of pontifical insignia be reserved to those ecclesiastical persons who have either episcopal rank or some definite jurisdiction.

# APPENDIX
## DECLARATION OF THE SECOND VATICAN ECUMENICAL COUNCIL ON REVISION OF THE CALENDAR

131. The Second Vatican Ecumenical Council recognizes the importance of the wishes expressed by many on assigning the feast of Easter to a fixed Sunday and on an unchanging calendar and has considered the effects that could result from the introduction of a new calendar. Accordingly the Council issues the following declaration:

1. The Council is not opposed to the assignment of the feast of Easter to a particular Sunday of the Gregorian Calendar, provided those whom it may concern, especially other Christians who are not in communion with the Apostolic See, give their assent.

2. The Council likewise declares that it does not oppose measures designed to introduce a perpetual calendar into civil society.

Among the various systems being suggested to establish a perpetual calendar and to introduce it into civil life, only those systems are acceptable to the Church that retain and safeguard a seven-day week with Sunday and introduce no days outside the week, so that the present sequence of weeks is left intact, unless the most serious reasons arise. Concerning these the Apostolic See will make its own judgment.

The Fathers of the Council have given assent to all and to each part of the matters set forth in this Constitution. And together with the venerable Fathers, we, by the apostolic power given to us by Christ, approve, enact, and establish in the Holy Spirit each and all the decrees in this Constitution and command that what has been thus established in the Council be promulgated for the glory of God.

# NOTES

1. RM, prayer over the gifts, Holy Thursday and 2d Sunday in Ordinary Time.

2. See Heb 13:14.

3. See Eph 2:21–22.

4. See Eph 4:13.

5. See Is 11:12.

6. See Jn 11:52.

7. See Jn 10:16.

## CHAPTER I

1. See Is 61:1; Lk 4:18.

2. Ignatius of Antioch, *To the Ephesians* 7, 2.

3. See 1 Tm 2:5.

4. *Sacramentarium Veronense* (ed. Mohlberg), no. 1265.

5. RM, preface I of Easter.

6. RM, prayer after the seventh reading, Easter Vigil.

7. See Mk 16:15.

8. See Acts 26:18.

9. See Rom 6:4; Eph 2:6; Col 3:1.

10. See Jn 4:23.

11. See 1 Cor 11:26.

12. Council of Trent, sess. 13, 11 Oct 1551, Decree on the Holy Eucharist, chap. 5.

13. Council of Trent, sess. 22, 17 Sept 1562, Doctrine on the Holy Sacrifice of the Mass, chap. 2.

14. See Augustine, *In Ioannis Evangelium Tractatus* 6, chap. 1, n. 7.

15. See Rv. 21:2; Col 3:1; Heb 8:2.

16. See Phil 3:20; Col 3:4.

17. See Jn 17:3; Lk 24:47; Acts 2:38.

18. See Mt 28:20.

19. RM, prayer after communion, Easter Vigil.

20. RM, opening prayer, Mass for Monday of Easter Week.

21. See 2 Cor 6:1.

22. See Mt 6:6.

23. See 1 Thes 5:17.

24. See 2 Cor 4:10–11.

25. RM, prayer over the gifts, Saturday after the 2d, 4th, and 6th Sundays of Easter.

26. Cyprian, *On the Unity of the Catholic Church* 7; see *Letter 66*, n. 8, 3.

27. See Council of Trent, sess. 22, 17 Sept 1562, Doctrine on the Holy Sacrifice of the Mass, chap. 8.

28. See Ignatius of Antioch, *To the Magnesians*, 7; *To the Philadelphians*, 4; *To the Smyrians*, 8.

## CHAPTER II

1. See Augustine, *In Ioannis Evangelium Tractatus 36*, chap. 6, n. 13.

2. Liturgy of the Hours, antiphon for Canticle of Mary, evening prayer II, feast of Corpus Christi.

3. See Cyril of Alexandria, *Commentary on the Gospel of John*, book 11, chap. 11–12.

4. See 1 Tm 2:1–2.

5. Council of Trent, sess. 21, Doctrine on Communion under Both Species, chap. 1–3.

## CHAPTER III

1. Council of Trent, sess. 24, Decree on Reform, chap. 1. See also RR, title 8, chap. 2, n. 6.

## CHAPTER VI

1. See Eph 5:19; Col 3:16.

# GENERAL INSTRUCTION
## OF THE
# ROMAN MISSAL

# OVERVIEW OF THE *GENERAL INSTRUCTION OF THE ROMAN MISSAL*

Mark R. Francis, CSV

Most people are familiar with a geographical resource book called an atlas—a book that contains a collection of two-dimensional views of the planet called maps. These views range from the general to the specific, from panoramic projections of the entire surface of the earth to focused representations of particular nations and cities. While maps are extremely useful in helping us situate ourselves and in getting a sense of the world as a whole, no one can ever confuse the maps themselves with the "real thing"—the world in which we live. The same relationship exists between the *General Instruction of the Roman Missal* and the celebration of the eucharist. Much as an atlas helps orient the reader to the world through both general and specific views of the globe, so the *General Instruction of the Roman Missal* provides both general and more focused perspectives on the celebration of the eucharist. No one can confuse the *General Instruction* with what it describes, but a careful reading of this document does provide the basic orientation necessary for anyone who would minister liturgically within the eucharistic celebration.

In addition to being a simple description of the structure of the eucharist, the *Instruction* also articulates the "whys" and "hows" of this celebration by explaining doctrinal principles and by outlining how these principles give shape to the present rite of Mass. Unlike the introductory section of the former Missal that only emphasized the rubrical "hows" of the Mass, the *General Instruction* is a guide that provides the all-important theological and pastoral "whys" regarding Roman Catholic eucharistic worship. Because it is such a guide, it really goes beyond the rather modest description of its purpose as stated in paragraph six: "to give the general guidelines for planning the eucharistic celebration properly and to set forth the rules for arranging individual forms of the celebration."

After the *Constitution on the Sacred Liturgy*, the *General Instruction* is probably the single most influential document of the liturgical reform promoted by the Second Vatican Council. With the sacramentary it helps to interpret, it is the product of more than a decade of international scholarly and pastoral work. Teams of experts in liturgy and theology, as well as pastors and others, were commissioned to revise the eucharistic worship of the church in accord with the mandate of the Council outlined in articles nos. 47–58 of the *Constitution on the Sacred Liturgy*. Their work resulted in the promulgation in Latin of the new Order of Mass in 1969, the subsequent publication of the new *Missale Romanum* in 1970, and the appearance of the English-language sacramentary, with its *General Instruction*, in 1974.

## THE DIFFERENCE BETWEEN A MISSAL AND A SACRAMENTARY

The attentive reader will note that there is an inconsistency between the title of this document and the title of the liturgical book that it interprets. The *General Instruction of the Roman Missal* perhaps would be more aptly translated *General*

*Instruction of the Roman Sacramentary.* In the United States, the more traditional term "sacramentary" is used to translate *Missale Romanum* (Roman Missal) following a classic definition of a sacramentary as a book containing only those prayers needed by the presider for the celebration of the eucharist. The term "missal" usually refers to a book that includes all the texts needed at Mass, for example, the scripture readings, the texts of the chants, as well as the presidential prayers. This is clearly not the case with the book currently in use in the United States, which is thus more a "sacramentary" than a "missal" in the strict sense of the word.

WHY IS THE *GENERAL INSTRUCTION* A NEGLECTED RESOURCE?

Unfortunately, this rich document often is overlooked by those engaged in liturgical ministry for two reasons. First, many assume that it has nothing to do with their particular ministry because it serves as the introduction to the "priest's book," the sacramentary. Even more common is the reaction of many who page through it and quickly put it down because they become perplexed by the way it is arranged. If one does not understand the general structure of the document and how the various aspects of the rite of Mass are presented in its pages, it is easy to be distracted by ritual details and miss the spirit that animates the reform of the new rite of Mass. It would be like someone looking in an atlas for the plan of a city in the section containing the maps of nations or entire continents, being unable to find the city, then concluding the book is irrelevant. Moreover, some "maps" in the *General Instruction* should be updated in light of subsequent developments in liturgy, developments in both the international and national church. The document has been slightly revised several times since it was first issued, but still it must always be read in light of its *Appendix for Dioceses in the United States* and other important liturgical documents such as the *Introduction to the Lectionary for Mass* and the *Directory for Masses with Children* that supplement and develop what is presented in the *General Instruction.*

THE INTRODUCTION

The *General Instruction* begins with an introduction that had not been written when the first version of this document appeared with the Order of Mass in 1969. At the behest of Pope Paul VI, the introduction was prefixed to the *General Instruction of the Roman Missal* to answer some of the critiques leveled against the new rite of Mass by those who misunderstood the reforms and labeled them illegitimate and unorthodox. For this reason, the introduction (nos. 1–15) emphasizes the historic and theological continuity of the new rite of Mass with the former rite contained in the Tridentine Missal of Pius V, which had been issued in 1570.

Despite the fact that it was prompted by criticism, the introduction to the document clearly describes the overall historical and theological premises that underlie the reformed eucharistic liturgy. Especially instructive is its treatment of two practices forbidden by the Council of Trent: the use of the vernacular and communion under both kinds. While presenting the liturgical tradition of the Roman Rite as a treasure of the church, the introduction maintains that to be faithful to the substance of that tradition, it often is necessary to modify liturgical practices based on that tradition in light of changing historical situations and cultural contexts (nos. 13–15).

At first glance, the arrangement of the *General Instruction* could seem rather confusing. Although this long document is divided into eight chapters, these chapters are not of equal length nor do they seem to follow the same approach in discussing the liturgy. Each chapter looks at the eucharistic celebration from a particular angle and with a particular purpose in mind. Again, like an atlas that begins with maps of the world and presents progressively more focused views of nations, states and even cities, each succeeding chapter takes a closer and closer look at particular aspects of the eucharistic celebration, beginning with general theological principles and ending with a discussion of specific celebrations, such as Masses for particular occasions.

The short first chapter speaks of the rite of Mass inspired by the theology of the eucharist found in the documents of Vatican II. The second chapter then develops this discussion by explaining how that theology is expressed in the general ritual structure of Mass as well as in its constitutive parts. The third chapter describes the various offices and ministries needed for the celebration. An important part of this chapter describes the "Office and Function of the People of God," thus emphasizing that the liturgy is indeed something performed by all the faithful and not just by the clerical leaders of the assembly. The fourth chapter is dedicated to a discussion of the principal forms of the eucharistic celebration, beginning with the normative form of this celebration, Mass with a congregation (nos. 77–152). Chapters five through eight deal with specific issues: church arrangement and furnishings, the basic requirements for celebrating the eucharist, the pastoral criteria for choosing among the alternatives provided in the sacramentary, and directives concerning both the celebration of the eucharist for occasional needs and Masses for the dead.

THREE IMPORTANT PARTS OF THE DOCUMENT

For those readers who are concerned primarily with the preparation of Sunday eucharist in the parish, the most immediately helpful parts of the document deal with the general structure and elements of the Mass (nos. 24–57) and the celebration of Mass with a congregation (nos. 77–152). Before looking at these two sections, however, it also is instructive to turn to paragraphs seven and eight, which rightly can be considered the two foundational articles for the whole document. Paragraph seven outlines the fourfold presence of the Christ in the eucharistic celebration—in the assembly, the minister, the word and the eucharistic elements. Paragraph eight addresses the two basic parts of the celebration— the liturgy of the word and the liturgy of the eucharist. The rest of the document, especially the part that describes Mass with a congregation, can be regarded as an extended explanation and illustration of the principles contained in these two paragraphs.

The *General Instruction* is an international document written to provide the broadest of guidelines in view of the many legitimate alternatives employed in the eucharistic liturgy around the world. For this reason, some of the specific practices mentioned in its pages may appear rather curious, such as the discussion of communion under both kinds using a spoon or a tube (nos. 248–252), for these methods never have been common in the United States.

The reader also should be aware that the specific topics treated by the *General Instruction* in chapters five through eight, such as issues in environment and art, liturgical music and funerals, have been supplemented and further developed by subsequent documents, many of which are contained in this volume.

Other parts of the document will have little appeal to anyone but priests— the articles dealing with Masses without a congregation (nos. 209–231) and the various ritual details concerning concelebration are obvious examples (nos. 153–208).

CONCLUSION

Although the *General Instruction of the Roman Missal* serves as the introduction to the liturgical book that traditionally belongs to the priest-presider, it is a document that belongs to all the people of God—especially to those serving their sisters and brothers in the eucharistic celebration in all of the liturgical ministries. Prayerful reflection on these pages only can enhance the ministry of those who have pledged to assist the church in constantly celebrating its identity as "one body, one Spirit in Christ."

# OUTLINE

# GENERAL INSTRUCTION OF THE ROMAN MISSAL

## INTRODUCTION

1.    When Christ the Lord was about to celebrate the passover meal with his disciples and institute the sacrifice of his body and blood, he directed them to prepare a large room, arranged for the supper (Luke 22:12). The Church has always regarded this command of Christ as applying to itself when it gives directions about the preparation of the sentiments of the worshipers, the place, rites, and texts for the celebration of the eucharist. The current norms, laid down on the basis of the intent of Vatican Council II, and the new Missal that will be used henceforth in the celebration of Mass by the Church of the Roman Rite, are fresh evidence of the great care, faith, and unchanged love that the Church shows toward the eucharist. They attest as well to its coherent tradition, continuing amid the introduction of some new elements.

### A WITNESS TO UNCHANGED FAITH

2.    The sacrificial nature of the Mass was solemnly proclaimed by the Council of Trent in agreement with the whole tradition of the Church.[1] Vatican Council II reaffirmed this teaching in these significant words: "At the Last Supper our Savior instituted the eucharistic sacrifice of his body and blood. He did this in order to perpetuate the sacrifice of the cross throughout the centuries until he should come again and in this way to entrust to his beloved Bride, the Church, a memorial of his death and resurrection."[2]

The Council's teaching is expressed constantly in the formularies of the Mass. This teaching, in the concise words of the Leonine Sacramentary, is that "the work of our redemption is carried out whenever we celebrate the memory of this sacrifice";[3] it is aptly and accurately brought out in the eucharistic prayers. At the anamnesis or memorial, the priest, addressing God in the name of all the people, offers in thanksgiving the holy and living sacrifice: the Church's offering and the Victim whose death has reconciled us with God.[4] The priest also prays that the body and blood of Christ may be a sacrifice acceptable to the Father, bringing salvation to the whole world.[5]

In this new Missal, then, the Church's rule of prayer (lex orandi) corresponds to its constant rule of faith (lex credendi). This rule of faith instructs us that the sacrifice of the cross and its sacramental renewal in the Mass, which Christ instituted at the Last Supper and commanded his apostles to do in his memory, are one and the same, differing only in the manner of offering, and that consequently the Mass is at once a sacrifice of praise and thanksgiving, of reconciliation and expiation.

3.      The celebration of Mass also proclaims the sublime mystery of the Lord's real presence under the eucharistic elements, which Vatican Council II[6] and other documents of the Church's magisterium[7] have reaffirmed in the same sense and as the same teaching that the Council of Trent had proposed as a matter of faith.[8] The Mass does this not only by means of the very words of consecration, by which Christ becomes present through transubstantiation, but also by that spirit and expression of reverence and adoration in which the eucharistic liturgy is carried out. For the same reason the Christian people are invited in Holy Week on Holy Thursday and on the solemnity of Corpus Christi to honor this wonderful sacrament in a special way by their adoration.

4.      Further, because of the priest's more prominent place and office in the rite, its form sheds light on the ministerial priesthood proper to the presbyter, who offers the sacrifice in the person of Christ and presides over the assembly of a holy people. The meaning of his office is declared and detailed in the preface for the chrism Mass on Thursday of Holy Week, the day celebrating the institution of the priesthood. The preface brings out the passing on of the sacerdotal power through the laying on of hands and, by listing its various offices, describes that power. It is the continuation of the power of Christ, High Priest of the New Testament.

5.      In addition, the ministerial priesthood puts into its proper light another reality of which much should be made, namely, the royal priesthood of believers. Through the ministry of presbyters the people's spiritual sacrifice to God is brought to completeness in union with the sacrifice of Christ, our one and only Mediator.[9] For the celebration of the eucharist is the action of the whole Church; in it all should do only, but all of, those parts that belong to them in virtue of their place within the people of God. In this way greater attention will be given to some aspects of the eucharistic celebration that have sometimes been neglected in the course of time. For these people are the people of God, purchased by Christ's blood, gathered together by the Lord, nourished by his word. They are a people called to offer God the prayers of the entire human family, a people giving thanks in Christ for the mystery of salvation by offering his sacrifice. Finally, they are a people growing together into unity by sharing in Christ's body and blood. These people are holy by their origin, but becoming ever more holy by conscious, active, and fruitful participation in the mystery of the eucharist.[10]

## A WITNESS TO UNBROKEN TRADITION

6.      In setting forth its decrees for the revision of the Order of Mass, Vatican Council II directed, among other things, that some rites be restored "to the vigor they had in the tradition of the Fathers";[11] this is a quotation from the Apostolic Constitution *Quo primum* of 1570, by which St. Pius V promulgated the Tridentine Missal. The fact that the same words are used in reference to both Roman Missals indicates how both of them, although separated by four centuries, embrace one and the same tradition. And when the more profound elements of

this tradition are considered, it becomes clear how remarkably and harmoniously this new Roman Missal improves on the older one.

7.    The older Missal belongs to the difficult period of attacks against Catholic teaching on the sacrificial nature of the Mass, the ministerial priesthood, and the real and permanent presence of Christ under the eucharistic elements. St. Pius V was therefore especially concerned with preserving the relatively recent developments in the Church's tradition, then unjustly being assailed, and introduced only very slight changes into the sacred rites. In fact, the Roman Missal of 1570 differs very little from the first printed edition of 1474, which in turn faithfully follows the Missal used at the time of Pope Innocent III (1198–1216). Manuscripts in the Vatican Library provided some verbal emendations, but they seldom allowed research into "ancient and approved authors" to extend beyond the examination of a few liturgical commentaries of the Middle Ages.

8.    Today, on the other hand, countless studies of scholars have enriched the "tradition of the Fathers" that the revisers of the Missal under St. Pius V followed. After the Gregorian Sacramentary was first published in 1571, many critical editions of other ancient Roman and Ambrosian sacramentaries appeared. Ancient Spanish and Gallican liturgical books also became available, bringing to light many prayers of profound spirituality that had hitherto been unknown.

Traditions dating back to the first centuries before the formation of the Eastern and Western rites are also better known today because so many liturgical documents have been discovered.

The continuing progress in patristic studies has also illumined eucharistic theology through the teachings of such illustrious saints of Christian antiquity as Irenaeus, Ambrose, Cyril of Jerusalem, and John Chrysostom.

9.    The "tradition of the Fathers" does not require merely the preservation of what our immediate predecessors have passed on to us. There must also be profound study and understanding of the Church's entire past and of all the ways in which its single faith has been expressed in the quite diverse human and social forms prevailing in Semitic, Greek, and Latin cultures. This broader view shows us how the Holy Spirit endows the people of God with a marvelous fidelity in preserving the deposit of faith unchanged, even though prayers and rites differ so greatly.

## ADAPTATION TO MODERN CONDITIONS

10.    As it bears witness to the Roman Church's rule of prayer *(lex orandi)* and guards the deposit of faith handed down by the later councils, the new Roman Missal in turn marks a major step forward in liturgical tradition.

The Fathers of Vatican Council II in reaffirming the dogmatic statements of the Council of Trent were speaking at a far different time in the world's history. They were able therefore to bring forward proposals and measures of a pastoral nature that could not have even been foreseen four centuries ago.

11.   The Council of Trent recognized the great catechetical value of the celebration of Mass, but was unable to bring out all its consequences for the actual life of the Church. Many were pressing for permission to use the vernacular in celebrating the eucharistic sacrifice, but the Council, judging the conditions of that age, felt bound to answer such a request with a reaffirmation of the Church's traditional teaching. This teaching is that the eucharistic sacrifice is, first and foremost, the action of Christ himself and therefore the manner in which the faithful take part in the Mass does not affect the efficacy belonging to it. The Council thus stated in firm but measured words: "Although the Mass contains much instruction for the faithful, it did not seem expedient to the Fathers that as a general rule it be celebrated in the vernacular."[12] The Council accordingly anathematized anyone maintaining that "the rite of the Roman Church, in which part of the canon and the words of consecration are spoken in a low voice, should be condemned or that the Mass must be celebrated only in the vernacular."[13] Although the Council of Trent on the one hand prohibited the use of the vernacular in the Mass, nevertheless, on the other, it did direct pastors to substitute appropriate catechesis: "Lest Christ's flock go hungry . . . the Council commands pastors and others having the care of souls that either personally or through others they frequently give instructions during Mass, especially on Sundays and holy days, on what is read at Mass and that among their instructions they include some explanation of the mystery of this sacrifice."[14]

12.   Convened in order to adapt the Church to the contemporary requirements of its apostolic task, Vatican Council II examined thoroughly, as had Trent, the pedagogic and pastoral character of the liturgy.[15] Since no Catholic would now deny the lawfulness and efficacy of a sacred rite celebrated in Latin, the Council was able to acknowledge that "the use of the mother tongue frequently may be of great advantage to the people" and gave permission for its use.[16] The enthusiasm in response to this decision was so great that, under the leadership of the bishops and the Apostolic See, it has resulted in the permission for all liturgical celebrations in which the faithful participate to be in the vernacular for the sake of a better comprehension of the mystery being celebrated.

13.   The use of the vernacular in the liturgy may certainly be considered an important means for presenting more clearly the catechesis on the mystery that is part of the celebration itself. Nevertheless, Vatican Council II also ordered the observance of certain directives, prescribed by the Council of Trent but not obeyed everywhere. Among these are the obligatory homily on Sundays and holy days[17] and the permission to interpose some commentary during the sacred rites themselves.[18]

Above all, Vatican Council II strongly endorsed "that more complete form of participation in the Mass by which the faithful, after the priest's communion, receive the Lord's body from the same sacrifice."[19] Thus the Council gave impetus to the fulfillment of the further desire of the Fathers of Trent that for fuller participation in the holy eucharist "the faithful present at each Mass should communicate not only by spiritual desire but also by sacramental communion."[20]

14.   Moved by the same spirit and pastoral concern, Vatican Council II was able to reevaluate the Tridentine norm on communion under both kinds. No one

today challenges the doctrinal principals on the completeness of eucharistic communion under the form of bread alone. The Council thus gave permission for the reception of communion under both kinds on some occasions, because this more explicit form of the sacramental sign offers a special means of deepening the understanding of the mystery in which the faithful are taking part.[21]

15.    Thus the Church remains faithful in its responsibility as a teacher of truth to guard "things old," that is, the deposit of tradition; at the same time it fulfills another duty, that of examining and prudently bringing forth "things new" (see Mt 13:52).

Accordingly, a part of the new Roman Missal directs the prayer of the Church expressly to the needs of our times. This is above all true of the ritual Masses and the Masses for various needs and occasions, which happily combine the traditional and the contemporary. Thus many expressions, drawn from the Church's most ancient tradition and become familiar through the many editions of the Roman Missal, have remained unchanged. Other expressions, however, have been adapted to today's needs and circumstances and still others—for example, the prayers for the Church, the laity, the sanctification of human work, the community of all peoples, certain needs proper to our era—are completely new compositions, drawing on the thoughts and even the very language of the recent conciliar documents.

The same awareness of the present state of the world also influenced the use of texts from very ancient tradition. It seemed that this cherished treasure would not be harmed if some phrases were changed so that the style of language would be more in accord with the language of modern theology and would faithfully reflect the actual state of the Church's discipline. Thus there have been changes of some expressions bearing on the evaluation and use of the good things of the earth and of allusions to a particular form of outward penance belonging to another age in the history of the Church.

In short, the liturgical norms of the Council of Trent have been completed and improved in many respects by those of Vatican Council II. This Council has brought to realization the efforts of the last four hundred years to move the faithful closer to the sacred liturgy, especially the efforts of recent times and above all the zeal for the liturgy promoted by St. Pius X and his successors.

# CHAPTER I
## IMPORTANCE AND DIGNITY
## OF THE EUCHARISTIC CELEBRATION

1.    The celebration of Mass, the action of Christ and the people of God arrayed hierarchically, is for the universal and the local Church as well as for each person the center of the whole Christian life.[1] In the Mass we have the high point of the work that in Christ, his Son, we offer to the Father.[2] During the cycle of the year, moreover, the mysteries of redemption are recalled in the Mass in such a way that they are somehow made present.[3] All other liturgical rites and all the works of the Christian life are linked with the eucharistic celebration, flow from it, and have it as their end.[4]

2.     Therefore, it is of the greatest importance that the celebration of the Mass, the Lord's Supper, be so arranged that the ministers and the faithful who take their own proper part in it may more fully receive its good effects.[5] This is the reason why Christ the Lord instituted the eucharistic sacrifice of his body and blood and entrusted it to the Church, his beloved Bride, as the memorial of his passion and resurrection.[6]

3.     This purpose will best be accomplished if, after due regard for the nature and circumstances of each assembly, the celebration is planned in such a way that it brings about in the faithful a participation in body and spirit that is conscious, active, full, and motivated by faith, hope, and charity. The Church desires this kind of participation, the nature of the celebration demands it, and for the Christian people it is a right and duty they have by reason of their baptism.[7]

4.     The presence and active participation of the people bring out more plainly the ecclesial nature of the celebration.[8] But even when their participation is not possible, the eucharistic celebration still retains its effectiveness and worth because it is the action of Christ and the Church,[9] in which the priest always acts on behalf of the people's salvation.

5.     The celebration of the eucharist, like the entire liturgy, involves the use of outward signs that foster, strengthen, and express faith.[10] There must be the utmost care therefore to choose and to make wise use of those forms and elements provided by the Church that, in view of the circumstances of the people and the place, will best foster active and full participation and serve the spiritual well-being of the faithful.

6.     The purpose of this Instruction is to give the general guidelines for planning the eucharistic celebration properly and to set forth the rules for arranging the individual forms of celebration.[11] In accord with the Constitution on the Liturgy, each conference of bishops has the power to lay down norms for its own territory that are suited to the traditions and character of peoples, regions, and various communities.[12]

# CHAPTER II
# STRUCTURE, ELEMENTS, AND PARTS OF THE MASS

## I. GENERAL STRUCTURE OF THE MASS

7.     At Mass or the Lord's Supper, the people of God are called together, with a priest presiding and acting in the person of Christ, to celebrate the memorial of the Lord or eucharistic sacrifice.[13] For this reason Christ's promise applies supremely to such a local gathering of the Church: "Where two or three come together in my name, there am I in their midst" (Mt 18:20). For at the celebration of Mass, which perpetuates the sacrifice of the cross,[14] Christ is really present to the assembly gathered in his name; he is present in the person of the minister, in his own word, and indeed substantially and permanently under the eucharistic elements.[15]

8. The Mass is made up as it were of the liturgy of the word and the liturgy of the eucharist, two parts so closely connected that they form but one single act of worship.[16] For in the Mass the table of God's word and of Christ's body is laid for the people of God to receive from it instruction and food.[17] There are also certain rites to open and conclude the celebration.

## II. DIFFERENT ELEMENTS OF THE MASS

READING AND EXPLAINING THE WORD OF GOD

9. When the Scriptures are read in the Church, God himself is speaking to his people, and Christ, present in his own word, is proclaiming the Gospel.

The readings must therefore be listened to by all with reverence; they make up a principal element of the liturgy. In the biblical readings God's word addresses all people of every era and is understandable to them, but a living commentary on the word, that is, the homily, as an integral part of the liturgy, increases the word's effectiveness.[18]

PRAYERS AND OTHER PARTS ASSIGNED TO THE PRIEST

10. Among the parts assigned to the priest, the eucharistic prayer is preeminent; it is the high point of the entire celebration. Next are the prayers: the opening prayer or collect, the prayer over the gifts, and the prayer after communion. The priest, presiding over the assembly in the person of Christ, addresses these prayers to God in the name of the entire holy people and all present.[19] Thus there is good reason to call them "the presidential prayers."

11. It is also up to the priest in the exercise of his office of presiding over the assembly to pronounce the instructions and words of introduction and conclusion that are provided in the rites themselves. By their very nature these introductions do not need to be expressed verbatim in the form in which they are given in the Missal; at least in certain cases it will be advisable to adapt them somewhat to the concrete situation of the community.[20] It also belongs to the priest presiding to proclaim the word of God and to give the final blessing. He may give the faithful a very brief introduction to the Mass of the day (before the celebration begins), to the liturgy of the word (before the readings), and to the eucharistic prayer (before the preface); he may also make comments concluding the entire sacred service before the dismissal.

12. The nature of the presidential prayers demands that they be spoken in a loud and clear voice and that everyone present listen with attention.[21] While the priest is reciting them there should be no other prayer and the organ or other instruments should not be played.

13. But the priest does not only pray in the name of the whole community as its president; he also prays at times in his own name that he may exercise his ministry with attention and devotion. Such prayers are said inaudibly.

14.   Since by nature the celebration of Mass has the character of being the act of a community,[22] both the dialogues between celebrant and congregation and the acclamations take on special value;[23] they are not simply outward signs of the community's celebration, but the means of greater communion between priest and people.

15.   The acclamations and the responses to the priest's greeting and prayers create a degree of the active participation that the gathered faithful must contribute in every form of the Mass, in order to express clearly and to further the entire community's involvement.[24]

16.   There are other parts, extremely useful for expressing and encouraging the people's active participation, that are assigned to the whole congregation: the penitential rite, the profession of faith, the general intercessions, and the Lord's Prayer.

17.   Finally, of the other texts:

a)  Some constitute an independent rite or act, such as the *Gloria*, the responsorial psalm, the *Alleluia* verse and the verse before the gospel, the *Sanctus*, the memorial acclamation, and the song after communion.

b)  Others accompany another rite, such as the songs at the entrance, at the preparation of the gifts, at the breaking of the bread *(Agnus Dei)*, and at communion.

## VOCAL EXPRESSION OF THE DIFFERENT TEXTS

18.   In texts that are to be delivered in a clear, loud voice, whether by the priest or by the ministers or by all, the tone of voice should correspond to the genre of the text, that is, accordingly as it is a reading, a prayer, an instruction, an acclamation, or a song; the tone should also be suited to the form of celebration and to the solemnity of the gathering. Other criteria are the idiom of different languages and the genius of peoples.

In the rubrics and in the norms that follow, the words *say (dicere)* or *proclaim (proferre)* are to be understood of both singing and speaking, and in accordance with the principles just stated.

## IMPORTANCE OF SINGING

19.   The faithful who gather together to await the Lord's coming are instructed by the Apostle Paul to sing psalms, hymns, and inspired songs (see Col 3:16). Song is the sign of the heart's joy (see Acts 2:46). Thus St. Augustine says rightly: "To sing belongs to lovers."[25] There is also the ancient proverb: "One who sings well prays twice."

With due consideration for the culture and ability of each congregation, great importance should be attached to the use of singing at Mass; but it is not always necessary to sing all the texts that are of themselves meant to be sung.

In choosing the parts actually to be sung, however, preference should be given to those that are more significant and especially to those to be sung by the priest or ministers with the congregation responding or by the priest and people together.[26]

Since the faithful from different countries come together ever more frequently, it is desirable that they know how to sing at least some parts of the Ordinary of the Mass in Latin, especially the profession of faith and the Lord's Prayer, set to simple melodies.[27]

MOVEMENTS AND POSTURES

20.   The uniformity in standing, kneeling, or sitting to be observed by all taking part is a sign of the community and the unity of the assembly; it both expresses and fosters the spiritual attitude of those taking part.[28]

21.   For the sake of uniformity in movement and posture, the people should follow the directions given during the celebration by the deacon, the priest, or another minister. Unless other provision is made, at every Mass the people should stand from the beginning of the entrance song or when the priest enters until the end of the opening prayer or collect; for the singing of the *Alleluia* before the gospel; while the gospel is proclaimed; during the profession of faith and the general intercessions; from the prayer over the gifts to the end of the Mass, except at the places indicated later in this paragraph. They should sit during the readings before the gospel and during the responsorial psalm, for the homily and the presentation of the gifts, and, if this seems helpful, during the period of silence after communion. They should kneel at the consecration unless prevented by the lack of space, the number of people present, or some other good reason.

But it is up to the conference of bishops to adapt the actions and postures described in the Order of the Roman Mass to the customs of the people.[29] But the conference must make sure that such adaptations correspond to the meaning and character of each part of the celebration. [See GIapp, no. 21.]

22.   Included among the external actions of the Mass are those of the priest going to the altar, of the faithful presenting the gifts, and their coming forward to receive communion. While the songs proper to these movements are being sung, they should be carried out becomingly in keeping with the norms prescribed for each.

SILENCE

23.   Silence should be observed at the designated times as part of the celebration.[30] Its function depends on the time it occurs in each part of the celebration. Thus at the penitential rite and again after the invitation to prayer, all recollect themselves; at the conclusion of a reading or the homily, all meditate briefly on what has been heard; after communion, all praise God in silent prayer.

# III. INDIVIDUAL PARTS OF THE MASS

## A. Introductory Rites

24. The parts preceding the liturgy of the word, namely, the entrance song, greeting, penitential rite, *Kyrie, Gloria,* and opening prayer or collect, have the character of a beginning, introduction, and preparation.

The purpose of these rites is that the faithful coming together take on the form of a community and prepare themselves to listen to God's word and celebrate the eucharist properly.

### ENTRANCE

25. After the people have assembled, the entrance song begins as the priest and the ministers come in. The purpose of this song is to open the celebration, intensify the unity of the gathered people, lead their thoughts to the mystery of the season or feast, and accompany the procession of priest and ministers.

26. The entrance song is sung alternately either by the choir and the congregation or by the cantor and the congregation; or it is sung entirely by the congregation or by the choir alone. The antiphon and psalm of the *Graduale Romanum* or *The Simple Gradual* may be used, or another song that is suited to this part of the Mass, the day, or the season and that has a text approved by the conference of bishops.

If there is no singing for the entrance, the antiphon in the Missal is recited either by the faithful, by some of them, or by a reader; otherwise it is recited by the priest after the greeting. [See GIapp, no. 26.]

### VENERATION OF THE ALTAR AND GREETING OF THE CONGREGATION

27. When the priest and the ministers enter the sanctuary, they reverence the altar. As a sign of veneration, the priest and deacon kiss the altar; when the occasion warrants, the priest may also incense the altar.

28. After the entrance song, the priest and the whole assembly make the sign of the cross. Then through his greeting the priest declares to the assembled community that the Lord is present. This greeting and the congregation's response express the mystery of the gathered Church.

### PENITENTIAL RITE

29. After greeting the congregation, the priest or other qualified minister may very briefly introduce the faithful to the Mass of the day. Then the priest invites them to take part in the penitential rite, which the entire community carries out through a communal confession and which the priest's absolution brings to an end.

30. The Kyrie begins, unless it has already been included as part of the penitential rite. Since it is a song by which the faithful praise the Lord and implore his mercy, it is ordinarily prayed by all, that is, alternately by the congregation and the choir or cantor.

As a rule each of the acclamations is said twice, but, because of the idiom of different languages, the music, or other circumstances, it may be said more than twice or a short verse (trope) may be interpolated. If the Kyrie is not sung, it is to be recited.

## GLORIA

31. The *Gloria* is an ancient hymn in which the Church, assembled in the Holy Spirit, praises and entreats the Father and the Lamb. It is sung by the congregation, or by the congregation alternately with the choir, or by the choir alone. If not sung, it is to be recited either by all together or in alternation.

The *Gloria* is sung or said on Sundays outside Advent and Lent, on solemnities and feasts, and in special, more solemn celebrations.

## OPENING PRAYER OR COLLECT

32. Next the priest invites the people to pray and together with him they observe a brief silence so that they may realize they are in God's presence and may call their petitions to mind. The priest then says the opening prayer, which custom has named the "collect." This expresses the theme of the celebration and the priest's words address a petition to God the Father through Christ in the Holy Spirit.

The people make the prayer their own and give their assent by the acclamation, *Amen.*

In the Mass only one opening prayer is said; this rule applies also to the prayer over the gifts and the prayer after communion.

The opening prayer ends with the longer conclusion, namely:

—if the prayer is directed to the Father: We ask this (Grant this) through our Lord Jesus Christ, your Son, who lives and reigns with you and the Holy Spirit, one God, for ever and ever;

—if it is directed to the Father, but the Son is mentioned at the end: Who lives and reigns with you and the Holy Spirit, one God, for ever and ever;

—if directed to the Son: You live and reign with the Father and the Holy Spirit, one God, for ever and ever.

The prayer over the gifts and the prayer after communion end with the shorter conclusion, namely:

—if the prayer is directed to the Father: We ask this (Grant this) through Christ our Lord;

—if it is directed to the Father, but the Son is mentioned at the end: Who lives and reigns with you for ever and ever;

—if it is directed to the Son: You live and reign for ever and ever.

### B. Liturgy of the Word

33. Readings from Scripture and the chants between the readings form the main part of the liturgy of the word. The homily, profession of faith, and general intercessions or prayer of the faithful expand and complete this part of the Mass. In the readings, explained by the homily, God is speaking to his people,[31] opening up to them the mystery of redemption and salvation, and nourishing their spirit; Christ is present to the faithful through his own word.[32] Through the chants the people make God's word their own and through the profession of faith affirm their adherence to it. Finally, having been fed by this word, they make their petitions in the general intercessions for the needs of the church and for the salvation of the whole world.

#### SCRIPTURE READINGS

34. The readings lay the table of God's word for the faithful and open up the riches of the Bible to them.[33] Since by tradition the reading of the Scripture is a ministerial, not a presidential function, it is proper that as a rule a deacon or, in his absence, a priest other than the one presiding read the gospel. A reader proclaims the other readings. In the absence of a deacon or another priest, the priest celebrant reads the gospel.[34]

35. The liturgy itself inculcates the great reverence to be shown toward the reading of the gospel, setting it off from the other readings by special marks of honor. A special minister is appointed to proclaim it and prepares himself by a blessing or prayer. The people, who by their acclamations acknowledge and confess Christ present and speaking to them, stand as they listen to it. Marks of reverence are given to the Book of the Gospels itself.

#### CHANTS BETWEEN THE READINGS

36. After the reading comes the responsorial psalm or gradual, an integral part of the liturgy of the word. The psalm as a rule is drawn from the Lectionary because the individual psalm texts are directly connected with the individual readings: the choice of psalm depends therefore on the readings. Nevertheless, in order that the people may be able to join in the responsorial psalm more readily, some texts of responses and psalms have been chosen, according to the different seasons of the years and classes of saints, for optional use, whenever the psalm is sung, in place of the text corresponding to the reading.

The psalmist or cantor of the psalm sings the verses of the psalm at the lectern or other suitable place. The people remain seated and listen, but also as a rule take part by singing the response, except when the psalm is sung straight through without the response.

The psalm when sung may be either the psalm assigned in the Lectionary or the gradual from the *Graduale Romanum* or the responsorial psalm or the psalm with *Alleluia* as the response from *The Simple Gradual* in the form they have in those books. [See GIapp, no. 36.]

37. As the season requires, the *Alleluia* or another chant follows the second reading.

a. The *Alleluia* is sung in every season outside Lent. It is begun either by all present or by the choir or cantor; it may then be repeated. The verses are taken from the Lectionary or the *Graduale*.

b. The other chant consists of the verse before the gospel or another psalm or tract, as found in the Lectionary or the *Graduale*.

38. When there is only one reading before the gospel:

a. during a season calling for the *Alleluia*, there is an option to use either the psalm with *Alleluia* as the response, or the responsorial psalm and the *Alleluia* with its verse, or just the psalm, or just the *Alleluia*.

b. during the season when the *Alleluia* is not allowed, either the responsorial psalm or the verse before the gospel may be used.

39. If the psalm after the reading is not sung, it is to be recited. If not sung, the *Alleluia* or the verse before the gospel may be omitted.

40. Sequences are optional, except on Easter Sunday and Pentecost.

HOMILY

41. The homily is an integral part of the liturgy and is strongly recommended:[35] it is necessary for the nurturing of the Christian life. It should develop some point of the readings or of another text from the Ordinary or from the Proper of the Mass of the day, and take into account the mystery being celebrated and the needs proper to the listeners.[36]

42. There must be a homily on Sundays and holy days of obligation at all Masses that are celebrated with a congregation; it may not be omitted without a serious reason. It is recommended on other days, especially on the weekdays of Advent, Lent, and the Easter season, as well as on other feasts and occasions when the people come to Church in large numbers.[37]

The homily should ordinarily be given by the priest celebrant.

PROFESSION OF FAITH

43. The symbol or profession of faith in the celebration of Mass serves as a way for the people to respond and to give their assent to the word of God heard in the readings and through the homily and for them to call to mind the truths of faith before they begin to celebrate the eucharist.

44. Recitation of the profession of faith by the priest together with the people is obligatory on Sundays and solemnities. It may be said also at special, more solemn celebrations.

If it is sung, as a rule all are to sing it together or in alternation.

GENERAL INTERCESSIONS

45. In the general intercessions or prayer of the faithful, the people, exercising their priestly function, intercede for all humanity. It is appropriate that this prayer be included in all Masses celebrated with a congregation, so that petitions will be offered for the Church, for civil authorities, for those oppressed by various needs, for all people, and for the salvation of the world.[38] [See GIapp, no. 45]

46. As a rule the sequence of intentions is to be:

   a. for the needs of the Church;

   b. for public authorities and the salvation of the world;

   c. for those oppressed by any need;

   d. for the local community.

In particular celebrations, such as confirmations, marriages, funerals, etc., the series of intercessions may refer more specifically to the occasion.

47. It belongs to the priest celebrant to direct the general intercessions, by means of a brief introduction to invite the congregation to pray, and after the intercessions to say the concluding prayer. It is desirable that a deacon, cantor, or other person announce the intentions.[39] The whole assembly gives expression to its supplication either by a response said together after each intention or by a silent prayer.

### C. Liturgy of the Eucharist

48. At the last supper Christ instituted the sacrifice and paschal meal that make the sacrifice of the cross to be continuously present in the Church, when the priest, representing Christ the Lord, carries out what the Lord did and handed over to his disciples to do in his memory.[40]

Christ took the bread and the cup and gave thanks; he broke the bread and gave it to his disciples, saying: "Take and eat, this is my body." Giving the cup, he said: "Take and drink, this is the cup of my blood. Do this in memory of me." Accordingly, the Church has planned the celebration of the eucharistic liturgy around the parts corresponding to these words and actions of Christ:

   1. In the preparation of the gifts, the bread and the wine with water are brought to the altar, that is, the same elements that Christ used.

   2. In the eucharistic prayer thanks is given to God for the whole work of salvation and the gifts of bread and wine become the body and blood of Christ.

   3. Through the breaking of the one bread the unity of the faithful is expressed and through communion they receive the Lord's body and blood in the same way the apostles received them from Christ's own hands.

49.   At the beginning of the liturgy of the eucharist the gifts, which will become Christ's body and blood, are brought to the altar.

First the altar, the Lord's table, which is the center of the whole eucharistic liturgy,[41] is prepared: the corporal, purificator, missal, and chalice are placed on it (unless the chalice is prepared at a side table).

The gifts are then brought forward. It is desirable for the faithful to present the bread and wine, which are accepted by the priest or deacon at a convenient place. The gifts are placed on the altar to the accompaniment of the prescribed texts. Even though the faithful no longer, as in the past, bring the bread and wine for the liturgy from their homes, the rite of carrying up the gifts retains the same spiritual value and meaning.

This is also the time to receive money or other gifts for the church or the poor brought by the faithful or collected at the Mass. These are to be put in a suitable place but not on the altar.

50.   The procession bringing the gifts is accompanied by the presentation song, which continues at least until the gifts have been placed on the altar. The rules for this song are the same as those for the entrance song (no. 26). If it is not sung, the presentation antiphon is omitted.

51.   The gifts on the altar and the altar itself may be incensed. This is a symbol of the Church's offering and prayer going up to God. Afterward the deacon or other minister may incense the priest and the people.

52.   The priest then washes his hands as an expression of his desire to be cleansed within.

53.   Once the gifts have been placed on the altar and the accompanying rites completed, the preparation of the gifts comes to an end through the invitation to pray with the priest and the prayer over the gifts, which are a preparation for the eucharistic prayer.

EUCHARISTIC PRAYER

54.   Now the center and summit of the entire celebration begins: the eucharistic prayer, a prayer of thanksgiving and sanctification. The priest invites the people to lift up their hearts to the Lord in prayer and thanks; he unites them with himself in the prayer he addresses in their name to the Father through Jesus Christ. The meaning of the prayer is that the entire congregation joins itself to Christ in acknowledging the great things God has done and in offering the sacrifice.

55.   The chief elements making up the eucharistic prayer are these:

a.   Thanksgiving (expressed especially in the preface): in the name of the entire people of God, the priest praises the Father and gives thanks to him for the whole work of salvation or for some special aspect of it that corresponds to the day, feast, or season.

b. Acclamation: joining with the angels, the congregation sings or recites the *Sanctus.* This acclamation is an intrinsic part of the eucharistic prayer and all the people join with the priest in singing or reciting it.

c. Epiclesis: in special invocations the Church calls on God's power and asks that the gifts offered by human hands be consecrated, that is, become Christ's body and blood, and that the victim to be received in communion be the source of salvation for those who will partake.

d. Institution narrative and consecration: in the words and actions of Christ, that sacrifice is celebrated which he himself instituted at the Last Supper, when, under the appearances of bread and wine, he offered his body and blood, gave them to his apostles to eat and drink, then commanded that they carry on this mystery.

e. Anamnesis: in fulfillment of the command received from Christ through the apostles, the Church keeps his memorial by recalling especially his passion, resurrection, and ascension.

f. Offering: in this memorial, the Church—and in particular the Church here and now assembled—offers the spotless victim to the Father in the Holy Spirit. The Church's intention is that the faithful not only offer this victim but also learn to offer themselves and so to surrender themselves, through Christ the Mediator, to an ever more complete union with the Father and with each other, so that at last God may be all in all.[42]

g. Intercessions: the intercessions make it clear that the eucharist is celebrated in communion with the entire Church of heaven and earth and that the offering is made for the Church and all its members, living and dead, who are called to share in the salvation and redemption purchased by Christ's body and blood.

h. Final doxology: the praise of God is expressed in the doxology, to which the people's acclamation is an assent and a conclusion.

The eucharistic prayer calls for all to listen in silent reverence, but also to take part through the acclamations for which the rite makes provision.

COMMUNION RITE

56. Since the eucharistic celebration is the paschal meal, it is right that the faithful who are properly disposed receive the Lord's body and blood as spiritual food as he commanded.[43] This is the purpose of the breaking of the bread and the other preparatory rites that lead directly to the communion of the people:

a. Lord's Prayer: this is a petition both for daily food, which for Christians means also the eucharistic bread, and for the forgiveness of sin, so that what is holy may be given to those who are holy. The priest offers the invitation to pray, but all the faithful say the prayer with him; he alone adds the embolism, *Deliver us,* which the people conclude with a doxology. The embolism, developing the last petition of the Lord's Prayer, begs on behalf of the entire community of the faithful deliverance from the power of evil. The invitation, the prayer itself, the embolism, and the people's doxology are sung or are recited aloud.

b. Rite of peace: before they share in the same bread, the faithful implore peace and unity for the Church and for the whole human family and offer some sign of their love for one another.

The form the sign of peace should take is left to the conference of bishops to determine, in accord with the culture and customs of the people. [See GIapp, no. 56b.]

c. Breaking of the bread: in apostolic times this gesture of Christ at the last supper gave the entire eucharistic action its name. This rite is not simply functional, but is a sign that in sharing in the one bread of life which is Christ we who are many are made one body (see 1 Corinthians 10:17).

d. Commingling: the celebrant drops a part of the host into the chalice.

e. Agnus Dei: during the breaking of the bread and the commingling, the *Agnus Dei* is as a rule sung by the choir or cantor with the congregation responding; otherwise it is recited aloud. This invocation may be repeated as often as necessary to accompany the breaking of the bread. The final reprise concludes with the words, *grant us peace.*

f. Personal preparation of the priest: the priest prepares himself by the prayer, said softly, that he may receive Christ's body and blood to good effect. The faithful do the same by silent prayer.

g. The priest then shows the eucharistic bread for communion to the faithful and with them recites the prayer of humility in words from the Gospels.

h. It is most desirable that the faithful receive the Lord's body from hosts consecrated at the same Mass and that, in the instances when it is permitted, they share in the chalice. Then even through the signs communion will stand out more clearly as a sharing in the sacrifice actually being celebrated.[44]

i. During the priest's and the faithful's reception of the sacrament the communion song is sung. Its function is to express outwardly the communicants' union in spirit by means of the unity of their voices, to give evidence of joy of heart, and to make the procession to receive Christ's body more fully an act of community. The song begins when the priest takes communion and continues for as long as seems appropriate while the faithful receive Christ's body. But the communion song should be ended in good time whenever there is to be a hymn after communion.

An antiphon from the *Graduale Romanum* may also be used, with or without the psalm, or an antiphon with psalm from *The Simple Gradual* or another suitable song approved by the conference of bishops. It is sung by the choir alone or by the choir or cantor with the congregation.

If there is no singing, the communion antiphon in the Missal is recited either by the people, by some of them, or by a reader. Otherwise the priest himself says it after he has received communion and before he gives communion to the faithful.

j. After communion, the priest and people may spend some time in silent prayer. If desired, a hymn, psalm, or other song of praise may be sung by the entire congregation.

k. In the prayer after communion, the priest petitions for the effects of the mystery just celebrated and by their acclamation, *Amen*, the people make the prayer their own.

### D. Concluding Rite

57. The concluding rite consists of:

a. the priest's greeting and blessing, which on certain days and occasions is expanded and expressed in the prayer over the people or another more solemn formulary;

b. the dismissal of the assembly, which sends each member back to doing good works, while praising and blessing the Lord.

# CHAPTER III
# OFFICES AND MINISTRIES IN THE MASS

58. All in the assembly gathered for the Mass have an individual right and duty to contribute their participation in ways differing according to the diversity of their order and liturgical function.[45] Thus in carrying out this function, all, whether ministers or laypersons, should do all and only those parts that belong to them,[46] so that the very arrangement of the celebration itself makes the Church stand out as being formed in a structure of different orders and ministries.

## I. OFFICES AND MINISTRIES OF HOLY ORDERS

59. Every authentic celebration of the eucharist is directed by the bishop, either in person or through the presbyters, who are his helpers.[47]

Whenever he is present at a Mass with a congregation, it is fitting that the bishop himself preside over the assembly and associate the presbyters with himself in the celebration, if possible by concelebrating with them.

This is done not to add external solemnity, but to express in a clearer light the mystery of the Church, which is the sacrament of unity.[48]

Even if the bishop is not the celebrant of the eucharist but assigns someone else, he should preside over the liturgy of the word and give the blessing at the end of Mass. [See GIapp, no. 59.]

60. Within the community of believers, the presbyter is another who possesses the power of orders to offer sacrifice in the person of Christ.[49] He therefore presides over the assembly and leads its prayer, proclaims the message of salvation, joins the people to himself in offering the sacrifice to the Father through Christ in the Spirit, gives them the bread of eternal life, and shares in it with them. At the eucharist he should, then, serve God and the people with dignity and humility; by his bearing and by the way he recites the words of the liturgy he should communicate to the faithful a sense of the living presence of Christ.

61.    Among ministers, the deacon, whose order has been held in high honor since the early Church, has first place. At Mass he has his own functions: he proclaims the gospel, sometimes preaches God's word, leads the general intercessions, assists the priest, gives communion to the people (in particular, ministering the chalice), and sometimes gives directions regarding the assembly's moving, standing, kneeling, or sitting.

## II. OFFICE AND FUNCTION OF THE PEOPLE OF GOD

62.    In the celebration of Mass the faithful are a holy people, a people God has made his own, a royal priesthood: they give thanks to the Father and offer the victim not only through the hands of the priest but also together with him and learn to offer themselves.[50] They should endeavor to make this clear by their deep sense of reverence for God and their charity toward all who share with them in the celebration.

They therefore are to shun any appearance of individualism or division, keeping before their mind that they have the one Father in heaven and therefore are all brothers and sisters to each other.

They should become one body, whether by hearing the word of God, or joining in prayers and song, or above all by offering the sacrifice together and sharing together in the Lord's table. There is a beautiful expression of this unity when the faithful maintain uniformity in their actions and in standing, sitting, or kneeling.

The faithful should serve the people of God willingly when asked to perform some particular ministry in the celebration.

63.    The *schola cantorum* or choir exercises its own liturgical function within the assembly. Its task is to ensure that the parts proper to it, in keeping with the different types of chants, are carried out becomingly and to encourage active participation of the people in the singing.[51] What is said about the choir applies in a similar way to other musicians, especially the organist.

64.    There should be a cantor or a choir director to lead and sustain the people in the singing. When in fact there is no choir, it is up to the cantor to lead the various songs, and the people take part in the way proper to them.[52]

## III. SPECIAL MINISTRIES

65.    The acolyte is instituted to serve at the altar and to assist the priest and deacon. In particular it is for him to prepare the altar and the vessels and, as a special minister of the eucharist, to give communion to the faithful.

66.    The reader is instituted to proclaim the readings from Scripture, with the exception of the gospel. He may also announce the intentions for the general intercessions and, in the absence of the psalmist, sing or read the psalm between the readings.

The reader has his own proper function in the eucharistic celebration and should exercise this even though ministers of a higher rank may be present.

Those who exercise the ministry of reader, even if they have not received institution, must be truly qualified and carefully prepared in order that the faithful will develop a warm and lively love for Scripture[53] from listening to the reading of the sacred texts. [See GIapp, no. 66.]

67. The cantor of the psalm is to sing the psalm or other biblical song that comes between the readings. To fulfill their function correctly, these cantors should possess singing talent and an aptitude for correct pronunciation and diction.

68. As for other ministers, some perform different functions inside the sanctuary, others outside.

The first kind include those deputed as special ministers of communion[54] and those who carry the missal, the cross, candles, the bread, wine, water, and the thurible.

The second kind include:

a. The commentator. This minister provides explanations and commentaries with the purpose of introducing the faithful to the celebration and preparing them to understand it better. The commentator's remarks must be meticulously prepared and marked by a simple brevity.

In performing this function the commentator stands in a convenient place visible to the faithful, but it is preferable that this not be at the lectern where the Scriptures are read.

b. Those who, in some places, meet the people at the church entrance, seat them, and direct processions.

c. Those who take up the collection.

69. Especially in larger churches and communities, a person should be assigned responsibility for planning the services properly and for their being carried out by the ministers with decorum, order, and devotion.

70. Laymen, even if they have not received institution as ministers, may perform all the functions below those reserved to deacons. At the discretion of the rector of the church, women may be appointed to ministries that are performed outside the sanctuary.

The conference of bishops may permit qualified women to proclaim the readings before the gospel and to announce the intentions of the general intercessions. The conference may also more precisely designate a suitable place for a woman to proclaim the word of God in the liturgical assembly.[55]

71. If there are several persons present who are empowered to exercise the same ministry, there is no objection to their being assigned different parts to perform. For example, one deacon may take the sung parts, another assist at the altar; if

there are several readings, it is better to distribute them among a number of readers. The same applies for the other ministries.

72.   If only one minister is present at a Mass with a congregation, he may carry out several different functions.

73.   All concerned should work together in the effective preparation of each liturgical celebration as to its rites, pastoral aspects and music. They should work under the direction of the rector of the church and should consult the faithful.

# CHAPTER IV
## THE DIFFERENT FORMS OF CELEBRATION

74.   In the local Church, first place should be given, because of its meaning, to the Mass at which the bishop presides surrounded by the college of presbyters and the ministers[56] and in which the people take full and active part. For this Mass is the preeminent expression of the Church.

75.   Great importance should be attached to a Mass celebrated by any community, but especially by the parish community, inasmuch as it represents the universal Church gathered at a given time and place. This is particularly true of the community's celebration of the Lord's Day.[57]

76.   Of those Masses celebrated by some communities, the conventual Mass, which is a part of the daily office, or the "community" Mass have particular significance. Although such Masses do not have a special form of celebration, it is most proper that they be celebrated with singing, with the full participation of all community members, whether religious or canons. In these Masses, therefore, individuals should exercise the function proper to the order or ministry they have received. All the priests who are not bound to celebrate individually for the pastoral benefit of the faithful should thus concelebrate at the conventual or community Mass, if possible. Further, all priests belonging to the community who are obliged to celebrate individually for the pastoral benefit of the faithful may also on the same day concelebrate at the conventual or community Mass.[58]

## I. MASS WITH A CONGREGATION

77.   Mass with a congregation means a Mass celebrated with the people taking part. As far as possible, and especially on Sundays and holy days of obligation, this Mass should be celebrated with song and with a suitable number of ministers.[59] But it may be celebrated without music and with only one minister.

78.   It is desirable that as a rule an acolyte, a reader, and a cantor assist the priest celebrant; this form of celebration will hereafter be referred to as the "basic" or "typical" form. But the rite to be described also allows for a greater number of ministers.

A deacon may exercise his office in any of the forms of celebration.

79.   The altar is to be covered with at least one cloth. On or near the altar there are to be candlesticks with lighted candles, at least two but even four, six, or, if the bishop of the diocese celebrates, seven. There is also to be a cross on or near the altar. The candles and cross may be carried in the entrance procession. The Book of the Gospels, if distinct from the book of other readings, may be placed on the altar, unless it is carried in the entrance procession.

80.   The following are also to be prepared:

a. next to the priest's chair: the missal and, as may be useful, a book with the chants;

b. at the lectern: the Lectionary;

c. on a side table: the chalice, corporal, purificator, and, if useful, a pall; a paten and ciboria, if needed, with the bread for the communion of the ministers and the people, together with cruets containing wine and water, unless all of these are brought in by the faithful at the presentation of the gifts; communion plate for the communion of the faithful; the requisites for the washing of hands. The chalice should be covered with a veil, which may always be white.

81.   In the sacristy the vestments for the priest and ministers are to be prepared according to the various forms of celebration:

a. for the priest: alb, stole, and chasuble;

b. for the deacon: alb, stole, and dalmatic; the last may be omitted either out of necessity or for less solemnity;

c. for the other ministers: albs or other lawfully approved vestments.

All who wear an alb should use a cincture and an amice, unless other provision is made.

### A. Basic Form of Celebration

INTRODUCTORY RITES

82.   Once the congregation has gathered, the priest and the ministers, clad in their vestments, go to the altar in this order:

a. a server with a lighted censer, if incense is used;

b. the servers, who, according to the occasion, carry lighted candles, and between them the cross bearer, if the cross is to be carried;

c. acolytes and other ministers;

d. a reader, who may carry the Book of the Gospels;

e. the priest who is to celebrate the Mass.

If incense is used, the priest puts some in the censer before the procession begins.

83. During the procession to the altar the entrance song is sung (see nos. 25–26).

84. On reaching the altar the priest and ministers make the proper reverence, that is, a low bow or, if there is a tabernacle containing the blessed sacrament, a genuflection.

If the cross has been carried in the procession, it is placed near the altar or at some other convenient place; the candles carried by the servers are placed near the altar or on a side table; the Book of the Gospels is placed on the altar.

85. The priest goes up to the altar and kisses it. If incense is used, he incenses the altar while circling it.

86. The priest then goes to the chair. After the entrance song, and with all standing, the priest and the faithful make the sign of the cross. The priest says: *In the name of the Father, and of the Son, and of the Holy Spirit;* the people answer: *Amen.*

Then, facing the people and with hands outstretched, the priest greets all present, using one of the formularies indicated. He or some other qualified minister may give the faithful a very brief introduction to the Mass of the day.

87. After the penitential rite, the *Kyrie* and *Gloria* are said, in keeping with the rubrics (nos. 30–31). Either the priest or the cantors or even everyone together may begin the *Gloria.*

88. With his hands joined, the priest then invites the people to pray, saying: *Let us pray.* All pray silently with the priest for a while. Then the priest with hands outstretched says the opening prayer, at the end of which the people respond: *Amen.*

LITURGY OF THE WORD

89. After the opening prayer, the reader goes to the lectern for the first reading. All sit and listen and make the acclamation at the end.

90. After the reading, the psalmist or cantor of the psalm, or even the reader, sings or recites the psalm and the congregation sings or recites the response (see no. 36).

91. Then, if there is a second reading before the gospel, the reader reads it at the lectern as before. All sit and listen and make the acclamation at the end.

92. The *Alleluia* or other chant, according to the season, follows (see nos. 37–39).

93. During the singing of the *Alleluia* or other chant, if incense is being used, the priest puts some into the censer. Then with hands joined he bows before the altar and inaudibly says the prayer, *Almighty God, cleanse my heart.*

94. If the Book of the Gospels is on the altar, he takes it and goes to the lectern, the servers, who may carry the censer and candles, walking ahead of him.

95. At the lectern the priest opens the book and says: *The Lord be with you.* Then he says: *A reading from . . . ,* making the sign of the cross with his thumb on the book and on his forehead, mouth, and breast. If incense is used, he then incenses the book. After the acclamation of the people, he proclaims the gospel and at the end kisses the book, saying inaudibly: *May the words of the gospel wipe away our sins.* After the reading the people make the acclamation customary to the region.

96. If no reader is present, the priest himself proclaims all the readings at the lectern and there also, if necessary, the chants between the readings. If incense is used, he puts some into the censer at the lectern and then, bowing, says the prayer, *Almighty God, cleanse my heart.*

97. The homily is given at the chair or at the lectern.

98. The profession of faith is said by the priest together with the people (see no. 44). At the words *by the power of the Holy Spirit,* etc., all bow; on the solemnities of the Annunciation and Christmas all kneel.

99. Next, with the people taking their proper part, follow the general intercessions (prayer of the faithful), which the priest directs from his chair or at the lectern (see nos. 45–47).

LITURGY OF THE EUCHARIST

100. After the general intercessions, the presentation song begins (see no. 50). The servers place the corporal, purificator, chalice, and missal on the altar.

101. It is fitting for the faithful's participation to be expressed by their presenting both the bread and wine for the celebration of the eucharist and other gifts to meet the needs of the church and of the poor.

The faithful's offerings are received by the priest, assisted by the ministers, and put in a suitable place; the bread and wine for the eucharist are taken to the altar.

102. At the altar the priest receives the paten with the bread from a minister. With both hands he holds it slightly raised above the altar and says the accompanying prayer. Then he places the paten with the bread on the corporal.

103. Next, as a minister presents the cruets, the priest stands at the side of the altar and pours wine and a little water into the chalice, saying the accompanying prayer softly. He returns to the middle of the altar, takes the chalice, raises it a little with both hands, and says the appointed prayer. Then he places the chalice on the corporal and may cover it with a pall.

104. The priest bows and says inaudibly the prayer, *Lord God, we ask you to receive.*

105. If incense is used, he incenses the gifts and the altar. A minister incenses the priest and the congregation.

106. After the prayer, *Lord God, we ask you to receive,* or after the incensation, the priest washes his hands at the side of the altar and softly says the prescribed prayer as a minister pours the water.

107. The priest returns to the center and, facing the people and extending then joining his hands, pronounces the invitation: *Pray, brothers and sisters.* After the people's response, he says the prayer over the gifts with hands outstretched. At the end the people make the acclamation: *Amen.*

108. The priest then begins the eucharistic prayer. With hands outstretched, he says: *The Lord be with you.* As he says: *Lift up your hearts,* he raises his hands; with hands outstretched, he adds: *Let us give thanks to the Lord our God.* When the people have answered, *It is right to give him thanks and praise,* the priest continues the preface. At its conclusion, he joins his hands and sings or says aloud with the ministers and people the *Sanctus-Benedictus* (see no. 55 b).

109. The priest continues the eucharistic prayer according to the rubrics that are given for each of them. If the priest celebrant is a bishop, after the words *N. our Pope* or the equivalent, he adds: *and for me your unworthy servant.* The local Ordinary must be mentioned in this way: *N. our Bishop* (or Vicar, Prelate, Prefect, Abbot). Coadjutor and auxiliary bishops may be mentioned in the eucharistic prayer. When several are named, this is done with the collective formula, *N. our bishop and his assistant bishops.*[60] All these phrases should be modified grammatically to fit each of the eucharistic prayers.

A little before the consecration, the server may ring a bell as a signal to the faithful. Depending on local custom, he also rings the bell at the showing of both the host and the chalice.

110. After the doxology at the end of the eucharistic prayer, the priest, with hands joined, says the introduction to the Lord's Prayer. With hands outstretched he then sings or says this prayer with the people.

111. After the Lord's Prayer, the priest alone, with hands outstretched, says the embolism, *Deliver us.* At the end the congregation makes the acclamation, *For the kingdom.*

112. Then the priest says aloud the prayer, *Lord Jesus Christ.* After this prayer, extending then joining his hands, he gives the greeting of peace: *The peace of the Lord be with you always.* The people answer: *And also with you.* Then the priest may add: *Let us offer each other a sign of peace.* All exchange some sign of peace and love, according to local custom. The priest may give the sign of peace to the ministers.

113. The priest then takes the eucharistic bread and breaks it over the paten. He places a small piece in the chalice, saying softly: *May this mingling.* Meanwhile the *Agnus Dei* is sung or recited by the choir and congregation (see no. 56 e).

114. Then the priest inaudibly says the prayer, *Lord, Jesus Christ, Son of the living God,* or *Lord Jesus Christ, with faith in your love and mercy.*

115. After the prayer the priest genuflects, takes the eucharistic bread, and, holding it slightly above the paten while facing the people, says: *This is the Lamb of God*. With the people he adds, once only: *Lord, I am not worthy to receive you.*

116. Next, facing the altar, the priest says inaudibly: *May the body of Christ bring me to everlasting life* and reverently consumes the body of Christ. Then he takes the chalice, saying: *May the blood of Christ bring me to everlasting life*, and reverently drinks the blood of Christ.

117. He then takes the paten or a ciborium and goes to the communicants. If communion is given only under the form of bread, he raises the eucharistic bread slightly and shows it to each one, saying: *The body of Christ*. The communicants reply: *Amen* and, holding the communion plate under their chin, receive the sacrament.

118. For communion under both kinds, the rite described in nos. 240–252 is followed.

119. The communion song is begun while the priest is receiving the sacrament (see no. 56 i).

120. After communion the priest returns to the altar and collects any remaining particles. Then, standing at the side of the altar or at a side table, he purifies the paten or ciborium over the chalice, then purifies the chalice, saying inaudibly: *Lord, may I receive these gifts*, etc., and dries it with a purificator. If this is done at the altar, the vessels are taken to a side table by a minister. It is also permitted, especially if there are several vessels to be purified, to leave them, properly covered and on a corporal, either at the altar or at a side table and to purify them after Mass when the people have left.

121. Afterward the priest may return to the chair. A period of silence may now be observed, or a hymn of praise or a psalm may be sung (see no. 56 j).

122. Then, standing at the altar or at the chair and facing the people, the priest says, with hands outstretched: *Let us pray*. There may be a brief period of silence, unless this has been already observed immediately after communion. He recites the prayer after communion, at the end of which the people make the response: *Amen*.

CONCLUDING RITES

123. If there are any brief announcements, they may be made at this time.

124. Then the priest, with hands outstretched, greets the people: *The Lord be with you*. They answer: *And also with you*. The priest immediately adds: *May almighty God bless you* and, as he blesses with the sign of the cross, continues: *the Father, and the Son, and the Holy Spirit*. All answer: *Amen*. On certain days and occasions another, more solemn form of blessing or the prayer over the people precedes this form of blessing as the rubrics direct.

Immediately after the blessing, with hands joined, the priest adds: *Go in the peace of Christ*, or: *Go in peace to love and serve the Lord*, or: *The Mass is ended, go in peace*, and the people answer: *Thanks be to God*.

125. As a rule, the priest then kisses the altar, makes the proper reverence with the ministers, and leaves.

126. If another liturgical service follows the Mass, the concluding rites (greeting, blessing, and dismissal) are omitted.

### B. Functions of the Deacon

127. When there is a deacon present to exercise his ministry, the norms in the preceding section apply, with the following exceptions.

In general the deacon: a. assists the priest and walks at his side; b. at the altar, assists with the chalice or the book; c. if there is no other minister present, carries out other ministerial functions as required.

INTRODUCTORY RITES

128. Vested and carrying the Book of the Gospels, the deacon precedes the priest on the way to the altar or else walks at the priest's side.

129. With the priest he makes the proper reverence and goes up to the altar. After placing the Book of the Gospels on it, along with the priest he kisses the altar. If incense is used, he assists the priest in putting some in the censer and in incensing the altar.

130. After the incensing, he goes to the chair with the priest, sits next to him, and assists him as required.

LITURGY OF THE WORD

131. If incense is used, the deacon assists the priest when he puts incense in the censer during the singing of the *Alleluia* or other chant. Then he bows before the priest and asks for the blessing, saying in a low voice: *Father, give me your blessing*. The priest blesses him: *The Lord be in your heart*. The deacon answers: *Amen*. If the Book of the Gospels is on the altar, he takes it and goes to the lectern; the servers, if there are any, precede, carrying candles and the censer when used. At the lectern the deacon greets the people, incenses the book, and proclaims the gospel. After the reading, he kisses the book, saying inaudibly: *May the words of the gospel wipe away our sins*, and returns to the priest. If there is no homily or profession of faith, he may remain at the lectern for the general intercessions, but the servers leave.

132. After the priest introduces the general intercessions, the deacon announces the intentions at the lectern or other suitable place.

133. At the presentation of the gifts, while the priest remains at the chair, the deacon prepares the altar, assisted by other ministers, but the care of the sacred vessels belongs to the deacon. He assists the priest in receiving the people's gifts. Next, he hands the priest the paten with the bread to be consecrated, pours wine and a little water into the chalice, saying inaudibly the prayer, *Through the mystery of this water and wine,* then passes the chalice to the priest. (He may also prepare the chalice and pour the wine and water at a side table.) If incense is used, the deacon assists the priest with the incensing of the gifts and the altar; afterward he, or another minister, incenses the priest and the people.

134. During the eucharistic prayer, the deacon stands near but slightly behind the priest, so that when necessary he may assist the priest with the chalice or the missal.

135. At the final doxology of the eucharistic prayer, the deacon stands next to the priest, holding up the chalice as the priest raises the paten with the eucharistic bread, until the people have said the acclamation: *Amen.*

136. After the priest has said the prayer for peace and the greeting: *The peace of the Lord be with you always,* and the people have made the response: *And also with you,* the deacon may invite all to exchange the sign of peace, saying: *Let us offer each other the sign of peace.* He himself receives the sign of peace from the priest and may offer it to other ministers near him.

137. After the priest's communion, the deacon receives under both kinds and then assists the priest in giving communion to the people. But if communion is given under both kinds, the deacon ministers the chalice to the communicants and is the last to drink from it.

138. After communion, the deacon returns to the altar with the priest and collects any remaining fragments. He then takes the chalice and other vessels to the side table, where he purifies them and arranges them in the usual way; the priest returns to the chair. But it is permissible to leave the vessels to be purified, properly covered and on a corporal, at a side table and to purify them after Mass, when the people have left.

CONCLUDING RITE

139. Following the prayer after communion, if there are any brief announcements, the deacon may make them, unless the priest prefers to do so himself.

140. After the priest's blessing, the deacon dismisses the people, saying: *Go in the peace of Christ,* or: *Go in peace to love and serve the Lord,* or: *The Mass is ended, go in peace.*

141. Along with the priest, the deacon kisses the altar, makes the proper reverence, and leaves in the manner followed for the entrance procession.

## C. Functions of the Acolyte

142. The acolyte may have functions of various kinds and several may occur at the same time. It is therefore desirable that these functions be suitably distributed among several acolytes. But if there is only a single acolyte present, he should perform the more important functions and the rest are distributed among other ministers.

### INTRODUCTORY RITES

143. In the procession to the altar the acolyte may carry the cross, walking between two servers with lighted candles. When he reaches the altar, he places the cross near it and takes his own place in the sanctuary.

144. Throughout the celebration it belongs to the acolyte to go to the priest or the deacon, whenever necessary, in order to present the book to them and to assist them in any other way required. Thus it is appropriate that, if possible, he have a place from which he can conveniently carry out his ministry both at the chair and at the altar.

### LITURGY OF THE EUCHARIST

145. After the general intercessions, when no deacon is present, the acolyte places the corporal, purificator, chalice, and missal on the altar, while the priest remains at the chair. Then, if necessary, the acolyte assists the priest in receiving the gifts of the people and he may bring the bread and wine to the altar and present them to the priest. If incense is used, the acolyte gives the censer to the priest and assists him in incensing the gifts and the altar.

146. The acolyte may assist the priest as a special minister in giving communion to the people.[61] If communion is given under both kinds, the acolyte ministers the chalice to the communicants or he holds the chalice when communion is given by intinction.

147. After communion, the acolyte helps the priest or deacon to purify and arrange the vessels. If no deacon is present, the acolyte takes the vessels to the side table, where he purifies and arranges them.

## D. Functions of the Reader

### INTRODUCTORY RITES

148. In the procession to the altar, when no deacon is present, the reader may carry the Book of the Gospels. In that case he walks in front of the priest; otherwise he walks with the other ministers.

149. Upon reaching the altar, the reader makes the proper reverence along with the priest, goes up to the altar, and places the Book of the Gospels on it. Then he takes his place in the sanctuary with the other ministers.

150. At the lectern the reader proclaims the readings that precede the gospel. If there is no cantor of the psalm, he may also sing or recite the responsorial psalm after the first reading.

151. After the priest gives the introduction to the general intercessions, the reader may announce the intentions when no deacon is present.

152. If there is no entrance song or communion song and the antiphons in the Missal are not said by the faithful, the reader recites them at the proper time.

## II. CONCELEBRATED MASSES

INTRODUCTION

153. Concelebration effectively brings out the unity of the priesthood, of the sacrifice, and of the whole people of God. The rite itself prescribes concelebration at the ordination of bishops and of priests and at the chrism Mass.

Unless the good of the faithful requires or suggests otherwise, concelebration is also recommended at:

   a. the evening Mass on Holy Thursday;

   b. the Mass for councils, meeting of bishops, and synods;

   c. the Mass for the blessing of an abbot;

   d. the conventual Mass and the principal Mass in churches and oratories;

   e. the Mass for any kind of meeting of priests, either secular or religious.[62] [See GIapp, no. 153.]

154. Where there is a large number of priests, the authorized superior may permit concelebration several times on the same day, but either at different times or in different places.[63]

155. The right to regulate, in accord with the law, the discipline for concelebration in his diocese, even in churches and oratories of exempt religious, belongs to the bishop.[64]

156. No one is ever to be admitted into a concelebration once Mass has already begun.[65]

157. A concelebration in which the priests of any diocese concelebrate with their own bishop, especially at the chrism Mass on Holy Thursday and on the occasion of a synod or pastoral visitation, is to be held in high regard. Concelebration is likewise recommended whenever priests gather together with their bishop during a retreat or at any other meeting. That sign of the unity of the priesthood and of the Church itself which marks every concelebration stands out even more clearly in the instances mentioned.[66]

158.  For a particular reason, having to do either with the meaning of the rite or of the liturgical feast, to celebrate or concelebrate more than once on the same day is permitted as follows:

a. One who has celebrated or concelebrated the chrism Mass on Holy Thursday may also celebrate or concelebrate the evening Mass.

b. One who has celebrated or concelebrated the Mass of the Easter Vigil may celebrate or concelebrate the second Mass of Easter.

c. All priests may celebrate or concelebrate the three Masses of Christmas, provided the Masses are at their proper times of day.

d. One who concelebrates with the bishop or his delegate at a synod or pastoral visitation, or concelebrates on the occasion of a meeting of priests, may celebrate another Mass for the benefit of the people.[67] This holds also, in analogous circumstances, for gatherings of religious.

159.  The structure of a concelebrated Mass, whatever its form, follows the norms for an individual celebration, except for the points prescribed or changed in the next section.

160.  If neither a deacon nor other ministers assist in a concelebrated Mass, their functions are carried out by the concelebrants.

INTRODUCTORY RITES

161.  In the sacristy or other suitable place the concelebrants put on the vestments usual for individual celebrants. For a good reason, however, as when there are more concelebrants than vestments, the concelebrants may omit the chasuble and simply wear the stole over the alb; but the principal celebrant always wears the chasuble.

162.  When everything is ready, there is the usual procession through the church to the altar. The concelebrating priests go ahead of the principal celebrant.

163.  On reaching the altar, the concelebrants and the celebrant make the prescribed reverence, kiss the altar, then go to their chairs. When incense is used, the principal celebrant incenses the altar, then goes to the chair.

LITURGY OF THE WORD

164.  During the liturgy of the word, the concelebrants remain at their places, sitting or standing as the principal celebrant does.

165.  As a rule the principal celebrant or one of the concelebrants gives the homily.

LITURGY OF THE EUCHARIST

166.  The rites for the preparation of the gifts are carried out by the principal celebrant; the other concelebrants remain at their places.

167. At the end of the preparation of the gifts, the concelebrants come near the altar and stand around it in such a way that they do not interfere with the actions of the rite and that the people have a clear view. They should not be in the deacon's way when he has to go to the altar in the performance of his ministry.

### Manner of Reciting the Eucharistic Prayer

168. The preface is said by the principal celebrant alone; the *Sanctus* is sung or recited by all the concelebrants with the congregation and the choir.

169. After the *Sanctus*, the concelebrants continue the eucharistic prayer in the way to be described. Unless otherwise indicated, only the principal celebrant makes the gestures.

170. The parts said by all the concelebrants together are to be recited in such a way that the concelebrants say them in a softer voice and the principal celebrant's voice stands out clearly. In this way the congregation should be able to hear the text without difficulty.

### A. Eucharistic Prayer I, the Roman Canon

171. The prayer, *We come to you, Father*, is said by the principal celebrant alone, with hands outstretched.

172. The intercessions, *Remember, Lord, your people* and *In union with the whole Church*, may be assigned to one of the concelebrants; he alone says these prayers, with hands outstretched and aloud.

173. The prayer, *Father, accept this offering*, is said by the principal celebrant alone, with hands outstretched.

174. From *Bless and approve our offering* to *Almighty God, we pray* inclusive, all the concelebrants recite everything together in this manner:

    a. They say *Bless and approve our offering* with hands outstretched toward the offerings.

    b. They say *The day before he suffered* and *When supper was ended* with hands joined.

    c. While saying the words of the Lord, each extends his right hand toward the bread and toward the chalice, if this seems appropriate; they look at the eucharistic bread and chalice as these are shown and afterward bow low.

    d. They say *Father, we celebrate the memory of Christ* and *Look with favor* with hands outstretched.

    e. From *Almighty God, we pray* to *the sacred body and blood of your Son* inclusive, they bow with hands joined; then they stand upright and cross themselves at the words, *let us be filled*.

175. The intercessions, *Remember, Lord, those who have died* and *For ourselves, too*, may be assigned to one of the concelebrants; he alone says these prayers, with hands outstretched and aloud.

176. At the words, *Though we are sinners,* all the concelebrants strike their breast.

177. The prayer, *Through Christ our Lord you give us all these gifts,* is said by the principal celebrant alone.

178. In this eucharistic prayer the parts from *Bless and approve our offering* to *Almighty God, we pray* inclusive and the concluding doxology may be sung.

### B. Eucharistic Prayer II

179. The prayer, *Lord, you are holy indeed,* is said by the principal celebrant alone, with hands outstretched.

180. From *Let your Spirit come* to *May all of us who share* inclusive, all the concelebrants together say the prayer in this manner:

a. They say *Let your Spirit come* with hands outstretched toward the offerings.

b. They say *Before he was given up to death* and *When supper was ended* with hands joined.

c. While saying the words of the Lord, each extends his right hand toward the bread and toward the chalice, if this seems appropriate; they look at the eucharistic bread and the chalice as they are shown and afterward bow low.

d. They say *In memory of his death* and *May all of us who share* with hands outstretched.

181. The intercessions for the living, *Lord, remember your Church,* and for the dead, *Remember our brothers and sisters,* may be assigned to one of the concelebrants; he alone says the intercessions, with hands outstretched.

182. In this eucharistic prayer the parts from *Before he was given up to death* to *In memory of his death* inclusive and the concluding doxology may be sung.

### C. Eucharistic Prayer III

183. The prayer, *Father, you are holy indeed,* is said by the principal celebrant alone, with hands outstretched.

184. From *And so, Father, we bring you these gifts* to *Look with favor* inclusive, all the concelebrants together say the prayer in this manner:

a. They say *And so, Father, we bring you these gifts* with hands outstretched toward the offerings.

b. They say *On the night he was betrayed* and *When supper was ended* with hands joined.

c. While saying the words of the Lord, each extends his right hand toward the bread and toward the chalice, if this seems appropriate; they look at the eucharistic bread and chalice as these are shown and afterward bow low.

d. They say *Father, calling to mind* and *Look with favor* with hands outstretched.

185. The intercessions, *May he make us an everlasting gift* and *Lord, may this sacrifice,* may be assigned to one of the concelebrants; he alone says these prayers, with hands outstretched.

186. In this eucharistic prayer the parts from *On the night he was betrayed* to *Father, calling to mind* inclusive and the concluding doxology may be sung.

### D. Eucharistic Prayer IV

187. The prayer, *Father, we acknowledge,* is said by the principal celebrant alone, with hands outstretched.

188. From *Father, may this Holy Spirit* to *Lord, look upon this sacrifice* inclusive, all the concelebrants together say the prayer in this manner:

a. They say *Father, may this Holy Spirit* with hands outstretched toward the offerings.

b. They say *He always loved those* and *In the same way* with hands joined.

c. While saying the words of the Lord, each extends his right hand toward the bread and toward the chalice, if this seems appropriate; they look at the eucharistic bread and chalice as these are shown and afterward bow low.

d. They say *Father, we now celebrate* and *Lord, look upon this sacrifice* with hands outstretched.

189. The intercessions, *Lord, remember those,* may be assigned to one of the concelebrants; he alone says them, with hands outstretched.

190. In this eucharistic prayer the parts from *He always loved those* to *Father, we now celebrate* inclusive and the concluding doxology may be sung.

191. The concluding doxology of the eucharistic prayer may be sung or said either by the principal celebrant alone or together with all the concelebrants.

COMMUNION RITE

192. Next, with hands joined, the celebrant introduces the Lord's Prayer; with hands outstretched, he then says this prayer itself with the other concelebrants and the congregation.

193. The embolism, *Deliver us,* is said by the principal celebrant alone, with hands outstretched. All the concelebrants together with the congregation say the final acclamation, *For the kingdom.*

194. After the deacon (or one of the concelebrants) says: *Let us offer each other the sign of peace,* all exchange the sign of peace. The concelebrants who are nearer the principal celebrant receive the sign of peace from him ahead of the deacon.

195. During the *Agnus Dei*, some of the concelebrants may help the principal celebrant break the eucharistic bread for communion, both for the concelebrants and for the congregation.

196. After the commingling, the principal celebrant alone inaudibly says the prayer, *Lord Jesus Christ, Son of the living God*, or *Lord Jesus Christ, with faith in your love and mercy.*

197. After this prayer, the principal celebrant genuflects and steps back a little. One by one the concelebrants come to the middle of the altar, genuflect, and reverently take the body of Christ from the altar. Then holding the eucharistic bread in the right hand, with the left hand under it, they return to their places. The concelebrants may, however, remain in their places and take the body of Christ from the paten presented to them by the principal celebrant or by one or more of the concelebrants, or from the paten as it is passed from one to the other.

198. Then the principal celebrant takes the eucharistic bread, holds it slightly raised above the paten, and, facing the congregation, says: *This is the Lamb of God.* With the concelebrants and the congregation he continues: *Lord, I am not worthy.*

199. Then the principal celebrant, facing the altar, says inaudibly: *May the body of Christ bring me to everlasting life* and reverently consumes the body of Christ. The concelebrants do the same. After them the deacon receives the body of Christ from the principal celebrant.

200. The blood of the Lord may be taken by drinking from the chalice directly, through a tube, with a spoon, or even by intinction.

201. If communion is received directly from the chalice, either of two procedures may be followed:

    a. The principal celebrant takes the chalice and says inaudibly: *May the blood of Christ bring me to everlasting life.* He drinks a little and hands the chalice to the deacon or a concelebrant. Then he gives communion to the faithful or returns to the chair. The concelebrants approach the altar one by one or, if two chalices are used, two by two. They drink the blood of Christ and return to their seats. The deacon or a concelebrant wipes the chalice with a purificator after each concelebrant communicates.

    b. The principal celebrant stands at the middle of the altar and drinks the blood of Christ in the usual manner.

    But the concelebrants may receive the blood of the Lord while remaining in their places. They drink from the chalice presented by the deacon or by one of their number, or else passed from one to the other. Either the one who drinks from the chalice or the one who presents it always wipes it off. After communicating, each one returns to his seat.

202. If communion is received through a tube, this is the procedure. The principal celebrant takes the tube and says inaudibly: *May the blood of Christ bring me to*

*everlasting life.* He drinks a little and immediately cleans the tube by sipping some water from a container at hand on the altar, then places the tube on the paten. The deacon or one of the concelebrants puts the chalice at a convenient place in the middle of the altar or at the right side on another corporal. A container of water for purifying the tubes is placed near the chalice, with a paten to hold them afterward.

The concelebrants come forward one by one, take a tube, and drink a little from the chalice. They then purify the tube, by sipping a little water, and place it on the paten.

203. If communion is received by using a spoon, the same procedure is followed as for communion with a tube. But care is to be taken that after each communion the spoon is placed in a container of water. After communion has been completed, the acolyte carries this container to a side table to wash and dry the spoons.

204. The deacon receives communion last. He then drinks what remains in the chalice and takes it to the side table. There he or the acolyte washes and dries the chalice and arranges it in the usual way.

205. The concelebrants may also receive from the chalice at the altar immediately after receiving the body of the Lord.

In this case the principal celebrant receives under both kinds as he would when celebrating Mass alone, but for the communion from the chalice he follows the rite that in each instance has been decided on for the concelebrants.

After the principal celebrant's communion, the chalice is placed on another corporal at the right side of the altar. The concelebrants come forward one by one, genuflect, and receive the body of the Lord; then they go to the side of the altar and drink the blood of the Lord, following the rite decided upon, as has just been said.

The communion of the deacon and the purification of the chalice take place as already described.

206. If the concelebrants receive communion by intinction, the principal celebrant receives the body and blood of the Lord in the usual way, making sure that enough remains in the chalice for their communion. Then the deacon or one of the concelebrants arranges the paten with the eucharistic bread and the chalice conveniently in the center of the altar or at the right side on another corporal. The concelebrants approach the altar one by one, genuflect, and take a particle, dip part of it into the chalice, and, holding a paten under their chin, communicate. Afterward they return to their places as at the beginning of Mass.

The deacon receives communion also by intinction and to the concelebrant's words: *The body and blood of Christ,* makes the response: *Amen.* At the altar the deacon drinks all that remains in the chalice, takes it to the side table and there he or the acolyte purifies and dries it, then arranges it in the usual way.

CONCLUDING RITE

207. The principal celebrant does everything else until the end of Mass in the usual way; the other concelebrants remain at their seats.

208. Before leaving, the concelebrants make the proper reverence to the altar; as a rule, the principal celebrant kisses the altar.

## III. MASS WITHOUT A CONGREGATION

INTRODUCTION

209. This section gives the norms for Mass celebrated by a priest with only one server to assist him and to make the responses.

210. In general this form of Mass follows the rite of Mass with a congregation. The server takes the people's part to the extent possible.

211. Mass should not be celebrated without a server or the participation of at least one of the faithful, except for some legitimate and reasonable cause. In this case the greetings and the blessing at the end of Mass are omitted.

212. The chalice is prepared before Mass, either on a side table near the altar or on the altar itself; the missal is placed on the left side of the altar.

INTRODUCTORY RITES

213. After he reverences the altar, the priest crosses himself, saying: *In the name of the Father*, etc. He turns to the server and gives one of the forms of greeting. For the penitential rite the priest stands at the foot of the altar.

214. The priest then goes up to the altar and kisses it, goes to the missal at the left side of the altar, and remains there until the end of the general intercessions.

215. He reads the entrance antiphon and says the *Kyrie* and the *Gloria*, in keeping with the rubrics.

216. Then, with hands joined, the priest says: *Let us pray.* After a suitable pause, he says the opening prayer, with hands outstretched. At the end the server responds: *Amen.*

LITURGY OF THE WORD

217. After the opening prayer, the server or the priest himself reads the first reading and psalm, the second reading, when it is to be said, and the *Alleluia* verse or other chant.

218. The priest remains in the same place, bows and says inaudibly: *Almighty God, cleanse my heart.* He then reads the gospel and at the conclusion kisses the book, saying: *May the words of the gospel wipe away our sins.* The server says the acclamation.

219. The priest then says the profession of faith with the server, if the rubrics call for it.

220. The general intercessions may be said even in this form of Mass; the priest gives the intentions and the server makes the response.

LITURGY OF THE EUCHARIST

221. The antiphon for the preparation of the gifts is omitted. The minister places the corporal, purificator, and chalice on the altar, unless they have already been put there at the beginning of Mass.

222. Preparation of the bread and wine, including the pouring of the water, are carried out as at a Mass with a congregation, with the formularies given in the Order of Mass. After placing the bread and wine on the altar, the priest washes his hands at the side of the altar as the server pours the water.

223. The priest says the prayer over the gifts and the eucharistic prayer, following the rite described for Mass with a congregation.

224. The Lord's Prayer and the embolism, *Deliver us,* are said as at Mass with a congregation.

225. After the acclamation concluding the embolism, the priest says the prayer, *Lord, Jesus Christ, you said.* He then adds: *The peace of the Lord be with you always,* and the server answers: *And also with you.* The priest may give the sign of peace to the server.

226. Then, while he says the *Agnus Dei* with the server, the priest breaks the eucharistic bread over the paten. After the *Agnus Dei,* he places a particle in the chalice, saying inaudibly: *May this mingling.*

227. After the commingling, the priest says inaudibly the prayer, *Lord Jesus Christ, Son of the living God,* or *Lord Jesus Christ, with faith in your love and mercy.* Then he genuflects and takes the eucharistic bread. If the server is to receive communion, the priest turns to him and, holding the eucharistic bread a little above the paten, says: *This is the Lamb of God,* adding once with the server: *Lord, I am not worthy.* Facing the altar, the priest then receives the body of Christ. If the server is not receiving communion, the priest, after making a genuflection, takes the host and, facing the altar, says once inaudibly: *Lord, I am not worthy,* and eats the body of Christ. The blood of Christ is received in the way described in the Order of Mass with a congregation.

228. Before giving communion to the server, the priest says the communion antiphon.

229. The chalice is washed at the side of the altar and then may be carried by the server to a side table or left on the altar, as at the beginning.

230. After the purification of the chalice, the priest may observe a period of silence. Then he says the prayer after communion.

231. The concluding rites are carried out as at Mass with a congregation, but the dismissal formulary is omitted.

## IV. SOME GENERAL RULES FOR ALL FORMS OF MASS

### VENERATION OF THE ALTAR AND THE BOOK OF THE GOSPELS

232. According to traditional liturgical practice, the altar and the Book of the Gospels are kissed as a sign of veneration. But if this sign of reverence is not in harmony with the traditions or the culture of the region, the conference of bishops may substitute some other sign, after informing the Apostolic See.

### GENUFLECTIONS AND BOWS

233. Three genuflections are made during Mass: after the showing of the eucharistic bread, after the showing of the chalice, and before communion.

If there is a tabernacle with the blessed sacrament in the sanctuary, a genuflection is made before and after Mass and whenever anyone passes in front of the blessed sacrament.

234. There are two kinds of bow, a bow of the head and a bow of the body:

a. A bow of the head is made when the three divine Persons are named together and at the name of Jesus, Mary and the saint in whose honor Mass is celebrated.

b. A bow of the body, or profound bow, is made: toward the altar if there is no tabernacle with the blessed sacrament; during the prayers, *Almighty God, cleanse* and *Lord God, we ask you to receive*; within the profession of faith at the words, *by the power of the Holy Spirit*; in Eucharistic Prayer I (Roman Canon) at the words, *Almighty God, we pray*. The same kind of bow is made by the deacon when he asks the blessing before the gospel. In addition, the priest bends over slightly as he says the words of the Lord at the consecration.

### INCENSATION

235. The use of incense is optional in any form of Mass:

a. during the entrance procession;

b. at the beginning of Mass, to incense the altar;

c. at the procession and proclamation of the gospel;

d. at the preparation of the gifts, to incense them, as well as the altar, priest, and people;

e. at the showing of the eucharistic bread and chalice after the consecration.

236. The priest puts the incense in the censer and blesses it with the sign of the cross, saying nothing.

This is the way to incense the altar:

a. If the altar is freestanding, the priest incenses it as he walks around it.

b. If the altar is not freestanding, he incenses it while walking first to the right side, then to the left.

If there is a cross on or beside the altar, he incenses it before he incenses the altar. If the cross is behind the altar, the priest incenses it when he passes in front of it.

## PURIFICATIONS

237. Whenever a particle of the eucharistic bread adheres to his fingers, especially after the breaking of the bread or the communion of the people, the priest cleanses his fingers over the paten or, if necessary, washes them. He also gathers any particles that may fall outside the paten.

238. The vessels are purified by the priest or else by the deacon or acolyte after the communion or after Mass, if possible at a side table. Wine and water or water alone are used for the purification of the chalice, then drunk by the one who purifies it. The paten is usually to be wiped with the purificator.

239. If the eucharistic bread or any particle of it should fall, it is to be picked up reverently. If any of the precious blood spills, the area should be washed and the water poured into the sacrarium.

## COMMUNION UNDER BOTH KINDS

240. Holy communion has a more complete form as a sign when it is received under both kinds. For in this manner of reception a fuller light shines on the sign of the eucharistic banquet. Moreover there is a clearer expression of that will by which the new and everlasting covenant is ratified in the blood of the Lord and of the relationship of the eucharistic banquet to the eschatological banquet in the Father's kingdom.[68]

241. For the faithful who take part in the rite or are present at it, pastors should take care to call to mind as clearly as possible Catholic teaching according to the Council of Trent on the manner of communion. Above all they should instruct the people that according to Catholic faith Christ, whole and entire, as well as the true sacrament are received even under one kind only; that, therefore, as far as the effects are concerned, those who receive in this manner are not deprived of any grace necessary for salvation.[69]

Pastors are also to teach that the Church has power in its stewardship of the sacraments, provided their substance remains intact. The Church may make those rules and changes that, in view of the different conditions, times, and places, it decides to be in the interest of reverence for the sacraments or the well-being of the recipients.[70] At the same time the faithful should be guided toward a desire to take part more intensely in a sacred rite in which the sign of the eucharistic meal stands out more explicitly.

242. At the discretion of the Ordinary and after the prerequisite catechesis, communion from the chalice is permitted in the case of:[71]

1. newly baptized adults at the Mass following their baptism; adults at the Mass at which they receive confirmation; baptized persons who are being received into the full communion of the Church;

2. the bride and bridegroom at their wedding Mass;

3. deacons at the Mass of their ordination;

4. an abbess at the Mass in which she is blessed; those consecrated to a life of virginity at the Mass of their consecration; professed religious, their relatives, friends, and the other members of their community at the Mass of first or perpetual vows or renewal of vows;

5. those who receive institution for a certain ministry at the Mass of their institution; lay missionary helpers at the Mass in which they publicly receive their mission; others at the Mass in which they receive an ecclesiastical mission;

6. the sick person and all present at the time viaticum is to be administered when Mass is celebrated in the sick person's home;

7. the deacon and ministers who exercise their office at Mass;

8. when there is a concelebration, in the case of:

a. all who exercise a liturgical function at this concelebration and also all seminarians present;

b. in their churches or oratories, all members of institutes professing the evangelical counsels and other societies whose members dedicate themselves to God by religious vows or by an offering or promise; also all those who reside in the houses of members of such institutes and societies;

9. priests who are present at major celebrations and are not able to celebrate or concelebrate;

10. all who make a retreat at a Mass in which they actively participate and which is specially celebrated for the group; also all who take part in the meeting of any pastoral body at a Mass they celebrate as a group;

11. those listed in nos. 2 and 4, at Masses celebrating their jubilees;

12. godparents, relatives, wife or husband, and lay catechists of newly baptized adults at the Mass of their initiation;

13. relatives, friends and special benefactors who take part in the Mass of a newly ordained priest;

14. members of communities at the conventual or community Mass, in accord with the provisions of this Instruction, no. 76.

Further, the conferences of bishops have the power to decide to what extent and under what considerations and conditions Ordinaries may allow communion under both kinds in other instances that are of special significance in the spiritual life of any community or group of the faithful.

Within such limits, Ordinaries may designate the particular instances, but on condition that they grant permission not indiscriminately but for clearly defined celebrations and that they point out matters for caution. They are also to exclude occasions when there will be a larger number of communicants. The groups receiving this permission must also be specific, well ordered, and homogeneous. [See GIapp, no. 242.]

243. Preparation for giving communion under both kinds:

a. If communion is received from the chalice with a tube, silver tubes are needed for the celebrant and each communicant. There should also be a container of water for purifying the tubes and a paten on which to put them afterward.

b. If communion is given with a spoon, only one spoon is necessary.

c. If communion is given by intinction, care is to be taken that the eucharistic bread is not too thin or too small, but a little thicker than usual so that after being partly dipped into the precious blood it can still easily be given to the communicant.

### 1. Rite of Communion under Both Kinds Directly from the Chalice

244. If there is a deacon or another assisting priest or an acolyte:

a. The celebrant receives the Lord's body and blood as usual, making sure enough remains in the chalice for the other communicants. He wipes the outside of the chalice with a purificator.

b. The priest gives the chalice with purificator to the minister and himself takes the paten or ciborium with the hosts; then both station themselves conveniently for the communion of the people.

c. The communicants approach, make the proper reverence, and stand in front of the priest. Showing the host he says: *The body of Christ.* The communicant answers: *Amen* and receives the body of Christ from the priest.

d. The communicant then moves to the minister of the chalice and stands before him. The minister says: *The blood of Christ*, the communicant answers: *Amen*, and the minister holds out the chalice with purificator. For the sake of convenience, communicants may raise the chalice to their mouths themselves. Holding the purificator under the mouth with one hand, they drink a little from the chalice, taking care not to spill it, and then return to their places. The minister wipes the outside of the chalice with the purificator.

e. The minister places the chalice on the altar after all who are receiving under both kinds have drunk from it. If there are others who are not receiving communion under both kinds, the priest gives these communion, then returns to the altar. The priest or minister drinks whatever remains in the chalice and carries out the usual purifications.

245. If there is no deacon, other priest or acolyte:

a. The priest receives the Lord's body and blood as usual, making sure enough remains in the chalice for the other communicants. He wipes the outside of the chalice with the purificator.

b. The priest then stations himself conveniently for communion and distributes the body of Christ in the usual way to all who are receiving under both kinds. The communicants approach, make the proper reverence, and stand in front of the priest. After receiving the body of Christ, they step back a little.

c. After all have received, the celebrant places the ciborium on the altar and takes the chalice with the purificator. All those receiving from the chalice come forward again and stand in front of the priest. He says: *The blood of Christ,* the communicant answers: *Amen,* and the priest presents the chalice with purificator. The communicants hold the purificator under their mouths with one hand, taking care that none of the precious blood is spilled, drink a little from the chalice, and then return to their places. The priest wipes the outside of the chalice with the purificator.

d. After the communion from the chalice, the priest places it on the altar and if there are others receiving under one kind only, he gives them communion in the usual way, then returns to the altar. He drinks whatever remains in the chalice and carries out the usual purifications.

### 2. Rite of Communion under Both Kinds by Intinction

246. If there is a deacon, another priest assisting, or an acolyte present:

a. The priest hands this minister the chalice with purificator and he himself takes the paten or ciborium with the hosts. The priest and the minister of the chalice station themselves conveniently for distributing communion.

b. The communicants approach, make the proper reverence, stand in front of the priest, and hold the communion plate below their chins. The celebrant dips a particle into the chalice and, showing it, says: *The body and blood of Christ.* The communicants respond: *Amen,* receive communion from the priest, and return to their places.

c. The communion of those who do not receive under both kinds and the rest of the rite take place as already described.

247. If there is no deacon, assisting priest, or acolyte present:

a. After drinking the blood of the Lord, the priest takes the ciborium or paten with the hosts, between the index and middle fingers of one hand and holds the chalice between the thumb and index finger of the same hand. Then he stations himself conveniently for communion.

b. The communicants approach, make the proper reverence, stand in front of the priest, and hold a plate beneath their chins. The priest takes a particle, dips it into the chalice, and, showing it, says: *The body and blood of Christ.* The communicants respond: *Amen,* receive communion from the priest, and return to their places.

c. It is also permitted to place a small table covered with a cloth and corporal at a suitable place. The priest places the chalice or ciborium on the table in order to make the distribution of communion easier.

d. The communion of those who do not receive under both kinds, the consumption of the blood remaining in the chalice, and the purifications take place as already described.

### 3. Rite of Communion under Both Kinds Using a Tube

248. In this case the priest celebrant also uses a tube when receiving the blood of the Lord.

249. If there is a deacon, another assisting priest, or an acolyte present:

a. For the communion of the body of the Lord, everything is done as described in nos. 224 b and c.

b. The communicant goes to the minister of the chalice and stands in front of him. The minister says: *The blood of Christ* and the communicant responds: *Amen.* The communicant receives the tube from the minister, places it in the chalice, and drinks a little. The communicant then removes the tube, careful not to spill any drops, and places it in a container of water held by the minister. The communicant sips a little water to purify the tube, then puts it into another container presented by the minister.

250. If there is no deacon, other assisting priest, or acolyte present, the priest celebrant offers the chalice to each communicant in a way described already for communion from the chalice (no. 245). The minister standing next to him holds the container of water for purifying the tube.

### 4. Rite of Communion under Both Kinds Using a Spoon

251. If a deacon, another assisting priest, or an acolyte is present, he holds the chalice and, saying: *The blood of Christ*, ministers the blood of the Lord with a spoon to the individual communicants, who hold the plate beneath their chins. He is to take care that the spoon does not touch the lips or tongues of the communicants.

252. If there is no deacon, other assisting priest, or acolyte present, the priest celebrant himself gives them the Lord's blood, after all receiving communion under both kinds have received the Lord's body.

# CHAPTER V
# ARRANGEMENT AND FURNISHING OF CHURCHES FOR THE EUCHARISTIC CELEBRATION
## I. GENERAL PRINCIPLES

253. For the celebration of the eucharist, the people of God normally assemble in a church or, if there is none, in some other fitting place worthy of so great a mystery. Churches and other places of worship should therefore be suited to celebrating the liturgy and to ensuring the active participation of the faithful.

Further, the places and requisites for worship should be truly worthy and beautiful, signs and symbols of heavenly realities.[72]

254. At all times, therefore, the Church seeks out the service of the arts and welcomes the artistic expressions of all peoples and regions.[73] The Church is intent on keeping the works of art and the treasures handed down from the past[74] and, when necessary, on adapting them to new needs. It strives as well to promote new works of art that appeal to the contemporary mentality.[75]

In commissioning artists and choosing works of art that are to become part of a church, the highest standard is therefore to be set, in order that art may aid faith and devotion and be true to the reality it is to symbolize and the purpose it is to serve.[76]

255. All churches are to be solemnly dedicated or at least blessed. But cathedral and parish churches are always to be dedicated. The faithful should give due honor to the cathedral of their diocese and to their own church as symbols of the spiritual Church that their Christian vocation commits them to build up and extend.

256. All who are involved in the construction, restoration, and remodeling of churches are to consult the diocesan commission on liturgy and art. The local Ordinary is to use the counsel and help of this commission whenever it comes to laying down norms on this matter, approving plans for new buildings, and making decisions on the more important issues.[77]

## II. ARRANGEMENT OF A CHURCH FOR THE LITURGICAL ASSEMBLY

257. The people of God assembled at Mass possess an organic and hierarchical structure, expressed by the various ministries and actions for each part of the celebration. The general plan of the sacred edifice should be such that in some way it conveys the image of the gathered assembly. It should also allow the participants to take the place most appropriate to them and assist all to carry out their individual functions properly.

The congregation and the choir should have a place that facilitates their active participation.[78]

The priest and his ministers have their place in the sanctuary, that is, in the part of the church that brings out their distinctive role, namely, to preside over the prayers, to proclaim the word of God, or to minister at the altar.

Even though these elements must express a hierarchical arrangement and the diversity of offices, they should at the same time form a complete and organic unity, clearly expressive of the unity of the entire holy people. The character and beauty of the place and all its appointments should foster devotion and show the holiness of the mysteries celebrated there.

## III. SANCTUARY

258. The sanctuary should be clearly marked off from the body of the church either by being somewhat elevated or by its distinctive design and appointments. It should be large enough to accommodate all the rites.[79]

## IV. ALTAR

259. At the altar the sacrifice of the cross is made present under sacramental signs. It is also the table of the Lord and the people of God are called together to share in it. The altar is, as well, the center of the thanksgiving that the eucharist accomplishes.[80]

260. In a place of worship, the celebration of the eucharist must be on an altar, either fixed or movable. Outside a place of worship, especially if the celebration is only for a single occasion, a suitable table may be used, but always with a cloth and corporal.

261. A fixed altar is one attached to the floor so that it cannot be moved; a movable altar is one that can be transferred from place to place.

262. In every church there should ordinarily be a fixed, dedicated altar, which should be freestanding to allow the ministers to walk around it easily and Mass to be celebrated facing the people. It should be so placed as to be a focal point on which the attention of the whole congregation centers naturally.[81]

263. According to the Church's traditional practice and the altar's symbolism, the table of a fixed altar should be of stone and indeed of natural stone. But at the discretion of the conference of bishops some other solid, becoming, and well-crafted material may be used. [See GIapp, no. 263.]

The pedestal or base of the table may be of any sort of material, as long as it is becoming and solid.

264. A movable altar may be constructed of any becoming, solid material suited to liturgical use, according to the traditions and customs of different regions.

265. Altars both fixed and movable are dedicated according to the rite described in the liturgical books, but movable altars may simply be blessed.

266. The practice of placing under the altar to be dedicated relics of saints, even of non-martyrs, is to be maintained. Care must be taken to have solid evidence of the authenticity of such relics.

267. Other altars should be fewer in number. In new churches they should be placed in chapels separated in some way from the body of the church.[82]

## V. ALTAR FURNISHINGS

268. At least one cloth should be placed on the altar out of reverence for the celebration of the memorial of the Lord and the banquet that gives us his body and

blood. The shape, size, and decoration of the altar cloth should be in keeping with the design of the altar.

269. Candles are to be used at every liturgical service as a sign of reverence and festiveness. The candlesticks are to be placed either on or around the altar in a way suited to the design of the altar and the sanctuary. Everything is to be well balanced and must not interfere with the faithful's clear view of what goes on at the altar or is placed on it.

270. There is also to be a cross, clearly visible to the congregation, either on the altar or near it.

## VI. CHAIR FOR THE PRIEST CELEBRANT AND THE MINISTERS, THAT IS, THE PLACE WHERE THE PRIEST PRESIDES

271. The priest celebrant's chair ought to stand as a symbol of his office of presiding over the assembly and of directing prayer. Thus the best place for the chair is at the back of the sanctuary and turned toward the congregation, unless the structure or other circumstances are an obstacle (for example, if too great a distance would interfere with communication between the priest and people). Anything resembling a throne is to be avoided. The seats for the ministers should be so placed in the sanctuary that they can readily carry out their appointed functions.[83]

## VII. LECTERN (AMBO) OR PLACE FROM WHICH THE WORD OF GOD IS PROCLAIMED

272. The dignity of the word of God requires the church to have a place that is suitable for proclamation of the word and is a natural focal point for the people during the liturgy of the word.[84]

As a rule the lectern or ambo should be stationary, not simply a movable stand. In keeping with the structure of each church, it must be so placed that the ministers may be easily seen and heard by the faithful.

The readings, responsorial psalm, and the Easter Proclamation (Exsultet) are proclaimed from the lectern; it may be used also for the homily and general intercessions (prayer of the faithful).

It is better for the commentator, cantor, or choir director not to use the lectern.

## VIII. PLACES FOR THE FAITHFUL

273. The places for the faithful should be arranged with care so that the people are able to take their rightful part in the celebration visually and mentally. As a rule, there should be benches or chairs for their use. But the custom of reserving seats for private persons must be abolished.[85] Chairs or benches should be set up in such a way that the people can easily take the positions required during various celebrations and have unimpeded access to receive communion.

The congregation must be enabled not only to see the priest and the other ministers but also, with the aid of modern sound equipment, to hear them without difficulty.

## IX. CHOIR, ORGAN AND OTHER MUSICAL INSTRUMENTS

274. In relation to the design of each church, the *schola cantorum* should be so placed that its character as a part of the assembly of the faithful that has a special function stands out clearly. The location should also assist the choir's liturgical ministry and readily allow each member complete, that is, sacramental participation in the Mass.[86]

275. The organ and other lawfully approved musical instruments are to be placed suitably in such a way that they can sustain the singing of the choir and congregation and be heard with ease when they are played alone. [See GIapp, no. 275.]

## X. RESERVATION OF THE EUCHARIST

276. Every encouragement should be given to the practice of eucharistic reservation in a chapel suited to the faithful's private adoration and prayer.[87] If this is impossible because of the structure of the church, the sacrament should be reserved at an altar or elsewhere, in keeping with local custom, and in a part of the church that is worthy and properly adorned.[88]

277. The eucharist is to be reserved in a single, solid, immovable tabernacle that is opaque and is locked in such a way as to provide every possible security against the danger of destruction. Thus as a rule there should be only one tabernacle in each church.[89]

## XI. IMAGES FOR VENERATION BY THE FAITHFUL

278. In keeping with the Church's very ancient tradition, it is lawful to set up in places of worship images of Christ, Mary, and the saints for veneration by the faithful. But there is need both to limit their number and to situate them in such a way that they do not distract the people's attention from the celebration.[90] There is to be only one image of any one saint. In general, the devotion of the entire community is to be the criterion regarding images in the adornment and arrangement of a church.

## XII. GENERAL PLAN OF THE CHURCH

279. The style in which a church is decorated should be a means to achieve noble simplicity, not ostentation. The choice of materials for church appointments must be marked by concern for genuineness and by the intent to foster instruction of the faithful and the dignity of the place of worship.

280. Proper planning of a church and its surroundings that meets contemporary needs requires attention not only to the elements belonging directly to liturgical

services but also to those facilities for the comfort of the people that are usual in places of public gatherings.

# CHAPTER VI
## REQUISITES FOR CELEBRATING MASS
### I. BREAD AND WINE

281. Following the example of Christ, the Church has always used bread and wine with water to celebrate the Lord's Supper.

282. The bread must be made only from wheat and must have been baked recently; according to the long-standing tradition of the Latin Church, it must be unleavened.

283. The nature of the sign demands that the material for the eucharistic celebration truly have the appearance of food. Accordingly, even though unleavened and baked in the traditional shape, the eucharistic bread should be made in such a way that in a Mass with a congregation the priest is able actually to break the host into parts and distribute them to at least some of the faithful. (When, however, the number of communicants is large or other pastoral needs require it, small hosts are in no way ruled out.) The action of the breaking of the bread, the simple term for the eucharist in apostolic times, will more clearly bring out the force and meaning of the sign of the unity of all in the one bread and of their charity, since the one bread is being distributed among the members of one family.

284. The wine for the eucharist must be from the fruit of the vine (see Luke 22:18), natural, and pure, that is not mixed with any foreign substance.

285. Care must be taken to ensure that the elements are kept in good condition: that the wine does not turn to vinegar or the bread spoil or become too hard to be broken easily.

286. If the priest notices after the consecration or as he receives communion that water instead of wine was poured into the chalice, he pours the water into another container, then pours wine with water into the chalice and consecrates it. He says only the part of the institution narrative related to the consecration of the chalice, without being obliged to consecrate the bread again.

### II. SACRED FURNISHINGS IN GENERAL

287. As in the case of architecture, the Church welcomes the artistic style of every region for all sacred furnishings and accepts adaptations in keeping with the genius and traditions of each people, provided they fit the purpose for which the sacred furnishings are intended.[91]

In this matter as well the concern is to be for the noble simplicity that is the perfect companion of genuine art.

288. In the choice of materials for sacred furnishings, others besides the traditional are acceptable that by contemporary standards are considered to be of high quality, are durable, and well suited to sacred uses. The conference of bishops is to make the decisions for each region. [See GIapp, no. 288.]

## III. SACRED VESSELS

289. Among the requisites for the celebration of Mass, the sacred vessels hold a place of honor, especially the chalice and paten, which are used in presenting, consecrating, and receiving the bread and wine.

290. Vessels should be made from materials that are solid and that in the particular region are regarded as noble. The conference of bishops will be the judge in this matter. But preference is to be given to materials that do not break easily or become unusable.

291. Chalices and other vessels that serve as receptacles for the blood of the Lord are to have a cup of nonabsorbent material. The base may be of any other solid and worthy material.

292. Vessels that serve as receptacles for the eucharistic bread, such as a paten, ciborium, pyx, monstrance, etc., may be made of other materials that are prized in the region, for example, ebony or other hard woods, as long as they are suited to sacred use.

293. For the consecration of hosts one rather large paten may properly be used; on it is placed the bread for the priest as well as for the ministers and the faithful.

294. Vessels made from metal should ordinarily be gilded on the inside if the metal is one that rusts; gilding is not necessary if the metal is more precious than gold and does not rust.

295. The artist may fashion the sacred vessels in a shape that is in keeping with the culture of each region, provided each type of vessel is suited to the intended liturgical use.

296. For the blessing or consecration of vessels the rites prescribed in the liturgical books are to be followed.

## IV. VESTMENTS

297. In the Church, the Body of Christ, not all members have the same function. This diversity of ministries is shown outwardly in worship by the diversity of vestments. These should therefore symbolize the function proper to each ministry. But at the same time the vestments should also contribute to the beauty of the rite.

298. The vestment common to ministers of every rank is the alb, tied at the waist with a cincture, unless it is made to fit without a cincture. An amice should be put on first if the alb does not completely cover the street clothing at the neck. A

surplice may not be substituted for the alb when the chasuble or dalmatic is to be worn or when a stole is used instead of the chasuble or dalmatic.

299. Unless otherwise indicated, the chasuble, worn over the alb and stole, is the vestment proper to the priest celebrant at Mass and other rites immediately connected with Mass.

300. The dalmatic, worn over the alb and stole, is the vestment proper to the deacon.

301. Ministers below the order of deacon may wear the alb or other vestment that is lawfully approved in each region.

302. The priest wears the stole around his neck and hanging down in front. The deacon wears it over his left shoulder and drawn across the chest to the right side, where it is fastened.

303. The cope is worn by the priest in processions and other services, in keeping with the rubrics proper to each rite.

304. Regarding the design of vestments, the conference of bishops may determine and propose to the Apostolic See adaptations that correspond to the needs and usages of their regions.[92]

305. In addition to the traditional materials, natural fabrics proper to the region may be used for making vestments; artificial fabrics that are in keeping with the dignity of the liturgy and the person wearing them may also be used. The conference of bishops will be the judge in this matter.[93] [See GIapp, no. 305.]

306. The beauty of a vestment should derive from its material and design rather than from lavish ornamentation. Representations on vestments should consist only of symbols, images, or pictures portraying the sacred. Anything out of keeping with the sacred is to be avoided.

307. Variety in the color of the vestments is meant to give effective, outward expression to the specific character of the mysteries of the faith being celebrated and, in the course of the year, to a sense of progress in the Christian life.

308. Traditional usage should be retained for the vestment colors.

a. White is used in the offices and Masses of the Easter and Christmas seasons; on feasts and memorials of the Lord, other than of his passion; on feasts and memorials of Mary, the angels, saints who were not martyrs, All Saints (November 1), John the Baptist (June 24), John the Evangelist (December 27), the Chair of St. Peter (February 22), and the Conversion of St. Paul (January 25).

b. Red is used on Passion Sunday (Palm Sunday) and Good Friday, Pentecost, celebrations of the Lord's passion, birthday feasts of the apostles and evangelists, and celebrations of martyrs.

c. Green is used in the offices and Masses of Ordinary Time.

d. Violet is used in Lent and Advent. It may also be worn in offices and Masses for the dead.

e. Black may be used in Masses for the dead.

f. Rose may be used on *Gaudete* Sunday (Third Sunday of Advent) and *Laetare* Sunday (Fourth Sunday of Lent).

The conference of bishops may choose and propose to the Apostolic See adaptations suited to the needs and culture of peoples. [See GIapp, no. 308.]

309. On solemn occasions more precious vestments may be used, even if not of the color of the day.

310. Ritual Masses are celebrated in their proper color, in white, or in a festive color; Masses for various needs and occasions are celebrated in the color proper to the day or the season or in violet if they bear a penitential character, for example, ritual Masses nos. 23, 28, and 40; votive Masses are celebrated in the color suited to the Mass itself or in the color proper to the day or season.

## V. OTHER REQUISITES FOR CHURCH USE

311. Besides vessels and vestments for which some special material is prescribed, any other furnishings that either have a liturgical use or are in any other way introduced into a church should be worthy and suited to their particular purpose.

312. Even in minor matters, every effort should be made to respect the canons of art and to combine cleanliness and a noble simplicity.

# CHAPTER VII
# CHOICE OF THE MASS AND ITS PARTS

313. The pastoral effectiveness of a celebration will be heightened if the texts of readings, prayers, and songs correspond as closely as possible to the needs, religious dispositions, and aptitude of the participants. This will be achieved by an intelligent use of the broad options described in this chapter.

In planning the celebration, then, the priest should consider the general spiritual good of the assembly rather than his personal outlook. He should be mindful that the choice of texts is to be made in consultation with the ministers and others who have a function in the celebration, including the faithful in regard to the parts that more directly belong to them.

Since a variety of options is provided for the different parts of the Mass, it is necessary for the deacon, readers, psalmists, cantors, commentator, and choir to be completely sure beforehand of those texts for which they are responsible so that nothing is improvised. A harmonious planning and execution will help dispose the people spiritually to take part in the eucharist.

# I. CHOICE OF MASS*

314. On solemnities the priest is bound to follow the calendar of the church where he is celebrating.

315. On Sundays, on weekdays of Advent, the Christmas season, Lent, and the Easter season, on feasts, and on obligatory memorials:

a. if Mass is celebrated with a congregation, the priest should follow the calendar of the church where he is celebrating;

b. if Mass is celebrated without a congregation, the priest may choose either the calendar of the church or his own calendar.

316. On optional memorials:

a. On the weekdays of Advent from December 17 to December 24, during the octave of Christmas, and on the weekdays of Lent, apart from Ash Wednesday and in Holy Week, the priest celebrates the Mass of the day; but he may take the opening prayer from a memorial listed in the General Roman Calendar for that day, except on Ash Wednesday and during Holy Week.

b. On the weekdays of Advent before December 17, the weekdays of the Christmas season from January 2 on, and the weekdays of the Easter season, the priest may choose the weekday Mass, the Mass of the saint or of one of the saints whose memorial is observed, or the Mass of a saint inscribed in the martyrology for that day.

c. On the weekdays in Ordinary Time, the priest may choose the weekday Mass, the Mass of an optional memorial, the Mass of a saint inscribed in the martyrology for that day, a Mass for various needs and occasions, or a votive Mass.

If he celebrates with a congregation, the priest should first consider the spiritual good of the faithful and avoid imposing his own personal preferences. In particular, he should not omit the readings assigned for each day in the weekday lectionary too frequently or without sufficient reason, since the Church desires that a richer portion of God's word be provided for the people.[94]

For similar reasons he should use Masses for the dead sparingly. Every Mass is offered for both the living and the dead and there is a remembrance of the dead in each eucharistic prayer.

Where the faithful are attached to the optional memorials of Mary or the saints, at least one Mass of the memorial should be celebrated to satisfy their devotion.

When an option is given between a memorial in the General Roman Calendar and one in a diocesan or religious calendar, the preference should be given, all things being equal and depending on tradition, to the memorial in the particular calendar.

# II. CHOICE OF INDIVIDUAL TEXTS

317. In the choice of texts for the several parts of the Mass, the following rules are to be observed. They apply to Masses of the season and of the saints.

318. Sundays and holy days have three readings, that is, from the Old Testament, from the writings of an apostle, and from a Gospel. Thus God's own teaching brings the Christian people to a knowledge of the continuity of the work of salvation.

Accordingly, it is expected that there will be three readings, but for pastoral reasons and by decree of the conference of bishops the use of only two readings is allowed in some places. In such a case, the choice between the first two readings should be based on the norms in the Lectionary and on the intention to lead the people to a deeper knowledge of Scripture; there should never be any thought of choosing a text because it is shorter or easier. [See GIapp, no. 318.]

319. In the weekday lectionary, readings are provided for each day of every week throughout the year; therefore, unless a solemnity or feast occurs, these readings are for the most part to be used on the days to which they are assigned.

The continuous reading during the week, however, is sometimes interrupted by the occurrence of a feast or particular celebration. In this case the priest, taking into consideration the entire week's plan of readings, is allowed either to combine omitted parts with other readings or to give preference to certain readings.

In Masses with special groups, the priest may choose texts more suited to the particular celebration, provided they are taken from the texts of an approved lectionary.

320. The Lectionary has a special selection of texts from Scripture for Masses that incorporate certain sacraments or sacramentals or that are celebrated by reason of special circumstances.

These selections or readings have been assigned so that by hearing a more pertinent passage from God's word the faithful may be led to a better understanding of the mystery they are taking part in and may be led to a more ardent love for God's word.

Therefore the texts for proclamation in the liturgical assembly are to be chosen on the basis of their pastoral relevance and the options allowed in this matter.

## PRAYERS

321. The many prefaces enriching the Roman Missal are intended to develop in different ways the theme of thanksgiving in the eucharistic prayer and bring out more clearly the different facets of the mystery of salvation.

322. The choice of the eucharistic prayer may be guided by the following norms.

a. Eucharistic Prayer I, the Roman Canon, which may be used on any day, is particularly apt on days when there is a special text for the prayer, *In union with the whole Church,* or in Masses that have a special form of the prayer, *Father, accept this offering;* also on the feasts of the apostles and saints mentioned in it and on Sundays, unless for pastoral considerations another eucharistic prayer is preferred.

b. Eucharistic Prayer II has features that make it particularly suitable for weekdays and special circumstances.

Although it has its own preface, it may also be used with other prefaces, especially those that summarize the mystery of salvation, such as the Sunday prefaces or the common prefaces.

When Mass is celebrated for a dead person, the special formulary may be inserted in the place indicated, namely, before the intercession, *Remember our brothers and sisters.*

c. Eucharistic Prayer III may be said with any preface. Its use is particularly suited to Sundays and holy days.

The special formulary for a dead person may be used with this prayer in the place indicated, namely, at the prayer, *In mercy and love unite all your children.*

d. Eucharistic Prayer IV has a fixed preface and provides a fuller summary of the history of salvation. It may be used when a Mass has no preface of its own.

Because of the structure of this prayer no special formulary for the dead may be inserted.

e. A eucharistic prayer that has its own preface may be used with that preface, even when the Mass calls for the preface of the season.

323. In any Mass the prayers belonging to that Mass are used, unless otherwise noted.

In Masses on a memorial, however, the opening prayer or collect may be from the Mass itself or from the common; the prayer over the gifts and prayer after communion, unless they are proper, may be taken either from the common or from the weekdays of the current season.

On the weekdays in Ordinary Time, the prayers may be taken from the preceding Sunday, from another Sunday in Ordinary Time, or from the prayers for various needs and occasions listed in the Missal. It is always permissible even to use the opening prayer from these Masses.

This provides a rich collection of texts that create an opportunity continually to rephrase the themes of prayer for the liturgical assembly and also to adapt the prayer to the needs of the people, the Church, and the world. During the more important seasons of the year, however, the proper seasonal prayers appointed for each day in the Missal already make this adaptation.

324. The norms laid down in their proper places are to be observed for the choice of chants between the readings and the songs for the processions at the entrance, presentation of the gifts, and communion.

SPECIAL PERMISSIONS

325. In addition to the permissions just given to choose more suitable texts, the conferences of bishops have the right in some circumstances to make further adaptations of readings, but on condition that the texts are taken from an approved lectionary.

# CHAPTER VIII
## MASSES AND PRAYERS FOR VARIOUS NEEDS AND OCCASIONS AND MASSES FOR THE DEAD
### I. MASSES AND PRAYERS FOR VARIOUS NEEDS AND OCCASIONS

326. For well-disposed Christians the liturgy of the sacraments and sacramentals causes almost every event in human life to be made holy by divine grace that flows from the paschal mystery.[95] The eucharist, in turn, is the sacrament of sacraments. Accordingly, the Missal provides formularies for Masses and prayers that may be used in the various circumstances of Christian life, for the needs of the whole world, and for the needs of the Church, both local and universal.

327. In view of the broad options for choosing the readings and prayers, the Masses for various needs and occasions should be used sparingly, that is, when the occasion requires.

328. In all the Masses for various needs and occasions, unless otherwise indicated, the weekday readings and the chants between them may be used, if they are suited to the celebration.

329. The Masses for various needs and occasions are of three types:

   a. the ritual Masses, which are related to the celebration of certain sacraments or sacramentals;

   b. the Masses for various needs and occasions, which are used either as circumstances arise or at fixed times;

   c. the votive Masses of the mysteries of the Lord or in honor of Mary or a particular saint or of all the saints, which are options provided in favor of the faithful's devotion.

330. Ritual Masses are prohibited on the Sundays of Advent, Lent and the Easter season, on solemnities, on days within the octave of Easter, on All Souls, on Ash Wednesday, and during Holy Week. In addition, the norms in the ritual books or in the Masses themselves also apply.

331. From the selection of Masses for various needs and occasions, the competent authority may choose Masses for those special days of prayer that the conferences of bishops may decree during the course of the year. [See GIapp, no. 331.]

332. In cases of serious need or pastoral advantage, at the direction of the local Ordinary or with his permission, an appropriate Mass may be celebrated on any day except solemnities, the Sundays of Advent, Lent, and the Easter season, days within the octave of Easter, on All Souls, Ash Wednesday, and during Holy Week.

333. On obligatory memorials, on the weekdays of Advent until December 16, of the Christmas season after January 2, and of the Easter season after the octave of Easter, Masses for various needs and occasions are *per se* forbidden. But if some real need or pastoral advantage requires, at the discretion of the rector of the church or the priest celebrant, the Masses corresponding to such need or advantage may be used in a celebration with a congregation.

334. On weekdays in Ordinary Time when there is an optional memorial or the office is of that weekday, any Mass or prayer for various needs and occasions is permitted, but ritual Masses are excluded.

## II. MASSES FOR THE DEAD

335. The Church offers Christ's paschal sacrifice for the dead so that on the basis of the communion existing between all Christ's members, the petition for spiritual help on behalf of some members may bring others comforting hope.

336. The funeral Mass has first place among the Masses for the dead and may be celebrated on any day except solemnities that are days of obligation, Holy Thursday, the Easter triduum, and the Sundays of Advent, Lent, and the Easter season.

337. On the occasions of news of a death, final burial, or the first anniversary, Mass for the dead may be celebrated even on days within the Christmas octave, on obligatory memorials, and on weekdays except Ash Wednesday and during Holy Week.

Other Masses for the dead, that is, daily Masses, may be celebrated on weekdays in Ordinary Time when there is an optional memorial or the office is of the weekday, provided such Masses are actually offered for the dead.

338. At the funeral Mass there should as a rule be a short homily, but never a eulogy of any kind. The homily is also recommended at other Masses for the dead celebrated with a congregation.

339. All the faithful, and especially the family, should be urged to share in the eucharistic sacrifice offered for the deceased person by receiving communion.

340. If the funeral Mass is directly joined to the burial rite, once the prayer after communion has been said and omitting the rite of dismissal, the rite of final commendation or of farewell takes place, but only when the body is present.

341. In the planning and choosing of the variable parts of the Mass for the dead, especially the funeral Mass (for example, prayers, readings, general intercessions) pastoral considerations bearing upon the deceased, the family, and those attending should rightly be foremost.

Pastors should, moreover, take into special account those who are present at a liturgical celebration or hear the Gospel only because of the funeral. These may be non-Catholics or Catholics who never or rarely share in the eucharist or who have apparently lost the faith. Priests are, after all, ministers of Christ's Gospel for all people.

# NOTES

## INTRODUCTION

1. See Council of Trent, sess. 22, 17 Sept 1562.
2. CSL 47; see LG 3, 28; PO, 2, 4, 5.
3. *Sacramentarium Veronense,* (ed. Mohlberg), 93.
4. See Eucharistic Prayer III.
5. See Eucharistic Prayer IV.
6. See CSL 7, 47; PO 5, 18.
7. See Pius XII, encyclical *Humani generis:* AAS 42 (1950) 570–571; Paul VI, encyclical *Mysterium fidei:* AAS 57 (1965) 762–769; Solemn Profession of Faith, 30 June 1968: AAS 60 (1968) 442–443; CR, instruction EM, 25 May 1967, 3, 9.
8. See Council of Trent, sess. 13, 11 Oct 1551.
9. See PO 2.
10. See CSL 11.
11. CSL 50.
12. Council of Trent, sess. 22, Doctrine on the Holy Sacrifice of the Mass, chap. 8.
13. Ibid., can. 9.
14. Ibid., chap. 8.
15. See CSL 33.
16. See CSL 36.
17. See CSL 52.
18. See CSL 35, 3.
19. CSL 55.
20. Council of Trent, sess. 22, Doctrine on the Holy Sacrifice of the Mass, chap. 6.
21. See CSL 55.

## CHAPTERS I–VIII

1. See CSL 41; LG 11; PO 2, 5, 6; Decree on the Pastoral Office of Bishops in the Church, *Christus Dominus,* 30; Decree on Ecumenism, *Unitatis redintegratio,* 15; EM 3e, 6.
2. See CSL 10.
3. See CSL 102.
4. See PO 5; CSL 10.
5. See CSL 14, 19, 26, 28, 30.
6. See CSL 47.
7. See CSL 14.
8. See CSL 41.
9. See PO 13.
10. See CSL 59.
11. For Masses with special groups see instruction CDW, *Actio pastoralis, 15 May 1969;* CDW, *Directory for Masses with Children;* for the manner of joining the liturgy of the hours with the Mass, General Instruction of the Liturgy of the Hours 93–98.
12. See CSL 37–40.
13. See PO 5; CSL 33.
14. See Council of Trent, sess. 22, chap. 1; Paul VI, Solemn Profession of Faith, 30 June 1968, 24.
15. See CSL 7; Paul VI encyclical *Mysterium fidei;* EM 9.
16. See CSL 56; EM 10.
17. See CSL 48, 51; DV 21; PO 4.
18. See CSL 7, 33, 52.
19. See CSL 33.
20. See CDW, circular letter on the eucharistic prayers. 27 April 1973, 14.
21. See MS 14.
22. See CSL 26, 27.
23. See CSL 30.
24. See MS 16a.
25. Augustine, Sermon 336, 1.
26. See MS 7, 16.
27. See CSL 54; IOe 59; MS 47.
28. See CSL 30.
29. See CSL 39.
30. See CSL 30; MS 17.
31. See CSL 33.
32. See CSL 7.
33. See CSL 51.
34. See IOe 50.
35. See CSL 52.
36. See IOe 54.

37. See IOe 56.

38. See CSL 53.

39. See IOe 56.

40. See CSL 47; EM 3a, b.

41. See IOe 91.

42. See CSL 48; PO 5, EM 12.

43. See EM 12, 33a.

44. EM 31, 32, on communion twice in one day. See also IC 2.

45. See CSL 14, 26.

46. See CSL 28.

47. See LG 26, 28; CSL 42.

48. See CSL 26.

49. See PO 2; LG 28.

50. See CSL 48; EM 12.

51. See MS 19.

52. See MS 21.

53. See CSL 24.

54. See IC 1.

55. See LI 7.

56. See CSL 41.

57. See CSL 42; EM 26; LG 28; PO 5.

58. See EM 47.

59. EM 26; MS 16, 27.

60. See CDW, Decree, 9 Oct 1972.

61. See MQ 6.

62. See CSL 57.

63. See EM 47.

64. See *Rite of Concelebration*, introduction, 3.

65. Ibid., 8.

66. See CR, general decree *Ecclesiae semper*, 7 Mar 1965; EM 47.

67. See *Rite of Concelebration*, introduction, 9; CDW, Declaration on Concelebration, 7 Aug 1972.

68. See EM 32.

69. See Council of Trent, sess. 21, Decree on Eucharistic Communion, chap. 1–3.

70. Ibid., chap. 2.

71. See CDW, instruction *Sacramentali Communione*, 29 June 1970.

72. See CSL, 122–124; PO 5; IOe 90; EM 24.

73. See CSL 123.

74. See EM 24.

75. See CSL 123, 129; IOe 13c.

76. See CSL 123.

77. See CSL 126.

78. See IOe 97–98.

79. IOe 91.

80. See EM 24.

81. See IOe 91.

82. IOe 93.

83. IOe 92.

84. IOe 96.

85. See CSL 32; IOe 98.

86. See MS 23.

87. See EM 53; RR, *Holy Communion and Worship of the Eucharist outside Mass*, introduction, 9.

88. EM 54, IOe 95.

89. See EM 52; IOe 96; CDW, instruction *Nullo umquam tempore*, 28 May 1938, 4; *Holy Communion and Worship of the Eucharist outside Mass*, 10–11.

90. See CSL 125.

91. See CSL 128; EM 24.

92. See CSL 128.

93. See CSL 128.

94. See CSL 51.

95. See CSL 61.

# APPENDIX
## TO THE
# GENERAL INSTRUCTION
### FOR THE DIOCESES
### OF THE UNITED STATES OF AMERICA

# OUTLINE

Adaptations for the dioceses of the United States are given on the following:

The numbers assigned to each entry refer to articles of the *General Instruction*.

# APPENDIX TO THE *GENERAL INSTRUCTION*
## FOR THE DIOCESES OF THE UNITED STATES

The following notes, related to the individual sections of the *General Instruction of the Roman Missal*, include adaptations made by the National Conference of Catholic Bishops for the dioceses of the United States, as well as supplementary references.

For further documentation concerning the Eucharistic celebration, see Congregation of Rites, *Instruction on Eucharistic Worship* (May 25, 1967), especially "Some General Principles of Particular Importance in the Catechesis of the People on the Mystery of the Eucharist" (nos. 5–15) and "The Celebration of the Memorial of the Lord" (nos. 16–48); and Sacred Congregation for the Sacraments and Divine Worship, *On Certain Norms concerning Worship of the Eucharistic Mystery* (April 17, 1980).

The number at the beginning of each section below refers to the respective section of the *General Instruction.* Unless otherwise indicated, decisions of the National Conference of Catholic Bishops were taken at the plenary session of November, 1969.

## 11. INTRODUCTIONS AND INVITATIONS

With regard to the adaptation of words of introduction, see the circular letter of the Congregation for Divine Worship, April 27, 1973. No. 14 reads:

Among the possibilities for further accommodating any individual celebration, it is important to consider the admonitions, the homily and the general intercessions. First of all are the admonitions. These enable the people to be drawn into a fuller understanding of the sacred action, or any of its parts, and lead them into a true spirit of participation. The *General Instruction of the Roman Missal* entrusts the more important admonitions to the priest for preparation and use. He may introduce the Mass to the people before the celebration begins, during the liturgy of the word prior to the actual readings, and in the Eucharistic prayer before the preface; he may also conclude the entire sacred action before the dismissal. The *Order of Mass* provides others as well, which are important to certain portions of the rite, such as during the penitential rite, or before the Lord's Prayer. By their very nature these brief admonitions do not require that everyone use them in the form in which they appear in the *Missal.* Provision can be made in certain cases that they be adapted to some degree to the varying circumstances of the community. In all cases it is well to remember the nature of an admonition, and not make them into a sermon or homily; care should be taken to keep them brief and not too wordy, for otherwise they become tedious.

# 19. SINGING

See the statements of the Bishops' Committee on the Liturgy, *The Place of Music in Eucharistic Celebrations* (1968), *Music in Catholic Worship* (revised edition, 1983), *Liturgical Music Today* (1982).

The settings for liturgical texts to be sung by the priest and ministers that are given in the *Sacramentary* are chant adaptations prepared by the International Commission on English in the Liturgy, rather than new melodies. Other settings for the ministerial chants are those approved by the National Conference of Catholic Bishops (November, 1965).

No official approbation is needed for new melodies for the Lord's Prayer at Mass or for the chants, acclamations and other songs of the congregation.

In accord with no. 55 of the instruction of the Congregation of Rites on music in the liturgy (March 5, 1967), the Conference of Bishops has determined that vernacular texts set to music composed in earlier periods may be used in liturgical services even though they may not conform in all details with the legitimately approved versions of liturgical texts (November, 1967). This decision authorizes the use of choral and other music in English when the older text is not precisely the same as the official version.

# 21. ACTIONS AND POSTURES

At its meeting in November, 1969, the National Conference of Catholic Bishops voted that in general, the directives of the *Roman Missal* concerning the posture of the congregation at Mass should be left unchanged, but that no. 21 of the *General Instruction* should be adapted so that the people kneel beginning after the singing or recitation of the Sanctus until after the Amen of the Eucharistic prayer, that is, before the Lord's Prayer.

# 26. ENTRANCE SONG

As a further alternative to the singing of the entrance antiphon and psalm of the *Roman Gradual (Missal)* or of the *Simple Gradual*, the Conference of Bishops has approved the use of other collections of psalms and antiphons in English, as supplements to the *Simple Gradual*, including psalms arranged in responsorial form, metrical and similar versions of psalms, provided they are used in accordance with the principles of the *Simple Gradual* and are selected in harmony with the liturgical season, feast or occasion (decree confirmed by the Consilium for the Implementation of the Constitution on the Liturgy, December 17, 1968).

With regard to texts of other sacred songs from the psalter that may be used as the entrance song, the following criterion was adopted by the Conference of Bishops in November, 1969:

The entrance rite should create an atmosphere of celebration. It serves the function of putting the assembly in the proper frame of mind for listening to the word of God. It helps people to become conscious of themselves as a worshiping community. The choice of texts for the entrance song should not conflict with these purposes.

In general, during the most important seasons of the Church year, Easter time, Lent, Christmas and Advent, it is preferable that most songs used at the entrance be seasonal in nature.

There are thus four options for the entrance song:
1. the entrance antiphon and psalm of the *Roman Gradual;*
2. the entrance antiphon and psalm of the *Simple Gradual;*
3. song from other collections of psalms and antiphons;
4. other sacred song chosen in accord with the above criterion.

The same options exist for the sacred song at the offertory and Communion, but not for the chants between the readings (below).

Only if none of the above alternatives is employed and there is no entrance song, is the antiphon in the Missal recited.

## 36. CHANTS BETWEEN THE READINGS

As a further alternative to (1) the singing of the psalm with its response in the *Lectionary,* (2) the gradual in the *Roman Gradual,* or (3) the responsorial or alleluia psalm in the *Simple Gradual,* the Conference of Bishops has approved the use of other collections of psalms and antiphons in English, as supplements to the *Simple Gradual,* including psalms arranged in responsorial form, metrical and similar versions of psalms, provided they are used in accordance with the principles of the *Simple Gradual* and are selected in harmony with the liturgical season, feast or occasion (decree confirmed by the Consilium for the Implementation of the Constitution on the Liturgy, December 17, 1968).

The choice of texts that are *not* from the psalter (permitted at the entrance, offertory and Communion) is not extended to the chants between the readings.

For further information concerning the use of the chants between the readings, see the Foreword and the Introduction (VIII) to the *Lectionary for Mass* (New York, Collegeville, Minn., 1970). In particular, see the common texts for sung responsorial psalms (nos. 174–175), which may be used in place of the text corresponding to the reading whenever the psalm is sung.

During Lent the alleluia is not sung with the verse before the Gospel. Instead one of the following (or similar) acclamations may be sung before and after the verse before the Gospel:

Praise and honor to you, Lord Jesus Christ,

King of endless glory!

Praise and honor to you, Lord Jesus Christ!

Glory and praise to you, Lord Jesus Christ!

Glory to you, Word of God, Lord Jesus Christ!

If the psalm after the reading is not sung, it is recited. The alleluia or the verse before the Gospel may be omitted if not sung (see no. 39 of the *General*

*Instruction).* The people stand for the singing of the alleluia before the Gospel (see no. 21 of the *General Instruction).*

## 45. GENERAL INTERCESSIONS

See the statements of the Bishops' Committee on the Liturgy, *General Prayer or Prayer of the Faithful* (1969) and *General Intercessions* (1979).

## 50. OFFERTORY SONG

The choice of texts for the offertory song is governed by the same rule as the entrance song, with the several options described above (no. 26). If there is no offertory song, the offertory antiphon is omitted.

With regard to texts not from the psalter that may be used as the offertory song, the following criterion was adopted by the National Conference of Bishops in November, 1969:

> The offertory song need not speak of bread and wine or of offering. The proper function of the offertory song is rather to accompany and celebrate the communal aspects of the procession. The text, therefore, may be an appropriate song of praise or of rejoicing in keeping with the season. Those texts are not acceptable that speak of the offering completely apart from the action of Christ.
>
> In general, during the most important seasons of the Church year, Easter time, Lent, Christmas and Advent, it is preferable that most songs used during the offertory be seasonal in character. During the remainder of the Church year, however, topical songs may be used during the offertory procession provided that these texts do not conflict with the paschal character of every Sunday *(Constitution on the Liturgy,* arts. 102, 106).

With regard to the offertory song, the statement of the Bishops' Committee on the Liturgy of 1968 *(The Place of Music in Eucharistic Celebrations)* gives additional comments:

> The procession can be accompanied by song. Song is not always necessary or desirable. Organ or instrumental music is also fitting at this time. The song need not speak of bread or wine or offering. The proper function of this song is to accompany and celebrate the communal aspects of the procession. The text, therefore, can be any appropriate song of praise or of rejoicing in keeping with the season. (See approved criterion above.) The song need not accompany the entire preparation rite. (The song, if any, continues at least until the priest has placed the bread and wine on the altar, while saying the accompanying prayers quietly; see no. 50 of the *General Instruction,* nos. 19–21 of the *Order of Mass.)*
>
> If there is no singing or organ or instrumental music, this may be a period of silence (see no. 23 of the *General Instruction).* In fact, it is good to give the assembly a period of quiet (that is, while the gifts are prepared and placed on the altar, until the introduction to the prayer over the gifts: "Pray,

brethren . . . ") before demanding, at the preface, their full attention to the Eucharistic prayer.

## 56b. SIGN OF PEACE

The Conference of Bishops has left the development of special modes of exchanging the sign of peace to local usage. Neither a specific form nor specific words are determined (November, 1969). See the statement of the Bishops' Committee on the Liturgy, *The Sign of Peace* (1977).

## 56i. COMMUNION SONG

The choice of texts for the Communion song is governed by the same rule as the entrance song, with the several options described above (no. 26).

With regard to the texts not from the psalter that may be used as the Communion song, the following criterion was adopted by the National Conference of Catholic Bishops in November, 1969:

> The Communion song should foster a sense of unity. It should be simple and not demand great effort. It gives expression to the joy of unity in the body of Christ and the fulfillment of the mystery being celebrated. Most benediction hymns, by reason of their concentration on adoration rather than on Communion, are not acceptable, as indicated in the instruction on music in the liturgy, no. 36.
>
> In general, during the most important seasons of the Church year, Easter time, Lent, Christmas and Advent, it is preferable that most songs used at the Communion be seasonal in nature. During the remainder of the Church year, however, topical songs may be used during the Communion procession provided these texts do not conflict with the paschal character of every Sunday *(Constitution on the Liturgy,* arts. 102, 106).
>
> Only if none of the above alternatives is employed and there is no Communion song, is the antiphon in the *Missal* recited. Until the publication of the complete new *Missal,* the antiphon from the present *Missal* is said in such cases (Congregation for Divine Worship, instruction, October 20, 1969, no. 13).

## 59. CELEBRATION BY THE BISHOP

See Congregation of Rites, instruction on the simplification of pontifical rites and insignia, June 21, 1968.

For occasions when the bishop is present at a celebration of the Eucharist but, for a just reason, does not elect to be the principal celebrant, he may assign another to celebrate the liturgy of the Eucharist while he presides over the introductory rites, the liturgy of the word and the concluding rite of the Mass. For directives on the manner in which this is done, see *Newsletter* of the Bishops' Committee on the Liturgy, May–June, 1981.

## 66. WOMEN AS READERS

The Conference of Bishops has given permission for women to serve as readers in accord with no. 66 of the *General Instruction* (November, 1969).

In February, 1971, the Bishops' Committee on the Liturgy prepared a commentary on the liturgical ministry of women:

a.    With the exception of service at the altar itself, women may be admitted to the exercise of other liturgical ministries. In particular the designation of women to serve in such ministries as reader, cantor, leader of song, commentator, director of liturgical participation, etc., is left to the judgment of the pastor or the priest who presides over the celebration, in the light of the culture and mentality of the congregation.

b.    Worthiness of life and character and other qualifications are required in women who exercise liturgical ministries in the same way as for men who exercise the same ministries.

c.    Women who read one or other biblical reading during the liturgy of the word (other than the Gospel, which is reserved to a deacon or priest) should do so from the lectern or ambo where the other readings are proclaimed: the reservation of a single place for all the biblical readings is more significant than the person of the reader, whether ordained or lay, whether woman or man (cf. *General Instruction*, no. 272).

d.    Other ministries performed by women, such as leading the singing or otherwise directing the congregation, should be done either within or outside the sanctuary area, depending on circumstances or convenience.

## 127. OFFICE OF THE DEACON

The various ministries of the deacon at Mass may be distributed among several deacons, present and wearing their vestments. (See Congregation of Rites, instruction, June 21, 1968, nos. 4, 5.) Other deacons who are present but not called upon to function in the celebration normally should not vest or occupy a specific place in the liturgy, unless they are participating as the *order of deacons*, e.g., at the liturgy of ordination of another deacon. (See Bishops' Committee on the Liturgy, *Newsletter*, October, 1981.) See also the guidelines established by the Bishops' Committee on the Liturgy for the liturgical ministry of the deacon in *Study Text 6: The Deacon, Minister of Word and Sacrament* (1979).

## 153. CONCELEBRATED MASS

See the statement of the Bishops' Committee on the Liturgy, "Concelebration," *Newsletter*, June, 1966, and guidelines of the Bishops' Committee on the Liturgy in *Study Text 5: Eucharistic Concelebration* (1978).

## 240. DISTRIBUTION OF COMMUNION

On June 17, 1977, the Congregation of Sacraments and Divine Worship approved the request of the National Conference of Catholic Bishops to permit the optional practice of Communion in the hand. The Bishops' Committee on the Liturgy, in its catechesis about this optional practice, drew attention to these considerations:

a.   Proper catechesis must be provided to assure the proper and reverent reception of Communion without any suggestion of wavering on the part of the Church in its faith in the Eucharistic presence.

b.   The practice must remain the option of the communicant. The priest or minister of Communion does not make the decision as to the manner of reception of Communion. It is the communicant's personal choice.

c.   When Communion is distributed under both kinds by intinction, the host is not placed in the hands of the communicants, nor may the communicants receive the host and dip it into the chalice. Intinction should not be introduced as a means of circumventing the practice of Communion in the hand.

d.   Children have the option to receive Communion in the hand or on the tongue. No limitations because of age have been established. Careful preparation for first reception of the Eucharist will provide the necessary instruction. (See also the Roman Ritual, *Holy Communion and Worship of the Eucharist outside Mass*, no. 21.)

### 242. COMMUNION UNDER BOTH KINDS

See the statement of the Bishops' Committee on the Liturgy, "Communion Under Both Kinds," *Newsletter*, July, 1966.

In accord with the instruction of the Congregation for Divine Worship on Communion under both kinds (June 29, 1970), the National Conference of Catholic Bishops in November, 1970, added the following cases:

15. other members of the faithful present on the special occasions enumerated in no. 242 of the *General Instruction*;

16. at funeral Masses and at Masses for a special family observance;

17. at Masses on days of special religious or civil significance for the people of the United States;

18. at Masses on Holy Thursday and at the Mass of the Easter Vigil, the norms of the instruction of June 29, 1970, being observed;

19. at weekday Masses.

At its meeting in November, 1978, the National Conference of Catholic Bishops further extended the occasions on which Holy Communion under both kinds might be given when it approved the motion that Holy Communion may be given under both kinds to the faithful at Masses on Sundays and holy days of obligation if, in the judgment of the ordinary, Communion may be given in an orderly and reverent manner. The Congregation for Divine Worship confirmed this decree of the National Conference of Catholic Bishops on October 13, 1984 (Prot. N. CD 1297/78). In all that pertains to Communion under Both Kinds the norms of *This Holy and Living Sacrifice: Directory for the Celebration and Reception of Communion under Both Kinds* are to be followed.

## 253. ARRANGEMENTS AND FURNISHINGS OF CHURCHES FOR EUCHARISTIC CELEBRATIONS

In those things which pertain to the arrangement and furnishing of churches and other requisites of liturgical art and architecture, the principles and directives of the 1978 statement of the Bishops' Committee on the Liturgy, *Environment and Art in Catholic Worship,* should be consulted and applied.

## 263. MATERIALS FOR FIXED ALTARS

Materials other than natural stone may be used for fixed altars provided these are worthy, solid and properly constructed, subject to the further judgment of the local ordinary in doubtful cases.

## 270. ALTAR CROSS

Only a single cross should be carried in a procession in order to give greater dignity and reverence to the cross. It is desirable to place the cross that has been carried in the procession near the altar so that it may serve as the cross of the altar. Otherwise it should be put away during the service. (See Congregation of Rites, instruction, June 21, 1968, no. 20.)

## 275. MUSICAL INSTRUMENTS

The Conference of Bishops has decreed that musical instruments other than the organ may be used in liturgical services provided they are played in a manner that is suitable to public worship (November, 1967; see *Constitution on the Liturgy,* art. 120). This decision deliberately refrains from singling out specific instruments. Their use depends on circumstances, the nature of the congregation, etc. In particular cases, if there should be doubt as to the suitability of the instruments, it is the responsibility of the diocesan bishop, in consultation with the diocesan liturgical and music commissions, to render a decision. See also the statements of the Bishops' Committee on the Liturgy, *Music in Catholic Worship* (revised edition, 1983) and *Liturgical Music Today* (1982).

## 288. MATERIALS FOR SACRED FURNISHINGS

Materials other than the traditional ones may be used for sacred furnishings provided they are suitable for liturgical use, subject to the further judgment of the local ordinary in doubtful cases.

## 305. MATERIALS FOR VESTMENTS

Fabrics, both natural and artificial, other than the traditional ones may be used for sacred vesture provided they are suitable for liturgical use, subject to the further judgment of the local ordinary in doubtful cases.

## 308. COLOR OF VESTMENTS

White, violet or black vestments may be worn at funeral services and at other offices and Masses for the dead (November, 1970).

## 318. READINGS ON SUNDAYS AND FEASTS

According to the decision of the National Conference of Catholic Bishops, the complete pattern of three readings for Sundays and feast days should be completely implemented.

## 331. DAYS OF PRAYER

The Conference of Bishops has decreed that there be observed in the dioceses of the United States, at times to be designated by the local ordinary in consultation with the diocesan liturgical commission, days or periods of prayer for the fruits of the earth, prayer for human rights and equality, prayer for world justice and peace, and penitential observance outside Lent (November, 1971). This is in addition to observances customary on certain civic occasions such as Independence Day, Labor Day and Thanksgiving Day, for which either proper text or texts of the *Sacramentary* and *Lectionary for Mass* are provided.

The Bishops' Committee on the Liturgy presented the above decision in these terms: The expression of such days or periods of prayer should be left as general as possible, so that the time, length, occasion, and more specific intentions of prayer should be determined locally rather than nationally. In this way no arbitrary rule is imposed until it becomes evident that a pattern of such supplications is emerging from practice. See also General Norms for the Liturgical Year and the Calendar, nos. 45–47.

## 340. FUNERAL MASS

Although the rite of final commendation at the catafalque or pall is excluded, it is permitted to celebrate the funeral service, including the commendations, in those cases where it is physically or morally impossible for the body of the deceased person to be present (November, 1970).

For other adaptations in the funeral Mass and service, see the *Rite of Funerals* (1971); *Newsletter* of the Bishops' Committee on the Liturgy, April–May, 1971. The following refer directly to the Eucharistic celebration:

It is appropriate that the paschal candle be carried in the entrance procession.

If the introductory rites have taken place at the church door, the priest venerates the altar and goes to his chair. The penitential rite is omitted, and the priest says or sings the opening prayer.

It is desirable that the first and second readings be read by relatives or friends of the deceased person.

The homily may properly include an expression of praise and gratitude to God for his gifts, particularly the gift of a Christian life, to the deceased person. The homily should relate Christian death to the paschal mystery of the Lord's victorious death and resurrection and to the hope of eternal life.

It is desirable that members of the family or friends of the deceased person participate in the usual offering of the bread and wine for the celebration of the Eucharist, together with other gifts for the needs of the Church and of the poor.

If incense is used, the priest, after incensing the gifts and the altar, may incense the body. The deacon or another minister then incenses the priest and people.

# LECTIONARY FOR MASS: INTRODUCTION

# OVERVIEW OF THE *LECTIONARY FOR MASS: INTRODUCTION*

Gerard S. Sloyan

Why should anyone read this *Introduction to the Lectionary for Mass* (LMIn), which is as much a defense as an exposition of a liturgical book that has been in use for more than 20 years?

—Many people who were engaged in the church's public worship when it first appeared (1970, revised in 1981) examined it with care and have not returned to it since. There are probably many more—presider-homilists, deacons and regular readers of the Bible in the liturgy—who have not read it for the first time. It provides the rationale underlying an aspect of the practice of the Western Church in which they have an intimate part. They should know what it has to say.

—There doubtless are liturgy committees in parishes, monasteries and convents of women and men that have not heard of the document, let alone explored it.

—There are regular complaints against the way the Roman lectionary is constructed, which a careful reading of this *Introduction* might dispel— or confirm.

—And, while there are certain practices regarding the use of the lectionary that this document does not condone, there are many more pastorally beneficial practices that go unemployed because priests and people are unaware of the freedoms it allows.

Two other matters leap out at the reader of this *Introduction*. One is its silence in no. 62 on the ecumenical advance represented by the Anglican and Protestant lectionaries that are based on the Roman lectionary and used world-wide. This lends a provincial tone to a piece of writing that bears the proud name of Catholic. The other is the mention of readers who have been "instituted" as such by a liturgical rite (nos. 51 and 52; these are men only, although this is not stated). The reference may surprise readers who have not heard of this understand-ably little-used rite.

## CATHOLIC LITURGY IS THOROUGHLY BIBLICAL

The best service a background paper can offer to liturgy committees that study the *Introduction* (with priests and deacons sitting in as members) is to high-light things to look for that might be missed. The first is the thoroughly biblical nature of the Catholic liturgy. As the *Introduction* proceeds to specifics, the impression might be derived that Bible readings *in* the eucharistic (or other sacramental) liturgy are the matter at issue. In fact, however, any liturgy is neither more nor less than a celebration of God's word as delivered in the Bible. The prayers of all the rites, including the eucharistic prayer or canon, are either tissues of biblical phrasing or are inspired by the Bible. The Lord's Supper is an act of obedience to a biblical injunction (Luke 22:14c). From the opening sign of the cross (Matthew 28:19) to the final dismissal (Psalm 29:11b; Judith 8:35), the participants are invited to live in the world of the Bible as one people with its people. That is why any Catholic should be able to invite a person who is not of this faith but has great veneration for the Bible to attend Sunday Mass saying: "Come to our Bible service." Any Catholic congregation where the Mass is not recognizable as such has not given sufficient attention to what the *Introduction* has to say (nos. 4–8; 44–48).

Obviously, the eucharistic rite peaks more visibly as biblical in what is called "the liturgy of the word" because there the texts that are read are extracted directly from the Holy Books and are commented on in what ought to be a Bible lesson. If they are not, the hope expressed in the *Constitution on the Sacred Liturgy* (CSL) that "the treasures of the Bible are to be opened up more lavishly, so that a richer share in God's word may be provided for the faithful" (CSL 51) will have been thwarted. Any visitor on a single Sunday can tell whether the opening up and sharing of the Bible is lavish or parsimonious, generous or grudging. The *Introduction* tries its best to convince congregations how to go the better route. "Christ himself is the center and fullness of all of the scripture, as he is of the entire liturgy. Thus the scriptures are the living waters from which all who seek life and salvation must drink" (LMIn 5).

READERS: AT HOME IN THE SACRED STORIES

Those who hear the scriptures proclaimed in liturgical celebrations should experience themselves as a new people in whom the covenant made in the past is fulfilled (no. 7). The ordained are *charged* with teaching God's word by virtue of their ordination, but they "or those who have been entrusted with that ministry" are the ones who must in fact *do* it. Bishops do the entrusting for the whole church. They wisely entrust with the task only those who *can* do it. The clearest impression that comes through from a line-by-line reading of the *Introduction* is that no one should be allowed to read publicly or preach but those who know the Bible.

The word that is heard and the eucharist that is offered and received may be the charge of different or the same ministers, but it is always "the one single divine act of worship" (no. 10). No person who has any ministerial function is absolved from an intimate knowledge of the Bible. That is why these persons have been designated or chosen, not for forensic gifts or personal piety only (although these are assumed), but because they have something of the wisdom that nourishes the church at the table of God's word (no. 10). That wisdom comes only from an intimate knowledge of the Bible.

This means in practice that the main task of a pastor of a small congregation or of a designated person in a larger one is not the business of recruiting lectors ("getting people to read") but getting the right people and only them to read. It does not matter if a team of four now does what 24 formerly did. The four have proved that they are fit for this task as the others are not. They not only read loudly, clearly and comprehensibly—the great minimum—but are so at home in the sacred stories, commands and exhortations that they never miss the rhetorical intent of the writings or the Anglicized pronunciation of Hebrew and Greek proper nouns. The qualified lector is a person who often reads the Bible privately. His or her intimate knowledge of it and enthusiasm for it is infectious. (See no. 6.)

Careful study of the *Introduction* regarding the homily (nos. 8, 24) will disclose that all that has been said about those who read the scriptures applies to homilists so much the more. This means, among other things, that not all who have been ordained to the order of deacon should be allowed to preach. All have had the same exposure to a modest theological education but not all have the homilist's gift. Many, in fact, were admitted to this order because they demonstrably had other gifts. Conversely, to reflect on all that is meant by "Christ himself is . . . always present and active in the preaching of his church" and "the homily . . . must always lead the community of the faithful to celebrate the eucharist wholeheartedly" (no. 24) is to realize that some among the nonordained are uniquely qualified to do that. Pastors must therefore ask bishops to authorize others than themselves at times to "explain the biblical word of God proclaimed in the readings," either as an integral part of the liturgy or before or after it (hence, a man or woman) as a "living explanation" of the word of God.

The remaining sticking point is the most important of all. What of men in the presbyteral order who do not seem qualified to expound the scriptures, even though many of these read them tolerably well? Two things must be remembered here: First, such priests were once deemed capable of acquiring the homilist's art and still may, and, second, the whole venture of proclaiming, explaining and being nourished by the scriptures is understood by the *Introduction* to be a corporate venture. (See nos. 8, 9, 19, 20, 24, 48 and especially 40, none of which can be realized without extensive consultation and exchange.) If priests regularly participate in planning sessions on the liturgy as prayerful celebration (not as orchestrated performance), there is everything to be hoped for in their prognosis as effective preachers. If not, then little or nothing.

## HOW THE LECTIONARY IS CONSTRUCTED

A word needs to be said about the *Introduction's* stress on the reading or chanting of the gospel (nos. 13, 17). Everything contained in these two sections must be affirmed strongly. Readings from the gospels always have had pride of place in Christian liturgies because there the Savior speaks directly to his people. In the four gospels, Jesus Christ the Word is embodied in words as nowhere else in the Bible. Hence, the acts of veneration of the book of gospels proposed in the *Introduction* must be taken seriously.

The preeminence of the gospels does not imply, however, that the gospel pericope should always or even usually be the one expounded. The very enlargement of offerings proposed by the three-year lectionary suggests otherwise. Israel's scriptures were not only the Bible of Jesus and the early church, but they are irrevocably the church's scriptures. Paul's letters, too, and perhaps some other New Testament writings were hailed as expressions of the apostolic faith before the first of the gospels was written. "There are certain passages in them hard to understand" the anonymous author of 2 Peter wrote of Paul's epistles (3:16b). He went on to acknowledge that the ignorant and the unstable were distorting them and the rest of scripture to their own ruin. In the present age, when Catholics everywhere are flooded with doubtful interpretations of the scriptures or confronted by those directly attacking Catholic faith, they must hear clear and accurate expositions of the representative passages contained in the three-year cycle.

The content of paragraphs 58–69, on the way the lectionary is constructed, should be mastered by liturgy committees and *a fortiori* by homilists. It may not give satisfaction but it will at least convey what the lectionary framers tried to achieve. Many people have expressed the wish that the principle of "harmony" among the three readings that marks the major feasts and Advent and Lent might prevail on every Sunday (see nos. 66, 93, 97). They are dismayed by the randomness that they see introduced by the "semicontinuous reading" principle. But if this were done, a false unity then might be imposed on the 72 books of the Catholic canon. The nonarticulation of the second reading with the first and third is a constant reminder of the diversity within this rich collection. If the reading from the First Testament were not in every case chosen because it somehow prefigures a gospel pericope from the Second (the present situation in the Roman and Protestant lectionaries but not always that of the *Common Lectionary* of the Consultation on Common Texts), the diversity would come through more clearly.

Yet the unity of the two testaments is something that never can be submerged. The life of the apostolic church always is seen as a continuation of the life of the people Israel, its ethnic exclusiveness apart. Any reading from either testament can be shown to be related to any other without strain. This is because all convey the relation of the God of Israel whom Jesus called "Father" to the people of God's special love.

Paragraph 64 rather confidently assumes that the selection and arrangement of readings is such that it will satisfy the requirements both of the liturgical seasons and the hermeneutical principles of contemporary biblical research. The Catholic scholars of pastoral bent (including women) who are at ease in the fields of liturgy and biblical interpretation, or who at least can engage in a profitable discussion with those of the other expertise than their own, are painfully few. One does not have to be an expert in gospel scholarship, for example, to see that the lectionary framers think that the incidents in Jesus' life are what must all be presented somehow over three years of Sundays. This is accomplished largely without regard to what Matthew, Mark, Luke and John made of them. People who have been active in adult initiation for several years and have undertaken the necessary study have concluded that the "baptismal and the penitential themes of this season" (no. 69) are sometimes in open conflict, with the medieval penitential emphasis usually winning out. The parishes that are taking seriously the "scrutinies" of candidates on the Third, Fourth and Fifth Sundays of Lent have long ago concluded that the readings proposed for Year A should be employed every year (as no. 97 allows). This is to say that the authors of the *Introduction* take for granted what may not be the case, namely, that the lectionary they have produced is perfectly at ease in face of the requirements of the liturgical seasons and the principles of contemporary biblical research.

TAKING LIBERTIES CAUTIOUSLY

Perhaps the best guidance for liturgy committees, some of whose members are regularly studying the shape of the Roman liturgy, is contained in paragraphs 76–78. There the *Introduction* shares with the prospective ministers of the liturgy its principles on including and omitting "difficult texts," including the ancient custom of lectionaries of not printing every verse in sequence in a given pericope for reasons of length or pastoral unsuitability. An ancient adage says that what is permissible to Jupiter is not necessarily the privilege of the cow (Quod licet Iovi non licet bovi). The more applicable adage in this case seems to be "What is sauce for the goose is sauce for the gander." If pastoral judgments were allowable to a team of scholars, some of them not engaged in pastoral work, in a distant city more than two decades ago, these scholars are clearly inviting pastoral teams to make similar wise judgments in their own situations. The options proposed in the choices of certain texts (nos. 78–84) therefore are not to be thought of as confining serious liturgy committees to the ones proposed. Much thought and study must of course go into any departure from the readings prescribed. There have to be good pastoral reasons in every case to justify it.

Some examples of the application of these principles follow. They are prefaced by the observation that omission of one of the three readings is an option that the United States bishops wisely have not entertained. (See no. 79.)

The gospel pericopes are consistently of sufficient length that the proposal of a shorter form normally does not work against the intended pastoral effect. The same is seldom the case with the first and second readings, many of which, if they were any weaker, would die. They always can be lengthened from a well-marked pulpit Bible. Such treatment might make their selection as lectionary readings understandable to the congregation for the first time. Needless to say, only a skilled hand will know how to lengthen a reading effectively.

In general, the weakness of the lectionary is the constant interruptions within interruptions that it allows. Until a fourth John year is introduced, no liturgical team should be discouraged from plotting either more sequential John readings or fewer. As it is, the lectionary framers give the impression of having ingeniously "worked John in," with the result that they have pitted him against the synoptics when what they wished was to have this gospel complement them.

When the first reading gives every appearance of being brief and inconsequential (because it was chosen for some glancing verbal similarity to the gospel or to have every book of the Bible represented), a powerful reading from that First Testament should be substituted. Paragraph 65 says that the "more significant parts of God's revealed word" have been chosen for the Sundays and solemnities of the Lord to which those chosen for weekdays are complementary; but this can be questioned. Often the nearby weekday first readings are more significant. If parishioners complain because there is departure from the paperback hand missal they take for an inspired book, they must be educated to the freedoms that the official Roman document proposes. The public reading must then be so effective that no one but the very deaf misses a word.

It is impossible for a liturgy committee to pay too much attention to paragraphs 19–22, on the responsorial psalm. The treatment of psalmody in Catholic worship is, after preaching and presiding, the largest liturgical problem the postconciliar church has had to face. In many churches the psalm is recited by the congregation, either antiphonally or in alternation with the lector, but such practices have not yet faced the problem. The problem is musical since the psalms are the lyrics of songs. Only good, simple musical renderings can solve it, in which the people are not exhausted by the feat of memorizing a long or musically difficult antiphon.

Some attention has been paid in this essay to perceived shortcomings in the present Sunday lectionary, but overall these are minor. The task the Consilium set for itself in appointing a subcommittee on the lectionary was major. The product this committee conceived is worthy of almost total admiration. These selections from the Bible, if consistently read well and just as consistently commented on, cannot but have the hoped-for effect. The readings and homilies can once again make Catholics what they were before the invention of printing, a people of the Bible. This means that in the eucharistic liturgy, they will "faithfully echo the Amen that Christ, the mediator between God and humanity, uttered once for all as he shed his blood to seal God's new covenant in the Holy Spirit" (LMIn 6).

A biblical liturgy is far from an archaic enterprise. It is not one that looks only to an historical past and a heavenly future. It is above all a thing of the present in which "the Holy Spirit makes our response effective, so that what we hear in the liturgy we can carry out in the way we live" (no. 6). To illustrate: unacceptable levels of employment in the labor force, total sexual liberty versus self-discipline, the consumer mentality, the rich nations and the poor—anything that is part of the people's lives is part of the life of the Bible, sometimes in joltingly specific language.

When the liturgy is celebrated well, it proclaims to every worshiper in church or chapel, "Be doers of the word and not hearers only" (James 1:22). Our day-to-day conduct is our chief praise of God. It is to this that the holy liturgy gives tongue.

# OUTLINE

PART TWO: STRUCTURE OF THE ORDER OF THE READINGS FOR MASS

CHAPTER VI: Adaptations, Translations, and Format of the Order of Readings

# LECTIONARY FOR MASS: INTRODUCTION

## PROLOGUE

### CHAPTER 1
### GENERAL PRINCIPLES FOR THE LITURGICAL
### CELEBRATION OF THE WORD OF GOD

*1. Preliminaries*

#### A. IMPORTANCE OF THE WORD OF GOD IN A LITURGICAL CELEBRATION

1.    Vatican Council II,[1] the teaching of the popes,[2] and various postconciliar documents of the Roman congregations[3] have already made many excellent statements about the importance of the word of God and about reestablishing the use of Scripture in every celebration of the liturgy. The Introduction of the 1969 edition of the Order of Readings for Mass has clearly stated and briefly explained some of the more important principles.[4]

On the occasion of this new edition of the Order of Readings for Mass, requests have come from many quarters for a more detailed exposition of the same principles. In response, this expanded and more helpful arrangement of the Introduction first gives a general statement on the close relationship between the word of God and the liturgical celebration,[5] then deals in greater detail with the word of God in the celebration of Mass, and, finally, explains the precise structure of the Order of Readings for Mass.

#### B. TERMS USED TO REFER TO THE WORD OF GOD

2.    For the sake of clear and precise language on this topic, a definition of terms might well be expected as a prerequisite. Nevertheless this Introduction will simply use the same terms employed in conciliar and postconciliar documents. Furthermore it will use "sacred Scripture" and "word of God" interchangeably throughout when referring to the books written under the inspiration of the Holy Spirit, thus avoiding any confusion of language or meaning.[6]

#### C. SIGNIFICANCE OF THE WORD OF GOD IN THE LITURGY

3.    The many riches contained in the one word of God are admirably brought out in the different kinds of liturgical celebrations and liturgical assemblies. This takes place as the unfolding mystery of Christ is recalled during the course of the liturgical year, as the Church's sacraments and sacramentals are celebrated, or as the faithful respond individually to the Holy Spirit working within them.[7] For then the liturgical celebration, based primarily on the word of God and sustained

by it, becomes a new event and enriches the word itself with new meaning and power. Thus in the liturgy the Church faithfully adheres to the way Christ himself read and explained the Scriptures, beginning with the "today" of his coming forward in the synagogue and urging all to search the Scriptures.[8]

*2. Liturgical celebration of the word of God*

A. PROPER CHARACTER OF THE WORD OF GOD IN THE LITURGICAL CELEBRATION

4.    In the celebration of the liturgy the word of God is not voiced in only one way[9] nor does it always stir the hearts of the hearers with the same power. Always, however, Christ is present in his word;[10] as he carries out the mystery of salvation, he sanctifies us and offers the Father perfect worship.[11]

Moreover, the word of God unceasingly calls to mind and extends the plan of salvation, which achieves its fullest expression in the liturgy. The liturgical celebration becomes therefore the continuing, complete, and effective presentation of God's word.

That word constantly proclaimed in the liturgy is always, then, a living, active word[12] through the power of the Holy Spirit. It expresses the Father's love that never fails in its effectiveness toward us.

B. THE WORD OF GOD IN THE PLAN OF SALVATION

5.    When in celebrating the liturgy the Church proclaims both the Old and New Testament, it is proclaiming one and the same mystery of Christ.

The New Testament lies hidden in the Old; the Old Testament comes fully to light in the New.[13] Christ himself is the center and fullness of all of Scripture, as he is of the entire liturgy.[14] Thus the Scriptures are the living waters from which all who seek life and salvation must drink.

The more profound our understanding of the liturgical celebration, the higher our appreciation of the importance of God's word. Whatever we say of the one, we can in turn say of the other, because each recalls the mystery of Christ and each in its own way causes that mystery to be ever present.

C. THE WORD OF GOD IN THE LITURGICAL PARTICIPATION OF THE FAITHFUL

6.    In celebrating the liturgy, the Church faithfully echoes the Amen that Christ, the meditator between God and humanity, uttered once for all as he shed his blood to seal God's new covenant in the Holy Spirit.[15]

When God shares his word with us, he awaits our response, that is, our listening and our adoring "in Spirit and in truth" (John 4:23). The Holy Spirit makes our response effective, so that what we hear in the celebration of the liturgy we carry out in the way we live: "Be doers of the word and not hearers only" (James 1:22).

The liturgical celebration and the faithful's participation receive outward expression in actions, gestures, and words. These derive their full meaning not simply from their origin in human experience but from the word of God and the economy of salvation, their point of reference. Accordingly, the faithful's participation in the liturgy increases to the degree that as they listen to the word of God spoken in the liturgy they strive harder to commit themselves to the Word of God made flesh in Christ. They endeavor to conform their way of life to what they celebrate in the liturgy, and then in turn to bring to the celebration of the liturgy all that they do in life.[16]

*3. The word of God in the life of the "People of the Covenant"*

A. THE WORD OF GOD IN THE CHURCH'S LIFE

7.     In the hearing of God's word the Church is built up and grows, and in the signs of the liturgical celebration God's many wonderful, past works in the history of salvation are symbolically presented anew. God in turn makes use of the assembly of the faithful who celebrate the liturgy in order that his word may speed on in triumph and his name be exalted among all peoples.[17]

Whenever, therefore, the Church, gathered by the Holy Spirit for liturgical celebration,[18] announces and proclaims the word of God, it has the experience of being a new people in whom the covenant made in the past is fulfilled. Baptism and confirmation in the Spirit have made all the faithful messengers of God's word because of the grace of hearing they have received. They must therefore be the bearers of the same word in the Church and in the world, at least by the witness of their way of life.

The word of God proclaimed in the celebration of his mysteries does not address present conditions alone but looks back to past events and forward to what is yet to come. Thus God's word shows us what we should hope for with such a longing that in this changing world our hearts will be set on the place of our true joy.[19]

B. HOW THE WORD OF GOD IS PROPOSED IN THE CHURCH

8.     By Christ's own will there is an ordered diversity of members in the new people of God and each has different duties and responsibilities toward the word of God. Accordingly, the faithful listen to God's word and dwell on its meaning, but only those expound the word of God who have the office of teaching by virtue of ordination or who have been entrusted with exercising that ministry.

This is how in teaching, life, and worship the Church keeps alive and passes on to every generation all that it is, all that it believes. Thus with the passage of the centuries, the Church is ever to advance toward the fullness of divine truth until God's word is wholly accomplished in it.[20]

C. CONNECTION BETWEEN THE WORD OF GOD PROCLAIMED
   AND THE WORKING OF THE HOLY SPIRIT

9.     The working of the Holy Spirit is needed if the word of God is to make what we hear outwardly have its effect inwardly. Because of the Holy Spirit's inspiration and support, the word of God becomes the foundation of the liturgical celebration and the rule and support of all our life.

The working of the Holy Spirit precedes, accompanies, and brings to completion the whole celebration of the liturgy. But the Spirit also brings home[21] to each person individually everything that in the proclamation of the word of God is spoken for the good of the whole assembly of the faithful. In strengthening the unity of all, the Holy Spirit at the same time fosters a diversity of gifts and furthers their multiform operation.

D. CLOSE RELATIONSHIP BETWEEN THE WORD OF GOD
   AND THE MYSTERY OF THE EUCHARIST

10.    The Church has honored the word of God and the eucharistic mystery with the same reverence, although not with the same worship, and has always and everywhere intended and endorsed such honor. Moved by the example of its Founder, the Church has never ceased to celebrate his paschal mystery of coming together to read "in all the Scriptures the things written about him" (Luke 24:27) and to carry out the work of salvation through the celebration of the memorial of the Lord and through the sacraments. "The preaching of the word is necessary for the sacramental ministry. For the sacraments are sacraments of faith and faith has its origin and sustenance in the word."[22]

The Church is nourished spiritually at the table of God's word and at the table of the eucharist:[23] from the one it grows in wisdom and from the other in holiness. In the word of God the divine covenant is announced; in the eucharist the new and everlasting covenant is renewed. The spoken word of God brings to mind the history of salvation; the eucharist embodies it in the sacramental signs of the liturgy.

It can never be forgotten, therefore, that the divine word read and proclaimed by the Church in the liturgy has as its one goal the sacrifice of the New Covenant and the banquet of grace, that is, the eucharist. The celebration of Mass in which the word is heard and the eucharist is offered and received forms but one single act of divine worship.[24] That act offers the sacrifice of praise to God and makes available to God's creatures the fullness of redemption.

# PART ONE
## THE WORD OF GOD IN THE CELEBRATION
## OF THE MASS
### CHAPTER II
### CELEBRATION OF THE LITURGY OF THE WORD AT MASS

*1. Elements of the liturgy of the word and their rites*

11.    "Readings from Scripture and the chants between the readings form the main part of the liturgy of the word. The homily, profession of faith and general intercessions or prayer of the faithful expand and complete this part of the Mass."[25]

12.  In the celebration of Mass the biblical readings with their accompanying scriptural chants may not be omitted, shortened, or, worse still, replaced by nonbiblical readings.[26] For it is from the word of God handed down in writing that even now "God is speaking to his people"[27] and it is from the continued use of Scripture that the people of God, docile to the Holy Spirit under the light of faith, receive the power to be Christ's living witnesses before the world.

13.  The reading of the gospel is the high point of the liturgy of the word. For this the other readings, in their established sequence from the Old to the New Testament, prepare the assembly.

14.  A speaking style on the part of the readers that is audible, clear, and intelligent is the first means of transmitting the word of God properly to the assembly. The readings, taken from the approved editions,[28] may be sung in a way suited to different languages. This singing, however, must serve to stress the words, not obscure them. On occasions when the readings are in Latin, they are to be sung to the melody given in the *Ordo cantus Missae.*[29]

15.  There may be concise introductions before the readings, especially the first. The style proper to such comments must be respected, that is, they must be simple, faithful to the text, brief, well prepared, and properly varied to suit the text they introduce.[30]

16.  In a Mass with a congregation the readings are always to be proclaimed at the lectern.[31]

17.  Of all the rites connected with the liturgy of the word, the reverence due to the gospel reading must receive special attention.[32] Where there is a Book of the Gospels that has been carried in by the deacon or reader during the entrance procession,[33] it is most fitting that the deacon or a priest, when there is no deacon, take the book from the altar[34] and carry it to the lectern. He is preceded by servers with candles and incense or other symbols of reverence that may be customary. As the faithful stand and acclaim the Lord, they show honor to the Book of the Gospels. The deacon who is to read the gospel, bowing in front of the one presiding, asks and receives the blessing. When no deacon is present, the priest, bowing before the altar, prays quietly: *Almighty God, cleanse my heart* . . . [35]

At the lectern the one who proclaims the gospel greets the people, who are standing, and announces the reading as he makes the sign of the cross on forehead, mouth, and breast. If incense is used, he next incenses the book, then reads the gospel. When finished, he kisses the book, saying the appointed words quietly.

Even if the gospel itself is not sung, it is appropriate for *The Lord be with you, A reading from the holy gospel* . . . , and at the end *This is the Gospel of the Lord* to be sung, in order that the assembly may also sing its acclamations. This is a way both of bringing out the importance of the gospel reading and of stirring up the faith of those who hear it.

18.    At the conclusion of the other readings, *This is the word of the Lord* may be sung, even by someone other than the reader; all respond with the acclamation. In this way the gathered assembly pays reverence to the word of God it has listened to in faith and gratitude.

## B. RESPONSORIAL PSALM

19.    The responsorial psalm, also called the gradual, has great liturgical and pastoral significance because it is "an integral part of the liturgy of the word."[36] Accordingly, the people must be continually instructed on the way to perceive the word of God speaking in the psalms and to turn these psalms into the prayer of the Church. This, of course, "will be achieved more readily if a deeper understanding of the psalms, in the meaning in which they are used in the liturgy, is more diligently promoted among the clergy and communicated to all the faithful by means of appropriate catechesis."[37]

A brief remark may be helpful about the choice of the psalm and response as well as their correspondence to the readings.

20.    As a rule the responsorial psalm should be sung. There are two established ways of singing the psalm after the first reading: responsorially and directly. In responsorial singing, which, as far as possible, is to be given preference, the psalmist or cantor of the psalm sings the psalm verse and the whole congregation joins in by singing the response. In direct singing of the psalm there is no intervening response by the community; either the psalmist or cantor of the psalm sings the psalm alone as the community listens or else all sing it together.

21.    The singing of the psalm, or even of the response alone, is a great help toward understanding and meditating on the psalm's spiritual meaning.

To foster the congregation's singing, every means available in the various cultures is to be employed. In particular use is to be made of all the relevant options provided in the Order of Readings for Mass[38] regarding responses corresponding to the different liturgical seasons.

22.    When not sung, the psalm after the reading is to be recited in a manner conducive to meditation on the word of God.[39]

The responsorial psalm is sung or recited by the psalmist or cantor at the lectern.[40]

## C. ACCLAMATION BEFORE THE READING OF THE GOSPEL

23.    The *Alleluia*, or, as the liturgical season requires, the verse before the gospel, is also a "rite or act standing by itself."[41] It serves as the assembled faithful's greeting of welcome to the Lord who is about to speak to them and as an expression of their faith through song.

The *Alleluia* or the verse before the gospel must be sung and during it all stand. It is not to be sung only by the cantor who intones it or by the choir, but by the whole congregation together.[42]

## D. HOMILY

24.    Through the course of the liturgical year the homily sets forth the mysteries of faith and the standards of the Christian life on the basis of the sacred text. Beginning with the Constitution on the Liturgy, the homily as part of the liturgy of the word[43] has been repeatedly and strongly recommended and in some cases it is obligatory. As a rule it is to be given by the one presiding.[44] The purpose of the homily at Mass is that the spoken word of God and the liturgy of the eucharist may together become "a proclamation of God's wonderful works in the history of salvation, the mystery of Christ."[45] Through the readings and homily Christ's paschal mystery is proclaimed; through the sacrifice of the Mass it becomes present.[46] Moreover Christ himself is also always present and active in the preaching of his Church.[47]

Whether the homily explains the biblical word of God proclaimed in the readings or some other texts of the liturgy,[48] it must always lead the community of the faithful to celebrate the eucharist wholeheartedly, "so that they may hold fast in their lives to what they have grasped by their faith."[49] From this living explanation, the word of God proclaimed in the readings and the Church's celebration of the day's liturgy will have greater impact. But this demands that the homily be truly the fruit of meditation, carefully prepared, neither too long nor too short, and suited to all those present, even children and the uneducated.[50]

At a concelebration, the celebrant or one of the concelebrants as a rule gives the homily.[51]

25.    On the prescribed days, that is, Sundays and holy days of obligation, there must be a homily in all Masses celebrated with a congregation, even Masses on the preceding evening; the homily may not be omitted without a serious reason.[52] There is also to be a homily in Masses with children and with special groups.[53]

A homily is strongly recommended on the weekdays of Advent, Lent, and the Easter season for the sake of the faithful who regularly take part in the celebration of Mass; also on other feasts and occasions when a large congregation is present.[54]

26.    The priest celebrant gives the homily either at the chair, standing or sitting, or at the lectern.[55]

27.    Any necessary announcements are to be kept completely separate from the homily; they must take place following the prayer after communion.[56]

## E. SILENCE

28.    The liturgy of the word must be celebrated in a way that fosters meditation; clearly, any sort of haste that hinders reflectiveness must be avoided. The dialogue between God and his people taking place through the Holy Spirit demands short intervals of silence, suited to the assembly, as an opportunity to take the word of God to heart and to prepare a response to it in prayer.

Proper times for silence during the liturgy of the word are, for example, before this liturgy begins, after the first and the second reading, after the homily.[57]

## F. PROFESSION OF FAITH

29.    The symbol or profession of faith, said when the rubrics require, has as its purpose in the celebration of Mass that the gathered faithful may respond and give assent to the word of God heard in the readings and through the homily, and that before they begin to celebrate in the eucharist the mystery of faith, they may call to mind the rule of faith in a formulary approved by the Church.[58]

## G. GENERAL INTERCESSIONS OR PRAYER OF THE FAITHFUL

30.    Enlightened by God's word and in a sense responding to it, the assembly of the faithful prays in the general intercessions as a rule for the needs of the universal Church and the local community, for the salvation of the world and those oppressed by any burden, and for special categories of people.

The celebrant introduces the prayer; the deacon, another minister, or some of the faithful may propose intentions that are short and phrased with a measure of flexibility. In these petitions "the people, exercising their priestly function, make intercession for all,"[59] with the result that, as the liturgy of the word has its full effects in them, they are better prepared to proceed to the liturgy of the eucharist.

31.    For the general intercessions the celebrant presides at the chair and the intentions are announced at the lectern.[60]

The congregation takes part in the general intercessions while standing and by saying or singing a common response after each intention or by silent prayer.[61]

### 2. Aids to the proper celebration of the liturgy of the word

## A. PLACE FOR PROCLAIMING THE WORD OF GOD

32.    There must be a place in the church that is somewhat elevated, fixed, and of a suitable design and nobility. It should reflect the dignity of God's word and be a clear reminder to the people that in the Mass the table of God's word and of Christ's body is placed before them.[62] The place for the readings must also truly help the people's listening and attention during the liturgy of the word. Great pains must therefore be taken, in keeping with the design of each church, over the harmonious and close relationship of the lectern with the altar.

33.    Either permanently or at least on occasions of greater solemnity, the lectern should be decorated simply and in keeping with its design.

Since the lectern is the place from which the ministers proclaim the word of God, it must of its nature be reserved for the readings, the responsorial psalm, and the Easter proclamation (Exsultet). The lectern may rightly be used for the homily and the general intercessions, however, because of their close connection with the entire liturgy of the word. It is better for the commentator, cantor, or director of singing, for example, not to use the lectern.[63]

34.    In order that the lectern may properly serve its liturgical purpose, it is to be rather large, since on occasion several ministers must use it at the same time.

Provisions must also be made for the readers to have enough light to read the text and, as required, to have sound equipment enabling the congregation to hear them without difficulty.

B. BOOKS FOR PROCLAMATION OF THE WORD OF GOD

35.   Along with the ministers, the actions, the lectern, and other elements, the books containing the readings of the word of God remind the hearers of the presence of God speaking to his people. Since, in liturgical celebrations the books too serve as signs and symbols of the sacred, care must be taken to ensure that they truly are worthy and beautiful.[64]

36.   The proclamation of the gospel always stands as the high point of the liturgy of the word. Thus the liturgical traditions of both the East and the West have consistently continued to preserve some distinction between the books for the readings. The Book of the Gospels was always designed with the utmost care and was more ornate and shown greater respect than any of the other books of readings. In our times also, then, it is very desirable that cathedrals and at least the larger, more populous parishes and the churches with a larger attendance possess a beautifully designed Book of the Gospels, separate from the other book of readings. For good reason it is the Book of the Gospels that is presented to the deacon at his ordination and that is laid upon the head of the bishop-elect and held there at his ordination.[65]

37.   Because of the dignity of the word of God, the books of readings used in the celebration are not to be replaced by other pastoral aids, for example, by leaflets printed for the faithful's preparation of the readings or for their personal meditation.

CHAPTER III
OFFICES AND MINISTRIES IN THE CELEBRATION OF THE
LITURGY OF THE WORD WITHIN MASS

*1. Function of the one presiding at the liturgy of the word*

38.   The one presiding at the liturgy of the word brings the spiritual nourishment it contains to those present, especially in the homily. Even if he too is a listener to the word of God proclaimed by others, the duty of proclaiming it has been entrusted above all to him. Personally or through others he sees to it that the word of God is properly proclaimed. He then as a rule reserves to himself the task of composing comments to help the people to listen more attentively and to preach a homily that fosters in them a richer understanding of the word of God.

39.   The first requirement for one who is to preside over the celebration is a thorough knowledge of the structure of the Order of Readings so that he will know how to inspire good effects in the hearts of the faithful. Through study and prayer he must also develop a full understanding of the coordination and connection of the various texts in the liturgy of the word, so that the Order of Readings will become the source of a sound understanding of the mystery of Christ and his saving work.

40.   The one presiding is to make ready use of the various options provided in the Lectionary regarding readings, responses, responsorial psalms, and gospel acclamations;[66] but he is to do so with the agreement[67] of all concerned and after listening to the faithful in regard to what belongs to them.[68]

41.   The one presiding exercises his proper office and the ministry of the word of God also as he preaches the homily.[69] In this way he leads his brothers and sisters to an affective knowledge of holy Scripture. He opens their souls to gratitude for the wonderful works of God. He strengthens their faith in the word that in the celebration becomes a sacrament through the Holy Spirit. Finally, he prepares them for a fruitful reception of communion and invites them to embrace the demands of the Christian life.

42.   The one presiding is responsible for preparing the faithful for the liturgy of the word on occasion by means of introductions before the readings.[70] These comments can help the gathered assembly toward a better hearing of the word of God, because they enliven the people's faith and their desire for good. He may also carry out this responsibility through other persons, the deacon, for example, or a commentator.[71]

43.   As he directs the general intercessions and through their introduction and conclusion connects them, if possible, with the day's readings and the homily, the one presiding leads the faithful toward the liturgy of the eucharist.[72]

*2. Role of the faithful in the liturgy of the word*

44.   Christ's word gathers the people of God as one and increases and sustains them. "This applies above all to the liturgy of the word in the celebration of Mass: there is an inseparable union between the proclamation of the death of the Lord, the response of the people listening, and the offering through which Christ has confirmed the New Covenant in his blood. The people share in this offering by their inner intentions and the reception of the sacrament."[73] For "not only when things are read 'that were written for our instruction' (Romans 15:4), but also when the Church prays or sings or acts, the faith of those taking part is nourished and their minds are raised to God, so that they may offer him their worship as intelligent beings and receive his grace more abundantly."[74]

45.   In the liturgy of the word, the congregation of the faithful still today receives from God the word of his covenant through the faith that comes by hearing. The faithful must respond to that word in the same faith so that more and more they may become the people of the New Covenant.

The people of God have a spiritual right to receive abundantly from the treasury of God's word. Its riches are presented to them through use of the Order of Readings, the homily, and pastoral efforts.

For their part, the faithful at the celebration of Mass are to listen to the word of God with an inward and outward reverence that will bring them continuous growth in the spiritual life and draw them more deeply into the mystery they celebrate.[75]

46.   As a help toward celebrating the memorial of the Lord with devotion, the faithful should be keenly aware of the one presence of Christ in both the word of God—"it is he who speaks when the holy Scriptures are read in the Church"— and "especially under the eucharistic elements."[76]

47.   To be received and integrated into the life of Christ's faithful, the word of God demands a living faith.[77] Hearing the word of God unceasingly proclaimed arouses that faith.

The Scriptures, and above all in their liturgical proclamation, are the source of life and power. As Paul attests, the Gospel is the saving power of God for everyone who believes.[78] Love of the Scriptures is therefore the force that renews the entire people of God.[79] All the faithful without exception must therefore always be ready to listen gladly to God's word.[80] When this word is proclaimed in the Church and put into living practice, it enlightens the faithful through the working of the Holy Spirit and draws them into the entire mystery of the Lord as a reality to be lived.[81] The word of God reverently received moves the heart and its desires toward conversion and toward a life filled with both individual and community faith,[82] since God's word is the sustenance of the Christian life and the source of the prayer of the entire Church.[83]

48.   The close connection between the liturgy of the word and the liturgy of the eucharist in the Mass should prompt the faithful to be present right from the beginning of the celebration,[84] to take part attentively, and to dispose themselves to hear the word, especially by learning beforehand more about Scripture. That same connection should also awaken in them a desire for a liturgical understanding of the texts read and for the willingness to respond through singing.[85]

When they hear the word of God and reflect deeply on it, the faithful receive the power to respond to it actively with full faith, hope, and charity through prayer and self-giving, and not only during Mass but in their entire Christian life.

### 3. Ministries in the liturgy of the word

49.   Liturgical tradition assigns responsibility for the biblical readings in the celebration of Mass to ministers: to readers and the deacon. But when there is no deacon or another priest present, the priest celebrant is to read the gospel[86] and when there is no reader present, all the readings.[87]

50.   The deacon's part in the liturgy of the word at Mass is to proclaim the gospel, sometimes to give the homily, as occasion suggests, and to propose the intentions of the general intercessions to the people.[88]

51.   "The reader has his own proper function in the eucharistic celebration and should exercise this even though ministers of a higher rank may be present."[89] The reader's ministry, which is conferred through a liturgical rite, must be held in respect. When there are instituted readers available, they are to carry out their office at least on Sundays and major feasts, especially at the principal Mass of the day. These readers may also be given responsibility for assisting in the planning of the liturgy of the word, and, to the extent necessary, of seeing to the preparation of

others of the faithful who may be appointed on a given occasion to serve as readers at Mass.[90]

52.   The liturgical assembly truly requires readers, even those not instituted. Proper measures must therefore be taken to ensure that there are qualifled laypersons who have been trained to carry out this ministry.[91] Whenever there is more than one reading, it is better to assign the readings to different readers, if available.

53.   In Masses without a deacon, the function of announcing the intentions for the general intercessions is to be assigned to the cantor, particularly when they are to be sung, to a reader, or to another person.[92]

54.   During the celebration of Mass with a congregation, a second priest, a deacon, and an instituted reader must wear the distinctive vestment of their office when they go to the lectern to read the word of God. Those who carry out the ministry of reader just for the occasion or even regularly but without institution may go to the lectern in ordinary attire that is in keeping with local custom.

55.   "It is necessary that those who exercise the ministry of reader, even if they have not received institution, be truly qualified and carefully prepared so that the faithful may develop a warm and living love for Scripture from listening to the sacred texts read."[93]

Their preparation must above all be spiritual, but what may be called a technical preparation is also needed. The spiritual preparation presupposes at least a biblical and liturgical formation. The purpose of their biblical formation is to give readers the ability to understand the readings in context and to perceive by the light of faith the central point of the revealed message. The liturgical formation ought to equip the readers to have some grasp of the meaning and structure of the liturgy of the word and of the significance of its connection with the liturgy of the eucharist. The technical preparation should make the readers more skilled in the art of reading publicly, either with power of their own voice or with the help of sound equipment.

56.   The psalmist, that is the cantor of the psalm, is responsible for singing, responsorially or directly, the chants between the readings—the psalm or other biblical canticle, the gradual and *Alleluia*, or other chant. The psalmist may, as occasion requires, intone the *Alleluia* and verse.[94]

For carrying out the function of psalmist it is advantageous to have in each ecclesial community laypersons with a talent for singing and correct diction. The points made about the formation of readers apply to cantors as well.

57.   The commentator also fulfills a genuine liturgical ministry, which consists in presenting to the assembly of the faithful, from a suitable place, relevant explanations and comments that are clear, of marked simplicity, meticulously prepared, as a rule written out, and approved beforehand by the celebrant.[95]

# PART TWO
## STRUCTURE OF THE ORDER OF READINGS FOR MASS

### CHAPTER IV
### GENERAL PLAN OF THE READINGS FOR MASS

*1. Pastoral aim of the Order of Readings for Mass*

58.   On the basis of the intention of Vatican Council II, the Order of Readings provided by the Lectionary of the Roman Missal has been composed above all for a pastoral purpose. To achieve this aim, not only the principles underlying this new Order of Readings but also the lists of texts that it provides have been discussed and revised over and over again, with the cooperation of a great many experts in exegesis, pastoral studies, catechetics, and liturgy from all parts of the world. The Order of Readings is the fruit of this combined effort.

The prolonged use of this Order of Readings to proclaim and explain sacred Scripture in the eucharistic celebration will, it is hoped, prove to be an effective step toward achieving the objective stated repeatedly by Vatican Council II.[96]

59.   The decision on revising the Lectionary for Mass was to draw up and edit a single, rich, and full Order of Readings that would be in complete accord with the intent and prescriptions of the Council.[97] At the same time, however, the Order was meant to be of a kind that would meet the requirements and usages of particular Churches and liturgical assemblies. For this reason, those responsible for the revision took pains to safeguard the liturgical tradition of the Roman Rite, but valued highly the merits of all the systems of selecting, arranging, and using the biblical readings in other liturgical families and in certain particular Churches. The revisers made use of those elements that experience has confirmed, but with an effort to avoid certain shortcomings found in the preceding form of the tradition.

60.   The present Order of Readings for Mass, then, is an arrangement of biblical readings that provides the faithful with a knowledge of the whole of God's word, in a pattern suited to the purpose. Throughout the liturgical year, but above all during the seasons of Easter, Lent, and Advent, the choice and sequence of readings are aimed at giving the faithful an ever-deepening perception of the faith they profess and of the history of salvation.[98] Accordingly, the Order of Readings corresponds to the requirements and interests of the Christian people.

61.   The celebration of the liturgy is not in itself simply a form of catechesis, but it does contain an element of teaching. The Lectionary of the Roman Missal brings this out[99] and therefore deserves to be regarded as a pedagogical resource aiding catechesis.

This is so because the Order of Readings for Mass aptly presents from Scripture the principal deeds and words belonging to the history of salvation. As its many phases and events are recalled in the liturgy of the word, the faithful will come to see that the history of salvation is contained here and now in the representation of Christ's paschal mystery celebrated through the eucharist.

62. The pastoral advantage of having in the Roman Rite a single Order of Readings for the Lectionary is obvious on other grounds. All the faithful, particularly those who for various reasons do not always take part in Mass with the same assembly, will everywhere be able to hear the same readings on any given day or in any liturgical season and to reflect on the application of these readings to their own circumstances. This is the case even in places that have no priest and where a deacon or someone else deputed by the bishop conducts a celebration of the word of God.[100]

63. Pastors may wish to respond specifically from the word of God to the concerns of their own congregations. Although they must be mindful that they are above all to be the heralds of the entire mystery of Christ and the Gospel, they may rightfully use the options provided in the Order of Readings for Mass. This applies particularly to the celebration of a ritual or votive Mass, a Mass in honor of the saints, or one of the Masses for various needs and occasions. In the light of the general norms, special faculties are granted for the readings in Masses with particular groups.[101]

### 2. Principles used in drawing up the Order of Readings for Mass

64. To achieve the purpose of the Order of Readings for Mass, the parts have been selected and arranged in such a way as to take into account the sequence of the liturgical seasons and the hermeneutical principles discovered and formulated through contemporary biblical research.

It was judged helpful to state here the principles guiding the composition of the Order of Readings for Mass.

#### A. SELECTION OF TEXTS

65. The course of readings in the Proper of Seasons is arranged as follows. Sundays and the solemnities of the Lord present the more important biblical passages. In this way the more significant parts of God's revealed word can be read to the assembly of the faithful within a reasonable period of time. Weekdays present a second series of texts from Scripture and in a sense these complement the message of salvation explained on Sundays and the solemnities of the Lord. But neither series in these main parts of the Order of Readings—the series for Sundays and the solemnities of the Lord and for weekdays—depends on the other. The Order of Readings for Sundays and the solemnities of the Lord extends over three years; for weekdays, over two. Thus each runs its course independently of the other.

The course of readings in other parts of the Order of Readings is governed by its own rules. This applies to the series of readings for celebrations of the saints, ritual Masses, Masses for various needs and occasions, votive Masses, or Masses for the dead.

66.    The following are features proper to the readings for Sundays and the solemnities of the Lord:

> 1. Each Mass has three readings: the first from the Old Testament, the second from an apostle (that is, either from a letter or from Revelation, depending on the season), and the third from the gospels. This arrangement brings out the unity of the Old and New Testaments and of the history of salvation, in which Christ is the central figure, commemorated in his paschal mystery.

> 2. A more varied and richer reading of Scripture on Sundays and the solemnities of the Lord results from the three-year cycle provided for these days, in that the same texts are read only every fourth year.[102]

> 3. The principles governing the Order of Readings for Sundays and the solemnities of the Lord are called the principles of "harmony" and of "semicontinuous reading." One or the other applies according to the different seasons of the year and the distinctive character of the particular liturgical season.

67.    The best instance of harmony between the Old and New Testament readings occurs when it is one that Scripture itself suggests. This is the case when the teaching and events recounted in texts of the New Testament bear a more or less explicit relationship to the teaching and events of the Old Testament. The present Order of Readings selects Old Testament texts mainly because of their correlation with New Testament texts read in the same Mass, and particularly with the gospel text.

Harmony of another kind exists between texts of the readings for each Mass during Advent, Lent, and Easter, the seasons that have a distinctive importance or character.

In contrast, the Sundays in Ordinary Time do not have a distinctive character. Thus the texts of both the apostolic and gospel readings are arranged in an order of semicontinuous reading, whereas the Old Testament reading is harmonized with the gospel.

68.    The decision was made not to extend to Sundays the arrangements suited to the liturgical seasons mentioned, that is, not to have an organic harmony of themes designed to aid homiletic instruction. Such an arrangement would be in conflict with the genuine conception of liturgical celebration. The liturgy is always the celebration of the mystery of Christ and makes use of the word of God on the basis of its own tradition, guided not by merely logical or extrinsic concerns but by the desire to proclaim the Gospel and to lead those who believe to the fullness of the truth.

## C. ARRANGEMENT OF THE READINGS FOR WEEKDAYS

69.   The weekday readings have been arranged in the following way:

1. Each Mass has two readings: the first is from the Old Testament or from an apostle (from a letter or Revelation), and during the Easter season from Acts; the second, from the gospels.

2. The yearly cycle for Lent has its proper principles of arrangement, which take into account the baptismal and penitential themes of this season.

3. The cycle for the weekdays of Advent, the Christmas season, and the Easter season is also yearly and the readings thus remain the same each year.

4. For the thirty-four weeks of Ordinary Time, the gospel readings are arranged in a single cycle, repeated each year. But the first reading is arranged in a two-year cycle and is thus read every other year. Year I is used during odd-numbered years; Year II, during even-numbered years.

Like the Order for Sundays and the solemnities of the Lord, then, the weekday Order of Readings is governed by similar application of the principles of harmony and of semicontinuous reading, especially in the case of seasons with their own distinctive character.

## D. READINGS FOR CELEBRATIONS OF THE SAINTS

70.   Two groups of readings are provided for celebrations of the saints:

1. The Proper of Saints provides the first group, for solemnities, feasts, or memorials and particularly when there are proper texts for such celebrations. Sometimes in the Proper, however, there is a reference to the most appropriate among the texts in the Commons as the one to be given preference.

2. The Commons of Saints provide the second, more extensive group of readings. There are, first, appropriate texts for the different classes of saints (martyrs, pastors, virgins, etc.), then a great many texts that deal with holiness in general. These are for alternative use whenever the Commons are indicated as the source for the choice of readings.

71.   As to their sequence, all the texts in this part of the Order of Readings appear in the order in which they are to be read at Mass. Thus the Old Testament texts are first, then the texts of an apostle, followed by the psalms and verses between the readings, and finally the texts from the gospels. The rationale of this arrangement is that, unless otherwise noted, the celebrant may choose at will from such texts, in view of the pastoral needs of the assembly taking part in the celebration.

## E. READINGS FOR RITUAL MASSES, MASSES FOR VARIOUS NEEDS AND OCCASIONS, VOTIVE MASSES, AND MASSES FOR THE DEAD

72.   For ritual Masses, Masses for various needs and occasions, votive Masses, and Masses for the dead, the texts for the readings are arranged as just described, that is, many texts are grouped together in the order of their use, as in the Commons of Saints.

73.   In addition to the guiding principles already given for the arrangement of readings in the individual parts of the Order of Readings, others of a more general nature are:

### 1. Reservation of some books on the basis of the liturgical seasons

74.   In this Order of Readings, some biblical books are set aside for particular liturgical seasons on the basis of both the intrinsic importance of subject matter and liturgical tradition. For example, the Western (Ambrosian and Hispanic) and Eastern tradition of reading Acts during the Easter season is respected. This usage results in a clear presentation of how the Church derives the beginning of its entire life from the paschal mystery. Another tradition of both the West and the East that is retained is the reading of the Gospel of John in the latter weeks of Lent and in the Easter season.

Tradition assigns the reading of Isaiah, especially the first part, to Advent. Some texts of this book, however, are read during the Christmas season, to which 1 John is also assigned.

### 2. Length of texts

75.   *A via media* is followed in regard to the length of texts. A distinction has been made between narratives, which require reading a fairly long passage but which usually hold the people's attention, and texts that should not be lengthy because of the profundity of their teaching.

In the case of certain rather long texts, longer and shorter versions are provided to suit different situations. The editing of the shorter version has been carried out with great caution.

### 3. Difficult texts

76.   In readings for Sundays and solemnities, texts that present real difficulties are avoided for pastoral reasons. The difficulties may be objective, in that the texts themselves raise complex literary, critical, or exegetical problems; or, at least to a certain extent, the difficulties may lie in the faithful's ability to understand the texts. But there could be no justification for depriving the faithful of the spiritual riches of certain texts on the grounds of difficulty if its source is the inadequacy either of the religious education that every Christian should have or of the biblical formation that every pastor should have. Often a difficult reading is clarified by its correlation with another in the same Mass.

### 4. Omission of texts

77.   The omission of verses in readings from Scripture has at times been the practice in many liturgical traditions, including the Roman. Admittedly such omissions may not be made lightly, for fear of distorting the meaning of the text or the intent and style of Scripture. Yet on pastoral grounds it was decided to continue the tradition in the present Order of Readings, but at the same time to ensure that the essential meaning of the text remained intact. One reason for the decision is that otherwise some texts would have been unduly long. It would also have been necessary to omit completely certain readings of high spiritual value

for the faithful because those readings include some verse that is unsuitable pastorally or that involves truly difficult problems.

*3. Principles to be followed in the use of the Order of Readings*

A. OPTIONS IN THE CHOICE OF SOME TEXTS

78. The Order of Readings sometimes leaves it to the celebrant to choose between alternative texts or to choose one from the several listed together for the same readings. The option seldom exists on Sundays, solemnities, or the greater feasts in order not to obscure the proper character of the particular liturgical season or needlessly interrupt the semicontinuous reading of some biblical book. On the other hand, the option is given readily in celebrations of the saints, in ritual Masses, Masses for various needs and occasions, votive Masses, and Masses for the dead.

These options, together with those indicated in the General Instruction of the Roman Missal and the *Ordo cantus Missae*,[103] have a pastoral aim. In planning the liturgy of the word, then, the priest should consider "the general spiritual good of the assembly rather than his personal outlook. He should be mindful that the choice of texts is to be made in consultation with the ministers and others who have a function in the celebration and should listen to the faithful in regard to the parts that more directly belong to them."[104]

1. The two readings before the gospel

79. In Masses assigned three readings, the three are to be used. If, however, for pastoral reasons the conference of bishops has permitted use of only two readings,[105] the choice between the two first readings is to be made in such a way as to safeguard the Church's intent to instruct the faithful more completely in the mystery of salvation. Thus, unless the contrary is indicated in the text of the Lectionary, the reading to be chosen as the first reading is the one that is closer to the theme of the gospel, or, in accord with the intent just mentioned, that is more helpful toward a coherent catechesis over an extended period, or that preserves the semicontinuous reading of some biblical book.[106]

2. Long and short forms of texts

80. A pastoral criterion must also guide the choice between the longer and shorter forms of a text. The main consideration must be the capacity of the hearers to listen profitably either to the longer or to the shorter reading; or to listen to a more complete text that will be explained through the homily.

3. When two texts are provided

81. When a choice is allowed between alternative texts, whether they are fixed or optional, the first consideration must be the best interests of those taking part. It may be a matter of using the easier text or the one more relevant to the gathered assembly or, as pastoral advantage may suggest, of repeating or replacing a text that is assigned as proper to one celebration and optional to another.

The issue may arise when it is feared that some text will create difficulties for a particular congregation or when the same text would have to be repeated within a few days, as on a Sunday and on a following weekday.

## 4. Weekday readings

82. The arrangement of weekday readings provides texts for every day of the week throughout the year. In most cases, therefore, these readings are to be used on their assigned days, unless a solemnity, feast, or memorial with proper readings occurs.[107]

The one using the Order of Readings for weekdays must check to see whether one reading or another from the same biblical book will have to be omitted because of some celebration occurring during the week. With the plan of readings for the entire week in mind, the priest in that case arranges to omit the less significant selections or suitably combines them with other readings, if they contribute to an integral view of a particular theme.

## 5. Celebrations of the saints

83. When they exist, proper readings are given for celebrations of the saints, that is, biblical passages about the saint or the event in the saint's life that the Mass is celebrating. Even in the case of a memorial these readings must take the place of the weekday readings for the same day. This Order of Readings makes explicit note of every case of proper readings on a memorial.

In some cases there are accommodated readings, those, namely, that bring out some particular aspect of a saint's spiritual life or apostolate. Use of such readings does not seem binding, except for compelling pastoral reasons. For the most part references are given to readings in the Commons in order to facilitate choice. But these are merely suggestions: in place of an accommodated reading or the particular reading proposed from a Common, any other reading from the Commons referred to may be selected.

The first concern of a priest celebrating with a congregation is the spiritual benefit of the faithful and he will be careful not to impose his personal preference on them. Above all he will make sure not to omit too often or needlessly the readings assigned for each day in the weekday Lectionary: the Church's desire is to provide the faithful with a richer share at the table of God's word.[108]

There are also general readings, that is, those placed in the Commons either for some determined class of saints (martyrs, virgins, pastors, etc.) or for the saints in general. Because in these cases several texts are listed for the same reading, it will be up to the priest to choose the one best suited to the congregation.

In all celebrations of saints the readings may be taken not only from the Commons to which the references are given in each case, but also from the Common of Holy Men and Women, whenever there is special reason for doing so.

84. For celebrations of the saints:

a. On solemnities and feasts the readings must be those that are given in the Proper or the Commons. For solemnities and feasts of the General Roman Calendar proper readings are always assigned.

b. On solemnities belonging to particular calendars, three readings are to be assigned, unless the conference of bishops has decreed that there are to be only two readings.[109] The first reading is from the Old Testament (but during the Easter season, from Acts or Revelation); the second from an apostle; the third, from the gospels.

c. On feasts and memorials, which have only two readings, the first can be chosen from either the Old Testament or from an apostle; the second is from the gospels. Following the Church's traditional practice, however, the first reading during the Easter season is to be taken from an apostle, the second, as far as possible, from the Gospel of John.

### 6. Other parts of the Order of Readings

85. In the Order of Readings for ritual Masses the references given are to the texts already published for the individual rites. This obviously does not include the texts belonging to celebrations that must not be integrated with Mass.[110]

86. The Order of Readings for Masses for various needs and occasions, votive Masses, and Masses for the dead provides many texts that can be of assistance in adapting such celebrations to the situation, circumstances, and concerns of the particular groups taking part.[111]

87. In ritual Masses, Masses for various needs and occasions, votive Masses, and Masses for the dead, since many texts are given for the same reading, the choice of readings follows the criteria already indicated for the choice of readings from the Common of Saints.

88. On a day when some ritual Mass is not permitted and the norms in the individual rite allow the choice of one reading from those provided for ritual Masses, the general spiritual welfare of the participants must be the primary consideration.[112]

### B. RESPONSORIAL PSALM AND ACCLAMATION BEFORE THE GOSPEL

89. Among the chants between the readings, the psalm after the first reading is very important. As a rule the psalm to be used is the one assigned to the reading. But in the case of readings for the Common of Saints, ritual Masses, Masses for various needs and occasions, votive Masses, and Masses for the dead the choice is left up to the priest celebrating. He will base his choice on the principle of the pastoral benefit of those participating.

But to make it easier for the people to join in the response to the psalm, the Order of Readings lists certain other texts of psalms and responses that have been chosen according to the various seasons or classes of saints. Whenever the psalm is sung, these texts may replace the text corresponding to the reading.[113]

90. The chant between the second reading and the gospel is either specified in each Mass and correlated with the gospel or else it is left as a choice to be made from those in the series belonging to a liturgical season or to one of the Commons.

91. During Lent one of the acclamations from those given in the text of the Order of Readings[114] may be used, depending on the occasion. This acclamation is made before and after the verse before the gospel.

[The forms customary for this acclamation are:
Praise to you, Lord Jesus Christ, king of endless glory!
Praise and honor to you, Lord Jesus Christ!
Glory and praise to you, Lord Jesus Christ!
Glory to you, Word of God, Lord Jesus Christ!]

## CHAPTER V
## DESCRIPTION OF THE ORDER OF READINGS

92.    It seems useful to provide here a brief description of the Order of Readings, at least for the principal celebrations and the different seasons of the liturgical year. With these in mind, readings were selected on the basis of the rules already stated. This description is meant to assist priests to understand the structure of the Order of Readings so that their use of it will become more perceptive and the Order of Readings a source of good for Christ's faithful.

### 1. Advent

A. SUNDAYS

93.    Each gospel reading has a distinctive theme: the Lord's coming at the end of time (First Sunday of Advent), John the Baptist (Second and Third Sunday), and the events that prepared immediately for the Lord's birth (Fourth Sunday).

The Old Testament readings are prophecies about the Messiah and the Messianic age especially from Isaiah.

The readings from an apostle serve as exhortations and as proclamations, in keeping with the different themes of Advent.

B. WEEKDAYS

94.    There are two series of readings: one to be used from the beginning of Advent until 16 December; the other from 17 to 24 December.

In the first part of Advent there are readings from Isaiah, distributed in accord with the sequence of the book itself and including salient texts that are also read on the Sundays. For the choice of the weekday gospel the first reading has been taken into consideration.

On Thursday of the second week the readings of the gospel about John the Baptist begin. The first reading is either a continuation of Isaiah or a text chosen in view of the gospel.

In the last week before Christmas the events that immediately prepared for the Lord's birth are presented from Matthew (Chapter 1) and Luke (Chapter 1). The texts in the first reading, chosen in view of the gospel reading, are from different Old Testament books and include important Messianic prophecies.

## 2. Christmas season

95.   For the vigil and the three Masses of Christmas both the prophetic readings and the others have been chosen from the Roman tradition.

The gospel on the Sunday within the octave of Christmas, feast of the Holy Family, is about Jesus' childhood and the other readings are about the virtues of family life.

On the octave of Christmas, solemnity of Mary, Mother of God, the readings are about the Virgin Mother of God and the giving of the holy Name of Jesus.

On the second Sunday after Christmas, the readings are about the mystery of the incarnation.

On Epiphany, the Old Testament reading and the gospel continue the Roman tradition; the text for the reading from the apostolic letters is about the calling of all peoples to salvation.

On the feast of the Baptism of the Lord, the texts chosen are about this mystery.

B. WEEKDAYS

96.   From 29 December on, there is a continuous reading of the whole of 1 John, which actually begins earlier, on 27 December, feast of St. John the Evangelist, and on 28 December, feast of the Holy Innocents. The gospels relate manifestations of the Lord: events of Jesus' childhood from Luke (29–30 December); passages from John 1 (31 December–5 January); other manifestations from the four gospels (7–18 January).

## 3. Lent

A. SUNDAYS

97.   The gospel readings are arranged as follows:

The first and second Sundays retain the accounts of the Lord's temptations and transfiguration, with readings, however, from all three Synoptics.

On the next three Sundays, the gospels about the Samaritan woman, the man born blind, and the raising of Lazarus have been restored in Year A. Because these gospels are of major importance in regard to Christian initiation, they may also be read in Year B and Year C, especially in places where there are catechumens.

Other texts, however, are provided for Year B and Year C: for Year B, a text from John about Christ's coming glorification through his cross and resurrection and for Year C, a text from Luke about conversion.

On Passion Sunday (Palm Sunday) the texts for the procession are selections from the Synoptic Gospels concerning the Lord's triumphal entrance into Jerusalem. For the Mass the reading is the account of the Lord's passion.

The Old Testament readings are about the history of salvation, which is one of the themes proper to the catechesis of Lent. The series of texts for each Year presents the main elements of salvation history from its beginning until the promise of the New Covenant.

The readings from the letters of the apostles have been selected to fit the gospel and the Old Testament readings and, to the extent possible, to provide a connection between them.

### B. WEEKDAYS

98.   The readings from the gospels and the Old Testament were selected because they are related to each other. They treat various themes of the Lenten catechesis that are suited to the spiritual significance of this season. Beginning with Monday of the fourth week of Lent, there is a semicontinuous reading of the Gospel of John, made up of texts that correspond more closely to the themes proper to Lent.

Because the readings about the Samaritan woman, the man born blind, and the raising of Lazarus are now assigned to Sundays, but only for Year A (in Year B and Year C they are optional), provision has been made for their use on weekdays. Thus at the beginning of the Third, Fourth, and Fifth Weeks of Lent optional Masses with these texts for the gospel have been inserted and may be used in place of the readings of the day on any weekday of the respective week.

In the first half of Holy Week the readings are about the mystery of Christ's passion. For the chrism Mass the readings bring out both Christ's messianic mission and its continuation in the Church by means of the sacraments.

*4. The Easter triduum and the Easter season*

### A. THE EASTER TRIDUUM

99.   On Holy Thursday at the evening Mass the remembrance of the supper preceding Christ's departure casts its own special light because of the Lord's example in washing the feet of his disciples and Paul's account of the institution of the Christian Passover in the eucharist.

On Good Friday the liturgical service has as its center John's narrative of the passion of him who was portrayed in Isaiah as the Servant of Yahweh and who became the one High Priest by offering himself to the Father.

On the holy night of the Easter Vigil there are seven Old Testament readings, recalling the wonderful works of God in the history of salvation. There are two New Testament readings, the announcement of the resurrection according to one of the Synoptic Gospels and a reading from St. Paul on Christian baptism as the sacrament of Christ's resurrection.

The gospel reading for the Mass on Easter day is from John on the finding of the empty tomb. There is also, however, the option to use the gospel texts from the Easter Vigil or, when there is an evening Mass on Easter Sunday, to use the account in Luke of the Lord's appearance to the disciples on the road to Emmaus. The first reading is from Acts, which throughout the Easter season replaces the

Old Testament reading. The reading from St. Paul concerns the living out of the paschal mystery in the Church.

## B. SUNDAYS

100. The gospel readings for the first three Sundays recount the appearances of the risen Christ. The readings about the Good Shepherd are assigned to the Fourth Sunday. On the Fifth, Sixth, and Seventh Sundays, there are excerpts from the Lord's discourse and prayer at the last supper.

The first reading is from Acts, in a three-year cycle of parallel and progressive selections: material is presented on the life of the primitive Church, its witness, and its growth.

For the reading from the apostles, 1 Peter is in Year A, 1 John in Year B, Revelation in Year C. These are the texts that seem to fit in especially well with the spirit of joyous faith and sure hope proper to this season.

## C. WEEKDAYS

101. As on the Sundays, the first reading is a semicontinuous reading from Acts. The gospel readings during the Easter octave are accounts of the Lord's appearances. After that there is a semicontinuous reading of the Gospel of John, but with texts that have a paschal character in order to complete the reading from John during Lent. This paschal reading is made up in large part of the Lord's discourse and prayer at the last supper.

## D. SOLEMNITIES OF THE ASCENSION AND PENTECOST

102. For the first reading the solemnity of the Ascension retains the account of the Ascension according to Acts. This text is complemented by the second reading from the apostolic reflections on Christ in exaltation at the right hand of the Father. For the gospel reading, each of the three Years has its own text in accord with the differences in the Synoptic Gospels.

In the evening Mass celebrated on the vigil of Pentecost four Old Testament texts are provided; any one of them may be used, in order to bring out the many aspects of Pentecost. The reading from the apostles shows the actual working of the Holy Spirit in the Church. The gospel reading recalls the promise of the Spirit made by Christ before his own glorification.

For the Mass on Pentecost itself, in accord with received usage, the account in Acts of the great occurrence on Pentecost is taken as the first reading. The texts from Paul bring out the effect of the action of the Holy Spirit in the life of the Church. The gospel reading is a remembrance of Jesus bestowing his Spirit on the disciples on Easter evening; other optional texts describe the action of the Spirit on the disciples and on the Church.

# 5. Ordinary Time

## A. ARRANGEMENT AND CHOICE OF TEXTS

103. Ordinary Time begins on the Monday after the Sunday following 6 January; it lasts until the Tuesday before Lent inclusive. It begins again on the Monday after Pentecost Sunday and finishes before evening prayer I of the first Sunday of Advent.

The Order of Readings provides readings for thirty-four Sundays and the weeks following them. In some years, however, there are only thirty-three weeks of Ordinary Time. Further, some Sundays either belong to another season (the Sunday on which the feast of the Baptism of the Lord falls and Pentecost) or else are impeded by a solemnity that coincides with Sunday (for example, Holy Trinity or Christ the King).

104. For the correct arrangement in the use of the readings for Ordinary Time, the following are to be respected:

1. The Sunday on which the feast of the Baptism of the Lord falls replaces the first Sunday in Ordinary Time. Therefore the readings of the First Week of Ordinary Time begin on the Monday after the Sunday following 6 January. When the feast of the Baptism of the Lord is celebrated on Monday because Epiphany has been celebrated on the Sunday, the readings of the First Week begin on Tuesday.

2. The Sunday following the feast of the Baptism of the Lord is the Second Sunday of Ordinary Time. The remaining Sundays are numbered consecutively up to the Sunday preceding the beginning of Lent. The readings for the week in which Ash Wednesday falls are suspended after the Tuesday readings.

3. For the resumption of the readings of Ordinary Time after Pentecost Sunday:

—When there are thirty-four Sundays in Ordinary Time, the week to be used is the one that immediately follows the last week used before Lent.[115]

—When there are thirty-three Sundays in Ordinary Time, the first week that would have been used after Pentecost is omitted in order to reserve for the end of the year the eschatological texts that are assigned to the last two weeks.[116]

## B. SUNDAY READINGS

### 1. Gospel readings

105. On the Second Sunday of Ordinary Time the gospel continues to center on the manifestation of the Lord, which Epiphany celebrates through the traditional passage about the wedding feast at Cana and two other passages from John.

Beginning with the Third Sunday, there is a semicontinuous reading of the Synoptic Gospels. This reading is arranged in such a way that as the Lord's life and preaching unfold the teaching proper to each of these Gospels is presented.

This distribution also provides a certain coordination between the meaning of each Gospel and the progress of the liturgical year. Thus after Epiphany the readings are on the beginning of the Lord's preaching and they fit in well with Christ's baptism and the first events in which he manifests himself. The liturgical year leads quite naturally to a termination in the eschatological theme proper to the last Sundays, since the chapters of the Synoptics that precede the account of the passion treat this eschatological theme rather extensively.

After the Sixteenth Sunday in Year B, five readings are incorporated from John 6 (the discourse on the bread of life). This is the proper place for these readings because the multiplication of the loaves from John takes the place of the same account in Mark. In the semicontinuous reading of Luke for Year C, the introduction of this Gospel has been prefixed to the first text (that is, on the Third Sunday). This passage expresses the author's intention very beautifully and there seemed to be no better place for it.

### 2. Old Testament readings

106. These readings have been chosen to correspond to the gospel passages in order to avoid an excessive diversity between the readings of different Masses and above all to bring out the unity between the Old and New Testament. The relationship between the readings of the same Mass is shown by a precise choice of the headings prefixed to the individual readings.

To the degree possible, the readings were chosen in such a way that they would be short and easy to grasp. But care has been taken to ensure that many Old Testament texts of major significance would be read on Sundays. Such readings are distributed not according to a logical order but on the basis of what the gospel reading requires. Still, the treasury of the word of God will be opened up in such a way that nearly all the principal pages of the Old Testament will become familiar to those taking part in the Mass on Sundays.

### 3. Readings from the apostles

107. There is a semicontinuous reading of the Letters of Paul and James. (The Letters of Peter and John are read during the Easter and Christmas seasons.)

Because it is quite long and deals with such diverse issues, the First Letter to the Corinthians has been spread over the three years of the cycle at the beginning of Ordinary Time. It also was thought best to divide Hebrews into two parts; the first part is read in Year B and the second part in Year C.

Only readings that are short and readily grasped by the people have been chosen.

Table II at the end of this Introduction[117] indicates the distribution of letters of the apostles over the three-year cycle of the Sundays of Ordinary Time.

### C. READINGS FOR SOLEMNITIES OF THE LORD DURING ORDINARY TIME

108. On the solemnities of Holy Trinity, Corpus Christi, and the Sacred Heart, the texts chosen correspond to the principal themes of these celebrations.

The readings of the Thirty-Fourth and last Sunday of Ordinary Time celebrate Christ the King. He was prefigured by David and heralded as king amid the humiliations of his passion and cross; he reigns in the Church and will come again at the end of time.

## D. WEEKDAY READINGS

109. 1. The *gospels* are so arranged that Mark is read first (First to Ninth Week), then Matthew (Tenth to Twenty-first Week), then Luke (Twenty-second to Thirty-fourth Week). Mark 1–12 are read in their entirety, with the exception only of the two passages of Mark 6 that are read on weekdays in other seasons. From Matthew and Luke the readings comprise all the matters not contained in Mark. From all three Synoptics or from two of them, as the case may be, all those passages are read that either are distinctively presented in each Gospel or are needed for a proper understanding of its progression. Jesus' eschatological discourse as contained in its entirety in Luke is read at the end of the liturgical year.

110. 2. The *first reading* is taken in periods of weeks first from the Old then from the New Testament; the number of weeks depends on the length of the biblical books read.

Rather large sections are read from the New Testament books in order to give the substance, as it were, of each of the letters of the apostles.

From the Old Testament there is room only for select passages that, as far as possible, bring out the character of the individual books. The historical texts have been chosen in such a way as to provide an overall view of the history of salvation before the Lord's incarnation. But lengthy narratives could hardly be presented; sometimes verses have been selected that make for a reading of moderate length. In addition, the religious significance of the historical events is sometimes brought out by means of certain texts from the wisdom books that are placed as prologues or conclusions to a series of historical readings.

Nearly all the Old Testament books have found a place in the Order of Readings for weekdays in the Proper of Seasons. The only omissions are the shortest of the prophetic books (Obadiah and Zephaniah) and the poetic book (Song of Solomon). Of those narratives written to edify and requiring a rather long reading to be understood, Tobit and Ruth are included, but Esther and Judith are omitted. (Texts from these two books are assigned to Sundays and weekdays at other times of the year.)

Table III at the end of this Introduction[118] lists the way the books of the Old and the New Testament are distributed over the weekdays in Ordinary Time in the course of two years.

At the end of the liturgical year the readings are from Daniel and Revelation, the books that correspond to the eschatological character of this period.

# CHAPTER VI
## ADAPTATIONS, TRANSLATIONS, AND FORMAT
## OF THE ORDER OF READINGS

### 1. Adaptations and translations

111.   In the liturgical assembly the word of God must always be read either from the Latin texts prepared by the Holy See or from vernacular translations approved by the conferences of bishops for liturgical use, according to existing norms.[119]

112.   The Lectionary for Mass must be translated integrally in all its parts, including the Introduction. If the conference of bishops has judged it necessary and useful to add certain adaptations, these are to be incorporated after their confirmation by the Holy See.[120]

113.   The size of the Lectionary will necessitate editions in more than one volume; no particular division of the volumes is prescribed. But each volume is to contain the explanatory texts on the structure and purpose of the section it contains.

   The ancient custom is recommended of having separate books, one for the gospels and the other for the readings for the Old and the New Testament.

   It may also be useful to publish separately a Sunday lectionary, which could also contain selected excerpts from the sanctoral cycle, and a weekday lectionary. A practical basis for dividing the Sunday lectionary is the three-year cycle, so that all the readings for each year are presented in sequence.

   But there is freedom to adopt other arrangements that may be devised and seem to have pastoral advantages.

114.   The texts for the chants are always to be adjoined to the readings, but separate books containing the chants alone are permitted. It is recommended that the texts be printed with divisions into stanzas.

115.   Whenever a text consists of different parts, the typography must make this structure of the text clear. It is likewise recommended that even nonpoetic texts be printed with division into sense lines to assist the proclamation of the readings.

116.   Where there are long and short forms of a text, they are to be printed separately so that each can be read with ease. But if such a separation does not seem feasible, a way is to be found to ensure that each text can be proclaimed without mistakes.

117.   In vernacular editions the texts are not to be printed without the headings prefixed. If it seems advisable, an introductory note on the general meaning of the passage may be added to the heading. This note is to carry some distinctive symbol or is to be set in different type to show clearly that it is an optional text.[121]

118.   It would be useful for every volume to have an index of the passages of the Bible, modeled on the biblical index of the present volume.[122] This will provide

ready access to texts of the lectionaries for Mass that may be needed or helpful for specific occasions.

## 2. Format of individual readings

For each reading the present volume carries the textual reference, the heading, and the *incipit*.

### A. TEXT REFERENCES

119. The text reference (that is, chapter and verse) is always given according to the Neo-Vulgate edition, except for the psalms.[123] But a second reference according to the original text (Hebrew, Aramaic, or Greek) has been added wherever there is a discrepancy. Depending on the decrees of the competent authorities for the individual languages, vernacular versions may retain the enumeration corresponding to the version of the Bible approved for liturgical use by the same authorities. Exact references to chapter and verses, however, must always appear and may be given in the text or in the margin.

120. These references provide liturgical books with the source of the "announcement" *(inscriptio)* of the text that must be read in the celebration, but which is not printed in this volume. This "announcement" of the text will observe the following norms, but they may be altered by decree of the competent authorities on the basis of what is customary and useful for different places and languages.

121. 1. The formula to be used is always: "A *reading* from the Book of . . . ," "A *reading* from the Letter of . . . ," or "A *reading* from the Gospel of . . . ," and not: "The *beginning* of . . ." (unless this seems advisable in particular instances) or: "*Continuation* of. . . ."

122. 2. The traditionally accepted titles for books are to be retained, with the following exceptions:

a. Where there are two books with the same name, the title is to be:
The First Book, The Second Book (e.g., of Kings, of Maccabees) or The First Letter, The Second Letter.

b. The title more common in current usage is to be accepted for the following books:
I and II Samuel instead of I and II Kings; I and II Kings instead of III and IV Kings; I and II Chronicles instead of I and II Paralipomenon; Books of Ezra and Nehemiah instead of I and II Ezra.

c. The distinguishing titles for the wisdom books are: Book of Job, Book of Proverbs, Book of Ecclesiastes or Qoheleth, Song of Songs, Book of Wisdom, Book of Ecclesiasticus or Sirach.

d. For all the books that are included among the prophets in the Neo-Vulgate, the formula is to be: "A reading from the Book of Isaiah, or of Jeremiah or of Baruch" and: "A reading from the Prophecy of Ezekiel, of Daniel, of Hosea, of Malachi," even in the case of books not universally regarded as in fact prophetic.

e.  The title is to be Book of Lamentations and Letter to the Hebrews, with no mention of Jeremiah and Paul.

## B. HEADING

123.  There is a *heading* prefixed to each text, chosen carefully (usually from the words of the text itself) in order to point out the main theme of the reading and, when necessary, to make the connection between the readings of the same Mass clear.

## C. INCIPIT

124.  In this Order of Readings the first element of the *incipit* is the customary introductory phrase, "At that time," "In those days," "Brothers and Sisters," "Dearly Beloved," or "Thus says the Lord." These words are not given when the text itself provides sufficient indication of the time or the persons involved or where such phrases would not fit in with the very nature of the texts. For the individual languages, such phrases may be changed or dropped by decree of the competent authorities.

After the first words of the *incipit* the Order of Readings gives the proper *beginning* of the reading, with some words deleted or supplied for intelligibility, inasmuch as the text is separated from its context. When the text for a reading is made up of nonconsecutive verses and this has required changes in wording, these are appropriately indicated.

## D. FINAL ACCLAMATION

125.  In order to facilitate the congregation's acclamation, the words for the reader, *This is the word of the Lord,* or similar words suited to local custom, are to be printed at the end of the reading for use by the reader.

# TABLES

# TABLE I

Seasonal Table of Principal Celebrations of the Liturgical Year

| YEAR | SUNDAY CYCLE | WEEKDAY CYCLE | ASH WEDNESDAY | EASTER | ASCENSION | PENTECOST |
|------|--------------|---------------|---------------|--------|-----------|-----------|
| 1992 | C | II | 4 March | 19 April | 28 May | 7 June |
| 1993 | A | I | 24 Feb. | 11 April | 20 May | 30 May |
| 1994 | B | II | 16 Feb. | 3 April | 12 May | 22 May |
| 1995 | C | I | 1 March | 16 April | 25 May | 4 June |
| 1996 | A | II | 21 Feb. | 7 April | 16 May | 26 May |
| 1997 | B | I | 12 Feb. | 30 March | 8 May | 18 May |
| 1998 | C | II | 25 Feb. | 12 April | 21 May | 31 May |
| 1999 | A | I | 17 Feb. | 4 April | 13 May | 23 May |
| 2000 | B | II | 8 March | 23 April | 1 June | 11 June |

| WEEKS OF ORDINARY TIME | | | | |
|---|---|---|---|---|
| BEFORE LENT | | AFTER EASTER SEASON | | |
| ENDING | IN WEEK NO. | BEGINNING | IN WEEK NO. | 1ST SUNDAY OF ADVENT |
| 3 March | 8 | 8 June | 10 | 29 Nov. |
| 23 Feb. | 7 | 31 May | 9 | 28 Nov. |
| 15 Feb. | 6 | 23 May | 8 | 27 Nov. |
| 28 Feb. | 8 | 5 June | 9 | 3 Dec. |
| 20 Feb. | 7 | 27 May | 8 | 1 Dec. |
| 11 Feb. | 5 | 19 May | 7 | 30 Nov. |
| 24 Feb. | 7 | 1 June | 9 | 29 Nov. |
| 16 Feb. | 6 | 24 May | 8 | 28 Nov. |
| 7 March | 9 | 12 June | 10 | 3 Dec. |

# TABLE II

## Arrangement of the Second Reading on the Sundays of Ordinary Time

| SUNDAY | YEAR A | YEAR B | YEAR C |
|---|---|---|---|
| 2 | 1 Corinthians 1–4 | 1 Corinthians 6–11 | 1 Corinthians 12–15 |
| 3 | " | " | " |
| 4 | " | " | " |
| 5 | " | " | " |
| 6 | " | " | " |
| 7 | " | 2 Corinthians | " |
| 8 | " | " | " |
| 9 | Romans | " | Galatians |
| 10 | " | " | " |
| 11 | " | " | " |
| 12 | " | " | " |
| 13 | " | " | " |
| 14 | " | " | " |
| 15 | " | Ephesians | Colossians |
| 16 | " | " | " |
| 17 | " | " | " |
| 18 | " | " | " |
| 19 | " | " | Hebrews 11–12 |
| 20 | " | " | " |
| 21 | " | " | " |
| 22 | " | James | " |
| 23 | " | " | Philemon |
| 24 | " | " | 1 Timothy |
| 25 | Philippians | " | " |
| 26 | " | " | " |
| 27 | " | Hebrews 2–10 | 2 Timothy |
| 28 | " | " | " |
| 29 | 1 Thessalonians | " | " |
| 30 | " | " | " |
| 31 | " | " | 2 Thessalonians |
| 32 | " | " | " |
| 33 | " | " | " |

# TABLE III

## Arrangement of the First Reading on the Weekdays of Ordinary Time

| WEEK | YEAR I | YEAR II |
|:---:|:---:|:---:|
| 1 | Hebrews | 1 Samuel |
| 2 | " | " |
| 3 | " | 2 Samuel |
| 4 | " | 2 Samuel; 1 Kings 1–16 |
| 5 | Genesis 1–11 | 1 Kings 1–16 |
| 6 | " | James |
| 7 | Sirach (Ecclesiasticus) | " |
| 8 | " | 1 Peter; Jude |
| 9 | Tobit | 2 Peter; 2 Timothy |
| 10 | 2 Corinthians | 1 Kings 17–22 |
| 11 | " | 1 Kings 17–22; 2 Kings |
| 12 | Genesis 12–50 | 2 Kings; Lamentations |
| 13 | " | Amos |
| 14 | " | Hosea; Isaiah |
| 15 | Exodus | Isaiah; Micah |
| 16 | " | Micah; Jeremiah |
| 17 | Exodus; Leviticus | Jeremiah |
| 18 | Numbers; Deuteronomy | Jeremiah; Nahum; Habakkuk |
| 19 | Deuteronomy; Joshua | Ezekiel |
| 20 | Judges; Ruth | " |
| 21 | 1 Thessalonians | 2 Thessalonians; 1 Corinthians |
| 22 | 1 Thessalonians; Colossians | 1 Corinthians |
| 23 | Colossians; 1 Timothy | " |
| 24 | 1 Timothy | " |
| 25 | Ezra; Haggai; Zechariah | Proverbs, Qoheleth (Ecclesiastes) |
| 26 | Zechariah; Nehemiah; Baruch | Job |
| 27 | Jonah; Malachi; Joel | Galatians |
| 28 | Romans | Galatians; Ephesians |
| 29 | " | Ephesians |
| 30 | " | " |
| 31 | " | Ephesians; Philippians |
| 32 | Wisdom | Titus; Philemon; 2 and 3 John |
| 33 | 1 and 2 Maccabees | Revelation |
| 34 | Daniel | " |

# NOTES

1. See CSL 7, 24, 33, 35, 48, 51, 52, 56; DV 21, 25, 26; AG 6; PO 18.

2. See MQ V; EN 28, 43, 47; CTr 23, 27, 48; DC 10.

3. See EM 10; LI 2; GCD 10–12, 25; GI 9, 11, 24, 33, 60, 62, 316, 320; ID 1, 2, 3.

4. See Lectionary for Mass, Introduction (1969) nos. 1–7; decree of promulgation: AAS 61 (1969) 548–549.

5. See CSL 35, 56; EN 28, 47; DC 10, 11, 12.

6. For example, the terms, *word of God, sacred Scripture, Old and New Testament, reading(s) of the word of God, reading(s) from sacred scripture, celebration(s) of the word of God,* etc.

7. Thus the same text may be read or used for diverse reasons on diverse occasions and celebrations of the liturgical year; this has to be remembered in the homily, pastoral exegesis, and catechesis.

8. See Lk 4:16–21; 24:25–35 and 44–49.

9. In the celebration of the Mass, for example, there is *proclamation, reading,* etc. (see GI 21, 23, 95, 131, 146, 234, 235). There are also other celebrations of the word of God in the Roman Pontifical, Ritual and Liturgy of the Hours.

10. See CSL 7, 33; Mk 16:19–20; Mt 28:20.

11. See CSL 7.

12. See Heb 4:12.

13. See Augustine, *Quaestionum in Hepta-teuchum,* book 2; DV 16.

14. See Jerome, "If, as St. Paul says (1 Cor 1:24), Christ is the power of God and the wisdom of God, anyone who does not know the Scriptures does not know the power of God or his wisdom. For not to know the Scriptures is not to know Christ" (*Commentarii in Isaiam prophe-tam,* prologue); DV ZS.

15. See 2 Cor 1:20–22.

16. See CSL 10.

17. See 2 Thes 3:1.

18. See RM, opening prayers A, B and C in Mass for the Universal Church.

19. See RM, opening prayer for the Twenty-first Sunday in Ordinary Time.

20. See DV 8.

21. See Jn 14:15–17, 25–26; 15:26—16:15.

22. See PO 4.

23. See CSL 51; PO 18; DV 21; AG 6; GI 8.

24. CSL 56.

25. GI 33.

26. See LI 2; DC 10; ID 1.

27. CSL 33.

28. See LMIn 111.

29. See RM, *Ordo cantus Missae* (ed. typ., 1972), Praenotanda, 4, 6, 10.

30. See GI 11 .

31. See GI 272; LMIn 32–34.

32. See GI 35, 95.

33. See GI 82–84.

34. See GI 94, 131.

35. See RM, Order of Mass, "Liturgy of the Word: The Gospel."

36. See GI 36.

37. Paul VI, apostolic constitution, *Laudis canticum,* in *The Liturgy of the Hours;* see also CSL 24, 90; MS 39.

38. See LMIn 89–90.

39. See GI 18, 39.

40. See GI 272; LMIn 32ff.

41. See GI 39 .

42. See GI 37—39; RM, *Ordo cantus Missae,* Praenotanda, 7–9; *Graduale Romanum* (1974), Praenotanda, 7, Graduale Simple (2d ed. typ., 1975); Praenotanda, 16.

43. See CSL 52; IOe 54.

44. See GI 42.

45. See CSL 35, 2.

46. See CSL 6, 47.

47. See Paul VI, encyclical, *Mysterium fidei,* 3 Sept 1965; AG 9; EN 43.

48. See CSL 35, 2; GI 41.

49. CSL 10.

50. See CTr 48.

51. See GI 165.

52. See GI 42; EM 28.

53. See AP 6g; DMC 48.

54. See GI 42, 338; RR, *Rite of Marriage* (1969), 22, 42, 57 and *Rite of Funerals* (1969), 41, 64.

55. See GI 97.

56. See GI 139.

57. See GI 23.

58. See GI 43.

59. See GI 45.

60. See GI 99.

61. See GI 47.

62. See LMln, note 23.

63. See GI 272.

64. See SCL 122.

65. See Roman Pontifical, *Ordination of Deacons, Priests and Bishops* (1968): of deacons, 24; of deacons and priests, 21; of a deacon, 24; of a bishop, 25; of bishops, 25.

66. See LMIn 78–91.

67. See GI 318–320; 324–325.

68. See GI 313.

69. See GI 42; ID 3.

70. See GI 11.

71. See GI 68.

72. See GI 33, 47.

73. PO 4.

74. CSL 33.

75. See GI 9.

76. See CSL 7.

77. See CSL 9.

78. See Rom 1:16.

79. See DV 21.

80. Ibid.

81. See Jn 14:15–26; 15:26—16:4, 5–15.

82. See AG 6, 15; DV 26.

83. See CSL 24; GCD 25.

84. See CSL 56; ID 1.

85. See CSL 24, 35.

86. See GI 34.

87. See GI 96.

88. See GI 47, 61, 132; ID 3.

89. GI 66.

90. See MQ, no. V.

91. See ID 2, 18; DMC 22, 24, 27.

92. See GI 47, 66, 151.

93. GI 66.

94. See GI 37a, 67.

95. See GI 68.

96. See Paul VI, apostolic constitution, *Missale Romanum.*

97. See CSL 35, 51.

98. See Paul VI, apostolic constitution, *Missale Romanum:* "This is meant to provide a fuller exposition of the continuing process of the mystery of salvation as shown in the words of divine revelation."

99. See CSL 9, 33; IOe 7; CTr 23.

100. See CSL 35,4; IOe 37–38.

101. See AP 6; DMC 41–47; Paul VI, apostolic exhortation *Marialis cultus,* 2 Feb 1974, no. 12.

102. Each of the years is designated by a letter, A, B or C. The following is the procedure to determine which year is A, B, or C. The letter C designates a year whose number is divisible into three equal parts, as though the cycle had taken its beginning from the first year of the Christian era. Thus the year 1 would have been Year A; year 2, Year B; year 3, Year C, (as would years 6, 9 and 12). Thus, year 1980 was Year C; 1981, Year A; 1982, Year B; and 1983, Year C again. Each cycle runs in accord with the plan of the liturgical year, that is, it begins with the first week of Advent which falls in the preceding year of the civil calendar. The distinguishing characteristic for the years in each cycle is based in a sense on the principal note of the synoptic gospel (Matthew, Mark or Luke) used for the semicontinuous reading of Ordinary Time.

103. See GI 36–40.

104. GI 313.

105. See GI 318; ID 1.

106. For example: in Lent the continuity of the Old Testament readings corresponds to the unfolding of the history of salvation; the Sundays in Ordinary Time provide the semicontinuous reading of one of the letters of the apostles. In these cases it is right that the priest choose one or other of the readings in a systematic way over a series of Sundays so that he may set up a

coherent plan for catechesis. It is not right to read indiscriminately on one day from the Old Testament, on another from the letter of an apostle, without any orderly plan for subsequent texts.

107. See GI 319.

108. See GI 316c; CSL 51.

109. See GI 318.

110. See RR, *Rite of Penance* (1974), introduction, no. 13.

111. See GI 320.

112. See GI 313.

113. See Lectionary for Mass, nos. 173–174.

114. See Lectionary for Mass, no. 223.

115. So when there are six weeks before Lent, the seventh week begins on the Monday after Pentecost. The solemnity of the Holy Trinity replaces the Sunday of Ordinary Time.

116. When there are five weeks before Lent, the Monday after Pentecost begins with the seventh week of Ordinary Time and the sixth week is dropped.

117. See LMIn, Table II.

118. See LMIn, Table III.

119. See Consilium, instruction *De Popularibus interpretationibus conficiendis*, 25 Jan 1969: Notitiae 5 (1969) 3–12; CDW, *Epistola ad Praesides Conferentiarum Episcoporum de linguis vulgaribus in S. Liturgiam inducendis:* Notitiae 12 (1976) 300–302.

120. See LI 11; GI 325.

121. See GI 11, 29, 68a, 139.

122. See Lectionary for Mass, index of readings.

123. The references for the psalms follow the order of the *Liber Psalmorum*, Pontifical Commission for the Neo-Vulgate.

# GENERAL NORMS
## FOR THE
# LITURGICAL YEAR
## AND THE
# CALENDAR

# OVERVIEW OF *GENERAL NORMS FOR THE LITURGICAL YEAR AND THE CALENDAR*

Kevin W. Irwin

The liturgical calendar is the basis and structure on which the liturgy of the eucharist and hours are celebrated. Hence the post–Vatican II study group charged with its reform was among the very first of the committees constituted to implement the directives of the *Constitution on the Sacred Liturgy.* This study group made two full reports to the Consilium (the group charged with the entire *Constitution*'s implementation), in 1965 and 1966. Pierre Jounel was particularly influential in the study group's work and in discussions of their proposals both in the Consilium and within the Roman Curia (1967–1969).

The two unequal parts of the document *General Norms for the Liturgical Year and the Calendar (Norms)* provide a useful description of how the church experiences Christ's paschal mystery in the course of the liturgical year during seasons, the week and each day (nos. 1–47) and of how the liturgical calendar is structured according to universal and particular church usages, e.g., a diocese or a religious order (nos. 48–59).

SUNDAY

Theologically and pastorally, the key insight in the document concerns the centrality of the paschal mystery in all liturgical celebrations (no. 1). Christ's paschal mystery (obedient life, suffering, passion, resurrection and ascension) is the theological center of what is celebrated at liturgy: the "mystery of faith" when "the work of our redemption is accomplished" (prayer over the gifts, Evening Mass of the Lord's Supper). The paschal mystery is actualized in all liturgy; it is experienced in a privileged way at Sunday eucharist. This leads to the priority placed in the document on reestablishing Sunday as the "first holy day of all" (no. 4). Apart from their celebration during special seasons, Sundays are designated as "Sundays of the Year" or of "Ordinary Time" (nos. 43–44). (Here "ordinary" derives from the Latin *"ordo,"* meaning "to set in order or in relation to each other.")

Postconciliar legislation has allowed for the celebration of the eucharist on Saturday evening for Sunday or on the previous evening for feasts and days of obligation (see *Eucharisticum Mysterium,* Instruction of the Congregation for Rites, May 25, 1967, no. 28). Despite the fact that this document insists that such "vigil Masses" should not lessen the meaning of Sunday (which has been repeated in a number of subsequent documents from the Holy See and bishops' conferences), a pastoral problem has arisen in the United States where the frequenting of Saturday evening Masses has diminished a proper understanding of the theology and liturgical experience of Sunday. This is compounded when solemnities of the Lord fall on a Saturday (see *Norms,* nos. 5, 11), which often means scheduling Masses of the solemnity on Friday evening for Saturday and Masses of Sunday on Saturday evening. That the solemnities of the Epiphany, Ascension and Corpus Christi are assigned to a Sunday when not observed as holy days of obligation (see *Norms,* 7 and *Code of Canon Law,* 1246) and that the liturgy for the Commemoration of All Souls (November 2) replaces the Sunday liturgy also can derogate from the Sunday eucharist as the primary celebration of the paschal mystery.

A particularly acute pastoral problem concerns parishes with no resident priest, hence no regular celebration of Sunday eucharist, a situation provided for in the *Order for Sunday Celebrations in the Absence of a Priest.* This document asserts the essential connection between the eucharist and the Lord's Day while at the same time providing for the sad anomaly of noneucharistic worship on Sunday.

THE SEASONS

The celebration of the annual seasons in the liturgical year, i.e., Lent-Easter and Advent-Christmas, derives from the annual repetition of seasons in nature and the cosmic phenomena of solstice and equinox, darkness and light. Specifically, the time when the sun "returns" is designated as the time for Christmas, and the date for Easter is established by the date of the first full moon of spring. Thus (in the northern hemisphere) the renewal of nature in the spring is the essential context for Lent-Easter-Pentecost and the darkness of winter is the essential context for Advent-Christmas-Epiphany.

The document appropriately cites "the Easter triduum of the passion and resurrection of Christ [as] the culmination of the entire liturgical year. Thus the solemnity of Easter has the same kind of preeminence in the liturgical year that Sunday has in the week" (no. 18). The restoration of the *Rite of Christian Initiation of Adults* has helped to make the season of Lent a time of intense preparation for sacramental initiation for the elect and of renewing initiation for the baptized (nos. 27–31). The initiation of adults also makes the Easter vigil "the mother of all vigils" (from St. Augustine, as quoted in no. 21) because the paschal sacraments of baptism, confirmation and eucharist are celebrated with particular solemnity. The primacy of the Easter triduum is asserted repeatedly in the *Norms*, particularly in the accompanying "Table of Liturgical Days according to Their Order of Precedence," as is the primacy of the Easter season, completed at Pentecost (nos. 22–26).

Sacramental initiation and the renewal of baptism at Easter help to focus on a theology of the liturgical year that emphasizes how "what is present is *our* being born anew in Christ, *our* entrance into new life through this coming of God to us *now*. For as St. Leo says in his famous aphorism . . . what Christ did visibly during his earthly ministry has now passed over into sacrament *(Quod itaque Redemptionis nostri conspicuum fuit, in sacramenta transivit).* Easter is essentially about the reawakening here and now of my baptismal death and resurrection in Christ" (Robert Taft, "Toward a Theology of the Christian Feast," in *Beyond East and West* [Washington DC: Pastoral Press, 1984], 11). Hence the appropriateness of the phrase "dying you destroyed our death, rising you restored our life" (*Norms*, no. 18, from Easter Preface I and the second memorial acclamation). A more complete description of the theology underlying the Easter triduum and the principles for correct liturgical celebration are found in the *Circular Letter Concerning the Preparation and Celebration of the Easter Feasts* (1988, from the Sacred Congregation for Divine Worship, published by the United States Catholic Conference Publications Office).

The Christmas season is placed after Easter in terms of preeminence. The extension of the season to the feast of the Baptism of the Lord (Sunday after Epiphany) reestablishes this feast as an essential part of experiencing anew

Christ's "early manifestations" (no. 32). The document asserts the ancient tradition of celebrating three Masses on Christmas, at midnight, at dawn and during the day (no. 34). With the establishment of "vigil Masses" for solemnities, however, the phenomenon in many American parishes is that vast numbers celebrate the Mass of Christmas Vigil and not these Masses of "ancient tradition."

A central theological and spiritual understanding of Christmas is that the Word became flesh so that the human race could be deified in and through Christ (derived from the gospel for Christmas day, John 1:1–14). Specific reference to our experience of the divine/human interchange in the incarnation is aptly expressed in the opening prayer of Christmas Day:

> Lord God,
> we praise you for creating [humankind],
> and still more in restoring it in Christ.
> Your Son shared our human weakness:
> may we share his glory.

Another expression is found in the third Christmas preface: "Your eternal Word has taken upon himself our human weakness, giving our mortal nature immortal value." The references to the celebration of Christmas as "the beginning of our redemption" (prayer over the gifts, Christmas Vigil) and to "the child born today [as] the Savior of the world" (prayer after communion, Christmas Day) help to bring out the intrinsic connection between the incarnation and the paschal mystery.

Advent is described in the *Norms* as a time of "devout and joyful expectation" for two comings of Christ, at the incarnation and at the end of time (no. 39). The rather clear separation between these two comings seen in the Sunday lectionary for Mass (e.g., the First Sunday is highly eschatological and the Fourth Sunday concerns to events immediately prior to Jesus' birth) is not so clear in the liturgy of the hours, where antiphons at the minor hours throughout Advent concern the incarnation. Hence the confluence of Advent themes emphasizing Christ's first and second comings should be respected as central, but not necessarily totally divisible, in celebration.

## SOLEMNITIES, FEASTS AND MEMORIALS

The section dealing with "solemnities, feasts and memorials" (nos. 8–15) vastly simplifies the previous classification of liturgical feasts. Solemnities have the highest rank; their liturgical observance begins with Evening Prayer I. The two greatest solemnities, Easter and Christmas (no. 12), continue for eight days. Feasts are ranked second and their celebration begins at midnight (hence there is no proper Evening Prayer I). Memorials are either obligatory or optional; some memorials in the American sacramentary are proper to the United States.

The rearrangement of some of the dates on which memorials are celebrated (e.g., transferring the commemoration of St. Dominic from August 4 to August 8) was influenced principally by a concern for historical accuracy. Now the celebrations of saints take place most usually on the dates of their deaths (*dies natalis*) or on the dates of the transferral of their bodies to other places. The rank of obligatory memorial is given to saints of greater importance for the whole church. In the previous calendar, heavy emphasis was placed on saints of antiquity and those from the Mediterranean world. In the present universal calendar, efforts were made to include recent saints, e.g., St. Maria Goretti, and saints from other parts of the world, e.g., the Nagasaki and Korean martyrs for the Far East, the martyrs of Uganda for South Central Africa, St. Peter Chanel for Oceania, the Canadian martyrs for North America, St. Martin de Porres for South America and St. Columbanus and St. Ansgar for northern Europe. (See Annibale Bugnini, *The Reform of the Liturgy* [Collegeville: The Liturgical Press, 1990], 321.)

The invitation in the document for establishing proper calendars for a local church (no. 48) has given rise to two phenomena. First is the reemphasis on patronal observances for dioceses, regions or countries, commemorations of founders or principal patrons of religious orders or congregations, or feasts proper to an individual church (see *Norms*, no. 59). Thus the Mass formula for the Dedication of a Church (with proper prefaces) is given important emphasis both in use and in its placement as the first common Mass formula in the sacramentary. The present use of particular sacramentaries for religious orders, e.g., Franciscans and Dominicans, shows the restored emphasis placed on observances proper to religious communities.

The second phenomenon regarding local observances is the actual development of calendars proper to various regions. In the United States, this takes shape in the *Proper Calendar for the Dioceses of the United States of America* (printed in the sacramentary). Several commemorations have been added since the 1985 edition of the sacramentary; what follows is a list of all dates for which the United States calendar is different from the General Roman Calendar. Obligatory memorials are designated for:

Elizabeth Ann Seton (January 4)
John Neumann (January 5)
Kateri Tekakwitha (July 14)
Peter Claver (September 9)
Isaac Jogues, John de Brébeuf and companions (October 19)
Frances Xavier Cabrini (November 13).

Optional memorials are designated for:

André Bessette (January 6)
Katharine Drexel (March 3)
Isidore (May 15)
Junipero Serra (July 1),
Independence Day (July 4)
Jane Frances de Chantal (August 18)
Marie Rose Durocher (October 6)
Paul of the Cross (October 20)
Rose Philippine Duchesne (November 18)
Miguel Agustin Pro (November 23)
Juan Diego (December 9)

The commemoration of Our Lady of Guadalupe (December 12) is raised to the status of a feast.

The theological and liturgical legitimacy of commemorating Independence Day has been the topic of much debate, especially because the present sacramentary texts for July 4 and the prefaces for Independence Day and Other Civic Observances I and II have been criticized as being nationalistic.

The designation of memorials in the new calendar has been less successful than the emphasis placed on Sunday or on the seasons as exemplified by the fact that the majority of memorials are still of European origin and that comparatively few laypersons are commemorated.

## HOLY DAYS OF OBLIGATION

Obligatory memorials are to be distinguished from holy days of obligation (days when participation in the eucharist is required). The *Code of Canon Law* lists Sundays and the following as days of obligation: Christmas; Epiphany; Ascension; the Body and Blood of Christ; Mary, Mother of God; Immaculate Conception; Assumption; St. Joseph; Sts. Peter and Paul; and All Saints (canon 1246; see also canons 1247–1248).

The issue of days of obligation has been debated by the United States bishops with the result that Epiphany and the Body and Blood of Christ are celebrated on Sundays, and the solemnities of St. Joseph and of Sts. Peter and Paul are not days of obligation. The chief difficulty here is that while many of these days are true "holidays" in other parts of the world, they are "workdays" in America, with the result that their observance is marked only by Mass attendance rather than as religious holidays of leisure.

In 1990, the Congregation for Divine Worship emended no. 5 of the *Norms* to specify what happens when certain solemnities fall on a Sunday. Henceforth when December 8 occurs on a Sunday, the solemnity of the Immaculate Conception will be celebrated on Monday, December 9. When either the solemnity of St. Joseph (March 19) or the Annunciation (March 25) occur on a Sunday in Lent, they will be celebrated on the following Monday except when either occurs on Passion (Palm) Sunday or Easter Sunday, in which case they will be celebrated on the Monday after the Second Sunday of Easter.

## OTHER ISSUES

The invitation in the *Norms* to designate rogation days (days of fast and outdoor procession interceding for a good harvest) and ember days (nos. 45–48) has been largely unanswered in the United States. This is unfortunate, considering recent important initiatives emphasizing environmental consciousness and liturgical symbolism that derives from human productivity, beginning with the symbolism related to planting and harvesting crops (e.g., bread and wine).

Missing from the *Norms* is a clear reference to the eschatological nature of the observances of the liturgical year. The welcome paschal emphasis in the document would be deepened by an understanding that when celebrating feasts or seasons the church always yearns for their fulfillment in the "eternal day of the Lord" in the kingdom. As the prayer after the Rite of Blessing and Sprinkling with Holy Water states:

> May almighty God cleanse us of our sins,
> and through the eucharist we celebrate
> make us worthy to sit at his table
> in his heavenly kingdom.

# OUTLINE

# GENERAL NORMS FOR THE LITURGICAL YEAR AND THE CALENDAR

## CHAPTER I
## THE LITURGICAL YEAR

1.    Christ's saving work is celebrated in sacred memory by the Church on fixed days throughout the year. Each week on the day called the Lord's Day the Church commemorates the Lord's resurrection. Once a year at Easter the Church honors this resurrection and passion with the utmost solemnity. In fact through the yearly cycle the Church unfolds the entire mystery of Christ and keeps the anniversaries of the saints.

During the different seasons of the liturgical year, the Church, in accord with traditional discipline, carries out the formation of the faithful by means of devotional practices, both interior and exterior, instruction, and works of penance and mercy.[1]

2.    The principles given here may and must be applied to both the Roman Rite and all others; but the practical rules are to be taken as pertaining solely to the Roman Rite, except in matters that of their nature also affect the other rites.[2]

### TITLE I: LITURGICAL DAYS

*I. The Liturgical Day in General*

3.    Each day is made holy through the liturgical celebrations of the people of God, especially through the eucharistic sacrifice and the divine office.

The liturgical day runs from midnight to midnight, but the observance of Sunday and solemnities begins with the evening of the preceding day.

*II. Sunday*

4.    The Church celebrates the paschal mystery on the first day of the week, known as the Lord's Day or Sunday. This follows a tradition handed down from the apostles and having its origin from the day of Christ's resurrection. Thus Sunday must be ranked as the first holy day of all.[3]

5.    Because of its special importance, the Sunday celebration gives way only to solemnities or feasts of the Lord. The Sundays of the seasons of Advent, Lent, and Easter, however, take precedence over all solemnities and feasts of the Lord. Solemnities occurring on these Sundays are observed on the Saturday preceding.

6. By its nature, Sunday excludes any other celebration's being permanently assigned to that day, with these exceptions:

    a. Sunday within the octave of Christmas is the feast of the Holy Family;

    b. Sunday following 6 January is the feast of the Baptism of the Lord;

    c. Sunday after Pentecost is the solemnity of the Holy Trinity;

    d. The last Sunday in Ordinary Time is the solemnity of Christ the King.

7. In those places where the solemnities of Epiphany, Ascension, and Corpus Christi are not observed as holy days of obligation, they are assigned to a Sunday, which is then considered their proper day in the calendar. Thus:

    a. Epiphany, to the Sunday falling between 2 January and 8 January;

    b. Ascension, to the Seventh Sunday of Easter;

    c. the solemnity of Corpus Christi, to the Sunday after Trinity Sunday.

*III. Solemnities, Feasts, and Memorials*

8. As it celebrates the mystery of Christ in yearly cycle, the Church also venerates with a particular love Mary, the Mother of God, and sets before the devotion of the faithful the memory of the martyrs and other saints.[4]

9. The saints of universal significance have celebrations obligatory throughout the entire Church. Other saints either are listed in the General Calendar for optional celebration or are left to the veneration of some particular Church, region, or religious family.[5]

10. According to their importance, celebrations are distinguished from each other and named as follows: solemnities, feasts, memorials.

11. Solemnities are counted as the principal days in the calendar and their observance begins with evening prayer I of the preceding day. Some also have their own vigil Mass for use when Mass is celebrated in the evening of the preceding day.

12. The celebration of Easter and Christmas, the two greatest solemnities, continues for eight days, with each octave governed by its own rules.

13. Feasts are celebrated within the limits of the natural day and accordingly do not have evening prayer I. Exceptions are feasts of the Lord that fall on a Sunday in Ordinary Time and in the Christmas season and that replace the Sunday office.

14. Memorials are either obligatory or optional. Their observance is integrated into the celebration of the occurring weekday in accord with the norms set forth in the *General Instruction of the Roman Missal* and the *Liturgy of the Hours.*

Obligatory memorials occurring on Lenten weekdays may only be celebrated as optional memorials.

Should more than one optional memorial fall on the same day, only one may be celebrated; the others are omitted.

15. On Saturdays in Ordinary Time when there is no obligatory memorial, an optional memorial of the Blessed Virgin Mary is allowed.

*IV. Weekdays*

16. The days following Sunday are called weekdays. They are celebrated in different ways according to the importance each one has.

a. Ash Wednesday and the days of Holy Week, from Monday to Thursday inclusive, have precedence over all other celebrations.

b. The weekdays of Advent from 17 December to 24 December inclusive and all the weekdays of Lent have precedence over obligatory memorials.

c. All other weekdays give way to solemnities and feasts and are combined with memorials.

### TITLE II: THE YEARLY CYCLE

17. By means of the yearly cycle the Church celebrates the whole mystery of Christ, from his incarnation until the day of Pentecost and the expectation of his coming again.[6]

*I. Easter Triduum*

18. Christ redeemed us all and gave perfect glory to God principally through his paschal mystery: dying he destroyed our death and rising he restored our life. Therefore the Easter triduum of the passion and resurrection of Christ is the culmination of the entire liturgical year.[7] Thus the solemnity of Easter has the same kind of preeminence in the liturgical year that Sunday has in the week.[8]

19. The Easter triduum begins with the evening Mass of the Lord's Supper, reaches its high point in the Easter Vigil, and closes with evening prayer on Easter Sunday.

20. On Good Friday[9] and, if possible, also on Holy Saturday until the Easter Vigil,[10] the Easter fast is observed everywhere.

21. The Easter Vigil, during the holy night when Christ rose from the dead, ranks as the "mother of all vigils."[11] Keeping watch, the Church awaits Christ's resurrection and celebrates it in the sacraments. Accordingly, the entire celebration of this vigil should take place at night, that is, it should either begin after nightfall or end before the dawn of Sunday.

## II. Easter Season

22. The fifty days from Easter Sunday to Pentecost are celebrated in joyful exultation as one feast day, or better as one "great Sunday."[12]

These above all others are the days for the singing of the *Alleluia*.

23. The Sundays of this season rank as the paschal Sundays and, after Easter Sunday itself, are called the Second, Third, Fourth, Fifth, Sixth, and Seventh Sundays of Easter. The period of fifty sacred days ends on Pentecost Sunday.

24. The first eight days of the Easter season make up the octave of Easter and are celebrated as solemnities of the Lord.

25. On the fortieth day after Easter the Ascension is celebrated, except in places where, not being a holy day of obligation, it has been transferred to the Seventh Sunday of Easter (see no. 7).

26. The weekdays after the Ascension until the Saturday before Pentecost inclusive are a preparation for the coming of the Holy Spirit.

## III. Lent

27. Lent is a preparation for the celebration of Easter. For the Lenten liturgy disposes both catechumens and the faithful to celebrate the paschal mystery: catechumens, through the several stages of Christian initiation; the faithful, through reminders of their own baptism and through penitential practices.[13]

28. Lent runs from Ash Wednesday until the Mass of the Lord's Supper exclusive.

The *Alleluia* is not used from the beginning of Lent until the Easter Vigil.

29. On Ash Wednesday, a universal day of fast,[14] ashes are distributed.

30. The Sundays of this season are called the First, Second, Third, Fourth, and Fifth Sundays of Lent. The Sixth Sunday, which marks the beginning of Holy Week, is called Passion Sunday (Palm Sunday).

31. Holy Week has as its purpose the remembrance of Christ's passion, beginning with his Messianic entrance into Jerusalem.

At the chrism Mass on Holy Thursday morning the bishop, concelebrating Mass with his body of priests, blesses the oils and consecrates the chrism.

## IV. Christmas Season

32. Next to the yearly celebration of the paschal mystery, the Church holds most sacred the memorial of Christ's birth and early manifestations. This is the purpose of the Christmas season.

33. The Christmas season runs from evening prayer I of Christmas until the Sunday after Epiphany or after 6 January, inclusive.

34.   The Mass of the vigil of Christmas is used in the evening of 24 December, either before or after evening prayer I.

On Christmas itself, following an ancient tradition of Rome, three Masses may be celebrated: namely, the Mass at Midnight, the Mass at Dawn, and the Mass during the Day.

35.   Christmas has its own octave, arranged as follows:

a. Sunday within the octave is the feast of the Holy Family;

b. 26 December is the feast of Saint Stephen, First Martyr;

c. 27 December is the feast of Saint John, Apostle and Evangelist;

d. 28 December is the feast of the Holy Innocents;

e. 29, 30, and 31 December are days within the octave;

f. 1 January, the octave day of Christmas, is the solemnity of Mary, Mother of God. It also recalls the conferral of the holy Name of Jesus.

36.   The Sunday falling between 2 January and 5 January is the Second Sunday after Christmas.

37.   Epiphany is celebrated on 6 January, unless (where it is not observed as a holy day of obligation) it has been assigned to the Sunday occurring between 2 January and 8 January (see no. 7).

38.   The Sunday falling after 6 January is the feast of the Baptism of the Lord.

## V. Advent

39.   Advent has a twofold character: as a season to prepare for Christmas when Christ's first coming to us is remembered; as a season when that remembrance directs the mind and heart to await Christ's Second Coming at the end of time. Advent is thus a period for devout and joyful expectation.

40.   Advent begins with evening prayer I of the Sunday falling on or closest to 30 November and ends before evening prayer I of Christmas.

41.   The Sundays of this season are named the First, Second, Third, and Fourth Sundays of Advent.

42.   The weekdays from 17 December to 24 December inclusive serve to prepare more directly for the Lord's birth.

## VI. Ordinary Time

43.   Apart from those seasons having their own distinctive character, thirty-three or thirty-four weeks remain in the yearly cycle that do not celebrate a specific aspect of the mystery of Christ. Rather, especially on the Sundays, they are devoted to the mystery of Christ in all its aspects. This period is known as Ordinary Time.

44. Ordinary Time begins on Monday after the Sunday following 6 January and continues until Tuesday before Ash Wednesday inclusive. It begins again on Monday after Pentecost and ends before evening prayer I of the First Sunday of Advent.

This is also the reason for the series of liturgical texts found in both the Roman Missal and *The Liturgy of the Hours* (vols. III–IV), for Sundays and weekdays in this season.

### VII. Rogation and Ember Days

45. On rogation and ember days the practice of the Church is to offer prayers to the Lord for the needs of all people, especially for the productivity of the earth and for human labor, and to give him public thanks.

46. In order to adapt the rogation and ember days to various regions and the different needs of the people, the conference of bishops should arrange the time and plan of their celebration.

Consequently, the competent authority should lay down norms, in view of local conditions, on extending such celebrations over one or several days and on repeating them during the year.

47. On each day of these celebrations the Mass should be one of the votive Masses for various needs and occasions that is best suited to the intentions of the petitioners.

# CHAPTER II
# THE CALENDAR
## TITLE I: CALENDAR AND CELEBRATIONS TO BE ENTERED

48. The arrangement for celebrating the liturgical year is governed by the calendar: the General Calendar, for use in the entire Roman Rite, or a particular calendar, for use in a particular Church or in families of religious.

49. In the General Calendar the entire cycle of celebrations is entered: celebrations of the mystery of salvation as found in the Proper of Seasons, of those saints having universal significance who must therefore be celebrated by everyone or of saints who show the universality and continuity of holiness within the people of God.

Particular calendars have more specialized celebrations, arranged to harmonize with the general cycle.[1] The individual Churches or families of religious should show a special honor to those saints who are properly their own.

Particular calendars, drawn up by the competent authority, must be approved by the Apostolic See.

50. The drawing up of a particular calendar is to be guided by the following considerations:

a. The Proper of Seasons (that is, the cycle of seasons, solemnities, and feasts that unfold and honor the mystery of redemption during the liturgical year) must be kept intact and retain its rightful preeminence over particular celebrations.

b. Particular celebrations must be coordinated harmoniously with universal celebrations, with care for the rank and precedence indicated for each in the Table of Liturgical Days. Lest particular calendars be enlarged disproportionately, individual saints may have only one feast in the liturgical year. For persuasive pastoral reasons there may be another celebration in the form of an optional memorial marking the transfer or discovery of the bodies of patrons or founders of Churches or of families of religious.

c. Feasts granted by indult may not duplicate other celebrations already contained in the cycle of the mystery of salvation, nor may they be multiplied out of proportion.

51. Although it is reasonable for each diocese to have its own calendar and propers for the Mass and office, there is no reason why entire provinces, regions, countries, or even larger areas may not have common calendars and propers, prepared with the cooperation of all the parties involved.

This principle may also be followed in the case of the calendars for several provinces of religious within the same civil territory.

52. A particular calendar is prepared by inserting in the General Calendar special solemnities, feasts, and memorials proper to that calendar:

a. in a diocesan calendar, in addition to celebrations of its patrons and the dedication of the cathedral, the saints and the blessed who bear some special connection with that diocese, for example, as their birthplace, residence over a long period, or place of death;

b. in the calendar of religious, besides celebrations of their title, founder, or patron, those saints and blesseds who were members of that religious family or had some special relationship with it;

c. in a calendar for individual churches, celebrations proper to a diocese or religious community, those celebrations that are proper to that church and are listed in the Table of Liturgical Days and also the saints who are buried in that church. Members of religious communities should join with the community of the local Church in celebrating the anniversary of the dedication of the cathedral and the principal patrons of the place and of the larger region where they live.

53. When a diocese or religious family has the distinction of having many saints and blessed, care must be taken not to overload the calendar of the entire diocese or institute. Consequently:

a. The first measure that can be taken is to have a common feast of all the saints and the blessed of a given diocese or religious family or of some category.

b. Only the saints and blessed of particular significance for an entire diocese or religious family may be entered in the calendar with an individual celebration.

c. The other saints or blessed are to be celebrated only in those places with which they have closer ties or where their bodies are buried.

54. Proper celebrations should be entered in the calendar as obligatory or optional memorials, unless other provisions have been made for them in the Table of Liturgical Days or there are special historical or pastoral reasons. But there is no reason why some celebrations may not be observed with greater solemnity in some places than in the rest of the diocese or religious community.

55. Celebrations entered in a particular calendar must be observed by all who are bound to follow that calendar. Only with the approval of the Apostolic See may celebrations be removed from a calendar or changed in rank.

## TITLE II: THE PROPER DATE FOR CELEBRATIONS

56. The Church's practice has been to celebrate the saints on the date of their death ("birthday"), a practice it would be well to follow when entering proper celebrations in particular calendars.

Even though proper celebrations have special importance for individual local Churches or religious families, it is of great advantage that there be as much unity as possible in the observance of solemnities, feasts, and obligatory memorials listed in the General Calendar.

In entering proper celebrations in a particular calendar, therefore, the following are to be observed.

a. Celebrations listed in the General Calendar are to be entered on the same date in a particular calendar, with a change in rank of celebration if necessary.

This also applies to diocesan or religious calendars when celebrations proper to an individual church alone are added.

b. Celebrations for saints not included in the General Calendar should be assigned to the date of their death. If the date of death is not known, the celebrations should be assigned to a date associated with the saint on some other grounds, such as the date of ordination or of the discovery or transfer of the saint's body; otherwise it is celebrated on a date unimpeded by other celebrations in that particular calendar.

c. If the date of death or other appropriate date is impeded in the General Calendar or in a particular calendar by another obligatory celebration, even of lower rank, the celebration should be assigned to the closest date not so impeded.

d. If, however, it is a question of celebrations that cannot be transferred to another date because of pastoral reasons, the impeding celebration should itself be transferred.

e. Other celebrations, called feasts granted by indult, should be entered on a date more pastorally appropriate.

f. The cycle of the liturgical year should stand out with its full preeminence, but at the same time the celebration of the saints should not be permanently impeded. Therefore, dates that most of the time fall during Lent and the octave of Easter, as well as the weekdays between 17 December and 31 December, should remain free of any particular celebration, unless it is a question of optional memorials, feasts found in the Table of Liturgical Days under no. 8 a, b, c, d, or solemnities that cannot be transferred to another season.

The solemnity of Saint Joseph (19 March), except where it is observed as a holy day of obligation, may be transferred by the conference of bishops to another day outside Lent.

57. If some saints or blessed are listed in the calendar on the same date, they are always celebrated together whenever they are of equal rank, even though one or more of them may be more proper to that calendar. If one or other of these saints or blessed is to be celebrated with a higher rank, that office alone is observed and the others are omitted, unless it is appropriate to assign them to another date in the form of an obligatory memorial.

58. For the pastoral advantage of the people, it is permissible to observe on the Sundays in Ordinary Time those celebrations that fall during the week and have special appeal to the devotion of the faithful, provided the celebrations take precedence over these Sundays in the Table of Liturgical Days. The Mass for such celebrations may be used at all the Masses at which a congregation is present.

59. Precedence among liturgical days relative to the celebration is governed solely by the following table.


TABLE OF LITURGICAL DAYS
ACCORDING TO THEIR ORDER OF PRECEDENCE

I

1. Easter triduum of the Lord's passion and resurrection.

2. Christmas, Epiphany, Ascension, and Pentecost.
Sundays of Advent, Lent, and the Easter season.
Ash Wednesday.
Weekdays of Holy Week from Monday to Thursday inclusive.
Days within the octave of Easter.

3. Solemnities of the Lord, the Blessed Virgin Mary, and saints listed in the General Calendar.
All Souls.

4. Proper solemnities, namely:

    a. Solemnity of the principal patron of the place, that is, the city or state.

    b. Solemnity of the dedication of a particular church and the anniversary.

    c. Solemnity of the title of a particular church.

    d. Solemnity of the title, or of the founder, or of the principal patron of a religious order or congregation.

## II

5. Feasts of the Lord in the General Calendar.

6. Sundays of the Christmas season and Sundays in Ordinary Time.

7. Feasts of the Blessed Virgin Mary and of the saints in the General Calendar.

8. Proper feasts, namely:

    a. Feast of the principal patron of the diocese.

    b. Feast of the anniversary of the dedication of the cathedral.

    c. Feast of the principal patron of a region or province, or a country, or of a wider territory.

    d. Feast of the title, founder, or principal patron of an order or congregation and of a religious province, without prejudice to the directives in no. 4.

    e. Other feasts proper to an individual church.

    f. Other feasts listed in the calendar of a diocese or of a religious order or congregation.

9. Weekdays of Advent from 17 December to 24 December inclusive.
Days within the octave of Christmas.
Weekdays of Lent.

## III

10. Obligatory memorials in the General Calendar.

11. Proper obligatory memorials, namely:

    a. Memorial of a secondary patron of the place, diocese, region, or province, country or wider territory, or of an order or congregation and of a religious province.

    b. Obligatory memorials listed in the calendar of a diocese, or of an order or congregation.

12. Optional memorials; but these may be celebrated even on the days listed in no. 9, in the special manner described by the General Instruction of the Roman Missal and of the Liturgy of the Hours.

In the same manner obligatory memorials may be celebrated as optional memorials if they happen to fall on the Lenten weekdays.

13. Weekdays of Advent up to 16 December inclusive.

Weekdays of the Christmas season from 2 January until the Saturday after Epiphany.

Weekdays of the Easter season from Monday after the octave of Easter until the Saturday before Pentecost inclusive.

Weekdays in Ordinary Time.

---

60. If several celebrations fall on the same day, the one that holds the highest rank according to the preceding Table of Liturgical Days is observed. But a solemnity impeded by a liturgical day that takes precedence over it should be transferred to the closest day not listed in nos. 1–8 in the table of the precedence; the rule of no. 5 remains in effect. Other celebrations are omitted that year.

61. If the same day were to call for celebration of evening prayer of that day's office and evening prayer I of the following day, evening prayer of the day with the higher rank in the Table of Liturgical Days takes precedence; in cases of equal rank, evening prayer of the actual day takes precedence.

# NOTES

## CHAPTER I

1. See CSL 102–105.

2. See CSL 5.

3. See CSL 106.

4. See CSL 103–104.

5. See CSL 111 .

6. See CSL 102.

7. See CSL 5.

8. See CSL 106.

9. See Paul VI, apostolic constitution, *Paenitemini*, 17 Feb 1966, II, §3.

10. See CSL 110.

11. Augustine, Sermo 219.

12. Athanasius, *Epist. fest.* 1.

13. See CSL 109.

14. See *Paenitemini*, 11, §3.

## CHAPTER II

1. See CDW, instruction, *Calendaria particularia*, 24 June 1970.

# CEREMONIAL
## OF
# BISHOPS

# OVERVIEW OF
# THE *CEREMONIAL OF BISHOPS*

G. Thomas Ryan

The *Ceremonial of Bishops* was published by the Congregation for Divine Worship after its approval by John Paul II in 1984. After its translation by the International Commission on English in the Liturgy, it was published by The Liturgical Press in 1989.

The current *Ceremonial* follows the tradition of the *Ordines Romani*, which collated norms for liturgies celebrated by the bishop of Rome as early as the seventh century. In 1600, a *Ceremoniale Episcoporum* was published by Clement VIII, collecting the Tridentine revisions of rites. That *Ceremoniale* evolved through various regional editions as the ritual reforms were received and were given particular shape in different parts of Europe. The latest edition, used through Vatican II, was published in 1886 by Leo XIII.

As the liturgical books were revised after Vatican II, work began on a new ceremonial volume that would outline the shape of these rites as celebrated by bishops. Its preparation took more than 20 years. The liturgical rites and the *Code of Canon Law* had to be revised first. Meanwhile, Vatican experts knew that many deemed such a ceremonial to be either useless or harmful. The various drafting groups, animated by sensitive liturgists (for example, A. - G. Martimort), responded to the reforms and the apprehensions, holding to their vision that a book collating ceremonial patterns would be a positive contribution to the life of local churches. The principles enunciated in the final edition are so important and so pervasive that the book turns out to be enormously useful in all Catholic communities, no matter how seldom a bishop visits.

## OVERVIEW OF THE *CEREMONIAL*

As noted in the decree accompanying the *Ceremonial*, this is not a liturgical book in the proper sense, for it is not used during actual celebrations. This document is to be used in the various stages of preparing a liturgical event.

The four chapters in Part I are reprinted in large part in this volume for they summarize many of the principles of good liturgy that we have come to learn over the past decades. The chapters begin with a vision of what a bishop is and how the liturgies at which he presides relate to all other actions of churches (nos. 1–17). Far from being occasions for extra pomp, these liturgies express and promote the real life of a local church and stand as shining examples of the full and active participation of all (no. 12).

The rest of the *Ceremonial* is divided according to the various rites of the church. The fairly exhaustive list of events and reformed rites makes the *Ceremonial* a useful review of the changes effected over the past 25 years:

—Part II, on the Mass, prescinds from language about surrounding the bishop with extra solemnity or signs of rank. Rather, it sees the Mass with a bishop as most expressive of the life and participation of an entire local church.

—Part III, on the Liturgy of the Hours, contains much information for parishes and a strong impetus for all to foster its frequent communal celebration (no. 190).

—Part IV, on various events in the liturgical year, contains admirable summaries of each season and many practical ideas for parishes. Several of the summary paragraphs are reprinted here. In the full document, all are followed by ceremonial details.

—Parts V and VI, on sacraments and sacramentals, describe the shared actions of just about every other rite (23 chapters on such diverse events as funerals, the blessing of a new cross for public veneration, and eucharistic exposition). The selections excerpted in this volume show how each of the chapters on sacraments and sacramentals is laid out—introductory paragraph; any notes regarding time, place or physical requisites; and a description of the rite. While the *Ceremonial* treats these topics in relation to the bishop's role, the insights are applicable to every parish.

—Parts VII and VIII contain notes on special days in the life of a bishop and on liturgical celebrations related to solemn acts of episcopal governance (see nos. 1177–1184 for suggestions for the pastoral visitation of bishops).

FIVE CONTRIBUTIONS MADE BY THE *CEREMONIAL*

### The Importance of Ceremony

The decades of liturgical renewal and ritual reforms have been marked by great and welcome attention to many aspects of the liturgy: Homiletics, the translation and composition of texts, music, interior design and architectural renovations often receive appropriate support. Less attention has been given to ceremony, to the right and orderly progression of processions, to the value of incensations and proper posture. Yet the life and health of local churches needs just as much attention to fully participatory ceremony as to singing. Time spent planning for gestures and movements need not lead to a "spectacle," but to a shared and ordered common action. Even the word "ceremonial" is somewhat forbidden, so great is the fear of many that we might be returning to a mindless repetition of meaningless gestures.

The liturgy is not just shared words and music. It is shared action, and the prospect of performing an act together necessitates common understandings about how we will do it. If all will bow or go in procession, then parents must be able to pass on to their children, and catechists and assemblies to the neophytes, how this church bows and moves in procession. Unless we want the liturgy to be private and domestic, we need commonly understood and regularly followed "rubrics" for common action. As noted by Aidan Kavanagh (*Elements of Rite* [New York: Pueblo, 1982], p. 3), rubrics are "helpful in securing a recognizable standard of usage deemed appropriate in worshiping assemblies enjoying each other's communion."

The ceremonial notes, grouped under general headings such as "signs of reverence" in chapter 4 of Part I, and scattered throughout the norms for the various feasts and rites, make this initial and necessary contribution to the church: Common participation in action is at least as important as common singing and shared texts.

Because this book was issued after all of the liturgical books, it consciously reviews the reforms. Certain modifications are made to various rites and both the decree and the preface of the *Ceremonial* call for these changes to take precedence. The changes generally are minor, bringing uniformity to rubrics prepared for various rites over a ten-year period. In some cases, the structure of the rites has been altered. One example of these slight but useful revisions is that the presider's hands now are to be outstretched (as at every other vocalization of collects) for the opening prayer at the Celebration of the Lord's Passion (no. 317).

The comprehensive review following the promulgation of all the liturgical books has allowed the *Ceremonial* to press for other advances. The encouragement of the full use of processions—for bringing a body to the church (no. 825ff.), for welcoming the bride and groom at the church's door (no. 602), for engaging the entire assembly in the blessing of candles (no. 242ff.), for bringing all the mourners to the cemetery (no. 399ff.)—is but one of the fruits of 25 years of reform. Still other contributions include reinvigorated traditions: the chanting of movable feasts on Epiphany (no. 240), penitential processions in Lent (no. 261), the removal of shoes for the veneration of the cross (no. 322) and the solemn bringing of flowers to the sanctuary during the Easter Vigil (no. 48).

## The Dignity and Customs of Particular Churches

The *Ceremonial* recognizes that the "traditions and requirements proper to each place can be retained" (Decree). As long as local customs are compatible with the reforms of Vatican II, they are encouraged by this book. This is but one reflection of the crucial presupposition that Christ's church is truly present in each local church (no. 1). Individual churches are far more than "branch offices" of Rome, far more than administrative or intentional or chance gatherings. In all of its chapters and in all of its prescriptions, the *Ceremonial* is careful to foster this awareness. Particular churches are a gift from God and their individual lights manifest and strengthen the universal church (nos. 2–4). Would that all the administrative departments of the Vatican grasped fully this liturgical vision of local churches!

## The Interrelationship of Ministries with the Bishop

Chapter 2 of Part I (nos. 18–41) is as fine a summary of the ministries reinvigorated by the recent reforms as one can find in any official document. Particularly noteworthy, because they are underplayed elsewhere, are the descriptions of the irreplaceable roles played by psalmists (no. 33), masters of ceremonies (nos. 34–36) and sacristans (nos. 37–38). The role of "chaplains" to bishops is not mentioned, but deacons are described as the assistants to bishops and as the ministers who facilitate the full participation of the assembly (see also no. 122).

The ministry of presiding exercised by bishops naturally receives fuller treatment. Pointless singularity and the needless multiplication of honors paid to the bishop are to be avoided. The reason for a bishop's presidership is not to add outward solemnity to a rite, but to allow the celebration to be a fuller manifestation of the entire local church. In this way, with ministries and leadership flowing from the nature of the local church, the rites led by a bishop should stand as models for the full participation and broad exercise of ministries demanded by all Roman rite liturgies.

### Advancing the Cause of Liturgical Architecture

Chapter 3 of Part I describes the cathedral church and, by implication, all parish churches. The paragraphs (nos. 42–54) gather the norms found in the praenotanda of the various rites found under the heading "Place of Celebration" and, in that review, advance the cause of appropriate architecture. Interior design, the disposition of sacred furnishings and the overall architecture of a church complex never are neutral matters. They make positive or negative contributions to the proper unfolding of the rites, to the full participation of all in the assembly. Of particular interest are the paragraph calling for the removal of any reserved eucharist if for some reason the tabernacle still is located in the eucharistic action hall (no. 49), the section describing the distinction between a vesting room and a sacristy (no. 53) and the clear call for a gathering place outside the eucharistic celebration hall where all the preparatory rites can unfold. These rites include the blessings of candles and palms and a variety of welcoming and preparatory rites—for catechumens, for infants to be baptized, for bridal parties, for the remains of deceased parishioners (no. 54).

## THE RECEPTION OF THIS DOCUMENT

The 1989 publication of the *Ceremonial* in this country was heralded by a publication of the Secretariat of the Bishops' Committee on the Liturgy (*The Bishop and the Liturgy* [Washington: USCC, 1986]); by an extraordinary convening of liturgists, masters of ceremonies and bishops; and by various articles in liturgical journals (see Peter Scagnelli, "Grace, Simplicity and Order: The Ceremonial of Bishops," in *Liturgy 90*, May/June, 1990). All of these praised the book and outlined its implications for all liturgies in the Catholic tradition.

Yet these positive recommendations all are marked by a fair amount of defensiveness. This tone was set from the start of the *Ceremonial* revision process right after Vatican II. As drafts were prepared, opposition and scorn were prevalent. It seems that the problems too often associated with the old pontifical ceremonies will not be forgotten by the middle-aged generation in positions of national and local leadership.

Commentators on the history of liturgical renewal commonly sketch out two periods in the liturgical reform since 1965: the revision of the books (through the 1970s) and the appropriation of these into local communities since then. A fuller analysis might add a third period, a most ungracious period of attention to the "margins." This gives voice to the experience of many—that the 1980s were not just a time of appropriation of the reforms, but that the lion's share of attention was given to people at the margins of reform. *Inestimabile Donum* began the decade with a list of abuses, and the following years were filled with official reactions and warnings in two extremes: the "pious," from Econe to Bayside who denied the orthodoxy of Roman reforms, and the "educated," from university chapel to suburban parish who went far beyond the official books. However few the Catholics were at the extreme positions, those in the middle tended to favor or excuse one of the extremes. Everyone had something to fear from a new *Ceremonial:* Those upset at the participation fostered by the reforms feared that this book would press bishops to model the reforms (it does); those who have gone so far as to consider the Roman rite books optional knew that this book would call all to a recognizable standard of behavior (it does).

The drafters of the *Ceremonial* accepted neither of these biases. They held to the terms and advances of the liturgical books that they were collating. Perhaps the apologetic nature of most recent introductions to the *Ceremonial*, the painful memories they try to answer and the careful language of the book itself are the best assurance we have that the worst excesses are over. Meanwhile, every lover of good liturgy, every minister responsible for promoting the full participation of all would do well to see more than the apologies and corrections. This volume is full of strategic advances, pastoral insight and practical detail.

# OUTLINE

*Parts of these sections are reproduced in this volume. For the complete texts,
refer to the *Ceremonial of Bishops.*

# CEREMONIAL OF BISHOPS

The following sections have been excerpted from the *Ceremonial of Bishops:* most of Part I, containing general considerations; from Part IV, on the liturgical year, one paragraph from the description of each season or celebration; from Parts V, VI and VIII, one chapter from each as an example. See the *Ceremonial* itself for further treatment of all the topics discussed here.

# PART I
## GENERAL CONSIDERATIONS

### CHAPTER 1
### CHARACTER AND IMPORTANCE OF A LITURGY AT WHICH THE BISHOP PRESIDES

#### I. DIGNITY OF THE PARTICULAR CHURCHES

1.  "The diocese forms that part of the people of God entrusted to the pastoral care of the bishop with the assistance of the presbyterate. In allegiance to its pastor and by him gathered together in the Holy Spirit through the Gospel and the eucharist, the diocese stands as a particular Church, in which Christ's one, holy, catholic, and apostolic Church is present and at work."[1] Indeed, Christ is present, since by his power the Church is gathered together in unity.[2] As Saint Ignatius of Antioch has truly written: "Just as where Christ Jesus is, there also is the Catholic Church, so also where the bishop is, there also should be the whole assembly of his people."[3]

2.  Hence the dignity of the Church of Christ is embodied in the particular Churches. Each such Church is not simply a group of people who on their own choose to band together for some common endeavor; rather each Church is a gift that comes down from the Father of lights. Nor are the particular Churches to be regarded merely as administrative divisions of the people of God. In their own proper way they contain and manifest the nature of the universal Church, which issued from the side of Christ crucified, which lives and grows through the eucharist, which is espoused to Christ, and which, as their mother, cares for all the faithful. The particular Churches "in their own locality are the new people called by God in the Holy Spirit and in great fullness (see 1 Thessalonians 1:5)."[4]

3.  But, as the Council also teaches, there is no lawful assembly of the faithful, no community of the altar except under the sacred ministry of the bishop.[5] The congregation making up the particular Church is situated and has its life in the many individual assemblies of the faithful, over which the bishop places his

presbyters, in order that under his authority they may sanctify and guide the portion of the Lord's flock that is assigned to them.[6]

4.    Just as the universal Church is present and manifested in the particular Churches,[7] so too each particular Church contributes its own distinctive gifts to the other Churches and to the Church as a whole, "so that from their sharing of gifts with one another and their common effort in unity toward perfection, the church achieves growth as a whole and in its particular parts."[8]

## II. THE BISHOP AS FOUNDATION AND SIGN OF COMMUNION IN THE PARTICULAR CHURCH

5.    As Christ's vicar and representative, marked with the fullness of the sacrament of orders, the bishop leads the particular Church in communion with the pope and under his authority.[9]

"Placed there by the Holy Spirit, bishops are the successors of the apostles as shepherds of souls, . . . for Christ gave the apostles and their successors the mandate and the power to teach all nations and to sanctify and to shepherd their people in truth. By the Holy Spirit who has been given to them, therefore, bishops have been made true and authentic teachers of the faith, high priests, and pastors."[10]

6.    Through the preaching of the Gospel and in the power of the Spirit the bishop calls men and women to faith or confirms them in the faith they already have, and he proclaims to them the mystery of Christ in its entirety.[11]

7.    The bishop's authority regulates the orderly and effective celebration of the sacraments and through them he sanctifies the faithful. He supervises the bestowal of baptism, since it brings with it a share in the royal priesthood of Christ. He is the primary minister of confirmation, he alone confers the sacrament of holy orders, and he oversees the penitential discipline in his diocese. He regulates every lawful celebration of the eucharist, from which the Church continually receives life and growth. He never ceases to exhort and to instruct his people to fulfill their part in the liturgy with faith and reverence, and especially in the eucharistic sacrifice.[12]

8.    In the person of the bishop, with the presbyters gathered round him, the Lord Jesus Christ, the High Priest, is present in the midst of the faithful. Seated at the right hand of the Father, Christ is not absent from the gathering of his high priests. They have been chosen to feed the Lord's flock and they are Christ's ministers and the stewards of the mysteries of God.[13] Therefore, "the bishop is to be looked on as the high priest of his flock, the faithful's life in Christ in some way deriving from and depending on him."[14]

9.    The bishop is "the steward of the grace of the supreme priesthood."[15] On him depend both presbyters and deacons in the exercise of their orders. Presbyters, appointed to be prudent co-workers of the order of bishops, are themselves consecrated as true priests of the New Testament; deacons serve as ministers ordained to service for the people of God in communion with the bishop and his

presbyters. The bishop himself is the chief steward of the mysteries of God and the overseer, promoter, and guardian of all liturgical life in the particular Church entrusted to his care.[16] To him "is committed the office of offering to the divine majesty the worship of Christian religion and administering it in accordance with the Lord's commandments and the Church's laws, as further specified by his particular judgment for his diocese."[17]

10.   The bishop rules the particular Church entrusted to him by counsel, persuasion, and example, but also by the authority and sacred power that he received through his ordination as bishop,[18] which he uses only for the building up of his flock in truth and holiness. "The faithful should cling to the bishop as the Church clings to Jesus Christ and as Jesus Christ clings to the Father, so that through such unity there may be harmony in everything and so that everything may conspire to the glory of God."[19]

## III. IMPORTANCE OF A LITURGY AT WHICH THE BISHOP PRESIDES

11.   The office of bishop as teacher, sanctifier, and pastor of his Church shines forth most clearly in a liturgy that he celebrates with his people.

"Therefore all should hold in great esteem the liturgical life of the diocese centered around the bishop, especially in his cathedral church; they must be convinced that the preeminent manifestation of the Church is present in the full, active participation of all God's holy people in these liturgical celebrations, especially in the same eucharist, in a single prayer, at one altar at which the bishop presides, surrounded by his college of presbyters and by his ministers."[20]

12.   Hence liturgical celebrations in which the bishop presides manifest the mystery of the Church as that mystery involves Christ's presence; such celebrations, then, are not a mere display of ceremony.

These celebrations should also serve as a model for the entire diocese and be shining examples of active participation by the people. The whole gathered community should thus take part through song, dialogue, prayerful silence, and attentiveness and by sharing in the sacraments.

13.   Provision should be made at appointed times and on the major dates of the liturgical year for the special manifestation of the particular Church that such a celebration means. The faithful from different areas of the diocese should be invited to gather and, as far as possible, the presbyters should join them. To encourage and make more convenient gatherings of the faithful and the presbyters, arrangement should be made for gatherings of this kind at different times in the various parts of the diocese.

14.   These gatherings should be occasions for the faithful to grow in their love for the entire Church and to heighten their desire to serve the Gospel and their neighbor.

## IV. THE BISHOP'S FULFILLMENT OF THE
## OFFICE OF PREACHING

15.    Among the principal duties of a bishop the preaching of the Gospel is preeminent. The bishop as herald of the faith leads new followers to Christ. As their authentic teacher, that is, one invested with the authority of Christ, he proclaims to the people entrusted to him the truths of faith they are to believe and to live by. Under the light of the Holy Spirit the bishop explains the teachings of faith, bringing forth from the treasure-house of revelation new things and old. He works to make faith yield its harvest and, like the good shepherd, he is vigilant in protecting his people from the threat of error.[21]

The liturgy is one of the ways in which the bishop discharges this responsibility: he preaches the homily at celebrations of the eucharist, celebrations of the word of God and, as occasion suggests, celebrations of morning and evening prayer; also when he imparts catechesis and in his introductions, invitations, or commentary during celebrations of the sacraments and sacramentals.

16.    This preaching "should draw its content mainly from scriptural and liturgical sources, being a proclamation of God's wonderful works in the history of salvation, the mystery of Christ, ever present and active within us, especially in the celebration of the liturgy."[22]

17.    Since the office of preaching is proper to the bishop, so that other ordained ministers fulfill this office only in his name, he should preach the homily himself whenever he presides at a celebration of the liturgy. Unless he decides that some other way is preferable, the bishop should preach while seated at the chair, wearing the miter and holding the pastoral staff.

# CHAPTER 2
# OFFICE AND MINISTRIES IN THE LITURGY OF BISHOPS

18.    "Any community of the altar, under the sacred ministry of the bishop, stands out clearly as a symbol of that charity and 'unity of the Mystical Body, without which there can be no salvation.' "[23]

Thus it is very fitting that when the bishop, who is marked by the fullness of the sacrament of orders, is present at a liturgical celebration in which a congregation takes part, he personally preside. The reason for this is not to give added outward solemnity to the rite, but to make the celebration a more striking sign of the mystery of the Church.

For the same reason it is fitting that the bishop associate presbyters with himself as concelebrants.

When a bishop presides at the eucharist but is not the celebrant, he does everything in the liturgy of the word that belongs to the celebrant and he concludes the Mass with the rite of dismissal,[24] following the provisions given in nos. 176–185.

19.   In every liturgical assembly, and especially one at which the bishop presides, all those present have the right and the duty to carry out their parts in the different ways corresponding to their differences in order and office. Each one, therefore, minister or layperson, should do all of, but only, those parts which pertain to that office by the nature of the rite and the principles of liturgy.[25] This way of celebration manifests the Church in its variety of orders and ministries as a body whose individual members form a unity.[26]

*Presbyters*

20.   Even though they do not possess the fullness of priesthood that belongs to the episcopate and in the exercise of their power depend upon the bishop, presbyters are nevertheless joined to the bishop by the bond of priestly dignity.

Presbyters, prudent co-workers with the episcopal order, its aid and instrument, called to serve the people of God, constitute one college of prebysters with their bishop and, under the bishop's authority, sanctify and govern that portion of the Lord's flock entrusted to them.[27]

21.   It is strongly recommended that in liturgical celebrations the bishop should have presbyters to assist him. In a eucharistic celebration presided over by the bishop, presbyters should concelebrate with him so that the mystery of the unity of the Church may be made manifest through the eucharistic celebration and so that the presbyters may be seen by the entire community to be the presbyterate of the bishop.

22.   Presbyters taking part in a liturgy with the bishop should do only what belongs to the order of presbyter;[28] in the absence of deacons they may perform some of the ministries proper to the deacon, but should never wear diaconal vestments.

*Deacons*

23.   Deacons hold the highest place among ministers and from the Church's earliest age the diaconate has been held in great honor. As men of good repute and full of wisdom,[29] they should act in such a way that, with the help of God, all may know them to be true disciples[30] of one who came, not to be served but to serve,[31] and who was among his disciples as one who serves.[32]

24.   Strengthened by the gift of the Holy Spirit, deacons assist the bishop and his presbyterate in the ministry of the word, the altar, and of charity. As ministers of the altar they proclaim the gospel reading, help at the celebration of the sacrifice, and serve as eucharistic ministers.

Deacons should therefore look upon the bishop as a father and assist him as they would the Lord Jesus Christ himself, who is the eternal High Priest, present in the midst of his people.

25.   In liturgical celebrations it belongs to the deacon to assist the celebrant, to minister at the altar with the book and the cup, to guide the assembly of

the faithful with suitable directions, to announce the intentions of the general intercessions.

If there is no other minister, the deacon also carries out other ministerial functions as required.[33]

When assisting at an altar that does not face the people, the deacon is always to turn toward the people when he addresses them.

26. At a liturgical celebration presided over by the bishop there should be at least three deacons, one to proclaim the gospel reading and to minister at the altar, and two to assist the bishop. If more than three deacons are present, they should divide the ministries accordingly,[34] and at least one of them should be charged with assisting the active participation of the faithful.

*Acolytes*

27. In the ministry of the altar, acolytes have their own proper functions and should exercise these even though ministers of a higher rank may be present.

28. Acolytes receive institution so that they may help the deacon and minister to the priest. Their proper ministry is to look after the service of the altar and to assist the deacon and priest in liturgical services, especially the celebration of Mass. In addition, acolytes may serve as special ministers of the eucharist, giving holy communion in accord with the provisions of the law.

When necessary, acolytes should instruct those who serve as ministers in liturgical rites by carrying the book, the cross, candles, or the censer or by performing other similar duties. But in celebrations presided over by the bishop it is fitting that all such ministerial functions be carried out by formally instituted acolytes, and if a number are present, they should divide the ministries accordingly.[35]

29. So that they may fulfill their responsibilities more worthily, acolytes should take part in the celebration of the eucharist with ever increasing devotion, as the source of their spiritual life and the object of an ever deeper appreciation. They should seek to acquire an interior and spiritual sense of their ministry so that each day they may offer themselves wholly to God and grow in sincere love for the Mystical Body of Christ, the people of God, and especially for the members who are weak and infirm.

*Readers*

30. In liturgical celebrations readers have their own proper function and should exercise this, even though ministers of a higher rank may be present.[36]

31. The office of reader was historically the first of the lesser ministries to emerge. This office exists in all the Churches and has never disappeared. Readers receive institution for an office proper to them: to proclaim the word of God in the liturgical assembly. Hence at Mass and in other rites of the liturgy readers proclaim the readings other than the gospel reading. When there is no cantor of the psalm present, the reader also leads the assembly in the responsorial

psalm; when no deacon is present, the reader announces the intentions of the general intercessions.

Whenever necessary, the reader should see to the preparation of any members of the faithful who may be appointed to proclaim the readings from Sacred Scripture in liturgical celebrations. But in celebrations presided over by the bishop it is fitting that readers formally instituted proclaim the readings and, if several readers are present, they should divide the readings accordingly.[37]

32.   Conscious of the dignity of God's word and the importance of their office, readers should be eager to learn how best to speak and proclaim, in order that those who listen may clearly hear and understand the word of God.

In proclaiming the word of God to others, readers should themselves receive it with docility and meditate on it with devotion so that they may bear witness to that word in their daily lives.

### Psalmist or Cantor of the Psalm

33.   The chants between the readings are very important liturgically and pastorally; it is therefore desirable in celebrations presided over by the bishop, especially in the cathedral church, that there be a psalmist or cantor who has the necessary musical ability and devotion to the liturgy. The cantor of the psalm is responsible for singing, either responsorially or directly, the chants between the readings—the psalm or other biblical canticle, the gradual and *Alleluia*, or other chant—in such a way as to assist the faithful to join in the singing and to reflect on the meaning of the texts.[38]

### Master of Ceremonies

34.   For a liturgical celebration, especially a celebration presided over by the bishop, to be distinguished by grace, simplicity, and order, a master of ceremonies is needed to prepare and direct the celebration in close cooperation with the bishop and others responsible for planning its several parts, and especially from a pastoral standpoint.

The master of ceremonies should be well-versed in the history and nature of the liturgy and in its laws and precepts. But equally he should be well-versed in pastoral science, so that he knows how to plan liturgical celebrations in a way that encourages fruitful participation by the people and enhances the beauty of the rites.

He should seek to ensure an observance of liturgical laws that is in accord with the true spirit of such laws and with those legitimate traditions of the particular Church that have pastoral value.

35.   In due time he should arrange with the cantors, assistants, ministers, and celebrants the actions to be carried out and the texts to be used, but during the celebration he should exercise the greatest discretion: he is not to speak more than is necessary, nor replace the deacons or assistants at the side of the celebrant. The master of ceremonies should carry out his responsibilities with reverence, patience, and careful attention.

36. The master of ceremonies wears either an alb or a cassock and surplice. Within a celebration a master of ceremonies who is an ordained deacon may wear a dalmatic and the other diaconal vestments.

*Sacristan*

37. Along with the master of ceremonies and under his direction, the sacristan sees to the preparation for a celebration with the bishop. The sacristan should carefully arrange the books needed for the proclamation of the word and for the presidential prayers; he or she should lay out the vestments and have ready whatever else is needed for the celebration. He or she should see to the ringing of bells for celebrations. He or she should ensure the observance of silence and quiet in the sacristy and the vesting room. Vestments, church furnishings, and decorative objects that have been handed down from the past are not to be treated carelessly, but kept in good condition. When anything new needs to be provided, it should be chosen to meet the standards of contemporary art, but not out of a desire simply for novelty.

38. The first of all the elements belonging to the beauty of the place where the liturgy is celebrated is the spotless condition of the floor and walls and of all the images and articles that will be used or seen during a service. In all the liturgical appurtenances both ostentation and shabbiness are to be avoided; instead the norms of noble simplicity, refinement, gracefulness, and artistic excellence are to be respected. The culture of the people and local tradition should guide the choice of objects and their arrangement, "on condition that they serve the places of worship and the sacred rites with the reverence and honor due to them."[39]

The adornment and decor of a church should be such as to make the church a visible sign of love and reverence toward God, and to remind the people of God of the real meaning of the feasts celebrated there and to inspire in them a sense of joy and devotion.

*Choir and Musicians*

39. All who have a special part in the singing and music for the liturgy—choir directors, cantors, organists, and others—should be careful to follow the provisions concerning their functions that are found in the liturgical books and other documents published by the Apostolic See.[40]

40. Musicians should constantly keep in mind those norms especially that regard the participation of the people in singing. In addition, they should take care that the singing expresses the note of universality belonging to celebrations presided over by the bishop; hence, the faithful should be able to recite or sing together not only in the vernacular but also in Latin the parts of the Order of Mass that pertain to them.

41. From Ash Wednesday until the singing of the *Gloria* at the Easter Vigil and in celebrations for the dead, the organ and other instruments should be played only to sustain the singing.[41] An exception is made for *Laetare* Sunday (the Fourth Sunday of Lent) and for solemnities and festive days.

From the end of the *Gloria* in the Mass of the Lord's Supper on Holy Thursday until the *Gloria* at the Easter Vigil, the organ and other musical instruments should be played only to sustain the singing.

During Advent musical instruments should be played with a moderation that is in keeping with the spirit of joyful expectation characteristic of this season, but does not anticipate the fullness of joy belonging to the celebration of the nativity of the Lord.

## CHAPTER 3
# CATHEDRAL CHURCH

42.   The cathedral church is the church that is the site of the bishop's cathedra or chair, the sign of his teaching office and pastoral power in the particular Church, and a sign also of the unity of believers in the faith that the bishop proclaims as shepherd of the Lord's flock.

In this church, on the more solemn liturgical days, the bishop presides at the liturgy. There also, unless pastoral considerations suggest otherwise, he consecrates the sacred chrism and confers the sacrament of holy orders.

43.   The diocesan cathedral "in the majesty of its building is a symbol of the spiritual temple that is built up in souls and is resplendent with the glory of divine grace. As Saint Paul says: 'We are the temple of the living God' (2 Corinthians 6:16). The cathedral, furthermore, should be regarded as the express image of Christ's visible Church, praying, singing, and worshiping on earth. The cathedral should be regarded as the image of Christ's Mystical Body, whose members are joined together in an organism of charity that is sustained by the outpouring of God's gifts."[42]

44.   With good reason, then, the cathedral church should be regarded as the center of the liturgical life of the diocese.

45.   Effective measures should be taken to instill esteem and reverence for the cathedral church in the hearts of the faithful. Among such measures are the annual celebration of the dedication of the cathedral and pilgrimages in which the faithful, especially in groups of parishes or sections of the diocese, visit the cathedral in a spirit of devotion.

46.   The cathedral church should be a model for the other churches of the diocese in its conformity to the directives laid down in liturgical documents and books with regard to the arrangement and adornment of churches.[43]

47.   The bishop's *cathedra* or *chair* mentioned in no. 42, should be a chair that stands alone and is permanently installed. Its placement should make it clear that the bishop is presiding over the whole community of the faithful.

Depending on the design of each church, the chair should have enough steps leading up to it for the bishop to be clearly visible to the faithful.

There is to be no baldachin over the bishop's chair; but valuable works of art from the past are to be preserved with utmost care.

Apart from the cases provided by law, only the diocesan bishop, or a bishop he permits to use it, occupies this chair.[44] Seats are to be provided in a convenient place for other bishops or prelates who may be present at a celebration, but such seats are not to be set up in the manner of a cathedra.[45]

The chair for a priest celebrant should be set up in a place separate from the site of the bishop's chair.

48. The *altar* should be constructed and adorned in accordance with the provisions of the law. It should be so placed as to be a focal point on which the attention of the whole congregation centers naturally.[46]

The altar of the cathedral church should normally be a fixed altar that has been dedicated. This altar should be freestanding to allow the ministers to walk around it easily and to permit celebration facing the people.[47] But when the cathedral has an old altar so constructed that it makes participation of the people difficult and that cannot be moved without damage to its artistic value, another fixed altar, of artistic merit and duly dedicated, should be erected. Only at this altar are liturgical celebrations to be carried out.

Flowers should not adorn the altar from Ash Wednesday until the *Gloria* at the Easter Vigil, nor in celebrations for the dead. Exceptions to this rule are *Laetare* Sunday (the Fourth Sunday of Lent), solemnities, and feasts.

49. It is recommended that the *tabernacle*, in accordance with a very ancient tradition in cathedral churches, should be located in a chapel separate from the main body of the church.[48]

But when, in a particular case, there is a tabernacle on the altar at which the bishop is to celebrate, the blessed sacrament should be transferred to another fitting place.

50. The *sanctuary* or *chancel*, that is, the place where the bishop, presbyters, and ministers carry out their ministries, should be set apart from the body of the church in some way—for example, by being at a somewhat higher level or by its distinctive design and ornamentation—in such a way that even the layout of the sanctuary highlights the hierarchic offices of the ministers. The sanctuary should be sufficiently spacious for the rites to be carried out without obstruction to movement or to the view of the assembly.

Seats, benches, or stools should be provided in the sanctuary, so that concelebrants, or canons and presbyters not concelebrating but assisting in choir dress, as well as the ministers, all have their own places, and in such a way as to facilitate the exercise of their various parts in a celebration.

A minister who is not wearing a vestment, a cassock and surplice, or other lawfully approved garb may not enter the sanctuary (chancel) during a celebration.[49]

51. The cathedral church should have an *ambo* or *lectern*, constructed in keeping with liturgical norms currently in force.[50] But the bishop should address

the people of God from the bishop's chair (cathedra), unless local conditions suggest otherwise.

The cantor, the commentator, or the choirmaster should not normally use the ambo or lectern, but should carry out their functions from another suitable place.

52. Even when it is not a parochial church, the cathedral should have a *baptistery*, at least for the celebration of baptism at the Easter Vigil. The baptistery should be designed and equipped in keeping with the provisions of The Roman Ritual.[51]

53. The cathedral church should have a *vesting room*, that is, a suitable place, as close as possible to the church entrance, where the bishop, concelebrants, and ministers can put on their liturgical vestments and from which the entrance procession can begin.

The sacristy, which should normally be separate from the vesting room, is a room where vestments and other liturgical materials are kept. It may also serve as the place where the celebrant and the ministers prepare for a celebration on ordinary occasions.

54. If at all possible, provision should be made for a *gathering place* of the people near the cathedral church—another church, a suitable hall, a square, or a cloister—where the blessings of candles, of palms, and of fire, as well as other preparatory celebrations, may take place and from which processions to the cathedral church may begin.

## CHAPTER 4
# GENERAL NORMS
## INTRODUCTION

55. According to the teaching of the Second Vatican Council, care must be taken to ensure that rites are marked by a noble simplicity.[52] This applies also to a liturgy in which the bishop presides, although the respect and reverence owed to a bishop are not to be disregarded. In him the Lord Jesus is present in the midst of those who believe and the faithful's life in Christ in some way depends on and derives from him.[53]

In addition, a liturgy in which the bishop presides is usually marked by the participation of those having the different orders existing in the Church and in this way the mystery of the Church is more clearly made visible. Thus celebrations with the bishop ought to be marked by love and mutual esteem between the members of the Mystical Body of Jesus Christ, so that the liturgy may truly fulfill the precept of Saint Paul: "Be first in showing honor to each other."[54]

Before describing the individual rites, it seems advisable to state some general norms that have proved valid by long use and that should be followed.

# I. VESTURE AND INSIGNIA

[See the *Ceremonial* for the norms regarding the vesture and insignia of the bishop.]

*Vesture of priests and other ministers*

65.   The vestment common to ministers of every rank is the alb, tied at the waist with a cincture, unless it is made to fit without a cincture. An amice should be put on first if the alb does not completely cover the minister's street clothing at the neck. A surplice may not be substituted for the alb when the chasuble or dalmatic is to be worn or when a stole is used instead of the chasuble or dalmatic.[60] When a surplice is worn, it must be worn with the cassock.

Acolytes, readers, and other ministers may wear other lawfully approved vesture in place of the vestments already mentioned.

66.   Unless otherwise indicated, the chasuble, worn over the alb and stole, is the vestment proper to the presbyter who is the celebrant at Mass and other rites immediately connected with Mass.

The priest wears the stole around his neck and hanging down in front.

The cope is worn by the priest in solemn liturgical services outside Mass and in processions; in other liturgical services, in keeping with the rubrics proper to each rite.[61]

Presbyters who take part in a liturgical service but not as concelebrants are to wear choir dress if they are prelates or canons,[62] cassock and surplice if they are not.

67.   The dalmatic, worn over the alb and stole, is the vestment proper to the deacon. The dalmatic may be omitted either out of necessity or for less solemnity. The deacon wears the stole over his left shoulder and drawn across the chest to the right side, where it is fastened.[63]

# II. SIGNS OF REVERENCE IN GENERAL

68.   A *bow* signifies reverence and honor toward persons or toward objects that represent persons.

There are two kinds of bows, a bow of the head and a bow of the body:

a. a bow of the head is made at the name of Jesus, the Blessed Virgin Mary, and the saint in whose honor the Mass or the liturgy of the hours is being celebrated;

b. a bow of the body, or deep bow, is made: to the altar if there is no tabernacle with the blessed sacrament on the altar; to the bishop, before and after incensation, as indicated in no. 91; whenever it is expressly called for by the rubrics of the various liturgical books.[64]

69.   A *genuflection*, made by bending only the right knee to the ground, signifies adoration, and is therefore reserved for the blessed sacrament, whether exposed or reserved in the tabernacle, and for the holy cross from the time of the solemn adoration in the liturgical celebration of Good Friday until the beginning of the Easter Vigil.

70.   Neither a genuflection nor a deep bow is made by those who are carrying articles used in a celebration, for example, the cross, candlesticks, the Book of the Gospels.

### Reverence toward the blessed sacrament

71.   No one who enters a church should fail to adore the blessed sacrament, either by visiting the blessed sacrament chapel or at least by genuflecting.

Similarly, those who pass before the blessed sacrament genuflect except when they are walking in procession.

### Reverence toward the altar

72.   A deep bow is made to the altar by all who enter the sanctuary (chancel), leave it, or pass before the altar.

73.   In addition, the celebrant and concelebrants at the beginning of Mass kiss the altar as a sign of reverence. The principal celebrant as a rule venerates the altar by kissing it before he leaves, while the other concelebrants, particularly if there are a number of them, venerate the altar by bowing.

When the bishop presides at a solemn celebration of morning or evening prayer, he kisses the altar at the beginning and, as circumstances suggest, at the end.

But if such a sign of reverence as kissing the altar is out of keeping with the traditions or the culture of the region, the conference of bishops may substitute some other sign, after informing the Apostolic See.[65]

### Reverence toward the gospel

74.   While the gospel reading is being proclaimed at Mass, at a celebration of the word, and at a prolonged vigil, all stand and, as a rule, face the reader.

The deacon solemnly carrying the Book of the Gospels to the ambo is preceded by the censerbearer with the censer[66] and acolytes with lighted candles.[67]

At the ambo the deacon stands facing the people and, with hands joined, says the greeting; then with his right thumb he makes the sign of the cross, first on the book at the beginning of the gospel passage that he is about to read, then on his forehead, lips, and breast, saying, A reading from the holy gospel. The bishop signs himself in the same way on forehead, lips, and breast, and all present do the same. Then, at least at a stational Mass, the deacon incenses the Book of the Gospels three times, that is, in the center, to the left, and to the right. Then he proclaims the gospel reading to its conclusion.

After the reading, the deacon takes the book to the bishop to be kissed, or the deacon himself kisses the book, unless, as mentioned in no. 73, another sign of reverence has been decided on by the conference of bishops.[68]

In the absence of a deacon, a presbyter asks for and receives a blessing from the bishop, and proclaims the gospel reading in the way just described.

75. All present also stand for the singing or recitation of the gospel canticles, the Canticles of Zechariah, of Mary, and of Simeon, and at the beginning of these canticles sign themselves with the sign of the cross.[69]

### Reverence toward the bishop and other persons

76. The bishop is greeted with a deep bow by the minister or others when they approach to assist him, when they leave after assisting him, or when they pass in front of him.[70]

77. When the bishop's chair is behind the altar, the ministers should reverence either the altar or the bishop, depending on whether they are approaching the altar or approaching the bishop; out of reverence for both, ministers should, as far as possible, avoid passing between the bishop and the altar.

78. If several bishops are present in the sanctuary (chancel), a reverence is made only to the one presiding.

79. When the bishop, vested as indicated in no. 63, proceeds to a church to celebrate some liturgical rite, he may, in accordance with local custom, be escorted publicly to the church by the canons or other presbyters and clerics in choir dress or wearing cassock and surplice, or he may be received by the clergy at the door after proceeding to the church in a less solemn way.

In both cases the bishop goes first: if he is an archbishop he is preceded by an acolyte carrying the archiepiscopal cross with the image of Christ facing forward; behind the bishop follow the canons, presbyters, and clergy, two by two. At the door of the church the senior of the presbyters hands the bishop the sprinkler, unless the blessing and sprinkling of water is to replace the penitential rite. With head uncovered, the bishop sprinkles himself and those around him, then returns the sprinkler. He next goes in procession to the place of reservation of the blessed sacrament and prays there for a short time; finally he goes to the vesting room (sacristy).

The bishop may, however, go directly to the vesting room (sacristy) and be received there by the clergy.

80. In a procession the bishop who presides at a liturgical celebration always walks vested and alone, following the presbyters, but preceding his assisting ministers, who walk a little behind him.

81. When the bishop presides at a celebration or only takes part in it wearing choir dress, he has as assistants two canons in choir dress or two presbyters or deacons in cassock and surplice.

82.    A head of state in official attendance at a liturgical celebration is received by the bishop, who waits in vestments at the door of the church. The bishop may offer holy water to a head of state who is a Catholic. After greeting the head of state in a manner that accords with local custom, the bishop, keeping to the left, escorts the head of state to an appointed place reserved in the church outside the sanctuary (chancel). At the end of the celebration the bishop as he leaves again greets the head of state.

83.    If such is the practice, other officials holding high position in the government of a nation, region, or city are received at the door of the church in a manner that accords with local custom by an ecclesiastic dignitary, who greets them and escorts them to their appointed place. The bishop may greet such personages during the entrance procession as he goes to the altar, and as he leaves.

## III. INCENSATION

84.    The rite of incensation or thurification is a sign of reverence and of prayer, as is clear from Psalm 141 (140):2 and Revelation 8:3.

85.    The substance placed in the censer should be pure sweet-scented incense alone or at least in larger proportion than any additive mixed with the incense.

86.    At the stational Mass of the bishop incense should be used:

a.  during the entrance procession;

b.  at the beginning of Mass to incense the altar;

c.  at the gospel, in the procession and at the proclamation of the gospel reading;

d.  at the presentation of the gifts, to incense the gifts, the altar, the cross, the bishop, the concelebrants, and the people;

e.  at the elevation of the consecrated bread and cup after their consecration.

At other Masses incense may be used as circumstances suggest.[71]

87.    Incense is also to be used as indicated in the liturgical books:

a.  in the rite of dedication of a church or altar;

b.  in the rite of the blessing of oils and consecrating the chrism, as the blessed oils and consecrated chrism are being taken away;

c.  at exposition of the blessed sacrament when the monstrance is used;

d.  at funerals.

88.    In addition, incense should as a rule be used during the processions for the feast of the Presentation of the Lord, Passion Sunday (Palm Sunday), the Mass of the Lord's Supper, the Easter Vigil, the solemnity of the Body and Blood of Christ (Corpus Christi), and the solemn translation of relics and, in general, in any procession of some solemnity.

89.   At the solemn celebration of morning or evening prayer the altar, the bishop, and the people may be incensed during the singing of the gospel canticle.

90.   If the bishop puts incense into the censer at his chair (cathedra) or another chair, he remains seated; otherwise he puts in the incense while standing. The deacon presents the incense boat[72] and the bishop blesses the incense with the sign of the cross, saying nothing.[73]

After the blessing, the deacon takes the censer from the acolyte and hands it to the bishop.[74]

91.   Before and after an incensation, a profound bow is made to the person or object that is incensed, except in the case of the incensation of the altar and the gifts for the eucharistic sacrifice.[75]

92.   The censer is swung back and forth three times for the incensation of: the blessed sacrament, a relic of the true cross and images of the Lord solemnly exposed, the gifts on the altar, the altar cross, the Book of the Gospels, the Easter candle, the bishop or presbyter who is celebrant, a representative of the civil authority in official attendance at a liturgical celebration, the choir and people, the body of a deceased person.

The censer is swung back and forth twice for the incensation of relics and images of the saints exposed for public veneration.

93.   The altar is incensed with a series of single swings of the censer in this way:

   a.   if the altar is freestanding, the bishop incenses it while walking around it;

   b.   if the altar is not freestanding, the bishop incenses it while walking first to the right side, then to the left.

If there is a cross on or beside the altar, he incenses it before he incenses the altar. If the cross is behind the altar, the bishop incenses it when he passes in front of it.[76]

The gifts of bread and wine are incensed before the incensation of the altar and the cross.

94.   The blessed sacrament is incensed from a kneeling position.

95.   Relics and images exposed for public veneration are incensed after the incensation of the altar; at Mass they are incensed only at the beginning of the celebration.

96.   Whether he is at the altar or at the chair (cathedra), the bishop receives the incensation standing and without the miter, unless he is already wearing it.

Concelebrants are incensed as a body by the deacon.

Lastly, the deacon incenses the people from the place most convenient. Canons who are not concelebrating or a community assembled in choir are incensed together with the people, unless the spatial arrangement suggests otherwise.

Bishops who may be present are also incensed along with the people.

97. A bishop who presides but does not concelebrate is incensed after the celebrant or concelebrants.

Where such a practice is customary, a head of state in official attendance at a liturgical celebration is incensed after the bishop.

98. The bishop should not begin any invitation, introduction, or prayer meant to be heard by all before the rite of incensation has been completed.

## IV. SIGN OF PEACE

99. After the deacon has said, Let us offer each other a sign of peace, the bishop who is celebrant gives the kiss of peace at least to the two concelebrants nearest to him, then to the first deacon.

100. Meanwhile the concelebrants and deacons and the other ministers as well as any bishops present also give each other the kiss of peace.

101. The faithful also exchange a sign of peace in the manner approved by the conference of bishops.

102. The deacon or one of the concelebrants goes to give a head of state in official attendance the sign of peace according to local custom.

103. The exchange of the sign of peace may be accompanied by the words, Peace be with you, and the response, And also with you. But other words may be used in accordance with local custom.

## V. POSITION OF THE HANDS

*Raised and outstretched hands*

104. Customarily in the Church, a bishop or presbyter addresses prayers to God while standing and with hands slightly raised and outstretched.

This practice appears already in the tradition of the Old Testament,[77] and was taken by Christians in memory of the Lord's passion: "Not only do we raise our hands, but also hold them outstretched, so that by imitating the Lord in his passion, we bear witness to him as we pray."[78]

*Outstretched hands over persons or objects*

105. The bishop holds his hands outstretched over the people when he blesses them solemnly and wherever the liturgical books call for such a gesture in the celebration of the sacraments or sacramentals.

106. The bishop and the concelebrants hold their hands outstretched over the offerings in Mass at the epiclesis before the consecration.

At the consecration, as the bishop holds the host or cup in his hands and says the words of consecration, the concelebrants say the words of institution and, if this seems appropriate, hold the right hand outstretched toward the bread and the cup.[79]

*Joined hands*

107.  Unless the bishop is holding the pastoral staff, he keeps his hands joined:[80] when, vested, he walks in procession for the celebration of a liturgy; when he is kneeling at prayer; when he moves from altar to chair or from chair to altar; when the liturgical books prescribe joined hands.

Similarly, concelebrants and ministers keep their hands joined when walking from place to place or when standing, unless they are holding something.

*Other positions for the hands*

108.  When the bishop signs himself with the sign of the cross or when he gives a blessing,[81] he places his left hand on his breast, unless he is holding something. When he is standing at the altar and blesses the offerings or something else with his right hand, he places his left hand on the altar, unless a rubric indicates otherwise.

109.  When the bishop is seated and wearing vestments, he places his palms on his knees, unless he is holding the pastoral staff.

## VI. USE OF HOLY WATER

110.  It is an old and honored practice for all who enter a church to dip their hand in a font (stoup) of holy water and sign themselves with the sign of the cross as a reminder of their baptism.

111.  If holy water is to be offered to the bishop as he enters the church, a senior cleric of the local Church offers it to him, presenting a sprinkler, with which the bishop sprinkles himself and those accompanying him. Then the bishop hands back the sprinkler.

112.  All this is omitted if the bishop enters the church already vested, as well as on Sunday whenever the blessing and sprinkling of water replace the penitential rite.

113.  The sprinkling of the people with water at the Easter Vigil and at the dedication of a church will be treated in nos. 369 and 892–893 of this *Ceremonial*.

114.  Objects being blessed are sprinkled with holy water in keeping with the provisions of the liturgical books.

115.   The liturgical books are to be treated with care and reverence, since it is from them that the word of God is proclaimed and the prayer of the Church offered. Care must therefore be taken, and especially in liturgical celebrations carried out by a bishop, to have on hand the official liturgical books in an edition that is current and is beautifully printed and bound.

116.   In texts that are to be delivered in a clear, audible voice, whether by the bishop or by the ministers or by all, the tone of voice should correspond to the genre of the text, that is, accordingly as it is a reading, a prayer, an instruction, an acclamation, or a song; the tone should also be suited to the form of celebration and to the solemnity of the gathering.

117.   Hence, in the rubrics and norms that follow in this *Ceremonial*, the words "say" *(dicere)*, "recite" *(recitare)*, "proclaim" *(proferre)* should be understood of both singing and speaking, in accordance with the principles set out in the respective liturgical books[82] and with the norms given in place in this *Ceremonial*.

118.   The phrase "sing or say," which is used frequently in this *Ceremonial*, is to be understood as referring to singing, unless some other consideration rules out singing.

# PART IV
# CELEBRATIONS OF THE MYSTERY OF THE LORD THROUGH THE CYCLE OF THE LITURGICAL YEAR

## INTRODUCTION

*Sunday, the Lord's Day*

228.   "The Church celebrates the paschal mystery on the first day of the week, known as the Lord's Day or Sunday. This follows a tradition handed down from the apostles and having its origin from the day of Christ's resurrection. Thus Sunday must be ranked as the first holy day of all."

Since Sunday is the nucleus and foundation of the yearly liturgical cycle by which the Church unfolds the entire mystery of Christ, the Sunday celebration gives way only to those solemnities or feasts of the Lord belonging to the General Roman Calendar. By its nature, then, Sunday excludes any other celebrations' being permanently assigned to that day, with these exceptions: the feasts of the Holy Family and the Baptism of the Lord, the solemnities of the Holy Trinity and Christ the King.

The Sundays of Advent, of Lent, and of the Easter season have precedence over all feasts of the Lord and over all solemnities.[2]

# CHAPTER 1
## ADVENT AND THE CHRISTMAS SEASON

234. Next to the yearly celebration of the paschal mystery, the Church holds most sacred the commemoration of Christ's birth and first manifestations. This is the purpose of the Christmas season.[7]

235. The season of Advent, the preparation for this commemoration, has a twofold character: it is a time to prepare for Christmas, when Christ's First Coming is remembered; it is a time when that remembrance directs the mind and heart to await Christ's Second Coming in the last days. In this way Advent is a period of devout and joyful expectation.[8]

# CHAPTER 2
## FEAST OF THE PRESENTATION OF THE LORD

241. On this day Christ's faithful people, with candles in their hands, go out to meet the Lord and to acclaim him with Simeon, who recognized Christ as "a light to reveal God to the nations."

They should therefore be taught to walk as children of the light in their entire way of life, because they have a duty to show the light of Christ to all by acting in the works that they do as lighted lamps.

# CHAPTER 3
## LENT

249. The annual observance of Lent is the special season for the ascent to the holy mountain of Easter.

Through its twofold theme of repentance and baptism, the season of Lent disposes both the catechumens and the faithful to celebrate the paschal mystery. Catechumens are led to the sacraments of initiation by means of the rite of election, the scrutinies, and catechesis. The faithful, listening more intently to the word of God and devoting themselves to prayer, are prepared through a spirit of repentance to renew their baptismal promises.[16]

# CHAPTER 4
## ASH WEDNESDAY

253. On the Wednesday before the First Sunday of Lent the faithful, by receiving ashes, enter upon the season appointed for spiritual purification. This sign of penance, biblical in origin[20] and preserved among the customs of the Church until our own day, expresses the human condition as affected by sin. In this sign we outwardly profess our guilt before God and thereby, prompted by the hope that the Lord is kind and compassionate, patient and bounding in mercy, express our desire for inward conversion. This sign is also the beginning of the journey of conversion

that will reach its goal in the celebration of the sacrament of reconciliation during the days leading to Easter.

## CHAPTER 5
## LITURGICAL ASSEMBLIES DURING LENT

260. All the elements of Lenten observance should conspire to manifest more clearly and to promote the life of the local Church. For this reason *The Roman Missal (Sacramentary)* strongly encourages the preservation and development of the traditional form of gathering the local Church after the fashion of the Roman "stations," at least in the larger cities and in a way suited to the particular place. Especially with the chief pastor of the diocese presiding, such assemblies of the faithful can gather on Sunday or on more convenient weekdays, at the tombs of the saints, in the principal churches or shrines of the city, or in other frequently visited places of pilgrimage in the diocese. This may be done on Sundays or weekdays, in parish churches or places of pilgrimage. The manner of celebration will vary according to local needs.[21]

## CHAPTER 6
## PASSION SUNDAY (PALM SUNDAY)

263. On Passion Sunday (Palm Sunday) the Church enters upon the mystery of its crucified, buried, and risen Lord, who, by his entrance into Jerusalem, gave a glimpse of his own majesty. Christians carry branches as a sign of the royal triumph that Christ won by his acceptance of the cross. Since Saint Paul says: "Provided we suffer with him in order that we may also be glorified with him,"[22] the link between these two aspects of the paschal mystery should stand out clearly in the liturgical celebration and catechesis of Palm Sunday.

## CHAPTER 7
## CHRISM MASS

274. This Mass, which the bishop concelebrates with his college of presbyters and at which he consecrates the holy chrism and blesses the other oils, manifests the communion of the presbyters with their bishop.[26]

The holy chrism consecrated by the bishop is used to anoint the newly baptized, to seal the candidates for confirmation, and to anoint the hands of presbyters and the heads of bishops at their ordination, as well as in the rites of anointing pertaining to the dedication of churches and altars. The oil of catechumens is used in the preparation of the catechumens for their baptism. The oil of the sick is used to bring comfort and support to the sick in their infirmity.

Presbyters are brought together and concelebrate this Mass as witnesses and cooperators with their bishop in the consecration of the chrism because they share in the sacred office of the bishop in building up, sanctifying, and ruling the people of God.[27] This Mass is therefore a clear expression of the unity of the priesthood and sacrifice of Christ, which continue to be present in the Church.

To show the unity of the college of presbyters, the presbyters who concelebrate with the bishop should come from different parts of the diocese.[28]

Presbyters who take part but for some reason do not celebrate may receive communion under both kinds.

## CHAPTER 8
# EASTER TRIDUUM

295. "Christ redeemed us all and gave perfect glory to God principally through his paschal mystery: dying he destroyed our death and rising he restored our life. Therefore the Easter Triduum of the Passion and Resurrection of the Lord is the culmination of the entire liturgical year. Thus the solemnity of Easter has the same kind of preeminence in the liturgical year that Sunday has in the week.[40]

Let the paschal fast be kept sacred. Let it be celebrated everywhere on Good Friday and, wherever possible, prolonged throughout Holy Saturday, as a way of coming to the joys of the Sunday of the resurrection with uplifted and welcoming heart.[41]

## CHAPTER 9
# MASS OF THE LORD'S SUPPER

297. With this Mass, celebrated in the evening of the Thursday in Holy Week, the Church begins the sacred Easter Triduum and devotes itself to the remembrance of the Last Supper. At this supper on the night he was betrayed, the Lord Jesus, loving those who were his own in the world even to the end, offered his body and blood to the father under the appearances of bread and wine, gave them to the apostles to eat and drink, then enjoined the apostles and their successors in the priesthood to offer them in turn.[42]

This Mass is, first of all, the memorial of the institution of the eucharist, that is, of the memorial of the Lord's Passover, by which under sacramental signs he perpetuated among us the sacrifice of the New Law. The Mass of the Lord's Supper is also the memorial of the institution of the priesthood, by which Christ's mission and sacrifice are perpetuated in the world. In addition this Mass is the memorial of that love by which the Lord loved us even to death. The bishop should see to it that all these considerations are suitably presented to the faithful through the ministry of the word so that by their devotion they may be able to deepen their grasp of such great mysteries and reflect them more faithfully in the conduct of their lives.

## CHAPTER 10
# CELEBRATION OF THE LORD'S PASSION
## INTRODUCTION

312. On this day, when "Christ our paschal lamb was sacrificed,"[56] what had long been promised in signs and figures was at last revealed and brought to fulfillment.

The true lamb replaced the symbolic lamb, and the many offerings of the past gave way to the single sacrifice of Christ.[57]

"The wonderful works of God among the people of the Old Testament were a prelude to the work of Christ the Lord. He achieved his task of redeeming humanity and giving perfect glory to God, principally by the paschal mystery of his blessed passion, resurrection from the dead, and glorious ascension, whereby 'dying he destroyed our death and rising he restored our life' (Preface of Easter). For it was from the side of Christ as he slept the sleep of death upon the cross that there came forth the sublime sacrament of the whole Church."[58]

In contemplating the cross of its Lord and Bridegroom, the Church commemorates its own origin and its mission to extend to all peoples the blessed effects of Christ's passion that it celebrates on this day in a spirit of thanksgiving for his marvelous gift.

## CHAPTER 11
# EASTER VIGIL
### INTRODUCTION

332. In accord with ancient tradition, this night is a night of vigil for the Lord,[77] and, as the memorial of the holy night of Christ's resurrection, the Vigil celebrated is "the mother of all holy vigils."[78] The Church this night awaits the Lord's resurrection and celebrates it with the sacrament of Christian initiation.

## CHAPTER 12
# EASTER SEASON

371. The fifty days from Easter Sunday to Pentecost are celebrated in joyful exultation as one feast day, or better as one "great Sunday."[123]

These above all others are the days for the singing of the *Alleluia.*

On Easter Sunday, wherever it is in force, the custom should be continued of celebrating a "baptismal" evening prayer, that is, a celebration in which the psalms are sung during a procession to the baptismal font.

## CHAPTER 13
# ORDINARY TIME

377. Apart from those seasons having their own distinctive character, thirty-three or thirty-four weeks remain in the yearly cycle that do not celebrate a particular element of the mystery of Christ. Rather, especially on the Sundays, these weeks are devoted to the mystery of Christ in its entirety. This period is known as Ordinary Time.[128]

378. Ordinary Time begins on Monday after the Sunday following 6 January and continues until Tuesday before Ash Wednesday inclusive. It begins again on

Monday after Pentecost and ends before Evening Prayer I of the First Sunday of Advent.[129]

379. Since Sunday is the first holy day of all, the nucleus and foundation of the liturgical year,[130] the bishop should ensure that, in view of nos. 228–230 of this *Ceremonial*, on the Sundays in Ordinary Time the proper Sunday liturgy is celebrated, even when such Sundays are days to which special themes are assigned.

380. For the pastoral advantage of the people, it is permissible to observe on the Sundays in Ordinary Time those celebrations that fall during the week and have special appeal to the devotion of the faithful, provided these celebrations take precedence over the Sundays in the table of liturgical days. The Mass for such celebrations may be used at all the Masses at which a congregation is present.[131]

## CHAPTER 14
# ROGATION AND EMBER DAYS

383. It is important that in each diocese, after taking into account local circumstance and customs, the bishop take great care that suitable means are found to preserve the liturgy of the rogation and ember days and to devote the liturgy of these days to the ministry of charity. In this way the devotion of the people of God will be fostered and their perception of the mystery of Christ deepened.

## CHAPTER 15
# SOLEMNITY OF THE BODY AND BLOOD OF CHRIST
## INTRODUCTION

385. The institution of the eucharist has as a special memorial the Mass of the Lord's Supper, when Christ the Lord shared a meal with his disciples and gave them the sacrament of his body and blood to be celebrated in the Church. The solemnity of the Body and Blood of Christ (Corpus Christi) further proposes the cultus of the blessed sacrament to the faithful so that they may celebrate the wonderful works of God, signified by the sacrament and accomplished by the paschal mystery of Christ. This solemnity is also intended to teach the faithful how to share in the eucharistic sacrifice and to have it more profoundly influence their life, to revere the presence of Christ the Lord in this sacrament, and to offer the thanks due for God's gifts.[135]

## CHAPTER 16
# ALL SOULS

395. The Church offers the eucharistic sacrifice and its own intercession for the dead not only at their funerals and anniversaries but also in the yearly remembrance of all the sons and daughters of the Church who sleep in Christ. The Church seeks to help the faithful departed by earnest prayer to God for their entry into the communion of the saints in heaven. In this way, because of the

communion of all Christ's members with one another, the Church obtains spiritual help for the dead and brings the consolation of hope to the living.[141]

# PART V
# SACRAMENTS

## CHAPTER 3
# SACRAMENT OF MARRIAGE
## INTRODUCTION

598. Mindful of Christ the Lord's attendance at the wedding feast of Cana, the bishop should make it his concern to bless occasionally the marriages of his people, and particularly those of the poor.

To prevent his participation from bearing the mark of favoritism[147] or from being a mere sign of outward show, it should be the bishop's normal practice not to assist at marriages in a private chapel or home but in the cathedral or parish church. In this way the ecclesial character of the celebration of the sacrament will more surely stand out and the local community will have the opportunity to participate in the celebration.

599. For the celebration of marriage, in addition to the usual requisites for the nuptial blessing imparted by a presbyter, a miter and pastoral staff should be made ready.

600. The bishop should be assisted by at least one presbyter, who as a rule will be the parish priest (pastor), and at least one deacon, along with several ministers.

## I. CELEBRATION OF MARRIAGE WITHIN MASS

601. If the bishop himself celebrates the Mass, he wears Mass vestments and uses the miter and pastoral staff. If a presbyter concelebrates, he also wears Mass vestments.

If the bishop presides at the Mass but does not celebrate, he wears an alb, pectoral cross, stole, and white cope, and uses the miter and pastoral staff.

A deacon wears the vestments of his order. The other ministers wear an alb or other lawfully approved vesture.

In addition to the requisites for the celebration of Mass, the following should be provided:

a. *Rite of Marriage*

b. vessel of holy water with sprinkler;

c. rings for the bridegroom and bride;

d. cup large enough for communion under both kinds.

602. At the appointed time the parish priest (pastor) or other presbyter, vested with a stole over a cassock and surplice or over an alb, or if he is to celebrate, vested for Mass, goes with the ministers to receive the bride and bridegroom at the door of the church or, if more suitable, at the altar. He greets them, then leads them to their places.[148]

Then the bishop goes to the altar and reverences it. The bride and bridegroom are presented to him by the parish priest (pastor) or another presbyter. Meanwhile, the entrance song is sung.

603. On days when ritual Masses are permitted[149] one of the wedding Masses (RM, Ritual Masses, IV. Wedding Mass, 1. For the Celebration of Marriage) may be celebrated, with its proper readings. The vestments for the Mass are white or of some other festive color.

On the days listed in nos. 1–4 of the table of liturgical days, the Mass of the day is celebrated, with the nuptial blessing included and, as circumstances suggest, the proper solemn blessing.

But if the Mass in which the sacrament of marriage is celebrated is a regular parish Mass, the Mass of the day is celebrated, even on the Sundays of the Christmas season and of Ordinary Time.

When the ritual Mass is not celebrated, one of the readings may be chosen from those provided for this ritual Mass in the Lectionary for Mass, except on those days listed in nos. 1–4 of the table of liturgical days.[150]

604. When a marriage is celebrated during Advent or Lent or on other days of penance, the parish priest (pastor) should advise the couple to take into consideration the special nature of these liturgical seasons.[151]

605. The introductory rites and the liturgy of the word take place in the usual way.

606. After the gospel reading, the bishop, seated and with miter and pastoral staff (unless he decides otherwise), gives the homily, drawn from the sacred text. He speaks about the mystery of Christian marriage, the dignity of wedded love, the grace of the sacrament, and the responsibilities of married people.[152]

607. After the homily, the bishop, with miter and pastoral staff, stands before the bride and bridegroom and questions them about their freedom, faithfulness to each other, and the acceptance and upbringing of children. He then invites the couple to declare their consent.[153]

608. Putting aside the pastoral staff (and also the miter if he uses the alternative, deprecatory formulary of blessing), the bishop blesses the rings and, as circumstances suggest, sprinkles them with holy water and hands them to the bridegroom and bride, who place them on each other's ring finger.[154]

609. When called for by the rubrics, the profession of faith is said; the general intercessions take place in the usual way.

610. In Eucharistic Prayer I there is a commemoration of the bride and bridegroom, in the formulary provided in *The Roman Missal (Sacramentary)* among the Ritual Masses (IV. Wedding Mass).

611. After the Lord's Prayer, the embolism Deliver us, Lord is omitted. The bishop, if he is celebrant of the eucharist, otherwise the presbyter who is the celebrant, faces the bride and bridegroom and, with hands joined, invites the assembly to pray: My dear friends, let us turn to the Lord. All pray silently for a short while. Then, with hands outstretched, the bishop pronounces the prayer of blessing, Father, by your power (or one of the other prayers of blessing provided in the *Rite of Marriage*).[155]

612. The married couple, their parents, witnesses, and relatives may receive communion under both kinds.[156]

613. In place of the usual blessing of the people at the end of Mass, the bishop uses one of the blessing formularies provided in the *Rite of Marriage* for this Mass.[157]

With miter and with hands outstretched, the bishop greets the people, saying, The Lord be with you. One of the deacons may then give the invitation before the blessing. With hands outstretched over the people, the bishop says the blessing invocations. Taking the pastoral staff, he then pronounces the blessing, as he makes the sign of the cross three times over the people.

The bishop may also impart the blessing by using one of the formularies given in nos. 1120–1121 of this *Ceremonial*.

## II. CELEBRATION OF MARRIAGE OUTSIDE MASS

614. The bishop is vested in the way indicated in no. 176 for a Mass at which he presides but does not celebrate. The presbyter assisting him wears a stole over a cassock and surplice or over an alb; the deacon wears the vestments of his order.

615. The bride and bridegroom and the bishop enter the church in the way already indicated in no. 602, while the entrance song is being sung.

616. After the singing, the bishop greets all present and says the opening prayer from *The Roman Missal (Sacramentary)* among the Ritual Masses (IV. Wedding Mass) or the *Rite of Marriage*. The liturgy of the word follows in the same way as at Mass.

617. The questions about freedom of choice, the expression of consent, and the exchange of rings take place in the manner already indicated in nos. 607–608.

618. The intercessions follow. Then, omitting the prayer that concludes the intercessions, the bishop, with hands outstretched, blesses the bride and bridegroom. He uses the text provided in the *Rite of Marriage* for this blessing within Mass.[158]

The Lord's Prayer is then recited.

619. If communion is to be given within this rite, the deacon takes the ciborium or pyx with the body of the Lord, places it on the altar, and, with the bishop, genuflects. Then the bishop introduces the Lord's Prayer, which all recite together.

Then the bishop genuflects. Taking the host, he raises it slightly over the ciborium or pyx and, facing those who will receive communion, says, This is the Lamb of God.

Communion is distributed as at Mass.

After communion, a period of silence may be observed, or a psalm or song of praise may be sung. Then the prayer Lord, we who have shared the food at your table, provided in the *Rite of Marriage,* or some other suitable prayer is said.[159]

620. The bishop then gives the final blessing in the manner already indicated in no. 613. The deacon says the dismissal formula, Go in peace, and all reply, Thanks be to God, and leave.

# PART VI
# SACRAMENTALS

## CHAPTER 16
## BLESSING OF A NEW CROSS FOR PUBLIC VENERATION
### INTRODUCTION

1011. Of all sacred images, the "figure of the precious, life-giving cross of Christ"[334] is preeminent, because it is the symbol of the entire paschal mystery. The cross is the image most cherished by the Christian people and the most ancient; it represents Christ's suffering and victory, and at the same time, as the Fathers of the Church have taught, it points to his Second Coming.

1012. The blessing of a new cross may be celebrated at any hour and on any day except Ash Wednesday, the Easter Triduum, and All Souls. But the preferred day is one that permits a large attendance of the faithful; they should receive proper preparation for their active participation in the rite.[335]

1013. The order presented in this chapter is meant for only two situations:

a. the solemn blessing of a cross erected in a public place, separate from a church;

b. the blessing of the principal cross that occupies a central place in the body of the church where the worshiping community assembles; in this case the rite of blessing begins at the point described here in no. 1020.

1014. The following should be prepared for the rite:

a. *Book of Blessings, Lectionary for Mass;*

b. censer and incense boat with spoon;

c. candlesticks for the acolytes;

The vestments for the celebration of the rite are white or some other festive color:

—for the bishop: alb, pectoral cross, stole, cope, miter, pastoral staff;

—for deacons: albs, stoles, and, as circumstances suggest, dalmatics;

—for other ministers: albs or other lawfully approved vesture.

## DESCRIPTION OF THE RITE

1015. When feasible, it is preferable for the community of the faithful to go in procession from the church or another location to the site where the cross that is to be blessed has been erected. When a procession either is not feasible or seems inadvisable, the faithful simply assemble at the site of the cross.[336]

When the people have gathered, the bishop, vested in alb, pectoral cross, stole, and cope, and with miter and pastoral staff, goes to them, accompanied by the ministers. Putting aside miter and pastoral staff, he greets the faithful in the words The grace of Jesus Christ or other suitable words. The people reply, And also with you, or make some other suitable reply.

1016. Then, using if he so chooses the words provided in the *Book of Blessings*, the bishop briefly addresses the faithful, in order to prepare them for the celebration and to explain the meaning of the rite.

After his introductory remarks, the bishop invites all to pray. After a period of silent prayer, the bishop, with hands outstretched, says the opening prayer, Lord, your Son reconciled us to you.[337]

1017. After the opening prayer, the bishop again takes the miter and pastoral staff, and the deacon may say, Let us proceed in peace. The procession to the site of the cross is then formed. During the procession Psalm 98 (97), with the antiphon "We should glory in the cross," or some other suitable song is sung.[338]

When there is no procession, the opening prayer is followed immediately by the reading of the word of God.

1018. After the opening prayer, the bishop puts on the miter and sits for the proclamation of the word of God. There may be one or two readings, each followed by a responsorial psalm related to it. The texts may be taken from those given in the *Lectionary for Mass* (Votive Masses, Holy Cross).[339]

1019. The bishop then gives the homily, in which he explains both the biblical texts and the power of the cross of Christ.

1020. After the homily, the bishop, putting aside the miter and standing before the cross, blesses it, saying the prayer Blessed are you, Lord God or the pray Lord God, Father all-holy.

After the prayer, he puts incense into the censer, stands before the cross, and incenses it, as all sing the antiphon We worship you, or the antiphon "Through the sign of the cross," or some other suitable song in honor of the cross.[340]

1021. After the incensation,* the bishop, the ministers, and the faithful venerate the new cross, if this can be done conveniently. One by one in procession all go to the cross and kneel before it or kiss it or offer some other sign of reverence in keeping with local custom.†

But if this procedure is impossible because of the large number in attendance or for some other good reason, the bishop speaks a few words, inviting the people to venerate the cross either by observing an interval of silent prayer or by some appropriate acclamation.[341]

1022. The veneration of the cross is followed by intercessions, either in the form usual at Mass or in the form provided in the *Book of Blessings*. The intercessions are concluded by the Lord's Prayer, sung or recited by all, and the prayer of the bishop.

Then, taking the miter and pastoral staff, the bishop blesses the people in the usual way, and the deacon assisting him dismisses them, saying, Go in peace, and all reply, Thanks be to God. Then a song in honor of the cross of Christ may be sung.[342]

# PART VIII
# LITURGICAL CELEBRATIONS IN CONNECTION WITH OFFICIAL ACTS PERTAINING TO THE GOVERNMENT OF A DIOCESE

## CHAPTER 2
## PASTORAL VISITATION

1177. The bishop in fulfilling the obligation to visit the parishes or local communities of his diocese should not appear to be satisfying a purely administrative duty. Rather the faithful should see in him the herald of the Gospel, the teacher, shepherd, and high priest of his flock.

1178. To ensure this happening, the visitation of the bishop should take place, if at all possible, on days that permit large numbers of the faithful to gather. Sufficient time should also be devoted to an apt, preparatory catechesis of the people by their presbyters. The visitation itself should be sufficiently long to enable the bishop to preside at celebrations of the liturgy and to evaluate, promote, encourage, and put into effect the apostolate of the clergy and laity and the works of charity.

1179. The bishop, in the vestments indicated in no. 63, should be received in a manner suited to the circumstances of the place and the situation. If this seems appropriate, the bishop may be solemnly received and greeted by the clergy at the door of the church. But the bishop may even be escorted to the church with festive song, when this is feasible and appropriate. A dignified solemnity in receiving the bishop is a sign of the love and devotion of the faithful toward their good shepherd.

1180. At the entrance of the church the parish priest (pastor), vested in cope, meets the bishop, offers him the crucifix to be kissed, and presents the sprinkler, with which the bishop sprinkles himself and those present. After a brief, silent prayer before the blessed sacrament, the bishop goes to the sanctuary (chancel); there the parish priest (pastor), standing before the altar, invites the faithful to join in prayer for the bishop and, after a brief pause for silent prayer, says the prayer God, eternal shepherd or God, our Father, our shepherd and guide, provided in *The Roman Missal (Sacramentary)*.[2]

The bishop then greets the people and announces his agenda for the visitation. He then says the collect for the titular of the church or the patron of the place, and, in the usual way, blesses the people. Then the parish priest (pastor) dismisses them.

1181. But when Mass is to follow the reception of the bishop, immediately after the prayer for the bishop has been said, the bishop, at the chair, puts on the vestments for Mass. The presbyters charged with the pastoral care of the parish or presbyters living within the parish confines concelebrate the Mass with the bishop, and the faithful take an active part. Such participation is particularly to be sought in the more remote parts of the diocese where the people rarely or never have the opportunity to take part in a stational Mass celebrated by the bishop in their own area.

1182. It is recommended that during the pastoral visitation the bishop confer not only the sacrament of confirmation but other sacraments as well, particularly in his visits to the sick. In this way he will more clearly appear to the faithful as the chief steward of the mysteries of God and as the overseer and guardian of the entire liturgical life in the Church entrusted to his care.

1183. When there is a lengthy visitation, there should be a celebration of the liturgy of the hours in the church or a celebration of the word of God, with the homily by the bishop and with intercessions for the universal Church and for the local Church.

1184. As circumstance suggest, the bishop should also go to the cemetery with the people and there offer prayers for the dead and sprinkle the graves with holy water, in the manner described already in nos. 399–402.

# NOTES

PART I

1. Vatican Council II, Decree on the Pastoral Office of Bishops *Christus Dominus* (hereafter, CD), no. 11: ICEL, *Documents on the Liturgy, 1963–1979: Conciliar, Papal, and Curial Texts* (hereafter, DOL; The Liturgical Press, Collegeville, Minn., 1982), 7, no. 191. See Vatican Council II, Dogmatic Constitution on the Church *Lumen Gentium* (hereafter, LG), no. 23.

2. See LG, no. 26; DOL 4, no. 146.

3. Ignatius of Antioch, *Ad Smyrnaeos*, 8, 2: Funk, ed., *Patres apostolici*, v. 1, p. 283.

4. LG, no. 26: DOL 4, no. 146.

5. See LG, no. 26: DOL 4, no. 146.

6. See LG, nos. 26, 28: DOL 4, nos. 146, 148. See Vatican Council II, Constitution on the Liturgy *Sacrosanctum Concilium* (hereafter, SC), art. 41: DOL 1, no. 41.

7. See LG, no. 23.

8. LG, no. 13.

9. See LG, nos. 26, 27: DOL 4, nos. 146–147. See CD, no. 3.

10. CD, no. 2.

11. See CD, no. 12: DOL 7, no. 192.

12. See LG, no. 26: DOL 4, no. 146. See CD, no. 15: DOL 7, no. 194.

13. See LG, no. 21: DOL 4, no. 145.

14. SC, art. 41: DOL 1, no. 41.

15. Prayer of consecration of a bishop in the Byzantine rite: *Euchologion to mega* (Rome, 1873), 139; LG, no. 26: DOL 4, no. 146.

16. See CD, no. 15: DOL 7, no. 194.

17. LG, no. 26: DOL 4, no. 146.

18. See LG, no. 21: DOL 4, no. 145. See CD, no. 3.

19. LG, no. 27.

20. SC, art. 41: DOL 1, no. 41.

21. See LG, no. 25.

22. SC, art. 35, 2: DOL 1, no. 35.

23. LG, no. 25: DOL 4, no. 146.

24. See Sacred Congregation of Rites (hereafter, SC Rites), Instruction *Pontificales ritus*, on the simplification of pontifical rites and insignia, 21 June 1968 (hereafter, PR), no. 24: AAS 60 (1968), p. 410; DOL 550, no. 4481.

25. See SC, art. 28: DOL 1, no. 28.

26. See SC, art. 26: DOL 1, no. 26.

27. See LG, no. 28: DOL 4, no 148.

28. See SC, art. 28: DOL 1, no. 28.

29. See Acts 6:3.

30. See John 13:35.

31. See Matthew 20:28.

32. See Luke 22:27.

33. See the General Instruction of the Roman Missal, 4th ed., 1975 (hereafter, GIRM), nos. 71, 127: DOL 208, nos. 1461, 1517.

34. See GIRM, no. 71: DOL 208, no. 1461.

35. See Paul VI, Motu Proprio *Ministeria quaedam*, on first tonsure, minor orders, and the subdiaconate, 15 August 1972 (hereafter, MQ), no. VI: AAS 64 (1972), p. 532; DOL 340, no. 2931.

36. GIRM, no. 66: DOL 208, no. 1456.

37. See MQ, no. V: AAS 64 (1972), p. 532; DOL 340, no. 2931. See The Roman Missal, *Lectionary for Mass*, 2nd English ed., 1981 (hereafter, LM), Introduction, nos. 51–55. See General Instruction of the Liturgy of the Hours (hereafter, GILH), no. 259: DOL 426, no. 3689.

38. See LM, Introduction, nos. 19–20, 56.

39. SC, art. 123: DOL 1, no. 123.

40. See GIRM, particularly nos. 12, 19, 22, 63, 64, 272, 274, 275, 313, 324: DOL 208, nos. 1402, 1409, 1412, 1453, 1454, 1662, 1664, 1665, 1703, 1714. See *Ordo cantus Missae*, Introduction: DOL 505, nos. 4276–4302; GILH, nos. 268–284: DOL 426, nos. 3698–3714. See The Roman Ritual, the *Rite of Baptism for Children, Christian Initiation*, General Introduction, no. 33: DOL 294, no. 2282. See The Roman Ritual, *Holy Communion and Worship of the Eucharist outside Mass*, nos. 12 and 104: DOL 279, nos. 2204 and 2222. See The Roman Ritual, *Rite of Penance*, nos. 24

and 36: DOL 368, nos. 3089 and 3101. See The Roman Ritual, *Pastoral Care of the Sick: Rites of Anointing and Viaticum,* nos. 38, d: DOL 411, no. 3358. See The Roman Ritual, *Order of Christian Funerals,* no. 12: DOL 416, no. 3384 (see English ed., nos. 30–33). See SC Rites, Instruction *Musicam sacrum,* 5 March 1967 (hereafter, MS): AAS 69 (1967), pp. 300–320; DOL 508, nos. 4122–4190. See Sacred Congregation for Bishops, Directory on the Pastoral Ministry of Bishops (1970), no. 90, d: DOL 329, no. 2660.

41. See MS, no. 66: AAS 69 (1967), p. 319; DOL 508, no. 4187.

42. Paul VI, Apostolic Constitution *Mirificus eventus,* declaring the jubilee of 1966, 7 December 1965: AAS 57 (1965), pp. 948–949; DOL 484, no. 4054.

43. See GIRM, nos. 253–312: DOL 208, nos. 1643–1702. See LM, Introduction, nos. 32–34. See The Roman Pontifical, *Dedication of a Church and an Altar,* ch. 2, no. 3, and ch. 4, nos. 6–11: DOL 547, no. 4371 and nos. 4403–4408. See The Roman Ritual, *Holy Communion and Worship of the Eucharist outside Mass,* General Introduction, nos. 9–11: DOL 279, nos. 2201–2203.

44. See *Codex Iuris Canonici (Code of Canon Law),* 1983 (hereafter, CIC), can. 463, §3. See in this *Ceremonial,* nos. 1171 and 1176.

45. See PR, nos. 10–13: AAS 60 (1968), pp. 408–409; DOL 550, nos. 4467–4470.

46. See GIRM, no. 262: DOL 208, no. 1652.

47. See GIRM, no. 262: DOL 208, no. 1652.

48. See SC Rites, Instruction *Eucharisticum mysterium,* on worship of the eucharist, 25 May 1967, no. 53: AAS 59 (1967), p. 568; DOL 179, no. 1282. See The Roman Ritual, *Holy Communion and Worship of the Eucharist outside Mass,* General Introduction, no. 9: DOL 279, no. 2201.

49. See in this *Ceremonial,* nos. 65–67. See LM, Introduction, no. 54.

50. See GIRM, no. 272: DOL 208, no. 1662. See LM, Introduction, nos. 32–34.

51. See The Roman Ritual, *Rite of Baptism for Children, Christian Initiation,* General Introduction, no. 25: DOL 294, no. 2274.

52. See SC, art. 34: DOL 1, no. 34.

53. See LG, no. 21: DOL 4, no. 145. See SC, art. 41: DOL 1, no. 41.

54. Romans 12:10.

60. See GIRM, no. 298: DOL 208, no. 1688.

61. See GIRM, nos. 299, 302, 303: DOL 208, nos. 1689, 1692, 1693.

62. See nos. 1207–1209 of this *Ceremonial.*

63. See GIRM, nos. 300, 81, b, 302: DOL 208, nos. 1690, 1471, 1692.

64. See GIRM, no. 234: DOL 208, no. 1624.

65. See GIRM, nos. 208 and 232: DOL 208, nos. 1598 and 1622.

66. See GIRM, nos. 93–95, 131: DOL 208, nos. 1483–1485, 1521. The Roman manner for the censer-bearer to walk in procession is that "he walks with hands somewhat raised, he should hold the censer with the right hand, with his thumb in the ring at the top, and the middle finger holding the chain, so that the cover of the censer is somewhat raised; he holds the boat containing incense and spoon with his left hand." (*Caeremoniale Episcoporum,* ed. 1886, I, XI, 7).

67. See GIRM, nos. 94, 131: DOL 208, nos. 1484, 1521. According to Roman practice acolytes "hold the candlesticks with their right hand, so that the acolyte walking on the right puts his left hand at the base of the candlestick and his right at the middle knob of the candlestick; the acolyte walking on the left puts his right hand at the base and his left at the middle knob of the candlestick" (*Caeremoniale Episcoporum,* ed 1886, I, XI, 8).

68. See GIRM, nos. 131, 232: DOL 208, nos. 1521, 1622.

69. See GILH, no 266, b: DOL 426, no. 3696.

70. See PR, no. 25: AAS 60 (1968), p. 411; DOL 550, no. 4482.

71. See GIRM, no. 235: DOL 208, no. 1625.

72. Two acolytes may go to the bishop with the censer and boat or one acolyte carrying both, the censer with burning charcoal in the left hand and the boat with the incense and spoon in the right (see *Caeremoniale Episcoporum,* ed. 1886, I, XIII, 1).

73. See GIRM, no. 236: DOL 208, no. 1626. From the acolyte the deacon takes the boat, half-opened and with the spoon resting in it, and offers the boat to the bishop. The bishop takes the spoon and with it three times scoops out incense, and three times puts the incense into the censer. After doing so, and having returned the

spoon to the minister, the bishop with his right hand makes the sign of the cross over the incense that has been deposited in the censer (see *Caeremoniale Episcoporum*, ed. 1886, I, XXII, 1–2).

74. The deacon "returns the boat to the acolyte and from him takes the censer, which he presents to the bishop, placing the top of the censer chain in the bishop's left hand and the censer itself in the bishop's right hand. *(Caeremoniale Episcoporum*, ed. 1886, I, IX, 1).

75. The one incensing "holds the top of the censer chain in the left hand, the bottom near the censer in the right hand, so that the censer can be swung back and forth easily." "The one incensing should take care to carry out this function with grave and graceful mien, not moving head or body while swinging the censer, holding the left hand with the top of the chains near the chest and moving the right arm back an forth with a measured beat" (See *Caeremoniale Episcoporum*, ed. 1886, I, XXIII, 4 and 8).

76. See GIRM, no. 236: DOL 208, no. 1626.

77. See Exodus 9:29; Psalm 28 (27):2, 63 (62):5, 134 (133):2; Isaiah 1:15.

78. Tertullian, *De oratione*, 14: CCL 1, 265; PL 1, 1273.

79. See GIRM, nos. 174, a and c, 180, a and c, 184, a and c, 188, a and c: DOL 208, nos. 1564, 1570, 1574, 1578. At the epiclesis preceding the consecration the hands are to be outstretched toward and above the offerings (see *Missale Romanum*, ed. 1962, *Ritus servandus in celebratione Missae*, VIII, 4). At the consecration the palm of the right hand is held sideward (see *Notitiae*, 1, 1965, p. 143: DOL 223, no. 1810, note R8).

80. "Hands joined" means: "Holding the palms sideward and together before the breast, with the right thumb crossed over the left" (*Caeremoniale Episcoporum*, ed. 1886, I, XIX, 1).

81. "When making the sign of the cross, he holds the palm of the right hand turned toward himself, with all the fingers joined and held straight, and makes the sign of the cross by moving this hand from head to chest and from left shoulder to right. If he blesses others or some object, he points the little finger at the person or thing to be blessed and in blessing extends the whole right hand with all the fingers joined and fully extended" (*Missale Romanum*, ed.

1962, *Ritus servandus in celebratione Missae*, III, 5).

82. See, for example, GIRM, nos. 18–19: DOL 208, nos. 1408–1409. See GILH, nos. 267–284: DOL 426, nos. 3697–3714. See MS, nos. 5–12: AAS 59 (1967), pp. 301–303; DOL 508, nos. 4126–4133. See Sacred Congregation for Divine Worship (hereafter, SC worship), Circular Letter *Eucharistiae participationem*, on the eucharistic prayers, 27 April 1973, no. 17: AAS 65 (1973), pp. 346–347; DOL 248, no. 1991.

## PART IV

2. See SC Rites, General Norms for the Liturgical Year and the Calendar, 21 March 1969 (hereafter, GNLYC), nos. 4–6: DOL 442, nos. 3770–3772.

7. Seen GNLYC, no. 32: DOL 442, no. 3798.

8. See GNLYC, nos. 32, 39: DOL 442, nos. 3798, 3805.

16. See SC, art. 109: DOL 1, no. 109. See GNLYC, no. 27: DOL 442, no. 3793.

20. See 2 Samuel 13:19; Esther 4:1; Job 42:6; 1 Maccabees 3:47, 4:39; Lamentations 2:10.

21. See RM, Proper of Seasons, the rubric printed at the beginning of the Lenten season.

22. Romans 8:17.

26. See GIRM, no 157: DOL 208, no. 1547. See RM, Proper of Seasons, Holy Thursday, rubrics preceding the text of the Chrism Mass.

27. See Vatican Council II, Decree on the Ministry and Life of Priests *Presbyterorum Ordinis*, no. 2: DOL 18, no. 257.

28. See RM, Proper of Seasons, Holy Thursday, rubrics preceding text of the Chrism Mass.

40. GNLYC, no. 18: DOL 442, no. 3784.

41. See SC, art. 110: DOL 1, no. 110.

42. See Council of Trent, sess. 22, 17 Sept. 1562, Doctr. *De ss. Missae sacrificio*, ch. 1: *Concilium Tridentinum, Diariorum, Actorum, Epistolarum, Tractatuum nova collectio*, ed. Görres Gesellschaft, vol. 8, *Actorum*, part 5 (Freiburg, Br., 1919), p. 960.

56. 1 Corinthians 5:7.

57. See Leo the Great, *Sermo* 58, *De Passione Domini* 1: PL 54, 332.

58. SC, art. 6: DOL 1, no. 5.

77. See Exodus 12:42.

78. See Augustine, *Sermo* 219: PL 38, 1088.

123. Anthanasius, *Epist. festal.*, 1: PG 26, 1366. See GNLYC, no. 22: DOL 442, no. 3788.

128. See GNLYC, no. 43: DOL 442, no. 3809.

129. See GNLYC, no. 44: DOL 442, no. 3810.

130. See SC, art. 106: DOL 1, no. 106. See GNLYC, no. 4: DOL 442, no. 3770.

131. See GNLYC, no. 58: DOL 442, no. 3809. See the Table of Liturgical Days in Appendix II of this *Ceremonial* (also in DOL 442, no. 3825).

135. See GIRM, no. 3: DOL 208, no. 1378.

141. See The Roman Ritual, *Rite of Funerals* (hereafter, RF), no. 1: DOL 416, no. 3373. In the English edition of 1985, The Roman Ritual, *Order of Christian Funerals* (hereafter, OCF), nos. 1–13.


PART V

147. See SC, art. 32: DOL 1, no. 32.

148. See The Roman Ritual, *Rite of Marriage*, English ed., 1969 (hereafter, RMar), no. 19.

149. See Appendix III of this *Ceremonial*.

150. See Appendix II of this *Ceremonial*; LM, nos. 801–805 (Ritual Masses, IV. Wedding Mass).

151. See RMar, Introduction, no. 11: DOL 349, no. 2979.

152. See RMar, no. 22.

153. See RMar, nos. 24–26.

154. See RMar, nos. 27–28.

155. See RMar, no. 33.

156. See RMar, no. 36

157. See RMar, nos. 125–127.

158. See RMar, nos. 33, 120–121.

159. See RMar, no. 123; HCWE, nos. 50 and 210–222.


PART VI

334. See Council of Nicaea II, Act. 7: Mansi 13, 378; Denzinger-Schönmetzer, *Enchiridion symbolorum, definitionum et declarationum de rebus fidei et morum*, ed. XXXIV, no. 601.

335. See The Roman Ritual, *Book of Blessings*, ch. 28, Order for the Blessing of a New Cross for Public Veneration (hereafter, OBNC), no. 964.

336. See OBNC, no. 966.

337. See OBNC, nos. 967–968.

338. See OBNC, no. 971.

339. See LM, nos. 969–975 (Votive Masses, Holy Cross); OBNC, nos. 973–975.

340. See OBNC, nos. 977–979.

* OBNC, no. 980, begins *Cantu expleto* ("After the singing"), not *Thurificatione completa* ("After the incensation").

† The rubrics for OBNC do not mention kneeling of kissing.

341. See OBNC, no. 980.

342. See OBNC, nos. 981–983.


PART VIII

2. See RM, Masses and Prayers for Various Needs and Occasions, 1. For the Church, 3. For the Bishop, A.

# DIRECTORY
### FOR
## MASSES
### WITH
## CHILDREN

# OVERVIEW OF THE *DIRECTORY FOR MASSES WITH CHILDREN*

Catherine Dooley, OP

The *Directory for Masses with Children* (1973) contains fundamental principles for the celebration of the eucharist with children that are equally valuable for the celebration of the eucharist with an adult assembly. The *Directory*, prepared by the Congregation for Divine Worship after several years of consultation with various national liturgical commissions, incorporates the "grass roots" experience of many local churches worldwide.

The *Directory*, written for use with children of catechetical age (those who have not yet reached preadolescence) supplements the *General Instruction of the Roman Missal* (GIRM). It offers principles and guidelines for adaptation of the liturgy to children so that they gradually may take a more active and conscious part in the full eucharistic assembly. These guidelines primarily are directed to the weekday celebration of Masses with children in which only a few adults participate. The document presumes that the children participate in the Sunday celebration with their parents, family members and their parish community, and urges that care be taken to include children consciously and carefully in the Sunday celebration. Children occasionally may have their own liturgy of the word, including the homily, in an area separate from the adult community, but the *Directory* consistently makes the integration of children into "a single assembly" a major value.

The primary place for the eucharistic celebration for children is the church, but any "appropriate and worthy" place can be chosen (no. 25) as long as the character and beauty of the place fosters devotion and shows the holiness of the mysteries celebrated there (GIRM, no. 257).

The *Directory* consists of an introduction and three chapters. The introduction outlines the historical development of the document, offers a rationale for the *Directory*, and identifies the social situation and parental indifference as factors that militate against the upbringing of children in the church. Chapter one (nos. 8–15) considers the ways that children are introduced to the eucharistic liturgy and the importance of the family and the broader faith community in the children's formation. The second chapter briefly treats Masses with adults in which children also take part (nos. 16–19), and the final chapter (nos. 20–55) deals with the ritual adaptation of the actual celebration for children with only a few adults participating. Throughout the document, the aspects of adaptation, participation and liturgical formation are recurring themes.

ADAPTATION

Over and over again, the document speaks of adapting to the age, abilities and capacities of the child. The purpose of adaptation is, on the one hand, to help the child better understand and participate, and on the other, to help the child realize that the eucharist is a community celebration and that the child is a member of this community. Liturgy for children is never to create a sense of separateness but always a sense of belonging to the entire ecclesial community.

In weekday Masses with children in which a few adults participate, adaptation should be made in the rites and texts used. The *Directory* insists that any changes made are not to be markedly different from the Order of Mass celebrated with an adult assembly. For the difference between the Masses with children and the Masses with adults not to become too pronounced, some rites and texts should never be adapted (no. 39). These are the acclamations, the responses to the priest's greeting, the Lord's Prayer and the Trinitarian formula at the end of the blessing with which Mass is concluded.

An adaptation that should be made is the omission of some of the elements of the introductory rites so that "an excess of rites" will not obscure their purposes, which are to gather the people into the form of a community and to prepare them to hear the word of God and to celebrate the eucharist properly (GIRM, no. 24). The introductory rites always should be completed by the opening prayer or collect.

The number of scripture readings may be reduced, but the reading of the gospel should never be omitted (no. 42). The *Directory* presumes that the liturgical calendar will be followed and that even when all the readings for the day are deemed unsuitable for the capacity of the children, the liturgical season still will be taken into account. The document urges that individual conferences of bishops prepare lectionaries for children so that suitable readings are available and paraphrases may be avoided. In the United States, a *Lectionary for Masses and Other Celebrations with Children* currently is being prepared.

The homily should be given prominence in Masses with children (no. 48). The presider should speak clearly and simply but never use a condescending or childish manner with children. With the consent of the pastor, the homily may be given by the catechist or an adult other than the presider. The homily is to unfold the word of God and is not catechectical instruction.

The question of eucharistic prayers for Masses with children was not addressed in the *Directory*. Subsequently, however, the Congregation for Divine Worship published three eucharistic prayers for children. The English versions approved for use in the United States are now included in the sacramentary.

PARTICIPATION

The corollary to the principle of adaptation is the principle of conscious and active participation. As with adaptation, the purpose is to help the child attain a sense of identity within and belonging to the ecclesial assembly. As many children as possible should have parts in the celebration (no. 22) either by singing, playing musical instruments, proclaiming the readings and preparing the general intercessions, bringing the gifts to the altar and performing similar activities, so that the Mass may stand out clearly as the celebration of the community (no. 24).

To encourage participation, the presider can insert introductory comments into the texts of the prayers. These are not to be didactic explanations, however, but rather invitations to prayer. The *Directory* affirms silence as another form of community participation and suggests that the presider focus the content of the silent prayer for the children to help them to reflect and pray.

Acclamations and responses should be sung by the children. Singing is to be especially encouraged in eucharistic celebrations with children because they have a special affinity for music, and the music chosen should reflect the capabilities of the children and the recognition of the culture of various groups. Music expresses the child's faith in a way that words alone cannot do. It promotes a sense of unity, fosters an awareness of the mystery of the feast or season, and lifts up the hearts of the children.

"All the forms of participation reach their high point in eucharistic communion" (no. 22). Communion is the preeminent sign of the unity of the Christian community, and all of the preparatory rites—the Lord's prayer, the breaking of the bread, the invitation to communion—are powerful signs of the assembly's oneness in eucharistic sharing. So that children may "go to the holy table calmly and with recollection" (no. 54), they must learn how to participate properly in the communion procession and how to receive communion reverently.

The purpose of conscious and active participation is that the children may "learn day by day, at home and away from home, to proclaim Christ" by living their faith and being conformed to the gospel in their daily lives (no. 55). The eucharist as a celebration leading to the service of others is not a strong theme throughout the document, so this final paragraph offers an important perspective.

LITURGICAL FORMATION

Another basic theme that runs through the document is that the liturgy is a major formative experience for children, that a "fully Christian life cannot be conceived without participation in the liturgical service in which the faithful, gathered into a single assembly, celebrate the paschal mystery" (no. 8). Catechesis should convey the meaning of the eucharist through the ritual action and the prayers of the Mass because "the liturgy itself always exerts its own inherent power to instruct" (no. 12). The liturgy brings the child into a relationship with Christ through assembly, word and eucharist. In the symbols, the ritual, the sacred space and time, the structured patterns of liturgical action, the child enters into a way of knowing that goes beyond words and only gradually will be able to be articulated. The music, the processions, the sign of the cross and the sign of peace, the sight and feel of water, oil, light and laying on of hands engage the child's imagination. Most of all, the community action of gathering and sending, of word and thanksgiving convey a sense of identity and belonging.

Various kinds of celebrations are important in the liturgical formation of children (no. 13) and it sometimes is preferable to conduct celebrations of the word of God rather than to celebrate the eucharist with children every day (no. 27). In these celebrations, children can develop an appreciation of the word of God and can become familiar with the liturgical elements of greetings, silence, acclamations and intercessions. Liturgical formation requires the use of the central symbols in a variety of ways.

The liturgical formation of children is based on and cannot be separated from human values (no. 9). Therefore, any eucharistic catechesis should develop the human values in community activity, the exchange of greetings, a capacity to listen and to seek and grant pardon, the expression of gratitude, the experience of symbolic actions, a meal of friendship and festive celebrations. The Christian family has the greatest role in instilling these Christian and human values and should be helped to see the importance of these ordinary actions for religious understanding.

The *Directory* was written before inclusive language became a general concern and it is important to give children an awareness of using language that does not omit or exclude anyone's participation. Moreover, liturgical prayer is trinitarian in nature but the Christian tradition has named and imaged God in a variety of ways and it is beneficial to offer children many different images and ways to call on God.

CONCLUSION

*The Directory for Masses with Children* is a major effort of the church to respect the nature of childhood and the age and abilities of the children (no. 2). The purpose of the adaptation is that the child might fully and actively participate in the assembly of the parish faith community. The principles in the document are therefore a means of evaluation by which the local community can examine and improve its liturgical practices so that what children have experienced in liturgies apart from the adult community also may be a part of their experience with the adult assembly.

# OUTLINE

# DIRECTORY FOR MASSES WITH CHILDREN

## INTRODUCTION

1.    The Church must show special concern for baptized children who have yet to be fully initiated through the sacraments of confirmation and eucharist as well as for children who have only recently been admitted to holy communion. Today the circumstances in which children grow up are not favorable to their spiritual progress.[1] In addition parents sometimes scarcely fulfill the obligations they accepted at the baptism of their children to bring them up as Christians.

2.    In the upbringing of children in the Church a special difficulty arises from the fact that liturgical celebrations, especially the eucharist, cannot fully exercise their inherent pedagogical force upon children.[2] Although the vernacular may now be used at Mass, still the words and signs have not been sufficiently adapted to the capacity of children.

In fact, even in daily life children do not always understand all their experiences with adults but rather may find them boring. It cannot therefore be expected of the liturgy that everything must always be intelligible to them. Nonetheless, we may fear spiritual harm if over the years children repeatedly experience in the Church things that are barely comprehensible: recent psychological study has established how profoundly children are formed by the religious experience of infancy and early childhood, because of the special religious receptivity proper to those years.[3]

3.    The Church follows its Master, who "put his arms around the children . . . and blessed them" (Mk 10:16). It cannot leave children in the condition described. Vatican Council II had spoken in the Constitution on the Liturgy about the need of liturgical adaptation for various groups.[4] Soon afterwards, especially in the first Synod of Bishops held in Rome in 1967, the Church began to consider how participation by children could be easier. On the occasion of the Synod, the President of the Consilium for the Implementation of the Constitution on the Liturgy said explicitly that it could not be a matter of "creating some entirely special rite but rather of retaining, shortening, or omitting some elements or of making a better selection of texts."[5]

4.    All the details of eucharistic celebration with a congregation were determined in the General Instruction of the revised Roman Missal published in 1969. Then this Congregation began to prepare a special Directory for Masses with Children, as a supplement to the General Instruction. This was done in response

to repeated petitions from the entire Catholic world and with the cooperation of men and women specialists from almost every nation.

5.     Like the *General Instruction of the Roman Missal,* this Directory reserves some adaptations to the conference of bishops or to individual bishops.[6]

Some adaptations of the Mass may be necessary for children in a given country but cannot be included in a general directory. In accord with the *Constitution on the Liturgy* art. 40, the conferences of bishops are to propose such adaptations to the Apostolic See for introduction into the liturgy with its consent.

6.     The Directory is concerned with children who have not yet entered the period of preadolescence. It does not speak directly of children who are physically or mentally handicapped, because a broader adaptation is sometimes necessary for them.[7] Nevertheless, the following norms may also be applied to the handicapped, with the necessary changes.

7.     The first chapter of the Directory (nos. 8–15) gives a kind of foundation by considering the different ways in which children are introduced to the eucharistic liturgy. The second chapter briefly treats Masses with adults in which children also take part (nos. 16–19). Finally, the third chapter (nos. 20–54) treats at greater length Masses with children in which only some adults take part.

# CHAPTER I
## THE INTRODUCTION OF CHILDREN TO THE EUCHARISTIC CELEBRATION

8.     A fully Christian life is inconceivable without participation in the liturgical services in which the faithful, gathered into a single assembly, celebrate the paschal mystery. Therefore, the religious initiation of children must be in harmony with this purpose.[8] The Church baptizes children and therefore, relying on the gifts conferred by this sacrament, it must be concerned that once baptized they grow in communion with Christ and each other. The sign and pledge of that communion is participation in the eucharistic table, for which children are being prepared or led to a deeper realization of its meaning. This liturgical and eucharistic formation may not be separated from their general education, both human and Christian; indeed it would be harmful if their liturgical formation lacked such a basis.

9.     For this reason all who have a part in the formation of children should consult and work together toward one objective: that even if children already have some feeling for God and the things of God, they may also experience in proportion to their age and personal development the human values that are present in the eucharistic celebration. These values include the community activity, exchange of greetings, capacity to listen and to seek and grant pardon, expression of gratitude, experience of symbolic actions, a meal of friendship, and festive celebration.[9]

Eucharistic catechesis, dealt with in no. 12, should develop such human values. Then, depending on their age and their psychological and social situation, children will gradually open their minds to the perception of Christian values and the celebration of the mystery of Christ.[10]

10. The Christian family has the greatest role in instilling these Christian and human values.[11] Thus Christian education, provided by parents and other educators, should be strongly encouraged in relation to the liturgical formation of children as well.

By reason of the duty in conscience freely accepted at the baptism of their children, parents are bound to teach them gradually how to pray. This they do by praying with them each day and by introducing them to prayers said privately.[12] If children, prepared in this way even from their early years, take part in the Mass with their family when they wish, they will easily begin to sing and to pray in the liturgical community and indeed will already have some initial idea of the eucharistic mystery.

If the parents are weak in faith but still wish their children to receive Christian formation, they should be urged at least to communicate to their children the human values mentioned already and, when the occasion arises, to participate in meetings of parents and in noneucharistic celebrations held with children.

11. The Christian communities to which the individual families belong or in which the children live also have a responsibility toward children baptized in the Church. By giving witness to the Gospel, living communal charity, and actively celebrating the mysteries of Christ, the Christian community is an excellent school of Christian and liturgical formation for the children who live in it.

Within the Christian community, godparents or other persons noted for their dedicated service can, out of apostolic zeal, contribute greatly to the necessary catechesis in the case of families that fail in their obligation toward the children's Christian upbringing.

Preschool programs, Catholic schools, and various kinds of associations for children serve these same ends in a special way.

12. Even in the case of children, the liturgy itself always exerts its own inherent power to instruct.[13] Yet within religious-education programs in the schools and parishes the necessary importance should be given to catechesis on the Mass.[14] This catechesis should be directed to the child's active, conscious, and authentic participation.[15] "Suited to children's age and capabilities, it should, by means of the main rites and prayers of the Mass, aim at conveying its meaning, including what relates to taking part in the Church's life."[16] This is especially true of the text of the eucharistic prayer and of the acclamations by which the children take part in this prayer.

The catechesis preparing children for first communion calls for special mention. In it they should learn not only the truths of faith regarding the eucharist but also how from first communion on—after being prepared according to their capacity by penance—they can as full members of Christ's Body take part actively with the people of God in the eucharist, sharing in the Lord's table and the community of their brothers and sisters.

13.   Various kinds of celebrations may also play a major role in the liturgical formation of children and in their preparation for the Church's liturgical life. By the very fact of such celebrations children easily come to appreciate some liturgical elements, for example, greetings, silence, and common praise (especially when this is sung together). But care must by taken that the instructive element does not become dominant in these celebrations.

14.   Depending on the capacity of the children, the word of God should have a greater and greater place in these celebrations. In fact, as the children's spiritual capacity develops, celebrations of the word of God in the strict sense should be held frequently, especially during Advent and Lent.[17] These will help greatly to develop in the children an appreciation of the word of God.

15.   While all that has been said remains true, the final purpose of all liturgical and eucharistic formation must be a greater and greater conformity to the Gospel in the daily life of the children.

## CHAPTER II
## MASSES WITH ADULTS IN WHICH CHILDREN ALSO PARTICIPATE

16.   In many places parish Masses are celebrated, especially on Sundays and holy days, at which a good many children take part along with the large number of adults. On such occasions the witness of adult believers can have a great effect upon the children. Adults can in turn benefit spiritually from experiencing the part that the children have within the Christian community. The Christian spirit of the family is greatly fostered when children take part in these Masses together with their parents and other family members.

   Infants who as yet are unable or unwilling to take part in the Mass may be brought in at the end of Mass to be blessed together with the rest of the community. This may be done, for example, if parish helpers have been taking care of them in a separate area.

17.   Nevertheless, in Masses of this kind it is necessary to take great care that the children present do not feel neglected because of their inability to participate or to understand what happens and what is proclaimed in the celebration. Some account should be taken of their presence: for example, by speaking to them directly in the introductory comments (as at the beginning and the end of Mass) and at some point in the homily.

   Sometimes, moreover, if the place itself and the nature of the community permit, it will be appropriate to celebrate the liturgy of the word, including a homily, with the children in a separate, but not too distant, room. Then, before the eucharistic liturgy begins, the children are led to the place where the adults have meanwhile celebrated their own liturgy of the word.

18.   It may also be very helpful to give some tasks to the children. They may, for example, bring forward the gifts or perform one or other of the songs of the Mass.

19. If the number of children is large, it may at times be suitable to plan the Mass so that it corresponds more closely to the needs of the children. In this case the homily should be directed to them but in such a way that adults may also benefit from it. Wherever the bishop permits, in addition to the adaptations already provided in the Order of Mass, one or other of the particular adaptations described later in the Directory may be employed in a Mass celebrated with adults in which children also participate.

# CHAPTER III
## MASSES WITH CHILDREN IN WHICH ONLY A FEW ADULTS PARTICIPATE

20. In addition to the Masses in which children take part with their parents and other family members (which are not always possible everywhere), Masses with children in which only a few adults take part are recommended, especially during the week. From the beginning of the liturgical reform it has been clear to everyone that some adaptations are necessary in these Masses.[18]

Such adaptations, but only those of a more general kind, will be considered later (nos. 38–54).

21. It is always necessary to keep in mind that these eucharistic celebrations must lead children toward the celebration of Mass with adults, especially the Masses at which the Christian community must come together on Sundays.[19] Thus, apart from adaptations that are necessary because of the children's age, the result should not be entirely special rites, markedly different from the Order of Mass celebrated with a congregation.[20] The purpose of the various elements should always correspond with what is said in the *General Instruction of the Roman Missal* on individual points, even if at times for pastoral reasons an absolute *identity* cannot be insisted upon.

### OFFICES AND MINISTRIES IN THE CELEBRATION

22. The principles of active and conscious participation are in a sense even more significant for Masses celebrated with children. Every effort should therefore be made to increase this participation and to make it more intense. For this reason as many children as possible should have special parts in the celebration: for example, preparing the place and the altar (see no. 29), acting as cantor (see no. 24), singing in a choir, playing musical instruments (see no. 32), proclaiming the readings (see nos. 24 and 47), responding during the homily (see no. 48), reciting the intentions of the general intercessions, bringing the gifts to the altar, and performing similar activities in accord with the usage of various peoples (see no. 34).

To encourage participation, it will sometimes be helpful to have several additions, for example, the insertion of motives for giving thanks before the priest begins the dialogue of the preface.

In all this, it should be kept in mind that external activities will be fruitless and even harmful if they do not serve the internal participation of the children. Thus religious silence has its importance even in Masses with children (see no.

37). The children should not be allowed to forget that all the forms of participation reach their high point in eucharistic communion, when the body and blood of Christ are received as spiritual nourishment.[21]

23. It is the responsibility of the priest who celebrates with children to make the celebration festive, familial, and meditative.[22] Even more than in Masses with adults, the priest is the one to create this kind of attitude, which depends on his personal preparation and his manner of acting and speaking with others.

The priest should be concerned above all about the dignity, clarity, and simplicity of his actions and gestures. In speaking to the children he should express himself so that he will be easily understood, while avoiding any childish style of speech.

The free use of introductory comments[23] will lead children to a genuine liturgical participation, but these should be more than mere explanatory remarks.

It will help him to reach the hearts of the children if the priest sometimes expresses the invitations in his own words, for example, at the penitential rite, the prayer over the gifts, the Lord's Prayer, the sign of peace, and communion.

24. Since the eucharist is always the action of the entire ecclesial community, the participation of at least some adults is desirable. These should be present not as monitors but as participants, praying with the children and helping them to the extent necessary.

With the consent of the pastor or rector of the church, one of the adults may speak to the children after the gospel, especially if the priest finds it difficult to adapt himself to the mentality of children. In this matter the norms soon to be issued by the Congregation for the Clergy should be observed.

Even in Masses with children attention is to be paid to the diversity of ministries so that the Mass may stand out clearly as the celebration of a community.[24] For example, readers and cantors, whether children or adults, should be employed. In this way a variety of voices will keep the children from becoming bored.

## PLACE AND TIME OF CELEBRATION

25. The primary place for the eucharistic celebration for children is the church. Within the church, however, a space should be carefully chosen, if available, that will be suited to the number of participants. It should be a place where the children can act with a feeling of ease according to the requirements of a living liturgy that is suited to their age.

If the church does not satisfy these demands, it will sometimes be suitable to celebrate the eucharist with children outside a place of worship. But in that case the place chosen should be appropriate and worthy of the celebration.[25]

26. The time of day chosen for Masses with children should correspond to the circumstances of their lives so that they may be most open to hearing the word of God and to celebrating the eucharist.

27. Weekday Mass in which children participate can certainly be celebrated with greater effect and less danger of boredom if it does not take place every day (for example, in boarding schools). Moreover, preparation can be more careful if there is a longer interval between diverse celebrations.

Sometimes it will be preferable to have common prayer, to which the children may contribute spontaneously, or else a common meditation, or a celebration of the word of God. These are ways of continuing the eucharistic celebrations already held and of leading to a deeper participation in subsequent celebrations.

28. When the number of children who celebrate the eucharist together is very great, attentive and conscious participation becomes more difficult. Therefore, if possible, several groups should be formed; these should not be set up rigidly according to age but with regard for the children's progress in religious formation and catechetical preparation.

During the week such groups may be invited to the sacrifice of the Mass on different days.

## PREPARATION FOR THE CELEBRATION

29. Each eucharistic celebration with children should be carefully prepared beforehand, especially with regard to the prayers, songs, readings, and intentions of the general intercessions. This should be done in discussion with the adults and with the children who will have a special ministry in these Masses. If possible, some of the children should take part in preparing and ornamenting the place of celebration and preparing the chalice with the paten and the cruets. Presupposing the appropriate internal participation, such activity will help to develop the spirit of community celebration.

## SINGING AND MUSIC

30. Singing must be given great importance in all celebrations, but it is to be especially encouraged in every way for Masses celebrated with children, in view of their special affinity for music.[26] The culture of various peoples and the capabilities of the children present should be taken into account.

If possible, the acclamations should be sung by the children rather than recited, especially the acclamations that form part of the eucharistic prayer.

31. To facilitate the children's participation in singing the *Gloria, Credo, Sanctus,* and *Agnus Dei*, it is permissible to use with the melodies appropriate vernacular texts, accepted by competent authority, even if these do not correspond exactly to the liturgical texts.[27]

32. The use of "musical instruments can add a great deal" in Masses with children, especially if they are played by the children themselves.[28] The playing of instruments will help to sustain the singing or to encourage the reflection of the children; sometimes in their own fashion instruments express festive joy and the praise of God.

Care should always be taken, however, that the musical accompaniment does not overpower the singing or become a distraction rather than a help to the children. Music should correspond to the purpose intended for the different periods at which it is played during the Mass.

With these precautions and with due and special discretion, recorded music may also be used in Masses with children, in accord with norms established by the conferences of bishops.

## GESTURES

33.   In view of the nature of the liturgy as an activity of the entire person and in view of the psychology of children, participation by means of gestures and posture should be strongly encouraged in Masses with children, with due regard for age and local customs. Much depends not only on the actions of the priest,[29] but also on the manner in which the children conduct themselves as a community.

If, in accord with the norms of the General Instruction of the Roman Missal,[30] a conference of bishops adapts the congregation's actions at Mass to the mentality of a people, it should take the special condition of children into account or should decide on adaptations that are for children only.

34.   Among the actions that are considered under this heading, processions and other activities that involve physical participation deserve special mention.

The children's entering in procession with the priest can serve to help them to experience a sense of the communion that is thus being created.[31] The participation of at least some children in the procession with the Book of the Gospels makes clear the presence of Christ announcing the word to his people. The procession of children with the chalice and the gifts expresses more clearly the value and meaning of the preparation of the gifts. The communion procession, if properly arranged, helps greatly to develop the children's devotion.

## VISUAL ELEMENTS

35.   The liturgy of the Mass contains many visual elements and these should be given great prominence with children. This is especially true of the particular visual elements in the course of the liturgical year, for example, the veneration of the cross, the Easter candle, the lights on the feast of the Presentation of the Lord, and the variety of colors and liturgical appointments.

In addition to the visual elements that belong to the celebration and to the place of celebration, it is appropriate to introduce other elements that will permit children to perceive visually the wonderful works of God in creation and redemption and thus support their prayer. The liturgy should never appear as something dry and merely intellectual.

36.   For the same reason, the use of art work prepared by the children themselves may be useful, for example, as illustrations of a homily, as visual expressions of the intentions of the general intercessions, or as inspirations to reflection.

# SILENCE

37.    Even in Masses with children "silence should be observed at the designated times as part of the celebration"[32] lest too great a place be given to external action. In their own way children are genuinely capable of reflection. They need some guidance, however, so that they will learn how, in keeping with the different moments of the Mass (for example, after the homily or after communion[33]), to recollect themselves, meditate briefly, or praise God and pray to him in their hearts.[34]

Besides this, with even greater care than in Masses with adults, the liturgical texts should be proclaimed intelligibly and unhurriedly, with the necessary pauses.

# PARTS OF THE MASS

38.    The general structure of the Mass, which "is made up as it were of the liturgy of the word and the liturgy of the eucharist," should always be maintained, as should certain rites to open and conclude the celebration.[35] Within individual parts of the celebration, the adaptations that follow seem necessary if children are truly to experience, in their own way and according to the psychological patterns of childhood, "the mystery of faith . . . by means of rites and prayers."[36]

39.    Some rites and texts should never be adapted for children lest the difference between Masses with children and the Masses with adults become too pronounced.[37] These are "the acclamations and the responses to the priest's greeting,"[38] the Lord's Prayer, and the Trinitarian formulary at the end of the blessing with which the priest concludes the Mass. It is urged, moreover, that children should become accustomed to the Nicene Creed little by little, the right to use the Apostles' Creed indicated in no. 49 remaining intact.

## A. Introductory Rite

40.    The introductory rite of Mass has as its purpose "that the faithful coming together take on the form of a community and prepare themselves to listen to God's word and celebrate the eucharist properly."[39] Therefore every effort should be made to create this disposition in the children and not to jeopardize it by any excess of rites in this part of Mass.

It is sometimes proper to omit one or other element of the introductory rite or perhaps to expand one of the elements. There should always be at least some introductory element, which is completed by the opening prayer. In choosing individual elements, care should be taken that each one be used from time to time and that none be entirely neglected.

## B. Reading and Explanation of the Word of God

41.    Since readings taken from holy Scripture "form the main part of the liturgy of the word,"[40] even in Masses celebrated with children biblical reading should never be omitted.

42.   With regard to the number of readings on Sundays and holy days, the decrees of the conferences of bishops are to be observed. If three or even two readings appointed on Sundays or weekdays can be understood by children only with difficulty, it is permissible to read two or only one of them, but the reading of the gospel should never be omitted.

43.   If all the readings assigned to the day seem to be unsuited to the capacity of the children, it is permissible to choose readings or a reading either from the Lectionary of the Roman Missal or directly from the Bible, but taking into account the liturgical seasons. It is recommended, moreover, that the individual conferences of bishops see to the composition of lectionaries for Masses with children.

If, because of the limited capabilities of the children, it seems necessary to omit one or other verse of a biblical reading, this should be done cautiously and in such a way "that the meaning of the text or the intent and, as it were, style of the Scriptures are not distorted."[41]

44.   In the choice of readings the criterion to be followed is the quality rather than the quantity of the texts from the Scriptures. A shorter reading is not as such always more suited to children than a lengthy reading. Everything depends on the spiritual advantage that the reading can bring to the children.

45.   In the biblical texts "God is speaking to his people . . . and Christ is present to the faithful through his own word."[42] Paraphrases of Scripture should therefore be avoided. On the other hand, the use of translations that may already exist for the catechesis of children and that are accepted by the competent authority is recommended.

46.   Verses of psalms, carefully selected in accord with the understanding of children, or singing in the form of psalmody or the *Alleluia* with a simple verse should be sung between the readings. The children should always have a part in this singing, but sometimes a reflective silence may be substituted for the singing.

If only a single reading is chosen, the singing may follow the homily.

47.   All the elements that will help explain the readings should be given great consideration so that the children may make the biblical readings their own and may come more and more to appreciate the value of God's word.

Among such elements are the introductory comments that may precede the readings[43] and that by explaining the context or by introducing the text itself help the children to listen better and more fruitfully. The interpretation and explanation of the readings from the Scriptures in the Mass on a saint's day may include an account of the saint's life, not only in the homily but even before the readings in the form of an introduction.

When the text of the readings lends itself to this, it may be helpful to have the children read it with parts distributed among them, as is provided for the reading of the Lord's passion during Holy Week.

48.   The homily explaining the word of God should be given great prominence in all Masses with children. Sometimes the homily intended for children should become a dialogue with them, unless it is preferred that they should listen in silence.

49.   If the profession of faith occurs at the end of the liturgy of the word, the Apostle's Creed may be used with children, especially because it is part of their catechetical formation.

### C. Presidential Prayers

50.   The priest is permitted to choose from the Roman Missal texts of presidential prayers more suited to children, so that he may truly associate the children with himself. But he is to take into account the liturgical season.

51.   Since these prayers were composed for adult Christians, however, the principle simply of choosing from among them does not serve the purpose of having the children regard the prayers as an expression of their own life and religious experience.[44] If this is the case, the text of prayers of the Roman Missal may be adapted to the needs of children, but this should be done in such a way that, preserving the purpose of the prayer and to some extent its substance as well, the priest avoids anything that is foreign to the literary genre of a presidential prayer, such as moral exhortations or a childish manner of speech.

52.   The eucharistic prayer is of the greatest importance in the eucharist celebrated with children because it is the high point of the entire celebration.[45] Much depends on the manner in which the priest proclaims this prayer[46] and on the way the children take part by listening and making their acclamations.

The disposition of mind required for this central part of the celebration and the calm and reverence with which everything is done must make the children as attentive as possible. Their attention should be on the real presence of Christ on the altar under the elements of bread and wine, on his offering, on the thanksgiving through him and with him and in him, and on the Church's offering, which is made during the prayer and by which the faithful offer themselves and their lives with Christ to the eternal Father in the Holy Spirit.

For the present, the four eucharistic prayers approved by the supreme authority for Masses with adults and introduced into liturgical use are to be employed until the Apostolic See makes other provision for Masses with children.

### D. Rites before Communion

53.   When the eucharistic prayer has ended, the Lord's Prayer, the breaking of bread, and the invitation to communion should always follow,[47] that is, the elements that have the principal significance in the structure of this part of the Mass.

54.　Everything should be done so that the children who are properly disposed and who have already been admitted to the eucharist may go to the holy table calmly and with recollection and thus take part fully in the eucharistic mystery. If possible, there should be singing, suited to the children, during the communion procession.[48]

The comments that precede the final blessing[49] are important in Masses with children. Before they are dismissed they need some repetition and application of what they have heard, but this should be done in a very few words. In particular, this is the appropriate time to express the connection between the liturgy and life.

At least sometimes, depending on the liturgical seasons and different occasions in the children's life, the priest should use more expanded forms of blessing, but at the end should always retain the Trinitarian formulary with the sign of the cross.[50]

*　　*　　*　　*　　*

55.　The contents of the Directory have as their purpose to help children readily and joyfully to encounter Christ together in the eucharistic celebration and to stand with him in the presence of the Father.[51] If they are formed by conscious and active participation in the eucharistic sacrifice and meal, they should learn day by day, at home and away from home, to proclaim Christ to others among their family and among their peers, by living the "faith, that works through love" (Gal 5:6).

This Directory was prepared by the Congregation for Divine Worship. On 22 October 1973, Pope Paul VI approved and confirmed it and ordered that it be published.

# NOTES

1. See GCD 5.

2. See CSL 33.

3. See GCD 78.

4. See CSL 38; also AP.

5. First Synod of Bishops, Liturgy: *Notitiae* 3 (1967) 368.

6. See DMC 19, 32, 33.

7. See Order of Mass with deaf and mute children of German-speaking regions approved, that is, confirmed by CDW, 26 June 1970 (Prot. no. 1546/70).

8. See CSL 14, 19.

9. See GCD 25.

10. See Vatican Council II, Declaration on Christian Education, *Gravissimum educationis*, no. 2.

11. See ibid, 3.

12. See GCD 78.

13. See CSL 33.

14. See EM 14.

15. See GCD 25.

16. See EM 14; GCD 57.

17. See CSL 35, 4.

18. See DMC 3.

19. See CSL 42, 106.

20. See First Synod of Bishops, Liturgy: *Notitiae* (1967) 368.

21. See GI 56.

22. See DMC 37.

23. See GI 11.

24. See CSL 28.

25. See GI 253.

26. See GI 19.

27. See MS 55.

28. MS 62.

29. See DMC 23.

30. See GI 21.

31. See GI 24.

32. GI 23.

33. See EM 38.

34. See GI 23.

35. GI 8.

36. CSL 48.

37. See DMC 21.

38. GI 15.

39. GI 24.

40. GI 33 .

41. Lectionary for Mass: Introduction, 1969 edition, no. 7d.

42. GI 33.

43. See GI 11.

44. See Consilium for the Implementation of the Constitution on the Sacred Liturgy, instruction on translations of liturgical texts for celebrations with a congregation, 25 Jan 1969, no. 20: *Notitiae* 5 (1969) 7.

45. GI 54.

46. See DMC 23, 37.

47. See DMC 23.

48. See MS 32.

49. See GI 11.

50. See DMC 39.

51. See RM, Eucharistic Prayer II.

# THIS HOLY
## AND
# LIVING SACRIFICE

DIRECTORY FOR THE CELEBRATION
AND RECEPTION OF COMMUNION
UNDER BOTH KINDS

# OVERVIEW OF
# THIS HOLY AND LIVING SACRIFICE

John M. Huels, OSM

*This Holy and Living Sacrifice: Directory for the Celebration and Reception of Communion under Both Kinds* (HLS) is a document that marks a change of major significance in the history of the liturgy. Its publication followed the approval by the Apostolic See in 1984 of the 1978 resolution of the National Conference of Catholic Bishops (NCCB) permitting the reception of communion under both kinds (under the form of wine as well as bread) on Sundays and holy days. Already in 1970 the NCCB had voted to permit the practice on weekdays.

During the thirteenth century, the practice of giving holy communion only in the form of bread became dominant in the Western church. Only the presiding priest communicated from the chalice. This custom, contrary to the practice of earlier centuries, was declared the general law of the Latin-rite church by the Council of Constance in 1415. Until recently, exceptions to that general rule had been few in number. In 1912, Pope Pius X permitted Latin-rite Catholics to receive holy communion in Eastern Catholic churches, where the administration of communion under both kinds always had been the rule. Nevertheless, the first *Code of Canon Law* (1917) reaffirmed the law that holy communion in Latin-rite churches could be distributed only in the form of bread (canon 852).

A principal aim of the twentieth-century liturgical movement had been the restoration of the chalice so that all communicants could participate fully in the Lord's Supper in the manner in which Christ had instituted it. After intense and prolonged debate, Vatican II, in 1963, approved an article in the *Constitution on the Sacred Liturgy*, no. 55b, that allowed the distribution of communion under both kinds to clerics, religious and laity at the discretion of the bishops in cases to be determined by the Apostolic See. In 1965, the Apostolic See published a rite for the distribution of communion under both kinds, permitting the practice in limited cases. This rite and a lengthier list of cases were later incorporated into the 1969 *General Instruction of the Roman Missal* (GIRM), nos. 240–252. (See also GIRM, nos. 48, 56h and 200–206, and no. 14 of the introduction to the GIRM.) In 1970, the Holy See permitted the conferences of bishops to determine when communion under both kinds could be given.

When the NCCB approved administering communion under both kinds at weekday Masses in 1970, the Bishops' Committee on the Liturgy also had proposed to extend the practice to Sundays and holy days, but this proposal failed to receive the necessary two-thirds majority approval of the nation's bishops. Opponents argued that there were not enough ordained ministers of communion for the large assemblies on those days of precept. With the introduction of lay ministers of communion in 1973, this obstacle was eliminated, and the way was paved for the 1978 NCCB resolution restoring communion under both kinds to all Masses on Sundays and holy days provided, in the judgment of the Ordinary, that communion could be distributed in an orderly and reverent manner.

The *General Instruction of the Roman Missal*, no. 242, lists the cases in which communion under both kinds may be distributed in the universal Latin-rite church. In the last paragraph of no. 242, communion under both kinds is said to be intended for clearly defined celebrations and for groups that are not too large but are specific, well ordered and homogeneous. The purpose of this requirement is to ensure the orderly distribution and reverent reception of holy communion. *This Holy and Living Sacrifice* provides helpful catechesis and directives in the attempt to fulfill this purpose, while at the same time it encourages the administration of communion under both kinds at nearly all eucharistic celebrations. There are only a few exceptions, listed in no. 22, when communion under both kinds is not permitted.

*This Holy and Living Sacrifice* is written in a style and format similar to the introductions to the postconciliar liturgical books, which are both doctrinal and disciplinary in content. Parts I and II are instructional in nature, giving key aspects of the church's eucharistic teaching—scriptural, theological and liturgical. The document recalls the doctrine of "concomitance," affirmed by the Council of Trent, which holds that Christ is truly present in the eucharist, body and blood, soul and divinity, under either species of bread or wine (no. 14). While it is doctrinally unnecessary to receive both the consecrated bread and wine to receive the whole Christ, the document points out many reasons why this is preferable to receiving only the bread. Drawing on church teachings found in the GIRM and elsewhere, HLS clarifies that communion under both kinds is a more complete sign of the eucharistic meal and a more faithful response to the Lord's command to "take and eat," "take and drink." Indeed, it says communion under both kinds "is to be desired in all celebrations of the Mass" (no. 19).

The preface of the directory notes its normative character. Its provisions are binding in all the Latin-rite dioceses of the United States. Part III of the document gives specific norms regulating the practice of communion under both kinds in order to ensure reverent and careful celebration and reception.

There are four different modes of distributing communion under both kinds, as established in GIRM, nos. 244–252. However, *This Holy and Living Sacrifice* states that the first mode—reception directly from the cup—"is always to be preferred to any other form of ministering the precious blood" (no. 44). This was the way it was done at the Last Supper in response to the Lord's command to "take and drink," and it was the dominant and preferred tradition in the Roman church before the practice died out. Today, communion from the cup is nearly the exclusive way that the precious blood is administered in the United States. The mode of intinction (whereby the host is dipped into the chalice and placed on the communicant's tongue) still is used in some places, but it is not favored by the NCCB, among other reasons because it does not allow communicants the option of receiving communion in the hand or the option of receiving communion under the form of bread alone (HLS, nos. 51, 52).

*This Holy and Living Sacrifice* marks for the United States the accomplishment of a major goal of the modern liturgical movement, the (nearly) total restoration of communion under both kinds. This advance in church law is not, however, reflected everywhere in actual practice. It is a disappointing fact that many Catholics do not regularly avail themselves of the cup, and it is even more regrettable that some pastors still do not offer the opportunity for it. One would hope that a great familiarity with the teachings and principles contained in HLS will contribute to the administration of the cup at a greater number of churches and to its reception by a greater number of communicants.

# OUTLINE

# THIS HOLY AND LIVING SACRIFICE
## DIRECTORY FOR THE CELEBRATION AND RECEPTION OF COMMUNION UNDER BOTH KINDS

## PART I
## INTRODUCTION

1.    From ancient times, the Church's teaching has clearly stated that the Eucharist is the center of Christian existence.[1] The Eucharist constitutes the very life of the Church, for the Lord said, "I myself am the bread of life. No one who comes to me shall ever be hungry, no one who believes in me shall ever thirst."[2] He who is the "living bread come down from heaven,"[3] assured the Church that "If anyone eats this bread he shall live forever; the bread I will give is my flesh, for the life of the world."[4] The Church places its trust and faith in Christ given in the Eucharist, for he said

> Let me solemnly assure you, if you do not eat the flesh of the Son of Man and drink his blood, you have no life in you. He who feeds on my flesh and drinks my blood has life eternal, and I will raise him up on the last day. For my flesh is real food; and my blood real drink.[5]

2.    Every time, then, that the Church assembles in the name of Jesus to celebrate the memorial of his passover from death to life and his glorification, it gathers to eat the bread of life and drink the cup of salvation.[6] "This means," as St. Paul admonishes us, "that whoever eats the bread or drinks the cup of the Lord unworthily sins against the body and blood of the Lord"[7] since eucharistic worship constitutes "the soul of Christian life."[8] The Eucharist which is the "sign of unity and bond of charity" is likewise "the school of active love for neighbor" for the Lord Jesus Christ "offers himself equally to each one, under the species of bread and wine."[9] This school of love is also called the Breaking of the Bread, for

> in apostolic times this gesture of Christ at the Last Supper gave the entire eucharistic action its name. This rite is not simply functional, but is a sign that in sharing in the one bread of life which is Christ we who are many are made one body (see 1 Cor 10:17).[10]

3.    The Eucharist has always been the source of Christian love and the center of ecclesial life,[11] daily building up the life of all Christians, "making of them a holy temple of the Lord, a dwelling-place for God in the Spirit, to the mature measure of the fullness of Christ."[12] The Eucharist "has the appearance of bread and wine, that is to say of food and drink; it is therefore familiar to people, as closely linked to their life, as food and drink."[13] This familiarity is linked also to a sense of great veneration and awe: the Lord who comes to the Church in the eucharistic banquet is also the God who is above all human experience. In Holy Communion the

faithful are at the same time brothers and sisters of the saving Christ and worshippers of the transcendent Holy One.[14]

4.     Therefore, the Church is concerned about all aspects of the eucharistic celebration, particularly the Rite of Holy Communion. The *Directory for the Celebration and Reception of Communion under Both Kinds* calls attention to the Church's eucharistic teaching on the nature of Christ's presence in the eucharistic elements and the underlying principles and norms by which the Rite of Communion under both kinds is ministered and received so that the Church's ministers of the Eucharist and all the faithful may have a deeper understanding of the very nature of the "Mystery of Faith."

# PART II
## THE CHURCH'S EUCHARISTIC TEACHING

5.     "The sacred character of the Eucharist has found and continues to find expression in the terminology of theology and the liturgy."[1] Thus in the prayer of remembrance or anamnesis, the one who presides proclaims: "we offer you in thanksgiving this holy and living sacrifice."[2] In the "memorial of our redemption"[3] the priest, in the person of Christ and in the name of the whole Church, implores the Spirit to "gather all who share this bread and wine into the one body of Christ, a living sacrifice of praise."[4] Through "this life-giving bread, this saving cup"[5] which have "become the body and blood of . . . our Lord Jesus Christ,"[6] God's People are renewed and refreshed by "the bread of life and the cup of eternal salvation,"[7] the one, holy, perfect and living sacrifice of praise, "the sacrifice of redemption and also the sacrifice of the New Covenant."[8]

### A. THE CENTER OF ECCLESIAL LIFE

6.     The sacred character and the magnitude of the Eucharistic Mystery "is so much a part of the faith of the People of God that their faith is enriched and strengthened by it."[9] The liturgical reforms required by the Second Vatican Council and embodied today in the Missal of Paul VI continue to renew the eucharistic life of the Church. For "when present at this mystery of faith," God's People "should not be there as strangers or silent spectators,"[10] for the Eucharist is also

> a sacrament of love, a sign of unity, a bond of charity, a paschal banquet in which Christ is consumed, the mind is filled with grace, and a pledge of future glory is given to us in the memorial of Christ's death and resurrection.[11]

The Eucharist

> is at one and the same time a Sacrifice-Sacrament, a Communion-Sacrament, and a Presence-Sacrament. And, although it is true to say that the Eucharist always was and must continue to be the most profound revelation of the human brotherhood of Christ's disciples and confessors, it cannot be treated merely as an occasion for manifesting this brotherhood.[12]

7.     In Holy Communion the faithful are joined to Christ and to one another in the reception of the Body and Blood of the Lord. In the great sacrament of the altar,

in which Christians remember and proclaim the wonderful works of God, it is Christ's will that the faithful

receive this sacrament for the preservation of his memory until he should come to judge the world. It was his will that this sacrament be received as the soul's spiritual food, to sustain and build up those who live with his life, as he said, "He who eats me, he also shall live because of me" (Jn 6:58). This sacrament is also to be a remedy to free us from our daily defects and to keep us from mortal sin. It was Christ's will, moreover, that this sacrament be a pledge of our future glory and our everlasting happiness and, likewise, a symbol of that one body of which he is the head. He willed that we, as members of this body should be united to it by firm bonds of faith, hope and love, so that we might all say the same thing, and that there might be no dissensions among us.[13]

## B. THE COMMON POSSESSION OF THE WHOLE CHURCH

8.   Because in the Liturgy of the Eucharist "the Church's rule of prayer *(lex orandi)* corresponds to its constant rule of faith *(lex credendi)*"[14] and likewise because "a very close and organic bond exists between the renewal of the liturgy and the renewal of the whole life of the Church,"[15] great care for the Eucharist, the sacrificial banquet, must be shown by all the faithful, ministers and assembly, even in the details of its celebration. For "the celebration of the Mass, the action of Christ and the people of God arrayed hierarchically, is for the universal and local Church as well as for each person the center of the whole Christian life."[16]

9.   The celebration of Mass, "the Lord's Supper,"[17] must be planned in such a way that it brings about in the faithful a participation in body and spirit that is conscious, active, full, and motivated by faith, hope, and charity."[18] The ecclesial nature of the Eucharist demands fidelity to the complete teaching of the Church on the nature of this great sacrament of love, at the same time as it requires the close collaboration of all, ministers and assembly, in the preparation and carrying out of each of its rites.[19] Thus no individual, no group, no local Church can be said to be the "sole proprietor" of the Eucharist.[20] "The Eucharist is the common possession of the whole Church as the sacrament of her unity. And thus the Church has the strict duty to specify everything which concerns participation in it and its celebration."[21]

10.   Fidelity to the Church's eucharistic doctrine and adherence to the Church's norms and directives concerning the eucharistic celebration interact with one another and express the ancient adage already alluded to, *"lex orandi, lex credendi."*[22] This teaching is nowhere more evident than in that rite toward which the Liturgy of the Word and the eucharistic prayer point, Holy Communion.[23] For Christ gave his body and blood to be eaten and drunk[24] so that all who participate share in the reality of his unique sacrifice and passover made present in sign and symbol in the Eucharist.[25]

For at the celebration of the Mass, which perpetuates the sacrifice of the Cross, Christ is really present to the assembly gathered in his name; he is present in the person of the minister, in his own word, and indeed substantially and permanently under the eucharistic elements.[26]

## C. PRESENCE OF CHRIST'S UNIQUE SACRIFICE

11.   The Church has taught the Real Presence of Christ in the eucharistic elements from time immemorial. At times that presence of love has been the cause of acrimonious debate among adherents of different theological points of view.[27] Ultimately it has always been the Liturgy of the Eucharist itself that has taught the true significance of Christ's presence, for in "the sacrifice and paschal meal that make the sacrifice of the cross to be continuously present in the Church . . . the priest, representing the Lord, carries out what the Lord did and handed over to his disciples to do in his memory."[28]

> Christ took the bread and the cup and gave thanks; he broke the bread, gave it to his disciples, saying: "Take and eat, this is my body." Giving the cup, he said: "Take and drink, this is the cup of my blood. Do this in memory of me." Accordingly, the Church has planned the celebration of the eucharistic liturgy around the parts corresponding to these words and actions of Christ. . . . [29]

12.   Bread and wine are brought to the altar and prepared. Thanks is given to God "for the whole work of salvation and the gifts of bread and wine become the body and blood of Christ" in the great eucharistic prayer of thanksgiving.[30] Finally, when the one bread is broken "the unity of the faithful is expressed and through communion they receive the Lord's body and blood in the same way the apostles received them from Christ's own hands."[31]

13.   These fundamental liturgical rites of the Mass embody Christ's actions at the Last Supper. For that Supper, in which his death, resurrection and ascension were proclaimed,[32] is also the legacy by which the mystery of his passover is made present today and the means by which the faithful share in that mystery.[33] In the bread and in the wine, over which the Church has pronounced its great thanksgiving, Christ is "truly, really, and substantially contained."[34] His presence is not momentary nor simply signified, but wholly and permanently real in both the consecrated bread and the consecrated wine.[35]

14.   As the Council of Trent teaches

> the true body and blood of our Lord, together with his soul and divinity, exist under the species of bread and wine. His body exists under the species of bread and his blood under the species of wine, according to the import of his words.[36]

The Church also teaches and believes that

> his body exists under the species of wine, his blood under the species of bread, and his soul under both species in virtue of the natural connection and concomitance which unite the parts of Christ our Lord who has risen from the dead and dies now no more. Moreover, Christ's divinity is present because of its admirable hypostatic union with his body and soul. It is, therefore, perfectly true that just as much is present under either species as

is present under both. For Christ, whole and entire, exists under the species of bread and under any part of that species, and similarly the whole Christ exists under the species of wine and under its parts.[37]

## D. FAITH IN THE PRESENCE OF CHRIST

15.    Christ's presence in the eucharistic elements surpasses all human understanding, all logic and ultimately all reason. His presence cannot be known by the senses but only through faith and through that communion which takes place between the Lord and his faithful in the very act of its celebration.

> For this reason the Fathers took special care to warn the faithful that in reflecting on this most august Sacrament, they should not trust to their senses, which reach only the properties of bread and wine, but rather to the words of Christ which have the power to transform, change and transmute the bread and wine into His Body and Blood.[38]

The teaching of St. Cyril of Jerusalem assists the Church even today to understand this great mystery:

> We have been instructed in these matters and filled with unshakable faith that that which seems to be bread is not bread, though it tastes like it, but the Body of Christ, and that which seems to be wine, is not wine, though it seems so to the taste, but the Blood of Christ. . . .[39]

16.    The act of Communion, therefore, is also an act of faith. For when the minister says, "The Body of Christ" or "The Blood of Christ," the communicant's "Amen" is a profession in the presence of the saving Christ, body, soul and divinity, who now gives life to the believer.[40]

The communicant makes this act of faith in the total presence of the Lord Jesus Christ whether in Communion under one form or in Communion under both kinds. It should never be construed, therefore, that Communion under the form of bread alone or Communion under the form of wine alone is somehow an incomplete act or that Christ is not fully present to the communicant. The Church's unchanging teaching from the time of the Fathers through ages of the ecumenical councils of the Lateran, Constance, Florence, Trent and the Second Vatican Council has witnessed to a constant unity of faith in the presence of Christ in both elements.[41]

## E. RESTORATION OF AN ANCIENT PRACTICE

17.    There has long been a desire among God's People for the restoration of the ancient practice of Communion under both kinds, not from any wavering or lack of faith or doubt of the Church's teaching. Rather the faithful have yearned that Christ's presence in the Eucharist be more fully expressed in the Rite of Communion under the form of bread and under the form of wine in one liturgical action. The restoration of this practice was not opportune when the Council of Trent was convened in 1545.[42] But with the passing of centuries of polemic and discord, and under the guidance of the Holy Spirit, the Fathers of the Second Vatican Council wished for a "more perfect form of participation in the Mass."[43] In the decrees set

forth in the *Constitution on the Sacred Liturgy*, the bishops of the world established the principles by which the entire eucharistic liturgy was to be revised. The reform of the Mass touched upon each element of its structure, including the Rite of Communion and Communion under both the forms of bread and wine.

> The dogmatic principles which were laid down by the Council of Trent remaining intact, Communion under both kinds may be granted when the bishops see fit, not only to clerics and religious, but also to the laity, in cases to be determined by the Apostolic See.[44]

18.   Thus, the Church's teaching on the Real Presence remaining unchanged, the *General Instruction of the Roman Missal*, promulgated by Pope Paul VI on April 3, 1969, states clearly the nature of the tradition of Communion under both kinds:

> Holy Communion has a more complete form as a sign when it is received under both kinds. For in this manner of reception a fuller light shines on the sign of the eucharistic banquet. Moreover, there is a clearer expression of that will by which the new and everlasting covenant is ratified in the blood of the Lord and of the relationship of the eucharistic banquet to the eschatological banquet in the Father's kingdom.[45]

19.   So that this "fuller light" may fall upon the import of Christ's words at the Last Supper[46] and in the eucharistic prayer, and for the sake of the faithful's greater participation in the mystery, Communion under both kinds is to be desired in all celebrations of the Mass, although this is not possible in all cases. For in this sacred rite "the sign of the eucharistic meal stands out more explicitly,"[47] and the act of drinking the consecrated wine, the Blood of Christ, strengthens the faith of communicants in the sacrificial nature of the Mass.[48] Communion under both kinds can therefore manifest more fully the nature of the Mass both as a sacrifice and as a sacred banquet, ritually expressing that "the sacrifice and the sacred Meal belong to the same mystery, to such an extent that they are linked to one another by a very close theological and sacramental bond."[49]

## F. WHEN COMMUNION UNDER BOTH KINDS MAY BE GIVEN

20.   At the discretion of the ordinary, and only after the proper catechesis of the faithful has taken place and the necessary cautions for its reverent celebration have been pointed out, Communion under both kinds is especially encouraged in the cases of:

a.   newly baptized adults at the Mass following their baptism; adults at the Mass at which they receive confirmation; baptized persons who are being received into the full communion of the Church;

b.   the bride and bridegroom at their wedding Mass;

c.   deacons at the Mass of their ordination;

d.   an abbess at the Mass in which she is blessed; those consecrated to a life of virginity at the Mass of their consecration; professed religious, their relatives, friends, and other members of their community at the Mass of first or perpetual vows or renewal of vows;

e.  those who receive institution for a certain ministry at the Mass of their institution; lay missionary helpers at the Mass in which they publicly receive their mission; others at the Mass in which they receive an ecclesiastical mission;

f.  the sick person and all present at the time viaticum is to be administered when Mass is lawfully celebrated in the sick person's home;

g.  the deacon and ministers who exercise their office at Mass;

h.  when there is a concelebration, in the case of:
    1.  all who exercise a liturgical function at this concelebration and also all seminarians present;
    2.  in their churches or oratories, all members of institutes professing the evangelical counsels and other societies whose members dedicate themselves to God by religious vows or by an offering or promise; also all those who reside in the houses of members of such institutes and societies;

i.  priests who are present at major celebrations and are not able to celebrate or concelebrate;

j.  all who make a retreat at a Mass in which they actively participate and which is specially celebrated for the group; also all who take part in the meeting of any pastoral body at a Mass they celebrate as a group;

k.  those listed in b and d above, at Masses celebrating their jubilees;

l.  godparents, relatives, wife or husband, and lay catechists of newly baptized adults at the Mass of their initiation;

m.  relatives, friends, and special benefactors who take part in the Mass of a newly ordained priest;

n.  members of communities at the conventual or community Mass, in accord with the provisions of the *General Instruction of the Roman Missal*, 76;[50]

o.  when other members of the faithful are present on the special occasions enumerated in no. 242 of the *General Instruction of the Roman Missal* (See no. 19 above);

p.  at funeral Masses and Masses for a special family observance;

q.  at Masses on days of special religious or civil significance for the people of the United States;

r.  at Masses on Holy Thursday and at the Mass of the Easter Vigil, the norms of *Sacramentali Communione* being observed;

s.  at weekday Masses.[51]

21.    Communion under both kinds is also permitted at parish and community Masses celebrated on Sundays and holy days of obligation in the dioceses of the United States.[52] However, because very often the number of the faithful in a liturgical assembly is great, the ordinary should be especially aware of the difficulties large assemblies pose for the reverent celebration of the Rite of Communion.

22.   Communion under both kinds, however, is not permitted in the following cases:

a.   at Masses celebrated in the open with a great number of communicants (e.g., in a stadium);

b.   at other Masses where the number of communicants is so great as to make it difficult for Communion under both kinds to be given in an orderly and reverent way (e.g., Masses celebrated in a civic square or building that would involve the carrying of the sacred species up and down a number of steps);

c.   at Masses where the assembled congregation is of such a diverse nature that it is difficult to ascertain whether those present have been sufficiently instructed about receiving Communion under both kinds;

d.   when circumstances do not permit the assurance that due reverence can be maintained towards the consecrated wine both during and after the celebration (cf. *Inaestimabile Donum,* 13–14).[53]

23.   When the ordinary permits Communion under both kinds on Sundays and holy days, he shall point out to pastors and others that it is of "special significance in the spiritual life of any community or group of the faithful."[54] Therefore, prior to its implementation, there must be proper diocesan norms concerning all matters touched upon in this directory. When, however, Communion under both kinds is requested in weekday or Sunday Masses celebrated outside the usual place (church, chapel, oratory, etc.), and the number of those participating in the liturgical celebration is especially great, the local ordinary, whose permission is always required, should determine whether Communion under both kinds is to be given, and, if so, he should review all preparations and plans according to the norms of this directory.

## G. MINISTERS OF COMMUNION

24.   The *General Instruction of the Roman Missal,* as a general rule, excludes Communion under both kinds at "occasions when there will be a large number of communicants,"[55] primarily because of the inherent difficulties of celebrating Communion reverently and also because there is usually an insufficient number of ordinary ministers, priests and deacons at such large celebrations. However, *Immensae Caritatis* in 1973 specifically addressed the problem of insufficient ministers of Communion by permitting the local ordinary to appoint suitable men and women to assist priests and deacons as special or extraordinary ministers of Communion. Among the occasions when the local ordinary is permitted to use the faculty of appointing extraordinary ministers are those times when "the number of the faithful requesting Holy Communion is such that the celebration of Mass or the distribution of the Eucharist outside Mass would be unduly prolonged."[56]

25.   The decrees of *Immensae Caritatis,* the catechesis on the Eucharist, and the familiarity of the faithful with Communion under both kinds made conditions favorable for an extension of Communion under both kinds on Sundays and holy days of obligation.[57]

26.  It seems opportune that both the Church's teaching on Christ's presence in Communion under both kinds, already stated above, and the norms and directives of the Church on all matters touching especially upon the proper celebration and reception of Communion under the form of wine, be restated and clarified. Therefore, the following norms and directives are to be followed by all parishes, religious communities and other groups of the faithful when Communion is given under the forms of both bread and wine.

# PART III
# NORMS FOR THE CELEBRATION AND RECEPTION OF COMMUNION UNDER BOTH KINDS
## A. THE PURPOSE OF THE NORMS

27.  The purpose and nature of these norms and directives are to ensure the reverent and careful celebration and reception of Communion under both kinds. Priests, deacons, acolytes, and special (extraordinary) ministers of Communion and all who are responsible for the preparation and planning of eucharistic worship should follow them with due attention.

## B. CATECHESIS

28.  When Communion under both kinds is first introduced by the diocesan or religious ordinary, and also whenever the opportunity for instruction is present, the faithful should be properly catechized on the following matters in the light of the teaching and directives of the *General Instruction of the Roman Missal* and other appropriate instructions and directives:

a.  the ecclesial nature of the Eucharist as the common possession of the whole Church;

b.  the Eucharist as the memorial of Christ's sacrifice, his death and resurrection, and as the sacred Banquet;

c.  the Real Presence of Christ in the eucharistic elements, whole and entire, in each element of bread and wine (the doctrine of concomitance);

d.  the kinds of reverence due at all times to the sacrament, whether within the eucharistic liturgy or outside the celebration.[1]

## C. MINISTERS OF COMMUNION

29.  In every celebration of the Eucharist there should always be a sufficient number of ministers for the distribution of Communion. Priority is always given to ordinary ministers (bishops, priests, deacons) and auxiliary ministers (instituted acolytes). When there are large numbers of the faithful present and there are insufficient ordinary and auxiliary ministers at hand, special or extraordinary ministers properly appointed beforehand should assist in the distribution of Communion.[2]

30.   It is desirable that all priests, deacons, acolytes and extraordinary ministers of Communion who assist the bishop or priest who presides over the celebration be present for and participate in the entire celebration of the Mass and not only for the Rite of Holy Communion. This may not, however, always be possible for the ordinary ministers, who must not, for this reason, be replaced by extraordinary ministers.

31.   Past experience and proper preparation for the celebration will enable those responsible to know exactly how many ministers are needed at each Mass.

32.   With the exception of those cases enumerated in no. 22 of this directory, when Communion under both kinds may not be given, at other eucharistic celebrations where extremely large numbers of the faithful are assembled, a careful judgment should be made by the ordinary whether or not Communion under both kinds is to be offered to all or only to as many as possible or convenient. Even when Communion will be ministered in the form of bread alone, there should always be sufficient consecrated wine for concelebrating bishops and priests, assisting deacons, acolytes, extraordinary ministers of Communion, and other ministers of the celebration.

33.   When Communion is to be given from the cup, generally there should be two ministers of the consecrated wine for each minister of the consecrated bread. In this way, the Rite of Holy Communion will not be unduly prolonged.

34.   Ministers shall always show the greatest reverence for the eucharistic species by their demeanor and in the manner in which they handle the consecrated bread or wine.

35.   Should there be any mishap, for example, if the consecrated wine is spilled from the chalice, the area should be washed and the water poured into the sacrarium.[3]

36.   After Communion the eucharistic bread that remains is to be stored in the tabernacle. Care should be taken in regard to any fragments remaining on the corporal or in the sacred vessels.[4] In those instances when there remains more consecrated wine than was necessary, the ministers shall consume it immediately at a side table before the Prayer After Communion, while the vessels themselves may be purified after Mass.[5] The amount of wine to be consecrated should be carefully measured before the celebration so that none remains afterward.

37.   The consecrated wine may not be reserved, except for someone who is ill.

Sick people who are unable to receive communion under the form of bread may receive it under the form of wine alone. If the wine is consecrated at a Mass not celebrated in the presence of the sick person, the blood of the Lord is kept in a properly covered vessel and is placed in the tabernacle after communion. The precious blood should be carried to the sick in a vessel which is closed in such a way as to eliminate all danger of spilling. If some of the precious blood remains, it should be consumed by the minister, who should also see to it that the vessel is properly purified.[6]

38.   It is strictly prohibited to pour the precious blood into the ground or into the sacrarium.

## D. PREPARATION

39.   From experience careful judgments should be made before the celebration of each Mass that enough bread and wine are made ready for the communication of the faithful in a particular eucharistic liturgy.[7] Wine may not be consecrated at one Mass and reserved for use at another.[8]

40.   The wine should be placed in flagons or pitchers of careful design and quality as befits the celebration of the eucharistic mystery. The bread should be placed on one large paten or plate, or in a ciborium in the style of a bowl appropriate as a container of bread. The vessels should be sturdy, made of materials which are solid and nonabsorbent. Preference is always to be given to materials that do not break easily or become unusable.[9] Before being used, vessels for the celebration must be blessed by the bishop or priest according to the Rite of Blessing of a Chalice and Paten.[10]

41.   Use is not to be made of simple baskets or other receptacles meant for ordinary use outside of the sacred celebrations, nor are the sacred vessels to be of poor quality or lacking any artistic merit.[11]

42.   When the altar is prepared after the general intercessions the wine may be brought forward in one chalice or, when the assembly is very large, one chalice and as many flagons as are necessary. Only one chalice (and the requisite number of flagons) and one large paten, ciborium or similar vessel, should be on the altar during the rites of preparation up to and including the rite of the fraction when other empty chalices and ciboria may be brought to the altar. At that time the consecrated bread is placed in several ciboria or plates and the consecrated wine is poured into enough chalices for use in the Rite of Communion. It should be remembered that enough eucharistic bread should be consecrated for each Mass.

43.   As soon as the *Agnus Dei* or "Lamb of God" is begun, the bishop or priest who presides, with the assistance of other priests, deacons, and acolytes or extraordinary ministers of Communion, if the former are not available, breaks the eucharistic bread and pours the consecrated wine into the chalices.[12] This action is performed generally at the altar, so that the sharing of all from the one cup is signified; in the case of large assemblies it may be done at the side table within the presbyterium.

## E. MINISTRATION OF THE CUP

44.   Because of its ancient sign value *"ex institutione Christi,"* Communion from the cup or chalice is always to be preferred to any other form of ministering the precious blood.[13]

45.   The chalice is always offered to the communicant with the words "The Blood of Christ," to which the communicant responds, "Amen."

When Communion is given by intinction, the minister shall say "The Body and Blood of Christ," to which the communicant responds, "Amen."[14]

46.    The chalice may never be left on the altar or another place to be picked up by the communicant for self-communication (except in the case of concelebrating bishops or priests), nor may the chalice be passed from one communicant to another. There shall always be a minister of the cup.[15]

47.    After each communicant has received the Blood of Christ, the minister shall carefully wipe both sides of the rim of the cup with a purificator. This action is both a matter of courtesy and hygiene. It is also customary for the minister to move the chalice a quarter turn after each communicant for the same reasons.

48.    When Communion from the cup is offered to the assembly, it shall always be clear that it is the option of the communicant and not of the minister whether the communicant shall receive the consecrated wine. Of course, pastors should encourage the whole assembly to receive Communion under both kinds.[16]

49.    Special care shall be given when children receive Communion from the chalice. Parents should be instructed that Communion under both kinds is an ancient tradition for children old enough to drink from a cup. However, children should have some familiarity with drinking wine at home before they are offered the chalice.

## F. OTHER FORMS OF COMMUNION UNDER BOTH KINDS

50.    *The General Instruction of the Roman Missal* allows for three other forms of receiving the consecrated wine:

a.    The Blood of Christ may be received from the chalice through a silver tube. In this form tubes are needed for the celebrant and for each communicant. There should also be a container of water for purifying the tubes and a paten on which to put them afterward.

b.    When communion is given with a spoon, only one spoon is necessary.

c.    Communion may also be given by intinction. However, care is to be taken that the eucharistic bread is not too thin or too small, but a little thicker than usual so that after being partly dipped into the precious blood, it can still be easily given to the communicant.[17]

51.    The forms of receiving the precious blood listed in no. 50 are not customary in the United States, since they are more fitting when the number of communicants is small and all in the assembly wish to receive Communion under both kinds. For in larger assemblies not all may be able or wish to receive the precious blood.

52.    Reception of the precious blood through a tube, in a spoon or by intinction may remove the communicant's legitimate option to receive Communion in the hand or, for valid reasons, not to receive the consecrated wine. However, if

Communion is given by intinction the communicant may never dip the eucharistic bread into the chalice. Communion under either the form of bread or wine must always be given by a minister with the usual words.

## G. CONCLUSION

53.   The norms and directives established by the Church for the celebration of any liturgical rite always have as their immediate goal the proper and careful celebration of those rites. However, such directives also have as their purpose celebrations which deepen the faith of the participants in liturgical worship. The ordered preparation and celebration of the Mass, Holy Communion in particular, should always profoundly affect the faith of communicants in all its aspects and dimensions. Not only will the faithful have a greater appreciation and deeper understanding of the nature of the Eucharist as both a sacrifice and a banquet, their faith in the presence of the Lord in the eucharistic species will also be strengthened by the reverence with which Communion is ministered and received. In the case of Communion under both kinds, now restored in the Church, Christian faith in the Real Presence of Christ can only be renewed and deepened in the life of all Christians.

54.   In all other matters pertaining to the Rite of Communion under both kinds the directives of the *General Instruction of the Roman Missal*, 244–252 and the instruction *Inaestimabile Donum*, "On Certain Norms Concerning Worship of the Eucharistic Mystery" (April 17, 1980), 9–17 are to be followed.

# NOTES

## PART I

1. "The Church lives by the Eucharist, by the fullness of this Sacrament, the stupendous content and meaning of which have often been expressed in the Church's Magisterium from the most distant times down to our own days" (Pope John Paul II, *Redemptor Hominis* (RH), [March 4, 1979] 20). See also Pope Paul VI, *Mysterium Fidei* (MF), "On the Holy Eucharist" (September 3, 1965) 57.

2. Jn 6:35.

3. Jn 6:51.

4. Ibid.

5. Jn 6:52–55.

6. Cf. 1 Cor 11:23–26.

7. 1 Cor 11:27.

8. Pope John Paul II, *Dominicae Cenae* (DC), "On the Mystery and Worship of the Holy Eucharist" (February 24, 1980) 5.

9. Ibid.

10. *Roman Missal*, General Instruction (GIRM) (4th edition, March 27, 1975) 56c.

11. DC 7.

12. CSL 2.

13. DC 7.

14. Ibid.

## PART II

1. DC 8.

2. Eucharistic Prayer (EP) III.

3. EP IV.

4. EP IV.

5. EP II.

6. EP III.

7. EP I (Roman Canon).

8. DC 9.

9. Ibid. 8.

10. CSL 48.

11. Ibid. 47.

12. RH 20.

13. Council of Trent, Session XIII, "Decree on the Most Holy Eucharist" (October 11, 1551), Chapter II: *De ratione institutionis ss. huius sacramenti* in Denzinger-Schönmetzer, *Enchiridion Symbolorum, Definitionum et Declarationum de rebus fidei et morum (editio xxxiv)* (DS), 1638; *The Church Teaches* (TCT) 720.

14. GIRM Introduction 2.

15. DC 13.

16. GIRM 1.

17. Ibid. 2.

18. Ibid. 3.

19. Cf. DC 11.

20. DC 12.

21. Ibid.

22. GIRM Introduction 6–10.

23. Cf. *The Lectionary for Mass*, Introduction (second typical edition, January 21, 1981) 10.

24. DS 1658 (TCT 735).

25. Cf. MF 52.

26. GIRM 7. Cf. CSL 7.

27. Cf. MF 52–54.

28. GIRM 48.

29. Ibid.

30. GIRM 48:2. Cf. also Sacred Congregation for the Sacraments and Divine Worship, *Inaestimabile Donum* (ID), "On Certain Norms Concerning Worship of the Eucharistic Mystery" (April 3, 1980) 8, on the bread and wine to be used in the celebration of the Lord's Supper.

31. Ibid. 48:3.

32. DC 11.

33. Ibid.

34. DS 1651 (TCT 728).

35. "Because Christ our Redeemer said that it was truly his body that he was offering under the species of bread (see Mt 26:26ff.; Mk 14:22ff.; Lk 22:19ff.; 1 Cor 11:24ff.), it has always been the conviction of the Church, and this holy council now again declares it that, by the consecration of the

bread and wine a change takes place in which the whole substance of bread is changed into the substance of the body of Christ our Lord and the whole substance of the wine into the substance of his blood. This change the holy Catholic Church fittingly and properly names transubstantiation" (Council of Trent, *Decree on the Most Holy Eucharist*, Chapter IV. *Transubstantiation* [DS 1642/TCT 722]).

36. DS 1640 (TCT 721).

37. Ibid.

38. MF 47.

39. Ibid. 48.

40. ID 11: "The *Amen* said by the faithful when receiving Communion is an act of personal faith in the presence of Christ." Holy Communion in the Eucharist also brings "protection," as St. Cyprian states: "Since the eucharist is meant to protect those who receive it, the people whom we want to see protected against the enemy should be given the help the Lord's food brings with it. How can we instruct and urge them to shed their blood in confession of Christ's name if we refuse them the blood of Christ when they go out to battle? How can we instill in them the strength to drink the cup of martyrdom if we do not first permit them to drink the cup of the Lord in the Church, in virtue of the right to do so that comes through communion with us?" (*Epist.* 57, 2,2).

41. Cf. note 35. The practice of *communione sub una* antedates these councils and was already a frequent occurrence in patristic times, permitted especially for infants and the elderly. (See Cyprian, *De Lapsis*, c. 25, on communion of infants and children; on communion of the sick and dying, see *Statuta eccles. antiqua*, can. 76, ed. Mansi, III, 957.) By the twelfth century theologians such as Peter Cantor ( + 1197) speak of communion under one kind as a "custom" of the Church. (See Petrus Cantor, *Summa de Sacramentis et Animae Consiliis*, ed. J.-A. Dugauquier, *Analecta Mediev. Namurcensia* 4, Louvain/Lille, 1954, I, 144.)

42. Cf. Council of Trent, Session XXI (July 16, 1562), *De Doctrina de communione sub utraque specie et parvulorum* (DS 1725–1734/TCT 739–745).

43. CSL 14, 19. See also, *Code of Canon Law* (1983), canons 912–923, "Participation in the Most Holy Eucharist," and canon 925

which states, "Holy Communion is to be given under the form of bread alone or under both kinds in accord with the norms of liturgical laws or even under the form of wine alone in case of necessity" (Canon Law Society of America, *Code of Canon Law*, Latin-English Edition, Washington, D.C., 1983).

44. Ibid. 55.

45. GIRM 240.

46. DS 1640 (TCT 721).

47. GIRM 241.

48. Sacred Congregation of Rites, *Eucharisticum Mysterium* (EM), "Instruction on Eucharistic Worship" (May 25, 1967), Introduction.

49. Congregation for Divine Worship, *Actio Pastoralis*, "Instruction on Masses for Special Gatherings" (May 15, 1969) 5.

50. GIRM 242.

51. The cases listed in 20a–e were authorized by the National Conference of Catholic Bishops in November 1970 in accord with the Instruction of the Sacred Congregation for Divine Worship, *Sacramentali Communione*, "On the Extension of the Faculty to Distribute Holy Communion under Both Kinds" (June 29, 1970). Cf. Appendix to the *General Instruction of the Roman Missal* for the Dioceses of the United States of America, 242 (*Liturgy Documentary Series 2: General Instruction of the Roman Missal*, Appendix I, p. 93).

52. In November 1978 the National Conference of Catholic Bishops authorized the extension of Communion under both kinds at Masses celebrated on Sundays and holy days of obligation, the norms of the *General Instruction of the Roman Missal* being observed, by the following resolution: "In addition to the instances already conceded by the Apostolic See and by the National Conference of Catholic Bishops, Holy Communion may be given under both kinds to the faithful at Masses on Sundays and holy days of obligation if, in the judgment of the ordinary, Communion may be given in an orderly and reverent manner." This decision was confirmed by the Congregation for Divine Worship on October 13, 1984 (Prot. CD 1297/78).

53. Letter of the Congregation for Divine Worship, October 13, 1984 (Prot. CD 1297/78).

54. GIRM 242.

55. Ibid.

56. Sacred Congregation for the Discipline of the Sacraments, *Immensae Caritatis* (IC), "Instruction on Facilitating Sacramental Communion in Particular Circumstances (January 29, 1973) I, 1c.

57. Cf. ID 12.


PART III

1. Cf. EM, Part I, "Some General Principles of Particular Importance in the Catechesis of the People on the Mystery of the Eucharist."

2. Cf. IC, Part I, "Extraordinary Ministers for the Distribution of Holy Communion"; also ID 10.

3. GIRM 239.

4. ID 13: "Even after Communion the Lord remains present under the species . Accordingly, when Communion has been distributed, the sacred particles remaining are to be consumed or taken by the competent minister to the place where the Eucharist is reserved."

5. ID 14; GIRM 120, 237–239.

6. *Pastoral Care of the Sick: Rites of Anointing and Viaticum* 74.

7. GIRM 56h; EM 31.

8. ID 14.

9. GIRM 288–296; ID 16.

10. Cf. *The Roman Pontifical: Dedication of a Church and an Altar,* Chapter 7. See also *Rituale Romanum: De benedictionibus,* 1068–1084.

11. ID 16.

12. GIRM 56c–e.

13. *Sacramentali Communione* 6.

14. GIRM 244c, 246b; ID 11.

15. GIRM 244–252; *Sacramentali Communione* 6.

16. GIRM 241.

17. GIRM 246–252.

# MUSIC
## IN
# CATHOLIC WORSHIP

# OVERVIEW OF *MUSIC IN CATHOLIC WORSHIP* AND *LITURGICAL MUSIC TODAY*

Edward Foley, Capuchin

In 1963, the *Constitution on the Sacred Liturgy* (CSL) asserted that music performs a particular ministerial function in worship and forms a necessary or integral part of the liturgy (CSL, no. 112). This statement was the culmination of almost 60 years of evolution in official church opinions on church music stretching back to Pius X (d. 1914), who maintained that music was an integral part of the solemn liturgy. By incorporating this revolutionary perspective into a document calling for the renewal of the liturgy, the CSL did more than simply reassert an old claim. Rather, it signaled the transformation of the church's worship music. It is notable, however, that the CSL offered few other principles to guide the transformation process.

In the years after the Council, various other documents and decrees began to spell out how our worship music was to be transformed. One of the earliest and most important of these was the 1967 instruction *Musicam Sacram* (Sacred Music) from the Sacred Congregation of Rites. In response to this instruction and in an attempt to offer more concrete guidelines for selecting and incorporating music into the worship of the church, the music advisory board of the Bishops' Committee on the Liturgy in the United States drafted a statement entitled "The Place of Music in Eucharistic Celebrations" (1967). Soon after its appearance, the Bishops' Committee on the Liturgy approved this statement, adopted it as its own and recommended it to the church of the United States (1968). This first major statement from the United States hierarchy on music in worship was a seminal piece of work, articulating with unusual clarity guidelines on liturgical music that were accessible to ordinary parochial ministers.

The importance of the topic led the Federation of Diocesan Liturgical Commissions to appoint a committee to study and critique the 1968 statement. Their critique, along with the intervening years of experimentation with sung English worship, was the ferment that eventually produced the 1972 document, *Music in Catholic Worship*.

## MUSIC IN CATHOLIC WORSHIP

*Music in Catholic Worship* (MCW) continues to be one of the finest pastoral documents on Christian liturgical music in existence today. Though written for the Roman Catholic Church in the United States, the breadth and insight of the document has resulted in the appropriation of its principles by other language groups and by other denominations.

The strength of the document is centered in two sections. The heart of the work is an exposition of the three critical judgments that the document considers central for determining the value of a given musical element in the liturgy (no. 25). These are the musical judgment (nos. 26–29), the liturgical judgment (nos. 30–38) and the pastoral judgment (nos. 39–41). The basic outline of this material first appeared in the 1968 document, "The Place of Music in Eucharistic Celebrations." The genius of this section is its concise articulation of principles that place the evaluation of worship music within the context of its usage by the particular people who are called to pray this music.

The second key section of this document is the theology of celebration found in the opening nine paragraphs. Also heavily dependent on the 1968 document, this section sets the theological context for understanding and considering music in worship. These paragraphs are influenced particularly by developments in twentieth-century thought on the nature of symbols. Such developments have prepared the way for MCW's assertion that symbols, including music, not only express our faith but they also shape our faith for good or for ill. Thus MCW baldly admits: "Good celebrations foster and nourish faith. Poor celebrations may weaken and destroy it" (no. 6).

Third, the section on pastoral planning for celebration (nos. 10–22) is notable. Though much of this material seems tame today, it was quite revolutionary when first published. This section has virtually no precedent in the 1968 document. Especially striking here is the keen assessment of the critical role of the presider or "celebrant" in worship. Significant, too, is the document's lucid acknowledgment that nothing affects the liturgy as much as the "attitude, style and bearing of the celebrant" (no. 21).

The section on "liturgical structures" (nos. 42–49) breaks little new ground. More important on this topic is the comparable section in the *General Instruction of the Roman Missal* (nos. 24–57), which serves as the basis for most of this material.

Of least enduring value in this document is the long section on the "Application of Principles of Celebration to Music in Eucharistic Worship" (nos. 50–78). Though undoubtedly progressive in the early 1970s, with the passing of time these paragraphs increasingly reveal how underdeveloped were our principles for wedding music to rite. This is clear, for example, in the way the document attends to the musical aspects of each individual moment in the eucharist such as the "Lord, have mercy" or the "Lamb of God," while paying virtually no attention to how music operates in the larger liturgical units such as the entrance or communion rites. Furthermore, some of the structural analysis and ensuing suggestions are untenable today. One such example is the suggestion that one of the five most important elements to be sung during the eucharist is the "doxology to the Lord's Prayer" (no. 54).

At the end of the document is a brief section on "Music in Sacramental Celebrations" (nos. 79–83). The brevity of this section underscores one of the overall weaknesses of MCW: its preoccupation with eucharistic liturgy. This weakness was one of the issues that *Liturgical Music Today* attempted to rectify.

*LITURGICAL MUSIC TODAY*

The decade after the appearance of *Music in Catholic Worship* was a period of unusual growth and development in the liturgical music industry in this country. It was also a period of significant musical activity and pastoral experimentation. Consequently, the 1970s served as an important testing period for MCW, during which some of the limitations of MCW became apparent. Besides the previously mentioned preoccupation with the eucharist, this included a great variety of issues ranging from the exclusive language of the document to major "missing pieces" such as the absence of any discussion of technology and musical worship.

Furthermore, developments in liturgical-musical scholarship, the emergence of various pastoral organizations and the work of groups such as *Universa Laus* provided new frameworks for understanding the role of music in worship. One emerging concept that goes unexplored in MCW, for example, is ritual music. Given these various developments, it was decided in the late 1970s to rewrite MCW. After some testing of the waters, however, it was decided that MCW was such an important document that its strength and integrity should not be jeopardized by a rewriting process that might weaken the work. Consequently, the rewriting of *Music in Catholic Worship* gave way to the composition of a new document, *Liturgical Music Today* (LMT).

The introduction of LMT notes that this document treats subjects not addressed in MCW. The introduction further observes that LMT attends to various developments that have taken place since the writing of MCW. Thus LMT should be read as a companion to the 1972 work (no. 3). These introductory remarks clearly indicate that LMT is not meant to supersede MCW in any way. This is an implicit acknowledgment of the continuing centrality of MCW today.

Following the introduction, LMT is divided into five sections. One of the most original and valuable of these is the first section on general principles (nos. 6–16). Among other things, these paragraphs attempt to articulate principles governing the function of music in the liturgy and the function and form of various musical elements (nos. 6–11). This section also reiterates the very important principle of progressive solemnity (no. 13) that originally appeared in the less well-known *General Instruction of the Liturgy of the Hours*. The inclusion of this principle in LMT has assured its broader dissemination among English-speaking liturgists and pastoral musicians.

The segment, "Music in the Eucharist" (nos. 16–21), offers reflections on specific elements such as acclamations and processional chants. This is followed by sections on "Music in the Celebration of Other Sacraments" (nos. 22–33), "Music in the Liturgy of the Hours" (nos. 34–45) and a catchall section entitled "Other Matters" (nos. 46–74). Of all these subdivisions, the last one contains some of the most valuable material in the document. Especially noteworthy is the document's willingness to address more specifically the issue of music and cultural heritage (nos. 54–55).

Unfortunately, LMT does a better job of raising issues than of offering strong principles; it reads like a catalog of questions and problems that need to be more fully explored. Thus LMT is useful for outlining parts of the musical-liturgical agenda for the coming decades. It is less useful, however, in moving that agenda along.

UNRESOLVED ISSUES

The past three decades have demonstrated the enduring strength of MCW and less so that of LMT. Despite the perennial value of the former, however, it is a document not without its faults. When reading MCW and its companion—especially the core sections on the musical, liturgical and pastoral judgments—it would be helpful to keep the following in mind. These may help the reader to take the next step beyond MCW and LMT.

When addressing the musical judgment (nos. 26–29), MCW draws an unnecessary distinction between popular music and what it calls "artistically sound" music. This language suggests that popular music is prone to be poor music and, conversely, that the opposite kind of music, i.e., music for the elite or concert-hall music, is better. A second problem in this section is MCW's ethnocentrism when it comes to musical judgments. Distinctions between "artistically sound" and "popular" music suggest a northern European perspective, generally adopted in the United States, in which art music and popular or folk music have developed separately. This distinction does not exist in many cultures and must be addressed if we are to cherish the "rich diversity of the cultural heritage of the many peoples of our country" of which LMT so eloquently speaks (no. 54). Third, MCW gives the impression that music is to be evaluated only in terms of the printed page and not the performance event. This again demonstrates the Western classical bias for judging a composition according to what is in the score and not necessarily by how it has been or could be performed.

Turning to the liturgical judgments (nos. 30–38), when discussing liturgical texts, MCW only addresses questions of orthodoxy and not the issue of poetics. Furthermore, MCW and LMT do not address issues of inclusive language. These are two critical topics that need further development as we face the deeper implications of sung worship in the vernacular. Turning to the question of the musical performance, neither document considers what performance styles are appropriate to pastoral musicians. Given the influence of the entertainment industry in the United States, this is a topic of crucial reflection.

One of the most problematic aspects of MCW that LMT does not resolve is the apparent opposition between the various judgments. *Music in Catholic Worship*, for example, notes that competent musicians decide on the compositional quality of a piece apart from it usage, while conversely giving the impression that pastoral leaders decide on the usage of a piece apart from its compositional quality. One reasonable interpretation of these paragraphs is that, ultimately, the pastoral decision is the most important and though the musical judgment is theoretically important, it can be discounted or ignored in the face of pastoral concerns. Because the various judgments have proved so helpful in developing new forms of musical worship in the United States, we must discover a further linkage between these judgments so that they can serve even more effectively in the future.

CONCLUSION

Almost 20 years after its first appearance, MCW retains a vitality and respect enjoyed by few other episcopal documents, particularly on worship and the arts. Though it is not without its flaws, this is by and large a splendid document that continues to influence the direction of liturgical music in the United States. The strength of the document is that it can generate companions such as LMT without being eclipsed. My hope is that the ongoing development of our theology and practice of sung worship in the United States will continue to draw on the insights of MCW and explore its implications for a church on the brink of its third millennium of sung praise.

# OUTLINE

# MUSIC IN CATHOLIC WORSHIP

## THE THEOLOGY OF CELEBRATION

1.    We are Christians because through the Christian community we have met Jesus Christ, heard his word in invitation, and responded to him in faith. We gather at Mass that we may hear and express our faith again in this assembly and, by expressing it, renew and deepen it.

2.    We do not come to meet Christ as if he were absent from the rest of our lives. We come together to deepen our awareness of, and commitment to, the action of his Spirit in the whole of our lives at every moment. We come together to acknowledge the love of God poured out among us in the work of the Spirit, to stand in awe and praise.

3.    We are celebrating when we involve ourselves meaningfully in the thoughts, words, songs, and gestures of the worshiping community—when everything we do is wholehearted and authentic for us—when we mean the words and want to do what is done.

4.    People in love make signs of love, not only to express their love but also to deepen it. Love never expressed dies. Christians' love for Christ and for one another and Christians' faith in Christ and in one another must be expressed in the signs and symbols of celebration or they will die.

5.    Celebrations need not fail, even on a particular Sunday when our feelings do not match the invitation of Christ and his Church to worship. Faith does not always permeate our feelings. But the signs and symbols of worship can give bodily expression to faith as we celebrate. Our own faith is stimulated. We become one with others whose faith is similarly expressed. We rise above our own feelings to respond to God in prayer.

6.    Faith grows when it is well expressed in celebration. Good celebrations foster and nourish faith. Poor celebrations may weaken and destroy it.

7.    To celebrate the liturgy means to do the action or perform the sign in such a way that its full meaning and impact shine forth in clear and compelling fashion. Since liturgical signs are vehicles of communication and instruments of faith, they must be simple and comprehensible. Since they are directed to fellow human beings, they must be humanly attractive. They must be meaningful and appealing to the body of worshipers or they will fail to stir up faith and people will fail to worship the Father.

8.    The signs of celebration should be short, clear, and unencumbered by useless repetition; they should be "within the people's powers of comprehension, and normally should not require much explanation."[1]

If the signs need explanation to communicate faith, they will often be watched instead of celebrated.

9.    In true celebration each sign or sacramental action will be invested with the personal and prayerful faith, care, attention, and enthusiasm of those who carry it out.

## PASTORAL PLANNING FOR CELEBRATION

10.    The responsibility for effective pastoral celebration in a parish community falls upon all those who exercise major roles in the liturgy. "The practical preparation for each liturgical celebration should be done in a spirit of cooperation by all parties concerned, under the guidance of the rector of the church, whether it be ritual, pastoral, or musical matters."[2] In practice this ordinarily means an organized "planning team" or committee which meets regularly to achieve creative and coordinated worship and a good use of the liturgical and musical options of a flexible liturgy.

11.    The power of a liturgical celebration to share faith will frequently depend upon its unity—a unity drawn from the liturgical feast or season or from the readings appointed in the lectionary as well as artistic unity flowing from the skillful and sensitive selection of options, music, and related arts. The sacred scriptures ought to be the source and inspiration of sound planning for it is of the very nature of celebration that people hear the saving words and works of the Lord and then respond in meaningful signs and symbols. Where the readings of the lectionary possess a thematic unity, the other elements ought to be so arranged as to constitute a setting for and response to the message of the Word.

12.    The planning team or committee is headed by the priest (celebrant and homilist) for no congregation can experience the richness of a unified celebration if that unity is not grasped by the one who presides, as well as by those who have special roles. The planning group should include those with the knowledge and artistic skills needed in celebration: men and women trained in music, poetry, and art, and familiar with current resources in these areas; men and women sensitive also to the present day thirst of so many for the riches of scripture, theology, and prayer. It is always good to include some members of the congregation who have not taken special roles in the celebrations so that honest evaluations can be made.

13.    The planning should go beyond the choosing of options, songs, and ministers to the composition of such texts as the brief introduction, general intercessions, and other appropriate comments as provided for in the *General Instruction of the Roman Missal*. How people are invited to join in a particular song may be as important as the choice of the song itself.

14.   In planning pastoral celebrations the congregation, the occasion, and the celebrant must be taken into consideration.

## THE CONGREGATION

15.   "The pastoral effectiveness of a celebration will be heightened if the texts of readings, prayers, and songs correspond as closely as possible to the needs, religious dispositions, and aptitude of the participants."[3] A type of celebration suitable for a youth group may not fit in a retirement home; a more formal style effective in a parish church may be inappropriate in a home liturgy. The music used should be within the competence of most of the worshipers. It should suit their age-level, cultural background, and level of faith.

16.   Variations in level of faith raise special problems. Liturgical celebration presupposes a minimum of biblical knowledge and a deep commitment of living faith. If these are lacking, there might arise the tendency to use the liturgy as a tool of evangelization. Greater liberty in the choice of music and style of celebration may be required as the participants are led toward that day when they can share their growing faith as members of the Christian community. Songs like the psalms may create rather than solve problems where faith is weak. Music, chosen with care, can serve as a bridge to faith as well as an expression of it.

17.   The diversity of people present at a parish liturgy gives rise to a further problem. Can the same parish liturgy be an authentic expression for a grade-school girl, her college-age brother, their married sister with her young family, their parents and grandparents? Can it satisfy the theologically and musically educated along with those lacking in training? Can it please those who seek a more informal style of celebration? The planning team must consider the general makeup of the total community. Each Christian must keep in mind that to live and worship in community often demands a personal sacrifice. All must be willing to share likes and dislikes with others whose ideas and experiences may be quite unlike their own.

18.   Often the problem of diversity can be mitigated by supplementing the parish Sunday celebration with special celebrations for smaller homogeneous groups. "The needs of the faithful of a particular cultural background or of a particular age level may often be met by a music that can serve as a congenial, liturgically oriented expression of prayer."[4] The music and other options may then be more easily suited to the particular group celebrating. Celebration in such groups, "in which the genuine sense of community is more readily experienced, can contribute significantly to growth in awareness of the parish as community, especially when all the faithful participate in the parish Mass on the Lord's day."[5] Nevertheless, it would be out of harmony with the Lord's wish for unity in his Church if believers were to worship only in such homogeneous groupings.[6]

## THE OCCASION

19.   The same congregation will want to celebrate in a variety of ways. During the course of the year the different mysteries of redemption are recalled in the

Mass so that in some way they are made present.[7] Each feast and season has its own spirit and its own music. The penitential occasions demand more restraint. The great feasts demand more solemnity. Solemnity, however, depends less on the ornateness of song and magnificence of ceremonial than on worthy and religious celebration.[8]

20.   Generally a congregation or choir will want to sing more on the great feasts like Christmas and Easter and less in the season through the year. Important events in family and parish life will suggest fuller programs of song. Sundays will be celebrated with variety but always as befits the day of the Lord. All liturgies, from the very simple to the most ornate, must be truly pastoral and prayerful.

## THE CELEBRANT

21.   No other single factor affects the liturgy as much as the attitude, style, and bearing of the celebrant: his sincere faith and warmth as he welcomes the worshiping community; his human naturalness combined with dignity and seriousness as he breaks the Bread of Word and Eucharist.

22.   The style and pattern of song ought to increase the effectiveness of a good celebrant. His role is enhanced when he is capable of rendering some of his parts in song, and he should be encouraged to do so. What he cannot sing well and effectively he ought to recite. If capable of singing, he ought, for the sake of people, to rehearse carefully the sung parts that contribute to their celebration.[9]

# THE PLACE OF MUSIC IN THE CELEBRATION

## MUSIC SERVES THE EXPRESSION OF FAITH

23.   Among the many signs and symbols used by the Church to celebrate its faith, music is of preeminent importance. As sacred song united to words it forms a necessary or integral part of the solemn liturgy.[10] Yet the function of music is ministerial; it must serve and never dominate. Music should assist the assembled believers to express and share the gift of faith that is within them and to nourish and strengthen their interior commitment of faith. It should heighten the texts so that they speak more fully and more effectively. The quality of joy and enthusiasm which music adds to community worship cannot be gained in any other way. It imparts a sense of unity to the congregation and sets the appropriate tone for a particular celebration.

24.   In addition to expressing texts, music can also unveil a dimension of meaning and feeling, a communication of ideas and intuitions which words alone cannot yield. This dimension is integral to the human personality and to growth in faith. It cannot be ignored if the signs of worship are to speak to the whole person. Ideally, every communal celebration of faith, including funerals and the sacraments of baptism, confirmation, penance, anointing, and matrimony, should include music and singing. Where it is possible to celebrate the Liturgy of the Hours in a community, it, too, should include music.

25.   To determine the value of a given musical element in a liturgical celebration a threefold judgment must be made: musical, liturgical, and pastoral.

## THE MUSICAL JUDGMENT

26.   Is the music technically, aesthetically, and expressively good? This judgment is basic and primary and should be made by competent musicians. Only artistically sound music will be effective in the long run. To admit the cheap, the trite, the musical cliché often found in popular songs for the purpose of "instant liturgy" is to cheapen the liturgy, to expose it to ridicule, and to invite failure.

27.   Musicians must search for and create music of quality for worship, especially the new musical settings for the new liturgical texts. They must also do the research needed to find new uses for the best of the old music. They must explore the repertory of good music used in other communions. They must find practical means of preserving and using our rich heritage of Latin chants and motets.[11]

In the meantime, however, the words of St. Augustine should not be forgotten: "Do not allow yourselves to be offended by the imperfect while you strive for the perfect."

28.   We do a disservice to musical values, however, when we confuse the judgment of music with the judgment of musical style. Style and value are two distinct judgments. Good music of new styles is finding a happy home in the celebrations of today. To chant and polyphony we have effectively added the chorale hymn, restored reponsorial singing to some extent, and employed many styles of contemporary composition. Music in folk idiom is finding acceptance in eucharistic celebrations. We must judge value within each style.

"In modern times the Church has consistently recognized and freely admitted the use of various styles of music as an aid to liturgical worship. Since the promulgation of the Constitution on the Liturgy and more especially since the introduction of vernacular languages into the liturgy, there has arisen a more pressing need for musical compositions in idioms that can be sung by the congregation and thus further communal participation."[12]

29.   The musician has every right to insist that the music be good. But although all liturgical music should be good, not all good music is suitable to the liturgy. The musical judgment is basic but not final. There remain the liturgical and pastoral judgments.

## THE LITURGICAL JUDGMENT

30.   The nature of the liturgy itself will help to determine what kind of music is called for, what parts are to be preferred for singing, and who is to sing them.

### A. Structural Requirements

31.   The choice of sung parts, the balance between them, and the style of musical setting used should reflect the relative importance of the parts of the Mass (or other service) and the nature of each part. Thus elaborate settings of the entrance

song, "Lord have Mercy" and "Glory to God" may make the proclamation of the word seem unimportant; and an overly elaborate offertory song with a spoken "Holy, Holy, Holy Lord" may make the eucharistic prayer seem less important.

### B. Textual Requirements

32. Does the music express and interpret the text correctly and make it more meaningful? Is the form of the text respected? In making these judgments the principal classes of texts must be kept in mind: proclamations, acclamations, psalms and hymns, and prayers. Each has a specific function which must be served by the music chosen for a text.

In most instances there is an official liturgical text approved by the episcopal conference. "Vernacular texts set to music composed in earlier periods," however, "may be used in liturgical texts."[13] As noted elsewhere, criteria have been provided for the texts which may replace the processional chants of Mass. In these cases and in the choice of all supplementary music, the texts "must always be in conformity with Catholic doctrine; indeed they should be drawn chiefly from holy scripture and from liturgical sources."[14]

### C. Role Differentiation

33. "In liturgical celebrations each one, minister or layperson, who has an office to perform, should do all of, but only, those parts which pertain to that office by the nature of the rite and the principles of liturgy."[15] Special musical concern must be given to the role of the congregation, the cantor, the choir, and the instrumentalists.

### D. The Congregation

34. Music for the congregation must be within its members' performance capability. The congregation must be comfortable and secure with what they are doing in order to celebrate well.

### E. The Cantor

35. While there is no place in the liturgy for display of virtuosity for its own sake, artistry is valued, and an individual singer can effectively lead the assembly, attractively proclaim the Word of God in the psalm sung between the readings, and take his or her part in other responsorial singing. "Provision should be made for at least one or two properly trained singers, especially where there is no possibility of setting up even a small choir. The singer will present some simpler musical settings, with the people taking part, and can lead and support the faithful as far as is needed. The presence of such a singer is desirable even in churches which have a choir, for those celebrations in which the choir cannot take part but which may fittingly be performed with some solemnity and therefore with singing."[16] Although a cantor "cannot enhance the service of worship in the same way as a choir, a trained and competent cantor can perform an important ministry by leading the congregation in common sacred song and in responsorial singing."[17]

## F. The Choir

36.   A well-trained choir adds beauty and solemnity to the liturgy and also assists and encourages the singing of the congregation. The Second Vatican Council, speaking of the choir, stated emphatically: "Choirs must be diligently promoted," provided that "the whole body of the faithful may be able to contribute that active participation which is rightly theirs."[18]

"At times the choir, within the congregation of the faithful and as part of it, will assume the role of leadership, while at other times it will retain its own distinctive ministry. This means that the choir will lead the people in sung prayer, by alternating or reinforcing the sacred song of the congregation, or by enhancing it with the addition of a musical elaboration. At other times in the course of liturgical celebration the choir alone will sing works whose musical demands enlist and challenge its competence."[19]

### G. The Organist and Other Instrumentalists

37.   Song is not the only kind of music suitable for liturgical celebration. Music performed on the organ and other instruments can stimulate feelings of joy and contemplation at appropriate times.[20] This can be done effectively at the following points: an instrumental prelude, a soft background to a spoken psalm, at the preparation of the gifts in place of singing, during portions of the communion rite, and the recessional.

In the dioceses of the United States, "musical instruments other than the organ may be used in liturgical services, provided they are played in a manner that is suitable to public worship."[21] This decision deliberately refrains from singling out specific instruments. Their use depends on circumstances, the nature of the congregation, etc.

38.   The *proper placing* of the organ and choir according to the arrangement and acoustics of the church will facilitate celebration. Practically speaking, the choir must be near the director and the organ (both console and sound). The choir ought to be able to perform without too much distraction; the acoustics ought to give a lively presence of sound in the choir area and allow both tone and word to reach the congregation with clarity. Visually it is desirable that the choir appear to be part of the worshiping community, yet a part which serves in a unique way. Locating the organ console too far from the congregation causes a time lag which tends to make the singing drag unless the organist is trained to cope with it. A location near the front pews will facilitate congregational singing.

## THE PASTORAL JUDGMENT

39.   The pastoral judgment governs the use and function of every element of celebration. Ideally this judgment is made by the planning team or committee. It is the judgment that must be made in this particular situation, in these concrete circumstances. Does music in the celebration enable these people to express their faith, in this place, in this age, in this culture?

40. The instruction of the Congregation for Divine Worship, issued September 5, 1970, encourages episcopal conferences to consider not only liturgical music's suitability to the time and circumstances of the celebration, "but also the needs of the faithful who will sing them. All means must be used to promote singing by the people. New forms should be used, which are adapted to the different mentalities and to modern tastes." The document adds that the music and the instruments "should correspond to the sacred character of the celebration and the place of worship."

41. A musician may judge that a certain composition or style of composition is good music, but this musical judgment really says nothing about whether and how this music is to be used in this celebration. The signs of the celebration must be accepted and received as meaningful for a genuinely human faith experience for these specific worshipers. This pastoral judgment can be aided by sensitivity to the cultural and social characteristics of the people who make up the congregation: their age, culture, and education. These factors influence the effectiveness of the liturgical signs, including music. No set of rubrics or regulations of itself will ever achieve a truly pastoral celebration of the sacramental rites. Such regulations must always be applied with a pastoral concern for the given worshiping community.

## GENERAL CONSIDERATIONS OF LITURGICAL STRUCTURE

42. Those responsible for planning the music for eucharistic celebrations in accord with the three preceding judgments must have a clear understanding of the structure of the liturgy. They must be aware of what is of primary importance. They should know the nature of each of the parts of the liturgy and the relationship of each part to the overall rhythm of the liturgical action.

43. The Mass is made up of the liturgy of the word and the liturgy of the Eucharist. These two parts are so closely connected as to form one act of worship. The table of the Lord is both the table of God's Word and the table of Christ's Body, and from it the faithful are instructed and refreshed. In addition, the Mass has introductory and concluding rites.[22] The introductory and concluding rites are secondary.

### THE INTRODUCTORY RITES

44. The parts preceding the liturgy of the word, namely, the entrance, greeting, penitential rite, Kyrie, Gloria, and opening prayer or collect, have the character of introduction and preparation. The purpose of these rites is to help the assembled people become a worshiping community and to prepare them for listening to God's Word and celebrating the Eucharist.[23] Of these parts the entrance song and the opening prayer are primary. All else is secondary.

If Mass begins with the sprinkling of the people with blessed water, the penitential rite is omitted; this may be done at all Sunday Masses.[24] Similarly, if the psalms of part of the Liturgy of the Hours precede Mass, the introductory rite is abbreviated in accord with the *General Instruction on The Liturgy of the Hours.*[25]

## THE LITURGY OF THE WORD

45.    Readings from scripture are the heart of the liturgy of the word. The homily, responsorial psalms, profession of faith, and general intercessions develop and complete it. In the readings, God speaks to his people and nourishes their spirit; Christ is present through his word. The homily explains the readings. The chants and the profession of faith comprise the people's acceptance of God's Word. It is of primary importance that the people hear God's message of love, digest it with the aid of psalms, silence, and the homily, and respond, involving themselves in the great covenant of love and redemption. All else is secondary.

## THE PREPARATION OF THE GIFTS

46.    The eucharistic prayer is preceded by the preparation of the gifts. The purpose of the rite is to prepare bread and wine for the sacrifice. The secondary character of the rite determines the manner of the celebration. It consists very simply of bringing the gifts to the altar, possibly accompanied by song, prayers to be said by the celebrant as he prepares the gifts, and the prayer over the gifts. Of these elements the bringing of the gifts, the placing of the gifts on the altar, and the prayer over the gifts are primary. All else is secondary.

## THE EUCHARISTIC PRAYER

47.    The eucharistic prayer, a prayer of thanksgiving and sanctification, is the center of the entire celebration. By an introductory dialogue the priest invites the people to lift their hearts to God in praise and thanks; he unites them with himself in the prayer he addresses in their name to the Father through Jesus Christ. The meaning of the prayer is that the whole congregation joins itself to Christ in acknowledging the works of God and in offering the sacrifice.[26] As a statement of the faith of the local assembly it is affirmed and ratified by all those present through acclamations of faith: the first acclamation or Sanctus, the memorial acclamation, and the Great Amen.

## THE COMMUNION RITE

48.    The eating and drinking of the Body and Blood of the Lord in a paschal meal is the climax of our eucharistic celebration. It is prepared for by several rites: the Lord's Prayer with embolism and doxology, the rite of peace, breaking of bread (and commingling) during the "Lamb of God," private preparation of the priest, and showing of the eucharistic bread. The eating and drinking are accompanied by a song expressing the unity of communicants and followed by a time of prayer after communion.[27] Those elements are primary which show forth signs that the first fruit of the Eucharist is the unity of the Body of Christ, Christians being loved by Christ and loving him through their love of one another. The principal texts to accompany or express the sacred action are the Lord's Prayer, the song during the communion procession, and the prayer after communion.

# THE CONCLUDING RITE

49. The concluding rite consists of the priest's greeting and blessing, which is sometimes expanded by the prayer over the people or another solemn form, and the dismissal which sends forth each member of the congregation to do good works, praising and blessing the Lord.[28]

A recessional song is optional. The greeting, blessing, dismissal, and recessional song or instrumental music ideally form one continuous action which may culminate in the priest's personal greetings and conversations at the church door.

# APPLICATION OF THE PRINCIPLES OF CELEBRATION TO MUSIC IN EUCHARISTIC WORSHIP
## GENERAL CONSIDERATIONS

50. Many and varied musical patterns are now possible within the liturgical structure. Musicians and composers need to respond creatively and responsibly to the challenge of developing new music for today's celebrations.

51. While it is possible to make technical distinctions in the forms of the Mass—all the way from the Mass in which nothing is sung to the Mass in which everything is sung—such distinctions are of little significance in themselves; almost unlimited combinations of sung and recited parts may be chosen. The important decision is whether or not this or that part may be or should be sung in this particular celebration and under these specific circumstances.[29] The former distinction between the ordinary and proper parts of the Mass with regard to musical settings and distribution of roles is no longer retained. For this reason the musical settings of the past are usually not helpful models for composing truly liturgical pieces today.

52. Two patterns formerly served as the basis for creating and planning liturgy. One was "High Mass" with its five movements, sung Ordinary and fourfold sung Proper. The other was the four-hymn "Low Mass" format that grew out of the *Instruction of Sacred Music* of 1958. The four-hymn pattern developed in the context of a Latin Mass which could accommodate song in the vernacular only at certain points. It is now outdated, and the Mass has more than a dozen parts that may be sung, as well as numerous options for the celebrant. Each of these parts must be understood according to its proper nature and function.

## SPECIFIC APPLICATIONS

### A. Acclamations

53. The acclamations are shouts of joy which arise from the whole assembly as forceful and meaningful assents to God's Word and Action. They are important because they make some of the most significant moments of the Mass (gospel, eucharistic prayer, Lord's Prayer) stand out. It is of their nature that they be rhythmically strong, melodically appealing, and affirmative. The people should know the acclamations by heart in order to sing them spontaneously. Some

variety is recommended and even imperative. The challenge to the composer and people alike is one of variety without confusion.

54.   In the eucharistic celebration there are five acclamations which ought to be sung even at Masses in which little else is sung: Alleluia; "Holy, Holy, Holy Lord"; Memorial Acclamation; Great Amen; Doxology to the Lord's Prayer.

## THE ALLELUIA

55.   This acclamation of paschal joy is both a reflection upon the Word of God proclaimed in the liturgy and a preparation for the gospel. All stand to sing it. After the cantor or choir sings the alleluia(s), the people customarily repeat it. Then a single proper verse is sung by the cantor or choir, and all repeat the alleluia(s). If not sung, the alleluia should be omitted.[30] A moment of silent reflection may be observed in its place. During Lent a brief verse of acclamatory character replaces the alleluia and is sung in the same way.

## HOLY, HOLY, HOLY LORD

56.   This is the people's acclamation of praise concluding the preface of the eucharistic prayer. We join the whole communion of saints in acclaiming the Lord. Settings which add harmony or descants on solemn feasts and occasions are appropriate, but since this chant belongs to priest and people, the choir parts must facilitate and make effective the people's parts.

## THE MEMORIAL ACCLAMATION

57.   We support one another's faith in the paschal mystery, the central mystery of our belief. This acclamation is properly a memorial of the Lord's suffering and glorification, with an expression of faith in his coming. Variety in text and music is desirable.

## THE GREAT AMEN

58.   The worshipers assent to the eucharistic prayer and make it their own in the Great Amen. To be most effective, the Amen may be repeated or augmented. Choirs may harmonize and expand upon the people's acclamation.

## DOXOLOGY TO THE LORD'S PRAYER

59.   These words of praise, "For the Kingdom, the power and the glory are yours, now and forever," are fittingly sung by all, especially when the Lord's Prayer is sung. Here, too, the choir may enhance the acclamation with harmony.

### B. Processional Songs

60.   The two processional chants—the entrance song and the communion song—are very important for creating and sustaining an awareness of community. Proper antiphons are given to be used with appropriate psalm verses. These may be replaced by the chants of the Simple Gradual, by other psalms and antiphons, or by other fitting songs.[31]

## THE ENTRANCE SONG

61.   The entrance song should create an atmosphere of celebration. It helps put the assembly in the proper frame of mind for listening to the Word of God. It helps people to become conscious of themselves as a worshiping community. The choice of texts for the entrance song should not conflict with these purposes. In general, during the most important seasons of the Church year—Easter, Lent, Christmas, and Advent—it is preferable that most songs used at the entrance be seasonal in nature.[32]

## THE COMMUNION SONG

62.   The communion song should foster a sense of unity. It should be simple and not demand great effort. It gives expression to the joy of unity in the body of Christ and the fulfillment of the mystery being celebrated. Because they emphasize adoration rather than communion, most benediction hymns are not suitable. In general, during the most important seasons of the Church year—Easter, Lent, Christmas, and Advent—it is preferable that most songs used at the communion be seasonal in nature. For the remainder of the Church year, however, topical songs may be used during the communion procession, provided these texts do not conflict with the paschal character of every Sunday."[33]

### C. Responsorial Psalm

63.   This unique and very important song is the response to the first lesson. The new lectionary's determination to match the content of the psalms to the theme of reading is reflected in its listing of 900 refrains. The liturgy of the Word comes more fully to life if between the first two readings a cantor sings the psalm and all sing the response. Since most groups cannot learn a new response every week, seasonal refrains are offered in the lectionary itself and in the *Simple Gradual*. Other psalms and refrains may also be used, including psalms arranged in responsorial form and metrical and similar versions of psalms, provided they are used in accordance with the principles of the *Simple Gradual* and are selected in harmony with the liturgical season, feast or occasion. The choice of the texts which are not from the psalter is not extended to the chants between the readings.[34] To facilitate reflection, there may be a brief period of silence between the first reading and the responsorial psalm.

### D. Ordinary Chants

64.   The fourth category is the ordinary chants, which now may be treated as individual choices. One or more may be sung; the others spoken. The pattern may vary according to the circumstances. These chants are the following:

## LORD HAVE MERCY

65.   This short litany was traditionally a prayer of praise to the risen Christ. He has been raised and made "Lord," and we beg him to show his loving kindness. The sixfold Kyrie of the new order of Mass may be sung in other ways, for example, as a ninefold chant.[35] It may also be incorporated in the penitential rite,

with invocations addressed to Christ. When sung, the setting should be brief and simple in order not to give undue importance to the introductory rites.

## GLORY TO GOD

66.    This ancient hymn of praise is now given in a new poetic and singable translation. It may be introduced by celebrant, cantor, or choir. The restricted use of the Gloria, i.e., only on Sundays outside Advent and Lent and on solemnities and feasts,[36] emphasizes its special and solemn character. The new text offers many opportunities for alternation of choir and people in poetic parallelisms. The "Glory to God" also provides an opportunity for the choir to sing alone on festive occasions.

## LORD'S PRAYER

67.    This prayer begins our immediate preparation for sharing in the Paschal Banquet. The traditional text is retained and may be set to music by composers with the same freedom as other parts of the Ordinary. All settings must provide for the participation of the priest and all present.

## LAMB OF GOD

68.    The Agnus Dei is a litany-song to accompany the breaking of the bread in preparation for communion. The invocation and response may be repeated as the action demands. The final response is always "grant us peace." Unlike the "Holy, Holy, Holy Lord," and the Lord's Prayer, the "Lamb of God" is not necessarily a song of the people. Hence it may be sung by the choir, though the people should generally make the response.

## PROFESSION OF FAITH

69.    This is a communal profession of faith in which". . . the people who have heard the Word of God in the lesson and in the homily may assent and respond to it, and may renew in themselves the rule of faith as they begin to celebrate the Eucharist."[37] It is usually preferable that the Creed be spoken in declamatory fashion rather than sung.[38] If it is sung, it might more effectively take the form of a simple musical declamation rather than an extensive and involved musical structure.

*E. Supplementary Songs*

70.    This category includes songs for which there are no specified texts nor any requirements that there should be a spoken or sung text. Here the choir may play a fuller role, for there is no question of usurping the people's part. This category includes the following:

## THE OFFERTORY SONG

71.    The offertory song may accompany the procession and preparation of the gifts. It is not always necessary or desirable. Organ or instrumental music is also fitting at the time. When song is used, it need not speak of bread and wine or of offering. The proper function of this song is to accompany and celebrate the

communal aspects of the procession. The text, therefore, can be any appropriate song of praise or of rejoicing in keeping with the season. The antiphons of the Roman Gradual, not included in the new Roman Missal, may be used with psalm verses. Instrumental interludes can effectively accompany the procession and preparation of the gifts and thus keep this part of the Mass in proper perspective relative to the eucharistic prayer which follows.

## THE PSALM OR SONG AFTER COMMUNION

72. The singing of a psalm or hymn of praise after the distribution of communion is optional. If the organ is played or the choir sings during the distribution of communion, a congregational song may well provide a fitting expression of oneness in the Eucharistic Lord. Since no particular text is specified, there is ample room for creativity.

## THE RECESSIONAL SONG

73. The recessional song has never been an official part of the rite; hence musicians are free to plan music which provides an appropriate closing to the liturgy. A song is one possible choice. However, if the people have sung a song after communion, it may be advisable to use only an instrumental or choir recessional.

### F. Litanies

74. Litanies are often more effective when sung. The repetition of melody and rhythm draws the people together in a strong and unified response. In addition to the "Lamb of God," already mentioned, the general intercessions (prayer of the faithful) offer an opportunity for litanical singing, as do the invocations of Christ in the penitential rite.

## PROGRESS AND NEW DIRECTIONS

75. Many new patterns and combinations of song are emerging in eucharistic celebrations. Congregations most frequently sing an entrance song, alleluia, "Holy, Holy, Holy Lord," memorial acclamation, Great Amen, and a song at communion (or a song after communion). Other parts are added in varying quantities, depending on season, degree of solemnity and musical resources. Choirs often add one or more of the following: a song before Mass, an Offertory song, the "Glory to God" on special occasions, additional communion songs or a song after communion or a recessional. They may also enhance the congregationally sung entrance song and acclamations with descants, harmony, and antiphonal arrangements. Harmony is desirable when, without confusing the people, it gives breadth and power to their voices in unison.

76. Flexibility is recognized today as an important value in liturgy. The musician with a sense of artistry and a deep knowledge of the rhythm of the liturgical action will be able to combine the many options into an effective whole. For the composer and performer alike there is an unprecedented challenge. They must enhance the liturgy with new creations of variety and richness and with those compositions from the time-honored treasury of liturgical music which can still

serve today's celebrations. Like the wise householder in Matthew's Gospel, the church musician must be one "who can produce from his store both the new and the old."

77.    The Church in the United States today needs the service of many qualified musicians as song leaders, organists, instrumentalists, cantors, choir directors, and composers. We have been blessed with many generous musicians who have given years of service despite receiving only meager financial compensation. For the art to grow and face the challenges of today and tomorrow, every diocese and parish should establish policies for hiring and paying living wages to competent musicians. Full-time musicians employed by the Church ought to be on the same salary scale as teachers with similar qualifications and workloads.[39]

78.    Likewise, to ensure that composers and publishers receive just compensation for their work, those engaged in parish music programs and those responsible for budgets must often be reminded that it is illegal and immoral to reproduce copyrighted texts and music by any means without written permission of the copyright owner. The fact that these duplicated materials are not for sale but for private use does not alter the legal or moral situation of copying without permission.[40]

## MUSIC IN SACRAMENTAL CELEBRATIONS

79.    While music has traditionally been part of the celebration of weddings, funerals, and confirmation, the communal celebration of baptism, anointing, and penance has only recently been restored. The renewed rituals, following the *Constitution on the Sacred Liturgy,* provide for and encourage communal celebrations, which, according to the capability of the congregation, should involve song.[41]

80.    The rite of baptism is best begun by an entrance song;[42] the liturgy of the word is enhanced by a sung psalm and/or alleluia. Where the processions to and from the place of the liturgy of the word and the baptistry take some time, they should be accompanied by music. Above all, the acclamations—the affirmation of faith by the people, the acclamation immediately after the baptism, the acclamation upon completion of the rite—should be sung by the whole congregation.

81.    Whenever rites like the anointing of the sick or the sacrament of penance are celebrated communally, music is important. The general structure is introductory rite, liturgy of the word, sacrament, and dismissal. The introductory rite and liturgy of the word follow the pattern of the Mass. At the time of the sacrament an acclamation or song by all the people is desirable.

82.    Confirmation and marriage are most often celebrated within a Mass. The norms given above pertain. Great care should be taken, especially at marriages, that all the people are involved at the important moments of the celebration, that the same general principles of planning worship and judging music are employed as at other liturgies, and, above all, that the liturgy is a prayer for all present, not a theatrical production.

83.   Music becomes particularly important in the new burial rites. Without it the themes of hope and resurrection are very difficult to express. The entrance song, the acclamations, and the song of farewell or commendation are of primary importance for the whole congregation. The choral and instrumental music should fit the paschal mystery theme.[43]

# CONCLUSION

84.   There is vital interest today in the Mass as prayer, and in this understanding of the Mass lies a principle of synthesis which is essential to good liturgical worship. When all strive with one accord to make the Mass a prayer, a sharing and celebration of Faith, the result is unity. Styles of music, choices of instruments, forms of celebration—all converge in a single purpose: that men and women of faith may proclaim and share that faith in prayer and Christ may grow among us all.

# NOTES

1. CSL 34.
2. MS 5e; GI 73.
3. GI 313.
4. BCLN, 18 April 1966.
5. BCLN, 17 Feb 1967.
6. AP.
7. GI 1; cf. CSL 102.
8. MS 11.
9. MS 8.
10. Cf. CSL 112.
11. Cf. CSL 114, 116.
12. BCLN, 18 April 1966.
13. National Conference of Catholic Bishops, [NCCB] Nov 1967.
14. CSL 121.
15. CSL 28.
16. MS 21.
17. BCLN, 18 April 1966.
18. CSL 114.
19. BCLN, 18 April 1966.
20. Cf. CSL 120; MS 63–65; LI 3c.
21. NCCB, Nov 1967; cf. CSL 120.
22. GI 8.
23. GI 24.
24. Cf. RM, Blessing and Sprinkling of Holy Water, 1.
25. The Liturgy of the Hours, General Instruction, 93–98.
26. GI 54.
27. GI 56.
28. GI 57.
29. Cf. GI 19; MS 28, 36.
30. GI 39. The first edition of this document had the word "may" instead of "should." This change has been made in the second edition in light of the norm found in LMI 23.
31. GI 56.
32. NCCB, Nov. 1969.
33. Ibid.
34. NCCB, Nov 1968; cf. GI 6.
35. Cf. GI 30.
36. GI 31.
37. GI 43.
38. NCCB, Nov 1967.
39. BCLN, 18 April 1966.
40. BCLN, April 1969.
41. Cf. CSL 27.
42. Baptism 5, 32, 35.
43. Rite of Funerals, 1.

# LITURGICAL MUSIC
# TODAY

# OUTLINE

# LITURGICAL MUSIC TODAY

## INTRODUCTION

1.    Liturgical music today exhibits signs of great vitality and creativity. During the nearly twenty years that have passed since the promulgation of the *Constitution on the Sacred Liturgy* of the Second Vatican Council, the ministerial role of liturgical music has received growing acceptance and greater appreciation by the Christian people. The sung prayer of our assemblies, often timid and weak but a few years ago, has taken on the characteristics of confidence and strength. In the liturgical ministry of music, more and more capable persons are assuming roles of leadership as cantors, instrumentalists and members of choirs. New musical compositions are appearing in great numbers and the quality of their craftsmanship and beauty is improving. All these developments serve as signs of hope for the present and future of liturgical music.

2.    Ten years ago the Bishops' Committee on the Liturgy published *Music in Catholic Worship*, itself the revision of an earlier statement.[1] That document has proven to be very useful in setting out the principles for Church music in the reformed liturgy. It has served well over these years.

3.    Since the Roman liturgical books were still in the process of revision ten years ago, the Committee recognizes that there are subjects that *Music in Catholic Worship* addressed only briefly or not at all, such as music within sacramental rites and in the Liturgy of the Hours. Moreover, the passage of time has raised a number of unforeseen issues in need of clarification and questions revealing new possibilities for liturgical music. We take this opportunity to note these developments. This statement, therefore, should be read as a companion to *Music in Catholic Worship* and *Environment and Art in Catholic Worship*.[2]

4.    The introduction to *Music in Catholic Worship* includes these words: " . . . mere observance of a pattern or rule of sung liturgy will not create a living and authentic celebration of worship in Christian congregations. That is the reason why statements such as this must take the form of recommendation and attempts at guidance."[3] These words continue to be true. Guidelines, far from being absolute, need to be adapted to particular circumstances. But first they must be read, reflected upon, and valued for the insights they contain. And ultimately they will be successful to the extent that they are implemented, to the extent that the context out of which they grow is communicated and understood.

5.    These guidelines concern the Church's liturgy, which is inherently musical. If music is not valued within the liturgy, then this statement will have little to

offer. On the other hand, if music is appreciated as a necessarily normal dimension of every experience of communal worship, then what follows may help to promote continued understanding of the liturgy, dialogue among those responsible for its implementation, and music itself as sung prayer.

# GENERAL PRINCIPLES
## THE STRUCTURE OF THE LITURGY

6.    A sacrament is celebrated either within Mass or with a liturgy of the word. This is the larger context for making judgments about what will be sung. This consideration will help to preserve the integrity of the entire liturgical prayer experience while, at the same time preventing the celebration from being top heavy in one or other part, and ensuring a good flow throughout.

7.    In all liturgical celebrations proper use should be made of the musical elements within the liturgy of the word, i.e., responsorial psalm, gospel acclamation, and sometimes an acclamation after the homily or profession of faith. *Music in Catholic Worship* treated these sung prayers in its discussion of eucharistic celebrations.[4] What was said there is applicable to all other liturgical celebrations which include a liturgy of the word. Further efforts are needed to make the assembly's responses in song the normal pastoral practice in the celebration of God's Word.

## THE PLACE OF SONG

8.    The structure of the liturgical unit will disclose the elements to be enhanced by music. For example, the liturgy of baptism or confirmation is placed between the liturgy of the word and the liturgy of the eucharist when celebrated at Mass. Each rite is composed of a number of elements, some of which lend themselves to singing. The first place to look for guidance in the use and choice of music is the rite itself. Often the rubrics contained in the approved liturgical books will indicate the place for song, and will also prescribe or suggest an appropriate text to be set musically. Thus, in confirmation, the ritual recommends singing at the end of the renewal of baptismal promises and during the anointing.[5] In baptism, the acclamations after the profession of faith and after the baptism itself demand song, since they are by nature musical forms.[6]

## THE FUNCTION OF SONG

9.    The various functions of sung prayer must be distinguished within liturgical rites. Sometimes song is meant to accompany ritual actions. In such cases the song is not independent but serves, rather, to support the prayer of the assembly when an action requires a longer period of time or when the action is going to be repeated several times. The music enriches the moments and keeps it from becoming burdensome. Ritual actions which employ such use of song include: the enrollment of names at the Election of Catechumens;[7] the processions in the celebration of baptism;[8] the vesting and sign of peace at an ordination;[9] the

presentation of the Bible at the institution of a reader;[10] the anointings with chrism at confirmation[11] and ordination.[12]

10. At other places in the liturgical action the sung prayer itself is a constituent element of the rite. While it is being prayed, no other ritual action is being performed. Such would be: the song of praise, which may be sung after communion;[13] the litany of saints at celebrations of Christian initiation,[14] ordination,[15] religious profession,[16] or the dedication of a church;[17] the proclamation of praise for God's mercy at the conclusion of the rite of reconciliation;[18] acclamations to conclude the baptismal profession of faith,[19] blessing of water,[20] or the thanksgiving over oil.[21] Even more important is the solemn chanting of the prayer of consecration by the bishop at ordinations,[22] or of the prayer of dedication of a church.[23] In each of these cases the music does not serve as a mere accompaniment, but as the integral mode by which the mystery is proclaimed and presented.

## THE FORM OF SONG

11. Beyond determining the moments when song is needed, the musical form employed must match its liturgical function. For instance, at the end of the baptismal profession of faith the assembly may express its assent by an acclamation. In place of the text provided ("This is our faith . . .") another appropriate formula or suitable song may be substituted.[24] An acclamation—a short, direct and strong declarative statement of the community's faith—will usually be more suitable for this than the several verses of a metrical hymn. The hymn form, appropriate in other contexts, may not work here because its form is usually less compact, less intense.

## PASTORAL CONCERNS

12. The pastoral judgment discussed in *Music in Catholic Worship* must always be applied when choosing music. Sacramental celebrations are significant moments in an individual's life, but just as importantly they are constitutive events of the community's life in Christ. The music selected must express the prayer of those who celebrate, while at the same time guarding against the imposition of private meanings on public rites. Individual preference is not, of itself, a sufficient principle for the choice of music in the liturgy. It must be balanced with liturgical and musical judgments and with the community's needs. Planning is a team undertaking, involving the presider, the musicians and the assembly.

## PROGRESSIVE SOLEMNITY

13. Music should be considered a normal and ordinary part of any liturgical celebration. However, this general principle is to be interpreted in the light of another one, namely, the principle of progressive solemnity.[25] This latter principle takes into account the abilities of the assembly, the relative importance of the individual rites and their constituent parts, and the relative festivity of the liturgical day. With regard to the Liturgy of the Hours, formerly a sung office meant a service in which everything was sung. Today the elements which lend

themselves to singing (the psalms and canticles with their antiphons, the hymns, responsories, litanies and prayers, and the acclamations, greetings and responses) should be sung in accordance with the relative solemnity of the celebration. This principle likewise applies to the music sung in all other liturgical celebrations.

## LANGUAGE AND MUSICAL IDIOMS

14.   Different languages may be used in the same celebration.[26] This may also be said of mixing different musical idioms and media. For example, pastoral reasons might suggest that in a given liturgical celebration some music reflect classical hymnody, with other music drawn from gospel or "folk" idioms, from contemporary service music, or from the plainsong or polyphonic repertoires. In the same celebration music may be rendered in various ways: unaccompanied; or accompanied by organ, piano, guitar or other instruments.

15.   While this principle upholding musical plurality has pastoral value, it should never be employed as a license for including poor music. At the same time, it needs to be recognized that a certain musical integrity within a liturgical prayer or rite can be achieved only by unity in the musical composition. Thus, it is recommended that for the acclamations in the eucharistic prayer one musical style be employed.

## MUSIC IN THE EUCHARIST

16.   The function of the various chants within the Eucharistic Liturgy has already been set out in *Music in Catholic Worship*, as well as above. Additional notes follow regarding specific elements.

## ACCLAMATIONS

17.   The acclamations (gospel acclamation, doxology after the Lord's Prayer, and eucharistic acclamations—including the special acclamations of praise in the *Eucharistic Prayers of Masses with Children*[27]) are the preeminent sung prayers of the eucharistic liturgy. Singing these acclamations makes their prayer all the more effective. They should, therefore, be sung, even at weekday celebrations of the Eucharist. The gospel acclamation, moreover, must always be sung.[28]

## PROCESSIONAL CHANTS

18.   Processional chants accompany an action. In some cases they have another function. The entrance song serves to gather and unite the assembly and set the tone for the celebration as much as to conduct the ministers into the sanctuary. The communion processional song serves a similiar purpose. Not only does it accompany movement, and thus give order to the assembly, it also assists each communicant in the realization and achievement of "the joy of all" and the fellowship of those "who join their voices in a single song."[29]

19.   While the responsorial form of singing is especially suitable for processions, the metrical hymn can also fulfill the function of the entrance song. If, however, a

metrical hymn with several verses is selected, its form should be respected. The progression of text and music must be allowed to play out its course and achieve its purpose musically and poetically. In other words, the hymn should not be ended indiscriminately at the end of the procession. For this same reason, metrical hymns may not be the most suitable choices to accompany the preparation of the gifts and altar at the Eucharist, since the music should not extend past the time necessary for the ritual.

## LITANIES

20.   The Lamb of God achieves greater significance at Masses when a larger sized eucharistic bread is broken for distribution and, when communion is given under both kinds, chalices must be filled. The litany is prolonged to accompany this action of breaking and pouring.[30] In this case one should not hesitate to add tropes to the litany so that the prayerfulness of the rite may be enriched.

21.   The litany of the third form of the penitential rite at Mass increasingly is being set to music for deacon (or cantor) and assembly, with the people's response made in Greek or English. This litany functions as a "general confession made by the entire assembly"[31] and as praise of Christ's compassionate love and mercy. It is appropriately sung at more solemn celebrations and in Advent and Lent when the Gloria is omitted.[32] Similar litanic forms of song could be employed when the rite of sprinkling replaces the penitential rite.

# MUSIC IN THE CELEBRATION
# OF OTHER SACRAMENTS AND RITES
## CHRISTIAN INITIATION

22.   As parish communities become more accustomed to initiate adults in stages, the opportunities for sung prayer within the *Rite of Christian Initiation of Adults* should become more apparent. The ritual book gives attention to the following: in the rite of becoming a catechumen, before the invitation to sponsors to present the candidates, and during their subsequent entry into the church building; in the rite of election, during the enrollment of names; in the Lenten scrutinies, after the prayer of exorcism; at the Easter Vigil celebration, an acclamation following baptism, song between the celebration of baptism and confirmation, and an acclamation during the anointing with chrism.[33]

23.   In the *Rite of Baptism of Children*, there is even greater emphasis on the sung prayer of the assembly: during the procession to the place where the Word of God will be celebrated; after the homily or after the short litany; during the procession to the place of baptism; an acclamation after the profession of faith and after each baptism; an acclamation or baptismal song during the procession to the altar.[34]

24.   At confirmation, the *Roman Pontifical* calls for song after the profession of faith and during the anointings with chrism.[35]

25.    Each of the various rites of initiation includes a liturgy of the word and is often followed by the Eucharist. Thus, in planning music for the celebration, proper emphasis should be given to each of the two or three primary liturgical rites. For instance, in the celebration of the baptism of a child, the assembly should not sing only at the times noted in the ritual for that sacrament while singing nothing during the celebration of the Word. Rather, a proper balance would require that singing be an essential element throughout the entire prayer experience.

26.    Composers of church music are encouraged to create musical settings of the acclamations from Sacred Scripture, the hymns in the style of the New Testament, and the songs from ancient liturgies which are included in the approved ritual books.[36] Much service music, set to texts in English, Spanish, and other vernacular languages, is still required for the full experience of these liturgical celebrations of initiation. Simpler musical settings would be especially welcome for use at celebrations where no musical accompanist is present.

## RECONCILIATION

27.    Communal celebrations of reconciliation (Forms 2 and 3 of the sacrament, as well as non-sacramental penance services) normally require an entrance song or song of gathering; a responsorial psalm and a gospel acclamation during the liturgy of the word; an optional hymn after the homily; and a hymn of praise for God's mercy following the absolution.[37] The litany within the General Confession of Sins (alternating between the deacon or cantor and the assembly) or another appropriate song may also be sung, as well as the Lord's Prayer. Singing or soft instrumental music may be used during the time of individual confessions, especially when there is a large number of people present for the celebration.

## CHRISTIAN MARRIAGE

28.    Weddings present particular challenges and opportunities to planners. It is helpful for a diocese or a parish to have a definite (but flexible) policy regarding wedding music. This policy should be communicated early to couples as a normal part of their preparation in order to avoid last-minute crises and misunderstandings. Both musician and pastor should make every effort to assist couples to understand and share in the planning of their marriage liturgy. Sometimes the only music familiar to the couple is a song heard at a friend's ceremony and one not necessarily suitable to the sacrament. The pastoral musician will make an effort to demonstrate a wider range of possibilities to the couple, particularly in the choice of music to be sung by the entire assembly present for the liturgy.

29.    Particular decisions about choice and placement of wedding music should grow out of the three judgments proposed in *Music in Catholic Worship*. The liturgical judgment: Is the music's text, form, placement and style congruent with the nature of liturgy?[38] The musical judgment: Is the music technically, aesthetically and expressively good irrespective of musical idiom or style?[39] The pastoral judgment: will it help this assembly to pray?[40] Such a process of dialogue may not

be as easy to apply as an absolute list of permitted or prohibited music, but in the long run it will be more effective pastorally.

## CHRISTIAN BURIAL

30.  Funerals, because of often difficult pastoral situations in which some family members and friends are overburdened with grief, unchurched or otherwise unable to enter into the liturgy, have frequently received little or no attention musically. In this respect, funerals may be the least successfully reformed of our liturgical rites.

31.  It is the pastoral responsibility of parishes to provide liturgical music at all Masses of Christian Burial. Attempts to involve the congregation more actively are to be encouraged. Appropriate participation aids should be prepared and provided for members of the praying assembly.

32.  Many parishes have found it helpful to form choirs of retired parishioners or others who are at home on weekdays, whose unique ministry it is to assist the grieving members of a funeral assembly by leading the sung prayer of the funeral liturgy. Where this is not possible, a cantor is able to perform a similar ministry. In all cases a serious effort should be made to move beyond the practice of employing a "funeral singer" to perform all the sung parts of the liturgy. Reconsideration should be given to the location of the singer, that person's role, and the kind of music that is sung. The cantor ought not individually sing or recite the congregational prayers as a substitute for the assembly. The same norms applicable to music at any Mass apply equally to the Mass of Christian Burial.[41]

33.  The principle of progressive solemnity, already mentioned, applies especially to the rites of Christian Burial. A few things sung well (the acclamations, responsorial psalm, entrance and communion processionals, and song of farewell during the final commendation) should be given priority at funerals and may be drawn from a parish's common musical repertoire.

# MUSIC IN THE LITURGY OF THE HOURS

34.  A growing number of parishes celebrate at least some part of the Liturgy of the Hours, usually Evening Prayer, during one or more of the liturgical seasons. The question of singing in the office is treated in the *General Instruction on the Liturgy of the Hours* and should be consulted along with *Study Text VII.*[42] The following observations expand on what is written there.

## METHODS OF SINGING THE PSALMS

35.  The psalms and canticles are songs; therefore they are most satisfying when sung. The *General Instruction* lists several ways in which the psalms may be sung: responsorially, antiphonally or straight through *(in directum.)*[43] Music may be of the formula type (e.g., psalm tones) or composed for each psalm or canticle.

## A. Responsorial

36.   The responsorial form of psalm singing appears to have been the original style for congregational use and still remains as the easiest method for engaging the congregation in the singing of psalms. In this model the psalmist or choir sings the verses of the psalm and the assembly responds with a brief antiphon (refrain). For pastoral or musical reasons, the *General Instruction* permits the substitution of other approved texts for these refrains.[44]

## B. Antiphonal

37.   In the antiphonal style, the praying assembly is divided into two groups. The text of the psalm is shared between them; generally the same musical configuration (e.g., a psalm tone) is used by both. A refrain is ordinarily sung before and after the psalm by the whole body. This method of singing has its roots in the choir and monastic traditions. Today where it is used by the congregation, care must be taken that the latter can be at ease with this form of sung prayer.

## C. Through-composed

38.   In a through-composed setting *(in directum)*, the musical material is ordinarily not repeated, unless the psalm calls for it. The music may be for soloist, soloist and choir or choir alone (e.g., an anthem). Only rarely will this form be found in settings designed for congregational use. The purpose of the *in directum* setting should be to complement the literary structure of the psalm and to capture its emotions.

## D. Metrical Psalms

39.   The *General Instruction on the Liturgy of the Hours* makes no mention of the practice of singing the psalms in metrical paraphrases. This manner of psalm singing developed with some of the Reformation churches. Due to its four hundred year tradition, a large and important repertoire of metrical psalms in English is available today. Poets and composers continue to add to this resource of psalm settings.

40.   While metrical psalmody may be employed fruitfully in the Church's liturgy (for instance, when a hymn is part of one of the rites), introduction of this musical form into the psalmody of the Liturgy of the Hours profoundly affects and alters the praying of the psalms as a ritual. Thus, metrical psalms should not be used as substitutes either for the responsorial psalm in a liturgy of the word of one of the rites or for the psalms in the Liturgy of the Hours.

## FORMULA TONES

41.   Formula tones (Gregorian plainsong tones, Anglican chants, faux-bourdons) are readily available and adaptable to modern use. Care should be taken in setting vernacular texts that the verbal accent pattern is not distorted by the musical cadence. These tones grew out of the paired half-line pattern of the Vulgate psalter. Modern translations of the psalms, however, have restored the Hebrew pattern of strophes (stanzas) of three, four, five or more lines. The sense unit

in a strophe will frequently run beyond the musical pattern of the classical formula tone and will often require some repetition and even some accommodation for half-lines.

42. Another kind of formula tone has more recently been developed (e.g., the Gelineau and Bevenot systems) which is based on the strophe as a unit. These tones are longer and make provisions for irregularities in the number of lines. They more naturally fit the Grail psalter, which is the approved translation of the psalms for the Liturgy of the Hours.

43. Where formula tones are employed for the hours of the office, especially with a parish congregation, variety should be sought in the use of other forms of sung prayer, particularly the responsorial style. The Old Testament Canticle in Morning Prayer and the New Testament Canticle in Evening Prayer are especially suitable for this latter method of singing.

### OTHER ELEMENTS

44. The principle mentioned earlier concerning the mixing of different musical idioms has special application in a sung celebration of the Liturgy of the Hours. Psalms may be sung in the manners discussed above. Certain psalms, however, might be sung by a choir alone. A few might lend themselves to recitation. The nature and literary form of the psalm itself should suggest the way it is to be prayed. Likewise, in the same office some parts may be rendered unaccompanied, others accompanied by organ, piano, guitar or other instruments.

45. Naturally, the hymns in the Liturgy of the Hours should be sung.[45] The responsories also lend themselves to singing, but as yet the number of published settings is few.[46] The readings are not usually chanted.[47] The introductory versicles and greetings can be easily learned and sung. The Lord's Prayer and the intercessions at Morning and Evening Prayer, either in the form of a litany with a fixed response (by far the easiest and most effective method for praying the intercessions) or as versicles and responses, are suited to singing.[48]

## OTHER MATTERS
### MUSIC AND THE LITURGICAL YEAR

46. The mystery of God's love in Christ is so great that a single celebration cannot exhaust its meaning. Over the course of the centuries the various seasons and feasts have developed to express the richness of the paschal mystery and of our need to celebrate it. While the liturgy celebrates but one "theme," the dying and rising of Christ, and while Sunday is the original Christian feast, even so the liturgical year shows forth this mystery like so many facets of a resplendent jewel.[49]

47. Music has been a unique means of celebrating this richness and diversity and of communicating the rhythm of the church year to the assembly. Music enhances the power of the readings and prayer to capture the special quality of the

liturgical seasons. What would Christmas be without its carols? How diminished would the fifty-day Easter feast be without the solemn, joyful Alleluia song?

48.     Great care must be shown in the selection of music for seasons and feasts. Contemporary culture seems increasingly unwilling either to prepare for or to prolong Christian feasts and seasons. The Church's pastors and ministers must be aware of cultural phenomena which run counter to the liturgical year or even devalue our feasts and seasons, especially through consumerism. The season of Advent should be preserved in its integrity, Christmas carols being reserved for the Christmas season alone. Hymns which emphasize the passion and death of Christ should be used only in the last week of the Lenten season. Easter should not be allowed to end in a day, but rather, the fifty days of its celebration should be planned as a unified experience.

## MUSIC OF THE PAST

49.     The *Constitution on the Sacred Liturgy* sets forth the principles for the recent reform of the liturgy. At the same time it called the heritage of sacred music "a treasure of inestimable value."[50] These purposes, while not opposed to each other, do exist in a certain tension. The restoration of active participation in the liturgy, the simplification of the rites, and the use of the vernacular have meant a massive change in the theory and practice of church music, a shift already detailed in *Music in Catholic Worship* and the present statement.

50.     Some have viewed this situation with profound regret. For some, the setting aside of the Latin repertoire of past centuries has been a painful experience, and a cause of bitter alienation. "Now is the time for healing."[51] It is also the time to make realistic assessments of what place the music of the past can still have in the liturgies of today.

51.     On the eve of the Council few parishes were performing the authentic repertoire recommended by Saint Pius X in his famous *motu proprio* on music.[52] Rather, most parishes generally used only a few of the simple chant Masses along with modern imitations of Renaissance motets and Masses. Moreover, the great music of the past was seldom the music of the ordinary parish church. Most often it was a product of the cathedrals and court chapels.

52.     However, singing and playing the music of the past is a way for Catholics to stay in touch with and preserve their rich heritage. A place can be found for this music, a place which does not conflict with the assembly's role and the other demands of the rite. Such a practice no longer envisions the performance of "Masses" as set pieces, but looks more to the repertoire of motets, antiphons and anthems which can be harmonized more easily with the nature of the renewed liturgy and with its pastoral celebration.[53]

53.     At Mass that place will typically include the time during the preparation of the gifts and the period after communion. A skillful director will also be able to find suitable choral repertoire to use as a prelude to the Mass, at the end of it, and

at the Glory to God. *Jubilate Deo*, the basic collection of simple Gregorian chants, should also be employed as a source for the assembly's participation.

## MUSIC AND CULTURAL HERITAGE

54.    Just as the great liturgical music of the past is to be remembered, cherished and used, so also the rich diversity of the cultural heritage of the many peoples of our country today must be recognized, fostered and celebrated. The United States of America is a nation of nations, a country in which people speak many tongues, live their lives in diverse ways, celebrate events in song and music in the folkways of their cultural, ethnic and racial roots.

55.    Liturgical music today must be as diverse and multi-cultural as the members of the assembly. Pastors and musicians must encourage not only the use of traditional music of other languages, but also the composition of new liturgical music appropriate to various cultures. Likewise the great musical gifts of the Hispanic, Black and other ethnic communities in the Church should enrich the whole Church in the United States in a dialogue of cultures.

## INSTRUMENTAL MUSIC

56.    The liturgy prefers song to instrumental music. "As a combination of sacred music and words it forms a necessary or integral part of the solemn liturgy."[54] Yet the contribution of instrumentalists is also important, both in accompanying the singing and in playing by themselves.

57.    Church music legislation of the past reflected a culture in which singing was not only primary, but was presumed to be unaccompanied (chant and polyphony). The music of today, as indeed musical culture today, regularly presumes that the song is accompanied. This places instruments in a different light. The song achieves much of its vitality from the rhythm and harmony of its accompaniment. Instrumental accompaniment is a great support to an assembly in learning new music and in giving full voice to its prayer and praise in worship.

58.    Instrumental music can also assist the assembly in preparing for worship, in meditating on the mysteries, and in joyfully progressing in its passage from liturgy to life. Instrumental music, used in this way, must be understood as more than an easily dispensable adornment to the rites, a decoration to dress up a ceremony. It is rather ministerial, helping the assembly to rejoice, to weep, to be of one mind, to be converted, to pray. There is a large repertoire of organ music which has always been closely associated with the liturgy. Much suitable music can be selected from the repertoires of other appropriate instruments as well.

59.    The proper place of silence must not be neglected, and the temptation must be resisted to cover every moment with music.[55] There are times when an instrumental interlude is able to bridge the gap between two parts of a ceremony and help to unify the liturgical action. But music's function is always ministerial and must never degenerate into idle background music.

60.    The liturgy is a complexus of signs expressed by living human beings. Music, being preeminent among those signs, ought to be "live." While recorded music, therefore, might be used to advantage outside the liturgy as an aid in the teaching of new music, it should, as a general norm, never be used within the liturgy to replace the congregation, the choir, the organist or other instrumentalists.

61.    Some exceptions to this principle should be noted, however. Recorded music may be used to accompany the community's song during a procession out-of-doors and, when used carefully, in Masses with children.[56] Occasionally it might be used as an aid to prayer, for example, during long periods of silence in a communal celebration of reconciliation. It may never become a substitute for the community's song, however, as in the case of the responsorial psalm after a reading from Scripture or during the optional hymn of praise after communion.

62.    A prerecorded sound track is sometimes used as a feature of contemporary "electronic music" composition. When combined with live voices and/or instruments, it is an integral part of the performance and, therefore, is a legitimate use of prerecorded music.

## MUSIC MINISTRY

63.    The entire worshiping assembly exercises a ministry of music. Some members of the community, however, are recognized for the special gifts they exhibit in leading the musical praise and thanksgiving of Christian assemblies. These are the pastoral musicians, whose ministry is especially cherished by the Church.

64.    What motivates the pastoral musician? Why does he or she give so much time and effort to the service of the church at prayer? The only answer can be that the church musician is first a disciple and then a minister. The musician belongs first of all to the assembly; he or she is a worshiper above all. Like any member of the assembly, the pastoral musician needs to be a believer, needs to experience conversion, needs to hear the Gospel and so proclaim the praise of God. Thus, the pastoral musician is not merely an employee or volunteer. He or she is a minister, someone who shares faith, serves the community, and expresses the love of God and neighbor through music.

65.    Additional efforts are needed to train men and women for the ministry of music. Colleges and universities offering courses of studies in liturgical music, as well as a growing number of regional and diocesan centers for the formation of liturgical ministers, are encouraged to initiate or to continue programs which develop musical skills and impart a thorough understanding of the liturgy of the Church.

66.    The musician's gift must be recognized as a valued part of the pastoral effort, and for which proper compensation must be made.[57] Clergy and musicians should strive for mutual respect and cooperation in the achievement of their common goals.

67.   As the assembly's principal liturgical leaders, priests and deacons must continue to be mindful of their own musical role in the liturgy. Priests should grow more familiar with chanting the presidential prayers of the Mass and other rites. Deacons, too, in the admonitions, exhortations, and especially in the litanies of the third penitential rite and in the general intercessions of the Mass, have a significant musical role to play in worship.

68.   Among music ministers, the cantor has come to be recognized as having a crucial role in the development of congregational singing. Besides being qualified to lead singing, he or she must have the skills to introduce and teach new music, and to encourage the assembly. This must be done with sensitivity so that the cantor does not intrude on the communal prayer or become manipulative. Introductions and announcements should be brief and avoid a homiletic style.

69.   The cantor's role is distinct from that of the psalmist, whose ministry is the singing of the verses of the responsorial psalm and communion psalm. Frequently the two roles will be combined in one person.

70.   A community will not grow in its ability either to appreciate or express its role in musical liturgy if each celebration is thought of as a discrete moment. A long-range plan must be developed which identifies how music will be used in the parish and how new music will be learned. The abilities of the congregation should never be misjudged. Some cannot or will not sing, for whatever reason. Most will take part and will enjoy learning new music if they have effective leaders.

## COPYRIGHT

71.   In the last decade pastors and musicians have become more aware of the legal and moral implications of copyright.[58] As a result parishes and institutions are now more sensitive to the need composers, poets and publishers have to receive a just compensation for their creative work. Publishers have cooperated in making their requirements known and their music available to reprint at reasonable rates, an effort for which they deserve the thanks of the Church in the United States.

72.   Additional education regarding copyright needs to continue. At the same time, parishes and other institutions should annually budget sufficient monies for the purchase of music necessary for the proper celebration of the liturgy. The need for much copying would then be lessened.

## CONCLUSION

73.   The past decade has shown important signs of growth. The eagerness of many congregations to make a beginning in singing has been matched by a second harvest of musical compositions. As time goes by, new generations will come to accept, as a matter of course, what was brand new and very strange only a few years ago, namely, that all should join in the songs and prayers of the liturgy.

74.   The Church in the United States continues on its journey of liturgical renewal and spiritual growth. It is the hope of the Bishops' Committee on the Liturgy that this statement will be a further encouragement in our progress along that course. The words of Saint Augustine remind us of our pilgrimage: "You should sing as wayfarers do—sing but continue your journey. Do not be lazy, but sing to make your journey more enjoyable. Sing, but keep going."[59]

# NOTES

1. Bishops' Committee on the Liturgy (BCL), *Music in Catholic Worship* (MCW), (Washington: USCC, 1972); BCL, "The Place of Music in Eucharistic Celebrations, November 1967.

2. Text appears in this volume.

3. MCW, Introduction, unpaged.

4. Ibid., 45, 55, 63.

5. *Roman Pontifical* (RP): *Rite of Confirmation* (Confirmation), 23, 29.

6. *Roman Ritual* (RR): *Rite of Baptism for Children* (Baptism), 59, 60.

7. RR: *Rite of Christian Initiation of Adults* (RCIA), 146.

8. RR: Baptism, 42, 52, 67.

9. RP: *Ordination of a Deacon* (Deacon), 25; *Ordination of a Priest* (Priest), 27; *Ordination of a Bishop* (Bishop), 35.

10. RP: *Institution of a Reader*, 7.

11. RP: Confirmation, 46.

12. RP: Priest, 25.

13. *Roman Missal*, General Instruction (GIRM), 56j.

14. RR: RCIA, 214; Baptism, 48.

15. RP: Deacon, 18; Priest, 17; Bishop, 21.

16. RP: *Consecration to a life of Virginity*, 20, 59.

17. RP: *Dedication of a Church and an Altar* (Dedication), 58.

18. RR: *Rite of Penance*, 56.

19. RR: Baptism, 59.

20. RR: RCIA, 389; Baptism, 223–4.

21. RR: *Pastoral Care of the Sick: Rites of Anointing and Viaticum*, 75b.

22. RP: Deacon, 21; Priest 22; Bishop 26.

23. RP: Dedication 62.

24. RR: Baptism, 96.

25. *The Liturgy of the Hours*, General Instruction (GILOTH), 273.

26. GILOTH, 276.

27. *Eucharistic Prayers for Masses with Children and for Masses of Reconciliation*, Provisional Text (Washington: USCC, 1975).

28. *The Lectionary for Mass*, Introduction (second typical edition, 1981), 23. "The *Alleluia* or the verse before the gospel must be sung and during it, all stand. It is not to be sung by the cantor who intones it or by the choir, but by the whole congregation together."

29. GIRM, 56i.

30. Ibid., 56e.

31. Ibid., 29.

32. Ibid., 31.

33. RR: RCIA. Becoming Catechumen, 74, 90. Election, 146, 171, 178. Initiation 221, 227, 231.

34. RR: Baptism. Procession, 42. Song after homily, 47. Procession to place of baptism, 52. Acclamation after profession of faith, 59. Acclamation after baptism, 60. Procession to altar, 67.

35. RP: Confirmation, 23, 29.

36. RR: RCIA, 390. RR: Baptism, 225–245. See Also "A Letter to Composers of Liturgical Music from the Bishops' Committee on the Liturgy" in BCL *Newsletter* XVI (December 1980), 237–239.

37. RR: *Rite of Penance*, 56. The ritual recommends the Canticle of Mary (Luke 1:46–55), Psalm 136 or another psalm listed in 206 as especially fitting as a song of praise.

38. MCW, 30–38.

39. MCW, 26–29.

40. MCW, 39–41.

41. RR: *Rite of Funerals*, 23–25, especially 25.5.

42. GILOTH, 267–284; BCL, *Study Text VII: The Liturgy of the Hours* (Washington: USCC, 1981).

43. GILOTH, 279, 121–123

44. Ibid., 274.

45. Ibid., 280.

46. Ibid. 281–282.

47. Ibid., 283.

48. Ibid., 284.

49. *Roman Calendar*, General Norms for the Liturgical Year and the Calendar, 4; Second Vatican Council, Constitution on the Liturgy (CSL), *Sacrosanctum Concilium* (4 December 1963), 104ff.

50. CSL, 112.

51. BCL, *A Commemorative Statement* (November 1978), in BCL *Newsletter* XIV (December 1978), 143.

52. Pius X, Motu Proprio, *Tra Le Sollecitudini* (22 November 1903).

53. Congregation of Rites, Instruction on Music in the Sacred Liturgy, *Musicam Sacram* (5 March 1967), 53.

54. CSL, 112.

55. GIRM, 23; GILOTH, 202; Paul VI, Apostolic Exhortation, *Evangelica Testificatio* (29 June 1971), 46.

56. *Notitiae* 127 (February 1977), 94; Congregation for Divine Worship, *Directory for Masses with Children* (1 November 1973), 32.

57. MCW, 77; BCL, *A Commemorative Statement* (November 1978), in BCL *Newsletter* XIV (December 1978), 143–144.

58. BCL *Newsletter* III, 12 (December 1967), 109; Ibid. V, 5 (May 1969), 177; Ibid. XVI (January 1980), 197; FDLC Liturgical Arts Committee, *Copyright Update: Reprint Permissions of Publishers of Liturgical Music and Sacred Scripture* (Washington: FDLC, 1982).

59. St. Augustine, Sermo 256, 3 (PL 38:1193)

# ENVIRONMENT AND ART
## IN
## CATHOLIC WORSHIP

# OVERVIEW OF *ENVIRONMENT AND ART IN CATHOLIC WORSHIP*

Andrew D. Ciferni, OPRAEM

With the promulgation of the Second Vatican Council's *Constitution on the Sacred Liturgy* (1963) and the publication of the revised *Roman Missal* (1969), most Roman Catholic worship spaces became obsolete. Paradoxically, some of our oldest spaces, for example, many of the Roman basilicas, are more amenable to the celebration of the reformed rites than churches built in this century. The task of adapting older spaces or building new ones adequate to the normative celebration of the reformed rites remains a challenge. The renewed understandings of God, church, sacrament and ministry that emerged in the reforms require a vastly different approach to church building than that used during the 400 years before Vatican II.

Thus the need for guidelines to assist communities and architects in the process of renovation and/or new building was and is a strong one. The response of the Bishops' Committee on the Liturgy (BCL) to that need was *Environment and Art in Catholic Worship* (EACW), issued in 1978.

The Foreword (see also no. 6) to the document states that it is intended to be a companion to the BCL's document on Catholic ritual music, *Music in Catholic Worship* (found in this volume). These and other BCL documents, such as *Liturgical Music Today* (also in this volume), are to aid the church in the United States in the implementation of the post–Vatican II revised rituals. It seems, however, that the complementary nature of these documents is rarely explored. For example, how does the processional nature of the eucharist in the Roman rite affect the shape of the worship space as well as the textual and musical shape of the entrance song? How might the judgments (musical, liturgical, pastoral) suggested for the choice of good ritual music be appropriately and fruitfully employed in making judgments about liturgical furnishings, vesture and seasonal appointments? How could the criteria of quality and appropriateness (EACW, nos. 20–21) be applied to judgments concerning ritual music?

CHALLENGES TO THE CHURCH

A tracking of the influence of EACW would indicate that the most consistently challenging questions have a remarkable correspondence with the divergence of diocesan guidelines from the directives of this document. They are 1) the need for adequate gathering-lingering space (nos. 40, 54); 2) the shape of the seating arrangement for the assembly (nos. 11, 24, 40, 53, 58–59, 68); 3) the shape, size and placement of the font (nos. 64, 76–77); 4) the space for music ministers and their instruments in relationship to the rest of the assembly (nos. 58, 69, 70, 83); and 5) the place for the altar of eucharistic celebration and that altar's relationship to the reservation of the blessed sacrament (nos. 71–73, 78–79).

On at least two of these issues, the place of the font and the place of the musicians, the tradition gives little strong guidance. It is only in the current liturgical reform—because the assembly sees and participates in the act of baptism—that the place of the font has become a major design question. The tradition placed greater emphasis on the candidates' (adults as well as infants) going down naked in the font. Thus the building of separate baptistries near the entry of the church for the sake of modesty and to signify the theological reality that we enter the church through baptism reflected values other than the current value of everyone's seeing the catechumens' baptism. It also should be evident that little in the tradition prepares us for placing a choir and their instruments in a position that expresses that the choir members are themselves members of the assembly (thus the inappropriateness of choir lofts) while serving in a role of musical leadership both within and vis-a-vis the rest of the congregation.

HELP FROM THE TRADITION

Contrary to some popular contemporary opinions, the tradition is extremely enlightening on the matter of gathering-lingering spaces. These can be found to this day in the form of the atriums that front most ancient basilicas. These provide a physical and psychological buffer between the street and the gathering of God's people for common prayer. At times, this space also is integral to the celebration of more processional liturgies such as the blessing of candles on February 2, the blessing of palms on Passion Sunday, the reception of the bride and groom for their wedding liturgy and the reception of the body in the funeral rites.

Section II, "The Subject of the Liturgical Action: The Church," asserts that the assembly of believers is the most important liturgical symbol (no. 28). The corollary: Seating arrangements in renovations or new buildings should be configured so that the assembly experiences itself as a face-to-face community (no. 11). By this criterion, the overwhelming majority of renovations completed since Vatican II are only sanctuary renovations, not church renovations. Until the Reformation and the introduction of fixed seating (pews) into Catholic churches, the shaping of the assembly simply was not an issue because the congregation could move unimpeded by fixed furniture in the body of the church.

The placement of the tabernacle is probably the directive of this document most contradicted by diocesan building guidelines and/or the rulings of diocesan bishops. The scholarship on this matter is clear. It was not until the late Middle Ages that the blessed sacrament came to be permanently reserved on the main altar of parish churches. It never was reserved on the main altar of cathedral and abbey churches and to this day is only reserved in separate chapels of the papal basilicas of Rome (see no. 49 of the *Ceremonial of Bishops*). Two of the master principles of this document are at stake here: 1) the primacy of the assembly (no. 28) and 2) the distinction between liturgical action and private devotion (no. 78), with the consequently different demands made on spaces designed for these two distinct but complementary modes of Catholic prayer (no. 70).

The principle of the symbolic primacy of the assembly relativizes centuries of Catholic devotional practice. This, in turn, calls for the renovation of most church buildings designed during those centuries when most worship spaces were designed to focus the entire congregation's attention on the tabernacle. To change direction in this regard is not to condemn the pastoral solutions of past ages, when the liturgy had ceased to function as the basic spiritual formation of our assemblies. On the other hand, to maintain that the tabernacle must remain within the main worship space is to cling to a former pastoral solution not in harmony with the present liturgical reforms.

Magisterial documents dealing with the eucharist consistently state that the reservation of the consecrated elements always has been and remains primarily a matter of having the sacrament available for communion for the sick and dying (*Eucharisticum mysterium,* no. 49, and *Holy Communion and Worship of the Eucharist outside Mass,* no. 5). This reservation has legitimately but secondarily become a focus of devotional adoration, and EACW's section on eucharistic reservation makes a clear distinction between the demands made on a space intended for liturgical action and one dedicated to devotional prayer.

DIRECTIONS FOR THE FUTURE: ACOUSTICS, HOSPITALITY, MYSTERY

One design element that comes to greater clarity in making the distinction between celebrational and devotional space and one that could benefit from further elucidation in any subsequent revision of this document is acoustics. Spaces designed for Catholic worship (celebration, action) must be "dry" or "live" (no. 51) because music is integral to ritual prayer. Not so for devotional spaces that are purposely deadened to facilitate the individual prayer proper to these spaces. Some of the most serious threats to the future success of Catholic liturgical reform are carpeted floors, sound-absorbent ceiling and/or wall finishes and upholstered assembly seating—which have a musical effect equivalent to lining a Steinway piano with a shag rug!

The conflicted issue of the placement of the blessed sacrament raises for many the elusive question of mystery, a topic not treated as adequately as it deserves in this document. Section I, "The Worship of God and Its Requirements," sets cheek by jowl "a climate of hospitality" (no. 11) and "the experience of mystery" (no. 12). Any revision of or supplement to this document could well devote space to further expounding the liturgical virtue of hospitality lest we confuse this hallmark of authentic Christian ritual with easy domestic comfort, casualness or weak design. This clarification could set the stage for a more adequate treatment of the experience of mystery in worship. Such treatment might well be grounded in the discovery of the mystery of God as it is encountered in daily pastoral care and comes to expression in the liturgy.

CONCLUSION

*Environment and Art in Catholic Worship* deals not only with the architectural requirements for normative celebration of the rites, but also with other vitally important ritual issues such as the body at prayer, the opening up of symbols and the quality of ritual furnishings, vesture, vessels and images. Since at least the period of the Reformation, the Roman Catholic tradition has been prone either to undervalue the importance of the arts in worship or to control them to such a degree that contemporary artists have felt alienated by the church. The development of the arts in the West therefore largely has taken place outside the sphere of ritual celebration. *Environment and Art in Catholic Worship* challenges architects and artists to creative activity in service to the ritual process (no. 25). It calls our worship communities to embody faith in ritual spaces, gestures, furnishings and other objects, which are both in continuity with our best liturgical tradition yet capable of proclaiming the incarnation of God's eternal word in new works that speak authentically to our time.

# OUTLINE

# ENVIRONMENT AND ART IN CATHOLIC WORSHIP

## INTRODUCTION

1.    Faith involves a good tension between human modes of expressive communications and God himself, whom our human tools can never adequately grasp. God transcends. God is mystery. God cannot be contained in or confined by any of our words or images or categories.

2.    While our words and art forms cannot contain or confine God, they can, like the world itself, be icons, avenues of approach, numinous presences, ways of touching without totally grasping or seizing. Flood, fire, the rock, the sea, the mountain, the cloud, the political situations and institutions of succeeding periods—in all of them Israel touched the face of God, found help for discerning a way, moved toward the reign of justice and peace. Biblical faith assures us that God covenants a people through human events and calls the covenanted people to shape human events.

3.    And then in Jesus, the Word of God is flesh: "This is what we proclaim to you: what was from the beginning, what we have heard, what we have seen with our eyes, what we have looked upon and our hands have touched—we speak of the word of life."[1]

4.    Christians have not hesitated to use every human art in their celebration of the saving work of God in Jesus Christ, although in every historical period they have been influenced, at times inhibited, by cultural circumstances. In the resurrection of the Lord, all things are made new. Wholeness and healthiness are restored, because the reign of sin and death is conquered. Human limits are still real and we must be conscious of them. But we must also praise God and give God thanks with the human means we have available. God does not need liturgy; people do, and people have only their own arts and styles of expression with which to celebrate.

5.    Like the covenant itself, the liturgical celebrations of the faith community (Church) involve the whole person. They are not purely religious or merely rational and intellectual exercises, but also human experiences calling on all human faculties: body, mind, senses, imagination, emotions, memory. Attention to these is one of the urgent needs of contemporary liturgical renewal.

6.    Historically, music has enjoyed a preeminence among the arts of public worship, and there is no clear evidence to justify denying it the same place today. The Bishops' Committee on the Liturgy, therefore, published guidelines (*Music in Catholic Worship*, 1972) encouraging attention to music, both instrumental and

choral/vocal. This companion booklet, *Environment and Art in Catholic Worship*, offers guidelines to encourage the other arts necessary for a full experience in public worship. The two booklets, therefore, should be used together, complementing one another, by those responsible for planning and conducting liturgical celebrations. For that reason, music is excluded from the specific concerns of the following pages.

7.    If we maintain that no human words or art forms can contain or exhaust the mystery of God's love, but that all words and art forms can be used to praise God in the liturgical assembly, then we look for criteria to judge music, architecture, and the other arts in relation to public worship.[2]

8.    The reason for offering principles to guide rather than blueprints to follow was stated clearly by the Council fathers: "The Church has not adopted any particular style of art as her very own; it has admitted styles from every period according to the natural talents and circumstances of peoples, and the needs of the various rites. Thus, in the course of the centuries, she has brought into being a treasury of art which must be carefully preserved. The art of our own days, coming from every race and region, shall also be given free scope in the Church, provided that it adorns the sacred buildings and holy rites with due reverence and honor; thereby it is enabled to contribute its own voice to that wonderful chorus of praise. . . . "[3]

## I. THE WORSHIP OF GOD AND ITS REQUIREMENTS

### LITURGY AND TRADITION

9.    Liturgy has a special and unique place in the life of Christians in the local churches, their communities of faith. Each Church gathers regularly to praise and thank God, to remember and make present God's great deeds, to offer common prayer, to realize and celebrate the kingdom of peace and justice. That action of the Christian assembly is liturgy.

10.    Common traditions carried on, developed and realized in each community make liturgy an experience of the Church which is both local and universal. The roots as well as the structure of its liturgical celebrations are biblical and ecclesial, asserting a communion with believers of all times and places. This tradition furnishes the symbol language of that action, along with structures and patterns refined through the centuries of experience, and gives the old meanings new life in our time, our place, with our new knowledge, talents, competencies, arts. Therefore, this celebration is that of a community at a given place and time, celebrated with the best of its resources, talents and arts in the light of our own tradition.[4]

### A CLIMATE OF HOSPITALITY

11.    As common prayer and ecclesial experience, liturgy flourishes in a climate of hospitality: a situation in which people are comfortable with one another, either knowing or being introduced to one another; a space in which people are

seated together, with mobility, in view of one another as well as the focal points of the rite, involved as participants and *not* as spectators.[5]

THE EXPERIENCE OF MYSTERY

12.    The experience of mystery which liturgy offers is found in its God-consciousness and God-centeredness. This involves a certain beneficial tension with the demands of hospitality, requiring a manner and an environment which invite contemplation (seeing beyond the face of the person or the thing, a sense of the holy, the numinous, mystery). A simple and attractive beauty in everything that is used or done in liturgy is the most effective invitation to this kind of experience. One should be able to sense something special (and nothing trivial) in everything that is seen and heard, touched and smelled, and tasted in liturgy.

13.    Incarnation, the paschal mystery and the Holy Spirit in us are faith's access to the transcendence, holiness, otherness of God. An action like liturgy, therefore, has special significance as a means of relating to God, or responding to God's relating to us. This does not mean that we have "captured" God in our symbols. It means only that God has graciously loved us on our own terms, in ways corresponding to our condition. Our response must be one of depth and totality, of authenticity, genuineness, and care with respect to everything we use and do in liturgical celebration.

THE OPENING UP OF SYMBOLS

14.    Every word, gesture, movement, object, appointment must be real in the sense that it is our own. It must come from the deepest understanding of ourselves (not careless, phony, counterfeit, pretentious, exaggerated, etc.). Liturgy has suffered historically from a kind of minimalism and an overriding concern for efficiency, partly because sacramental causality and efficacy have been emphasized at the expense of sacramental signification. As our symbols tended in practice to shrivel up and petrify, they became much more manageable and efficient. They still "caused," were still "efficacious" even though they had often ceased to signify in the richest, fullest sense.

15.    Renewal requires the opening up of our symbols, especially the fundamental ones of bread and wine, water, oil, the laying on of hands, until we can experience all of them as authentic and appreciate their symbolic value.

THE PERSONAL-COMMUNAL EXPERIENCE

16.    A culture which is oriented to efficiency and production has made us insensitive to the symbolic function of persons and things. Also, the same cultural emphasis on individuality and competition has made it more difficult for us to appreciate the liturgy as a *personal-communal* experience. As a consequence, we tend to identify anything private and individual as "personal." But, by inference, anything communal and social is considered impersonal. For the sake of good liturgy, this misconception must be changed.

17.    To identify liturgy as an important *personal-communal* religious experience is to see the virtue of simplicity and commonness in liturgical texts, gestures,

music, etc. This is easier said than done. But it does require a persevering effort to respect the Church's mind in terms of its common feelings and simplicity, for example, by not drowning the action in a flood of words or by not making the action more complex than necessary in order to signify the gospel essentials.

## THE SACRED

18. An important part of contemporary Church renewal is the awareness of the community's recognition of the sacred. Environment and art are to foster this awareness. Because different cultural and subcultural groups in our society may have quite different styles of artistic expression, one cannot demand any universal sacred forms.[6]

## QUALITY AND APPROPRIATENESS

19. This is not to say that liturgy makes no demand upon architecture, music and the other arts. To be true to itself and to protect its own integrity, liturgy must make demands. Basically, its demands are two: *quality* and *appropriateness*. Whatever the style or type, no art has a right to a place in liturgical celebration if it is not of high quality and if it is not appropriate.[7]

20. *Quality* is perceived only by contemplation, by standing back from things and really trying to *see* them, trying to let them speak to the beholder. Cultural habit has conditioned the contemporary person to look at things in a more pragmatic way: "What is it worth?" "What will it do?" Contemplation sees the hand stamp of the artist, the honesty and care that went into an object's making, the pleasing form and color and texture. Quality means love and care in the making of something, honesty and genuineness with any materials used, and the artist's special gift in producing a harmonious whole, a well-crafted work. This applies to music, architecture, sculpture, painting, pottery making, furniture making, as well as to dance, mime or drama—in other words, to any art form that might be employed in the liturgical environment or action.

21. *Appropriateness* is another demand that liturgy rightfully makes upon any art that would serve its action. The work of art must be appropriate in two ways: 1) it must be capable of bearing the weight of mystery, awe, reverence, and wonder which the liturgical action expresses; 2) it must clearly *serve* (and not interrupt) ritual action which has its own structure, rhythm and movement.

22. The first point rules out anything trivial and self-centered, anything fake, cheap or shoddy, anything pretentious or superficial. That kind of appropriateness, obviously, is related to quality. But it demands more than quality. It demands a kind of transparency, so that we see and experience both the work of art and something beyond it.

23. The second point (to serve) refers both to the physical environment of public worship and to any art forms which might be employed as part of the liturgical action (e.g., ritual movement, gestures, audio-visuals, etc.).

24.    By environment we mean the larger space in which the action of the assembly takes place. At its broadest, it is the setting of the building in its neighborhood, including outdoor spaces. More specifically it means the character of a particular space and how it affects the action of the assembly. There are elements in the environment, therefore, which contribute to the overall experience, e.g., the seating arrangement, the placement of liturgical centers of action, temporary decoration, light, acoustics, spaciousness, etc. The environment is appropriate when it is beautiful, when it is hospitable, when it clearly invites and needs an assembly of people to complete it.

Furthermore, it is appropriate when it brings people close together so that they can see and hear the entire liturgical action, when it helps people feel involved and become involved. Such an environment works with the liturgy, not against it.

## THE SERVICE OF THE ARTS

25.    If an art form is used in liturgy it must aid and serve the action of liturgy since liturgy has its own structure, rhythm and pace: a gathering, a building up, a climax, and a descent to dismissal. It alternates between persons and groups of persons, between sound and silence, speech and song, movement and stillness, proclamation and reflection, word and action. The art form must never seem to interrupt, replace, or bring the course of liturgy to a halt. If one uses film, for example, in such a way that one seems to be saying, "We will stop the liturgy for a few moments now in order to experience this art form," then that use is inappropriate. If, however, an art form is used to enhance, support and illumine a part or parts of the liturgical action or the whole action, it can be both appropriate and rewarding.

26.    A major and continuing educational effort is required among believers in order to restore respect for competence and expertise in all the arts and a desire for their best use in public worship. This means winning back to the service of the Church professional people whose places have long since been taken by "commercial" producers, or volunteers who do not have the appropriate qualifications. Both sensitivity to the arts and willingness to budget resources for these are the conditions of progress so that quality and appropriateness can be real.

# II. THE SUBJECT OF LITURGICAL ACTION: THE CHURCH

27.    To speak of environmental and artistic requirements in Catholic worship, we have to begin with ourselves—we who are the Church, the baptized, the initiated.

## THE ASSEMBLY OF BELIEVERS

28.    Among the symbols with which liturgy deals, none is more important than this assembly of believers. It is common to use the same name to speak of the

building in which those persons worship, but that use is misleading. In the words of ancient Christians, the building used for worship is called *domus ecclesiae*, the house of the Church.

THE ACTION OF THE ASSEMBLY

29.   The most powerful experience of the sacred is found in the celebration and the persons celebrating, that is, it is found in the action of the assembly: the living words, the living gestures, the living sacrifice, the living meal. This was at the heart of the earliest liturgies. Evidence of this is found in their architectural floor plans which were designed as general gathering spaces, spaces which allowed the whole assembly to be part of the action.

30.   Because liturgical celebration is the worship action of the entire Church, it is desirable that persons representing the diversity of ages, sexes, ethnic and cultural groups in the congregation should be involved in planning and ministering in the liturgies of the community. Special competencies in music, public reading, and any other skills and arts related to public worship should be sought, respected and used in celebration. Not only the planners and ministers, however, are active in the liturgy. The entire congregation is an active component. There is no audience, no passive element in the liturgical celebration. This fact alone distinguishes it from most other public assemblies.

31.   The assembly's celebration, that is, celebration in the midst of the faith community, by the whole community, is the normal and normative way of celebrating any sacrament or other liturgy. Even when the communal dimension is not apparent, as sometimes in communion for the sick or for prisoners, the clergy or minister functions within the context of the entire community.

32.   The action of the assembly is also unique since it is not merely a "celebration of life," reflecting all of the distinctions stemming from color, sex, class, etc. Quite the contrary, liturgy requires the faith community to set aside all those distinctions and divisions and classifications. By doing this the liturgy celebrates the reign of God, and as such maintains the tension between what is (the status quo of our daily lives) and what must be (God's will for human salvation—liberation and solidarity). This uniqueness gives liturgy its key and central place in Christian life as seen from the perspective of an actual community. Just as liturgy makes its own demands on the environment and the arts, so, too, does the assembly. When the assembly gathers with its own varied background, there is a commonness demanded which stems from our human condition. The commonality here seeks the best which people can bring together rather than what is compromised or less noble. For the assembly seeks its own expression in an atmosphere which is beautiful, amidst actions which probe the entire human experience. This is what is most basic and most noble. It is what the assembly seeks in order to express the heart of the Church's liturgy.

CONTEMPORARY

33.   Contemporary art forms belong to the liturgical expressions of the assembly as surely as the art forms of the past. The latter are part of our common memory,

our communion (which extends over time as well as over geographical boundaries). Contemporary art is our own, the work of artists of our time and place, and belongs in our celebrations as surely as we do. If liturgy were to incorporate only the acceptable art of the past, conversion, commitment and tradition would have ceased to live. The assembly should, therefore, be equally unhesitating in searching out, patronizing and using the arts and media of past and present. Because it is symbolic communication, liturgy is more dependent on past tradition than many human activities are. Because it is the action of a contemporary assembly, it has to clothe its basically traditional structures with the living flesh and blood of our times and our arts.

BEAUTIFUL

34. Because the assembly gathers in the presence of God to celebrate his saving deeds, liturgy's climate is one of awe, mystery, wonder, reverence, thanksgiving and praise. So it cannot be satisfied with anything less than the *beautiful* in its environment and all its artifacts, movements, and appeals to the senses.[8] Admittedly difficult to define, the beautiful is related to the sense of the numinous, the holy. Where there is evidently no care for this, there is an environment basically unfriendly to mystery and awe, an environment too casual, if not careless, for the liturgical action. In a world dominated by science and technology, liturgy's quest for the beautiful is a particularly necessary contribution to full and balanced human life.

THE HUMAN EXPERIENCE

35. To gather intentionally in God's presence is to gather our total selves, our complete persons—a "living sacrifice." Other human activities tend to be more incomplete, specialized, and to claim one or the other facet of ourselves, lives, talents, roles. Liturgy is total, and therefore must be much more than a merely rational or intellectual exercise. Valid tradition reflects this attention to the whole person. In view of our culture's emphasis on reason, it is critically important for the Church to reemphasize a more total approach to the human person by opening up and developing the non-rational elements of liturgical celebration: the concerns for feelings of conversion, support, joy, repentance, trust, love, memory, movement, gesture, wonder.

SINFUL

36. The Church is a church of sinners, and the fact that God forgives, accepts and loves sinners places the liturgical assembly under a fundamental obligation to be honest and unpretentious, without deceit or affectation, in all it does. If all distinctions have been stripped away, then basic honesty has to be carried through in all the words, gestures and movements, art forms, objects, furnishings of public worship. Nothing which pretends to be other than it is has a place in celebration, whether it is a person, cup, table or sculpture.

SERVANT

37. Different ministries in such an assembly do not imply "superiority" or "inferiority." Different functions are necessary in the liturgy as they are in any

human, social activity. The recognition of different gifts and talents and the ordination, institution or delegation for the different services required (priest, reader, acolyte, musician, usher, etc.) is to facilitate worship. These are services to the assembly and those who perform them are servants of God who render services to the assembly. Those who perform such ministries are indeed servants of the assembly.

38.   The liturgical assembly, as presented, is Church, and as Church is servant to the world. It has a commitment to be sign, witness, and instrument of the reign of God. That commitment must be reflected and implemented not only in the individual lives of its members but also in the community's choices and in its use of its money, property and other resources. Liturgical buildings and spaces should have the same witness value. Their planning should involve representatives of oppressed and disadvantaged parts of the communities in which they are located.

## III. A HOUSE FOR THE CHURCH'S LITURGICAL CELEBRATIONS

39.   The congregation, its liturgical action, the furniture and the other objects it needs for its liturgical action—these indicate the necessity of a space, a place, a hall, or a building for the liturgy. It will be a place for praying and singing, for listening and speaking—a place for human interaction and active participation—where the mysteries of God are recalled and celebrated in human history. The servant nature of the Church in relation to the rest of the community in its area (and in the world) invites it to consider the broader needs of the community, especially in the community's deprived, handicapped and suffering members, and therefore to consider a breadth of possible uses of its buildings.

PRIMARY DEMAND: THE ASSEMBLY

40.   In no case, however, should this mean a lack of attention to the requirements of the liturgical celebration or a yielding of the primary demands that liturgy must make upon the space: the gathering of the faith community in a participatory and hospitable atmosphere for word and eucharist, for initiation and reconciliation, for prayer and praise and song.

41.   Such a space acquires a sacredness from the sacred action of the faith community which uses it. As a place, then, it becomes quite naturally a reference and orientation point for believers. The historical problem of the church as a *place* attaining a dominance over the faith community need not be repeated as long as Christians respect the primacy of the living assembly.

42.   The norm for designing liturgical space is the assembly and its liturgies. The building or cover enclosing the architectural space is a shelter or "skin" for a liturgical action. It does not have to "look like" anything else, past or present. Its integrity, simplicity and beauty, its physical location and landscaping should take into account the neighborhood, city and area in which it is built.

43.   Many local Churches must use spaces designed and built in a former period, spaces which may now be unsuitable for the liturgy. In the renovation of these spaces for contemporary liturgical use, there is no substitute for an ecclesiology that is both ancient and modern in the fullest sense. Nor is there any substitute for a thorough understanding of ritual needs in human life and the varied liturgical tradition of the Church. With these competencies, a renovation can respect both the best qualities of the original structure and the requirements of contemporary worship.

TEAMWORK

44.   Whether designing a new space for the liturgical action or renovating an old one, teamwork and preparation by the congregation (particularly its liturgy committee), clergy, architect and consultant (liturgy and art) are essential.[9] A competent architect should have the assistance of a consultant in liturgy and art both in the discussion stages of the project (dialogue with congregation and clergy as well as among themselves) and throughout the stages of design and building. Recent competitions in the design of buildings for liturgy have indicated the advantages of such consultation.

45.   The congregation, or local Church, commonly acting through its delegates, is a basic and primary component in the team. The congregation's work is to acquaint the architect and consultant with its own self-image as Church and its sense of the larger community in which it exists. It is important for the congregation and clergy to recognize the area of their own competence. This will also define the limits beyond which they should not go. Respect for the competence of others in their respective fields is essential for good teamwork.

46.   If a community has selected competent and skilled persons, they will receive from the architect and the consultant a design which will stimulate and inspire, as well as serve the assembly's needs as they have been described. When financial benefactors are involved, they have the same part in this process as the congregation and the clergy, subject to the same prior requirements of good liturgy.

47.   A good architect will possess both the willingness to learn from the congregation and sufficient integrity not to allow the community's design taste or preference to limit the freedom necessary for a creative design. The architect will look to the congregation and clergy for an understanding of the character and purpose of the liturgical assembly. With that rapport, it is the architect's task to design the space, using contemporary materials and modes of construction, in dialogue with consultants who are expert in the areas of liturgical art, rites, acoustics and other specialized issues.

48.   The liturgical-artistic consultant is an invaluable partner of the architect, for the purposes of space can be imagined and the place creatively designed only by a competent designer (architect) who is nourished with liturgy's tradition, its current shape, together with the appropriate furniture and other objects used. The feeling of liturgical action is as crucial as the craft of the designer in producing a worthy space and place.

## VISIBILITY AND AUDIBILITY

49.  One of the primary requirements of the space is visibility of all in the assembly: others in the congregation as well as the principal focal point of the ritual action.

50.  Visibility speaks more to the quality of view than merely the mechanics of seeing. A space must create a sense that what is seen is proximate, important and personal. The arrangement of the space should consider levels of priority in what is seen, allowing visual flow from one center of liturgical action to another. Furthermore, the sense and variety of light, artificial or natural, contribute greatly to what is seen.

51.  Audibility of all (congregation and ministers) is another primary require-ment. A space that does not require voice amplification is ideal. Where an amplifying system is necessary, provision for multiple microphone jacks should be made (e.g., at the altar, ambo, chair, font, space immediately in front of the congregation, and a few spots through the congregation). Since the liturgical space must accommodate both speech and song, there must be a serious acoustical consideration of the conflicting demands of the two. The services of an acoustical engineer can enable architect and builder to be aware of certain disadvantages in rooms that are exclusively "dry" or "live." A room designed to deaden all sounds is doomed to kill liturgical participation.

## THE SCALE OF A SPACE

52.  The liturgical space should have a "good feeling" in terms of human scale, hospitality and graciousness. It does not seek to impress, or even less, to dominate, but its clear aim is to facilitate the public worship and common prayer of the faith community.

## UNITY OF SPACE

53.  Special attention must be given to the unity of the entire liturgical space. Before considering the distinction of roles within the liturgy, the space should communicate an integrity (a sense of oneness, of wholeness) and a sense of being the gathering place of the initiated community. Within that one space there are different areas corresponding to different roles and functions, but the wholeness of the total space should be strikingly evident.

54.  Planning for a convergence of pathways to the liturgical space in a concourse or foyer or other place adequate for gathering before or after liturgies is recom-mended. In some climates this might be outdoors. Such a gathering space can encourage introductions, conversations, the sharing of refreshments after a liturgy, the building of the kind of community sense and feeling recognized now to be a prerequisite of good celebration.

# IV. THE ARTS AND THE
# BODY LANGUAGE OF LITURGY

55. Liturgical celebration, because of its public and corporate nature, and because it is an expression of the total person within a community, involves not only the use of a common language and ritual tradition, but also the use of a common place, common furnishings, common art forms and symbols, common gestures, movements and postures. But when one examines the quality of these common elements, one finds that an uncommon sensitivity is demanded. For these common elements create a tremendous impact on the assembly visually, environmentally and bodily. This section and those following will offer a basic orientation and some principles with regard to each of these elements. We will begin with the sense of the person in the space: the bodily movement.

### PERSONAL GESTURES

56. The liturgy of the Church has been rich in a tradition of ritual movement and gestures. These actions, subtly, yet really, contribute to an environment which can foster prayer or which can distract from prayer. When the gestures are done in common, they contribute to the unity of the worshiping assembly. Gestures which are broad and full in both a visual and tactile sense, support the entire symbolic ritual. When the gestures are done by the presiding minister, they can either engage the entire assembly and bring them into an even greater unity, or if done poorly, they can isolate.[10]

### POSTURE

57. In an atmosphere of hospitality, posture will never be a marshaled, forced uniformity. It is important that the liturgical space can accommodate certain common postures: sitting for preparations, for listening, for silent reflection; standing for the gospel, solemn prayer, praise and acclamation; kneeling for adoration, penitential rites. Those who suffer from handicaps of one sort or another must be carefully planned for so that they can participate in the liturgy without unnecessary strain or burden.

58. Attentiveness, expressed in posture and eye contact, is a requirement for full participation and involvement in the liturgy. It is part of one's share in the life of the community and something one owes the rest of the assembly. Because of this, a space and its seating should be so designed that one can see the places of the ritual action, but further, that these spaces cannot be so distant that eye contact is impossible, for eye contact is important in any act of ministry—in reading, preaching, in leading the congregation in music and prayer. Not only are the ministers to be visible to all present, but among themselves the faithful should be able to have visual contact, being attentive to one another as they celebrate the liturgy.

59.   Beyond seeing what is done, because good liturgy is a ritual action, it is important that worship space allow for movement.[11] Processions and interpretations through bodily movement (dance) can become meaningful parts of the liturgical celebration if done by truly competent persons in the manner that benefits the total liturgical action. A procession should move from one place to another with some purpose (not simply around the same space), and should normally include the congregation, sometimes with stops of stations for particular prayers, readings, or actions. The design of the space and arrangement of the seating should allow for this sort of movement. There should be concern for the quality, the gracefulness, and the surety of this movement. Seating arrangements which prohibit the freedom of action to take place are inappropriate.

60.   In the general movement of the liturgical rite, the role of the one who presides is critical and central. The area of presiding should allow that person to be attentive to and present to the entire congregation, the other ministers, and each part of the liturgical action, even if not personally leading the action at that moment. The place should allow one to conduct the various ministers in their specific activity and roles of leadership, as well as the congregation in its common prayer.

61.   In the above instances, audibility and visibility to all in the assembly are minimal requirements. The chair, the lectern and the altar should be constructed so that all can see and hear the person of the reader or the one who presides.

EASE OF MOVEMENT

62.   The proper use of furniture and other objects which have a symbolic function is important in ritual action. These objects are next in importance to the people themselves and their total environment. They are part of a total rite which everyone present should be able to experience as fully as possible. Thus, their placement and use should allow for ease of movement.

# V. FURNISHINGS
## FOR LITURGICAL CELEBRATION

63.   Because the Sunday eucharistic assembly is the most fundamental ecclesial symbol, the requirements of that celebration will have the strongest claim in the provision of furnishings for liturgy. Consequently, any liturgical space must take into consideration not only the general requirements of the assembly but also the need for a feeling of contact with altar, ambo and celebrant's chair.

64.   This primacy of the eucharistic assembly, however, should not discourage a liturgical life of greater richness and variety in the local Church. In planning construction, renovation or refurnishing of liturgical spaces, baptism and the other sacraments, morning and evening prayer, services of the word, prayer meetings and other community events should be kept in mind.

65.  When multi-functional use of the space is indicated by the needs either of the faith community or of the surrounding city, town or rural area which the faith community services, a certain flexibility or movability should be considered even for the essential furnishings. Great care, however, should be taken in the design and care of movable furnishings that none of the dignity, noble and simple beauty proper to such objects is sacrificed. There is no reason why a movable altar or ambo need have a flimsy, cheap or disposable appearance.

66.  Normally the furnishings used in a liturgical celebration of any kind should be placed before the celebration begins and remain stationary during the celebration. Ritual action is not enhanced by the moving of furniture during a rite. A careful arrangement of furnishings is an integral part of liturgical planning.

## DIGNITY AND BEAUTY

67.  Consultation with persons who are experts, at least one in liturgy and one in the arts, is not a luxury but a necessity for those responsible for furnishing the liturgical space. Each piece of furniture has its own requirements, but at least two criteria are applicable to all of them, in fact, to any object used in any way in liturgy: 1) None should be made in such a way that it is far removed from the print of the human hand and human craft. When mass-produced items are chosen, care must be taken that they are truly suitable. Dignity and beauty in materials used, in design and form, in color and texture—these are concerns of artists for their work, for the furniture they build, and are not, unfortunately, the evident concerns of many mass manufacturers and merchandisers. 2) All furnishings taken together should possess a unity and harmony with each other and with the architecture of the place.

## BENCHES OR CHAIRS

68.  Benches or chairs for seating the assembly should be so constructed and arranged that they maximize feelings of community and involvement.[12] The arrangement should facilitate a clear view not only of the one who presides and the multiple focal points of reading, preaching, praying, music and movement during the rite, but also of other members of the congregation. This means striving for a seating pattern and furniture that do not constrict people, but encourage them to move about when it is appropriate.

69.  Benches or chairs for the seating of those engaged in the ministry of music, instrumental or choral, should be so constructed and arranged that they have the advantages described above for congregational seating and also that they are clearly part of the assembly.[13] Yet, the ministers of music should be able to sing and play facing the rest of the assembly in order to elicit the participation of the community without distracting from the central action of the liturgy. The same should be said of an individual cantor or song leader.

## THE CHAIR

70.  Chairs or benches for the presiding minister and other ministers should be so constructed and arranged that they too are clearly part of the one assembly, yet

conveniently situated for the exercise of their respective offices. The importance of the personal symbol and function of the one who presides in liturgical celebration should not be underrated or underplayed, because it is essential for good celebration. The chair of that person should be clearly in a presiding position, although it should not suggest either domination or remoteness.[14]

## THE ALTAR

71. The altar, the holy table, should be the most noble, the most beautifully designed and constructed table the community can provide.[15] It is the common table of the assembly, a symbol of the Lord, at which the presiding minister stands and upon which are placed the bread and wine and their vessels and the book. It is holy and sacred to this assembly's action and sharing, so it is never used as a table of convenience or as a resting place for papers, notes, cruets, or anything else. It stands free, approachable from every side, capable of being encircled. It is desirable that candles, cross, any flowers or other decoration in the area should not be so close to the altar as to constitute impediments to anyone's approach or movement around the common table.

72. The altar is designed and constructed for the action of a community and the functioning of a single priest—not for concelebrants. The holy table, therefore, should not be elongated, but square or slightly rectangular, an attractive, impressive, dignified, noble table, constructed with solid and beautiful materials, in pure and simple proportions. Its symbolic function, of course, is rendered negligible when there are other altars in sight. The liturgical space has room for but one.

73. The location of the altar will be central in any eucharistic celebration, but this does not mean it must be spatially in the center or on a central axis. In fact, an off-center location may be a good solution in many cases. Focus and importance in any celebration move with the movement of the rite. Placement and elevation must take into account the necessity of visibility and audibility for all.

## THE AMBO

74. The ambo or lectern is a standing desk for reading and preaching (although preaching can be done from the chair or elsewhere).[16] One main ambo should be reserved for these functions and therefore not used by commentators, song leaders, etc. Like the altar, it should be beautifully designed, constructed of fine materials, and proportioned carefully and simply for its function. The ambo represents the dignity and uniqueness of the Word of God and of reflection upon that Word.

75. A very simple lectern, in no way competing or conflicting with the main ambo, and placed for the necessary visibility and audibility, can be used by a cantor, song leader, commentator, and reader of the announcements. It should be located for easy communication with both musicians and congregation.

## BAPTISTRY

76. To speak of symbols and of sacramental signification is to indicate that immersion is the fuller and more appropriate symbolic action in baptism.[17] New

baptismal fonts, therefore, should be constructed to allow for the immersion of infants, at least, and to allow for the pouring of water over the entire body of a child or adult. Where fonts are not so constructed, the use of a portable one is recommended.

77.    The place of the font, whether it is an area near the main entrance of the liturgical space or one in the midst of the congregation, should facilitate full congregational participation, regularly in the Easter Vigil.[18] If the baptismal space is in a gathering place or entry way, it can have living, moving water, and include provision for warming the water for immersion. When a portable font is used, it should be placed for maximum visibility and audibility, without crowding or obscuring the altar, ambo and chair.

EUCHARISTIC CHAPEL

78.    The *celebration* of the eucharist is the focus of the normal Sunday assembly. As such, the major space of a church is designed for this *action*. Beyond the celebration of the eucharist, the Church has had a most ancient tradition of reserving the eucharistic bread. The purpose of this reservation is to bring communion to the sick and to be the object of private devotion. Most appropriately, this reservation should be designated in a space designed for individual devotion. A room or chapel specifically designed and separate from the major space is important so that no confusion can take place between the celebration of the eucharist and reservation.[19] Active and static aspects of the same reality cannot claim the same human attention at the same time. Having the eucharist reserved in a place apart does not mean it has been relegated to a secondary place of no importance. Rather, a space carefully designed and appointed can give proper attention to the reserved sacrament.

79.    This space should offer easy access from the porch areas, garden or street as well as the main space. The devotional character of the space should create an atmosphere of warmth while acknowledging the mystery of the Lord. It should support private meditation without distractions. If iconography or statuary are present, they should not obscure the primary focus of reservation.

THE TABERNACLE

80.    The tabernacle, as a receptacle for the reservation of the eucharist, should be solid and unbreakable, dignified and properly ornamented.[20] It may be placed in a wall niche, on a pillar, eucharistic tower. It should not be placed on an altar for the altar is a place for action not for reservation. There should be only one tabernacle in a church building. A lamp should burn continously near it.

RECONCILIATION CHAPEL

81.    A room or rooms for the reconciliation of individual penitents may be located near the baptismal area (when that is at the entrance) or in another convenient place.[21] Furnishings and decoration should be simple and austere, offering the penitent a choice between face-to-face encounter or the anonymity provided by a screen, with nothing superfluous in evidence beyond a simple cross,

table and bible. The purpose of this room is primarily for the celebration of the reconciliation liturgy; it is not a lounge, counseling room, etc. The word "chapel" more appropriately describes this space.

## SACRISTY

82.   A sacristy or vesting space should be located to favor the procession of cross, candles, book and ministers through the midst of the congregation to the altar area.

## MUSICAL INSTRUMENTS

83.   Because choir, instrumentalists and organ often function as an ensemble, they need to be located together in such a way that the organist can see the other musicians and the liturgical action directly or by means of a simple mirror.[22] Organ consoles can be detached from the pipework and their connection supplied by flexible means. This allows for movable consoles, which may be an advantage, especially when the liturgical space serves other functions as well. However, self-contained organs, where console and pipework are united in a single element, are a possibility also, and can be designed so that the whole organ is movable. Organs designed for liturgical rather than concert purposes need not be very large; they should not be grandiose or visually dominating. But they should be superior musically, and as with all artifacts, the instrument and its casework should be authentic, beautiful and coherent with its environment. Proper space must also be planned for other musical instruments used in liturgical celebrations.

# VI. OBJECTS USED IN LITURGICAL CELEBRATION

84.   Like the furniture, all other objects used in liturgical celebrations should be designed or selected in consultation with experts in both liturgy and art. Each should be not only suitable for its purpose but also capable of making a visual or other sensory contribution to the beauty of the action. The two principles cited above are applicable to everything employed in liturgy.

## DUPLICATED AND MINIMIZED

85.   There is a cultural tendency to minimize symbols and symbolic gestures and to cover them with a heavy curtain of texts, words and commentary. As a result there are two other problems in our use of objects in worship.

86.   One problem is the tendency to duplicate signs and objects, a practice which seems to have multiplied in proportion to the symbols' diminution. (The converse is also true: the multiplication of the symbols causes their very diminution.) A symbol claims human attention and consciousness with a power that seems to be adversely affected by overdose. For example, the multiplication of crosses in a liturgical space or as an ornamentation on objects may lessen rather than increase attention to that symbol.

87.   A second common problem in the use of symbolic objects is a tendency to "make up" for weak primary symbols by secondary ones. It is not uncommon, for

example, to make extensive and expensive efforts to enrich and enliven a Sunday eucharistic celebration without paying any attention to the bread that is used or to the sharing of the cup. Bread and wine are primary eucharistic symbols, yet peripheral elements frequently get more attention. It is important to focus on central symbols and to allow them to be expressed with full depth of their vision. This may mean solutions which are less efficient and pragmatic.

## THE CROSS

88. A cross is a basic symbol in any Christian liturgical celebration. The advantage of a processional cross with a floor standard, in contrast to one that is permanently hung or affixed to a wall, is that it can be placed differently according to the celebration and the other environmental factors.[23] While it is permissible for the cross to rest on the altar, it is preferable that it be elsewhere, not only for non-eucharistic liturgies but also so that in eucharistic celebrations the altar is used only for bread and wine and book.

## CANDLESTICKS AND CANDLES

89. The same can be said of candlesticks and candles. When they are floor-standing, they can be arranged differently from time to time. The number can be varied according to the season and feast and the solemnity of the celebration. Like the cross, the candles should be visible without impeding the sight of the altar, ambo, chair and action.[24]

90. The Easter Candle and its standard call for very special dimensions and design. They occupy a central location in the assembly during the Easter season and a place at the baptismal font thereafter.[25]

## BOOKS

91. Any book which is used by an officiating minister in a liturgical celebration should be of a large (public, noble) size, good paper, strong design, handsome typography and binding.[26] The Book of the Gospels or lectionary, of course, is central and should be handled and carried in a special way. The other liturgical books of the Church, which contain the rites of our public worship tradition, are also worthy of venerable treatment and are a significant part of the liturgical environment. Each should be visually attractive and impressive. The use of pamphlets and leaflets detracts from the visual integrity of the total liturgical action. This applies not only to books used by ministers at the altar, chair and font, but also to those used in any other public or semipublic rite.

92. When a liturgical book is employed at a place other than altar or ambo, the book should be held by an assistant or acolyte so that the hands and body of the one who reads are free.

## VESTMENTS

93. The wearing of ritual vestment by those charged with leadership in a ritual action is an appropriate symbol of their service as well as a helpful aesthetic component of the rite.[27] That service is a function which demands attention from

the assembly and which operates in the focal area of the assembly's liturgical action. The color and form of the vestments and their difference from everyday clothing invite an appropriate attention and are part of the ritual experience essential to the festive character of a liturgical celebration.[28]

94.   The more these vestments fulfill their function by their color, design and enveloping form, the less they will need the signs, slogans and symbols which an unkind history has fastened on them. The tendency to place symbols upon symbols seems to accompany the symbolic deterioration and diminution already discussed.[29]

95.   Vesture may also be used appropriately on an altar or ambo or other objects at times, especially for festive occasions, not as "frontals" or "facades," but as decorative covering which respects the integrity and totality of the particular object.[30] The fabrics used in these instances should be chosen because of the quality of design, texture and color.

## VESSELS

96.   In a eucharistic celebration, the vessels for the bread and wine deserve attention and care.[31] Just as in other types of celebration those objects which are central in the rite are a natural focus. When the eucharistic assembly is large, it is desirable not to have the additional plates and cups necessary for communion on the altar. A solution is to use one large breadplate and either one large chalice or a large flagon until the breaking of the bread. At the fraction, any other chalices or plates needed are brought to the altar. While the bread is broken on sufficient plates for sharing, the ministers of the cups pour from the flagon into the communion chalices. The number and design of such vessels will depend on the size of the community they serve. To eat and drink is of the essence of the symbolic fullness of this sacrament. Communion under one kind is an example of the minimizing of primary symbols.

97.   Like the plates and chalices or flagons, all other vessels and implements used in the liturgical celebration should be of such quality and design that they speak of the importance of the ritual action. Pitchers, vessels for holy oils, bowls, cruets, sprinklers, censers, baskets for collection, etc.—all are presented to the assembly in one way or another and speak well or ill of the deed in which the assembly is engaged.

## IMAGES

98.   Images in painting or sculpture, as well as tapestries, cloth hangings, banners and other permanent or seasonal decorations, should be introduced into the liturgical space upon consultation with an art consultant.[32] Like the furniture and other objects used in worship, they become part of the environment and are subject to its criteria of quality and appropriateness. In addition, their appropriateness must take into account the current renewed emphasis on the action of the assembly. If instead of serving and aiding that action, they threaten it or compete with it, then they are unsuitable.

99.   In a period of Church and liturgical renewal, the attempt to recover a solid grasp of Church and faith and rites involves the rejection of certain embellishments which have in the course of history become hindrances. In many areas of religious practice, this means a simplifying and refocusing on primary symbols. In building, this effort has resulted in more austere interiors, with fewer objects on the walls and in the corners.

DECORATIONS

100.  Many new or renovated liturgical spaces, therefore, invite temporary decoration for particular celebrations, feasts and seasons. Banners and hangings of various sorts are both popular and appropriate, as long as the nature of these art forms is respected. They are creations of forms, colors, and textures, rather than signboards to which words must be attached. Their purpose is to appeal to the senses and thereby create an atmosphere and a mood, rather than to impress a slogan upon the minds of observers or deliver a verbal message.

101.  Although the art and decoration of the liturgical space will be that of the local culture, identifying symbols of particular cultures, groups, or nations are not appropriate as permanent parts of the liturgical environment. While such symbols might be used for a particular occasion or holiday, they should not regularly constitute a part of the environment of common prayer.

102.  Flowers, plants and trees—genuine, of course—are particularly apt for the decoration of liturgical space, since they are of nature, always discreet in their message, never cheap or tawdry or ill-made. Decoration should never impede the approach to or the encircling of the altar or any of the ritual movement and action, but there are places in most liturgical spaces where it is appropriate and where it can be enhancing. The whole space is to be considered the arena of decoration, not merely the sanctuary.

103.  Suitable decoration need not and should not be confined to the altar area, since the unity of the celebration space and the active participation of the entire assembly are fundamental principles. The negative aspect of this attention to the whole space invites a thorough housecleaning in which superfluities, things that have no use or are no longer used, are removed. Both beauty and simplicity demand careful attention to each piece of furniture, each object, each decorative element, as well as to the whole ensemble, so that there is no clutter, no crowding. These various objects and elements must be able to breathe and function without being smothered by excess.

AUDIOVISUALS

104.  It is too early to predict the effect of contemporary audiovisual media—films, videotape, records, tapes—on the public worship of Christians. It is safe to say that a new church building or renovation project should make provision for screens and/or walls which will make the projection of films, slides, and filmstrips visible to the entire assembly, as well as an audio system capable for fine electronic reproduction of sound.[33]

105. There seems to be a parallel between the new visual media and the traditional function of stained glass. Now that the easily printed word has lost its grip on popular communication, the neglect of audiovisual possibilities is a serious fault. Skill in using these media in ways which will not reduce the congregation to an audience or passive state can be gained only by experience.

106. Such media, of course, should never be used to replace essential congregational action. At least two ways in which they may be used to enhance celebration and participation are already apparent: 1) visual media may be used to create an environment for the liturgical action, surrounding the rite with appropriate color and form; 2) visual and audio media may be used to assist in the communication of appropriate content, a use which requires great delicacy and a careful, balanced integration into the liturgy taken as a whole.

## VII. CONCLUSION

107. When the Christian community gathers to celebrate its faith and vision, it gathers to celebrate what is most personally theirs and most nobly human and truly Church. The actions of the assembly witness the great deeds God has done; they confirm an age-old covenant. With such vision and depth of the assembly can the environment be anything less than a vehicle to meet the Lord and to encounter one another? The challenge of our environment is the final challenge of Christ: We must make ready until he returns in glory.

# NOTES

1. 1 Jn 1.

2. Among the official conciliar and postconciliar documents which specifically address these questions are: *The Constitution on the Sacred Liturgy* (CSL), Chapters 6 and 7; *Instructions for the Proper Implementation of the Constitution on the Sacred Liturgy*, Chapter 6; and the *General Instruction of the Roman Missal* (GI), Chapters 5 and 6.

3. CSL no. 123.

4. GI introduction nos. 6–15.

5. GI nos. 4, 5.

6. CSL no. 123.

7. GI no. 254.

8. GI no. 253.

9. CSL no. 126; GI no. 258.

10. *The Directory for Masses with Children* (DMC) bases the importance of the development of gestures, postures and actions in the liturgy on the fact that liturgy, by its nature, is the activity of the entire person (see no. 33).

11. See *Holy Communion and Worship of the Eucharist Outside Mass* (EOM), nos. 101–108; DMC no. 34.

12. GI no. 273.

13. GI no. 274.

14. GI no. 271.

15. GI nos. 259–270; Appendix to GI no. 263.

16. GI no. 272.

17. *Rite of Baptism for Children* (BC), introduction.

18. Ibid. no. 25.

19. GI no. 276.

20. GI no. 277.

21. *Rite of Penance*, nos. 12, 18b; *Bishops' Committee on the Liturgy Newsletter* 1965–1975, p. 450.

22. GI nos. 274, 275; *Music in Catholic Worship* no. 38.

23. GI nos. 84, 270; Appendix to GI no. 270.

24. GI no. 269; EOM no. 85.

25. BC no. 25.

26. *Bishops' Committee on the Liturgy Newsletter* 1965–1975, p. 417.

27. GI nos. 297–310; Appendix GI nos. 305–306.

28. GI no. 308; Appendix GI no. 308.

29. GI no. 306.

30. GI no. 268.

31. GI nos. 289–296.

32. CSL no. 125; GI no. 278.

33. See DMC nos. 35–36.

# FULFILLED
# IN
# YOUR HEARING

## THE HOMILY IN THE SUNDAY ASSEMBLY

# OVERVIEW OF *FULFILLED IN YOUR HEARING: THE HOMILY IN THE SUNDAY ASSEMBLY*

Kathleen Cannon, OP

*Fulfilled in Your Hearing* is an extraordinary document. First, it grew out of the concern of the American bishops for the quality of preaching in the church. In 1979, the National Conference of Catholic Bishops (NCCB) authorized the Bishops' Committee on Priestly Life and Ministry to address the matter of the Sunday homily. *Fulfilled in Your Hearing* is the fruit of their study.

Second, the document represents the work of a committee, although William Skudlarek, OSB, was the principal author of the final text. Skudlarek holds a doctorate in homiletics from Princeton Theological Seminary. In addition to his doctoral dissertation, which addressed the lay-preaching controversy of the late Middle Ages, he has authored an excellent study of liturgical preaching entitled *The Word in Worship* (Nashville: Abingdon, 1981). He was well chosen for the task and those familiar with his writing will spot similarities between his book and this document.

It is in its structure and content, however, the uniqueness of *Fulfilled in Your Hearing* is most evident. The Introduction opens with a statement from the Vatican II *Decree on the Ministry and Life of Priests* that asserts that "the primary duty of priests is the proclamation of the gospel of God to all" (no. 4). That chord is sounded many times in the document, stressing that all the other activities of the ordained derive from and are supportive of the proclamation of the word of God. Just as Vatican II intended the statement as a corrective to the overemphasis on sacrament in Roman Catholic thought, so, too, *Fulfilled in Your Hearing* reasserts the primacy of the ministry of the word.

This stress on the responsibility that the ordained have for the proclamation of the word is held in conjunction with another statement in the Introduction, which serves as the organizing principle for the entire document. "Indeed the proclamation of the word of God is the responsibility of the entire Christian community by virtue of the sacrament of baptism" (par. 2). With this as its point of departure, Chapter I describes not the homily nor the preacher, but the assembly. The authors claim this is not only appropriate, but is, on ecclesiological grounds, essential.

THE ASSEMBLY

The church is a gathering of those who have responded to God's call into a covenant relationship; it is the place where the word of God is sustained and safeguarded and from which it is proclaimed. The proclamation of the gospel, then, belongs to the whole of God's people. Within that proclamation, the priest has a special function or ministry, but not the sole responsibility to preach the word. The primary reality is Christ in the assembly (the church); the preacher articulates the faith of the community in the name of the community (par. 4).

Beginning with the assembly rather than the preacher or the homily is, to my mind, as momentous as was the decision to reverse the order of chapters in *Lumen Gentium* to consider first the church as the whole People of God and only then to consider ministry. Ministry, including the primary ministry of preaching, is not prior to but in service of the community.

## THE PREACHER

Chapter II describes the role of the homilist as enabling the community to hear God's word. As a mediator of meaning, the preacher first must identify with the people in their joys and sorrows, struggles and concerns, a task that demands attentive listening as well as prayer. Theological study is also an indispensable requirement for one who would preach.

## THE HOMILY

In Chapter III, the homily is described as "a scriptural interpretation of human existence which enables a community to recognize God's active presence, to respond to that presence in faith through liturgical word and gesture, and beyond the liturgical word and gesture, and beyond the liturgical assembly, through a life lived in conformity with the gospel" (par. 29). While the document affirms the preeminent position of sacred scripture in preaching, it carefully distinguishes preaching *from* or *through* the scriptures from preaching *on* them.

In other words, scripture is employed to interpret life. The preacher must listen to human experience for an echo of the gospel. Rather than an exposition of the scriptural texts, then, the homily is an interpretation of life and attempts to name what God is doing at the heart of human existence. Consequently, God's word never is something spoken once and for all in the past, but has the character of present address. The response of the community to God's summons of us is gratitude and eucharist.

## A METHOD FOR PREPARING THE HOMILY

Chapter IV outlines a homiletic method, one that respects the nature of preaching as an art. It recommends spreading the preparation over a period of several days, allowing time for prayer, study and reflection. The chapter further recommends the formation of homily preparation groups to assist the homilist and suggests specific steps for their formation. A brief epilogue on the power of God's word recalls that God's word must make do with our human sounds and images and experiences.

## HAS IT MADE A DIFFERENCE?

Since its publication in 1982, more than 50,000 copies of *Fulfilled in Your Hearing* have been sold. I do not know whether the content has affected the quality of preaching. I do know that not much has been done to carry out the recommendations made in the appendix for follow-up on the national, diocesan and parish levels. On the national level, the document recommended the establishment of a doctoral program in homiletics, but as of 1991, one does not exist at a Catholic seminary or theologate in the United States. This means that those who are to be teachers of preaching have to do their study at Protestant schools that lack a Catholic liturgical context and tradition.

At the diocesan level, the document was taken in hand by several continuing-education directors. They worked with the writers to develop a method of helping preachers become aware of the insights of this document. A model was developed and workshops were offered in several dioceses. Many dioceses, of course, have sponsored workshops on preaching, but three-day workshops will not change habits that took years to acquire. Short workshops are valuable, but more is needed.

The document also calls for clearly formulated criteria for granting faculties to preach. If this were implemented, it would perhaps facilitate the improvement of the quality of preaching.

To conclude, here are the final words of *Fulfilled in Your Hearing:* "At all levels, national, diocesan and parish, bishops and priests are urged to invite religious and laity to read this document so as to assist, encourage and support priests in efforts toward a renewal of preaching in the church." Read on!

# OUTLINE

# FULFILLED IN YOUR HEARING
## THE HOMILY IN THE SUNDAY ASSEMBLY

## INTRODUCTION

"The primary duty of priests is the proclamation of the Gospel of God to all."
These clear, straightforward words of the Second Vatican Council (*Decree on the Ministry and Life of Priests*, #4) may still come as something of a surprise to us. We might more spontaneously think that the primary duty of priests is the celebration of the Church's sacraments, or the pastoral care of the People of God, or the leadership of a Christian community. Yet, the words of the document are clear: the proclamation of the Gospel is primary. The other duties of the priest are to be considered properly presbyteral to the degree that they support the proclamation of the Gospel.

"Proclamation" can cover a wide variety of activities in the church. A life of quiet faith and generous loving deeds is proclamation; the celebration of the Eucharist is the proclamation "of the death of the Lord until he comes." But a key moment in the proclamation of the Gospel is preaching, preaching which is characterized by "proclamation of God's wonderful works in the history of salvation, that is, the mystery of Christ, which is ever made present and active within us, especially in the celebration of the liturgy" (Constitution on the Sacred Liturgy, #35, 2).

The *Decree on the Ministry and Life of Priests* is especially clear in relating the ministry of preaching to that of the celebration of the sacraments. Since these sacraments are sacraments of faith, and since "faith is born of the Word and nourished by it," the preaching of the Word is an essential part of the celebration of the sacraments. This is especially true in the celebration of the Eucharist, the document goes on to note, for "in this celebration the proclamation of the death and resurrection of the Lord is inseparably joined both to the response of the people who hear, and to the very offering whereby Christ ratified the New Testament in His blood."

This intimate link between preaching and the celebration of the sacraments, especially of the Sunday Eucharist, is what we intend to address in this document on preaching. We recognize that preaching is not limited to priests. Deacons are also ordained ministers of the Word. Indeed, the proclamation of the Word of God is the responsibility of the entire Christian community by virtue of the sacrament of baptism. Moreover, we recognize that preaching is not limited to the Eucharist, and we are pleased to support the ways in which more and more Catholics are celebrating the power of God's Word in evangelistic gatherings, in the catechumenate, and in groups devoted to the study of the Bible and to prayer. We also recognize that for the vast majority of Catholics the Sunday homily is the normal and frequently the formal way in which they hear the Word of God proclaimed. For these Catholics the Sunday homily may well be the most decisive factor in determining the depth of their faith and strengthening the level of their commitment to the church.

The focus of this document, therefore, will be the Sunday homily, and even more specifically, the homily preached by the bishop or priest who presides at the celebration of the Eucharist. Again, we recognize that there are occasions when the homily may be preached by someone other than the presider, by a deacon serving in the parish or a guest priest preacher, for example. Yet, in terms of common practice and of liturgical norm, the preaching of the homily belongs to the presiding minister. (See *The General Instruction of the Roman Missal*, #42: "The homily should ordinarily be given by the celebrant.") The unity of Word and Sacrament is thus symbolized in the person of the presiding minister of the Eucharist.

While this document is addressed specifically to priests who have a pastoral ministry that involves regular Sunday preaching, we hope that all who are concerned with effective proclamation of the Gospel will find it helpful. This document may also prove useful in the preparation for and continuing formation of permanent deacons as ministers of the Word.

We propose that this document be used as a basis of discussion among priests and bishops, and by priests with members of their congregations. In such sharing of personal experiences, of expectations and frustrations, and by mutual support, we find hope for a renewal of preaching in the church today.

## I. THE ASSEMBLY

[1]    Jesus came to Nazareth where he had been reared, and entering the synagogue on the sabbath as he was in the habit of doing, he stood up to do the reading. When the book of the prophet Isaiah was handed him, he unrolled the scroll and found the passage where it was written:

"The spirit of the Lord is upon me;
   therefore he has anointed me.
He has sent me to bring glad tidings to the poor,
   to proclaim liberty to captives,
Recovery of sight to the blind
   and release to prisoners,
To announce a year of favor from the Lord."

Rolling up the scroll he gave it back to the assistant and sat down. All in the synagogue had their eyes fixed on him. Then he began by saying to them, "Today this Scripture passage is fulfilled in your hearing." All who were present spoke favorably of him; they marveled at the appealing discourse which came from his lips. (Lk 4:14–22a)

[2]    These verses from the fourth chapter of the Gospel of Saint Luke present us with a picture of Jesus as reader and homilist in the synagogue at Nazareth. He

stands up to read the lesson from the prophet which was placed at the end of the service. He then draws on this passage to speak to the here-and-now situation. All who listened to him were favorably impressed.

[3]   The three major elements of liturgical preaching are all here: the preacher, the word drawn from the Scriptures, and the gathered community. Each element is essential and each must be considered carefully if we are to understand the challenge and the possibilities of liturgical preaching.

[4]   We believe that it is appropriate, indeed essential, to begin this treatment of the Sunday homily with the assembly rather than with the preacher or the homily, and this for two principal reasons. First of all we can point to the great emphasis which communication theorists place on an accurate understanding of the audience if communication is to be effective. Unless a preacher knows what a congregation needs, wants, or is able to hear, there is every possibility that the message offered in the homily will not meet the needs of the people who hear it. To say this is by no means to imply that preachers are only to preach what their congregations want to hear. Only when preachers know what their congregations want to hear will they be able to communicate what a congregation needs to hear. Homilists may indeed preach on what they understand to be the real issues, but if they are not in touch with what the people think are the real issues, they will very likely be misunderstood or not heard at all. What is communicated is not what is said, but it is what is heard, and what is heard is determined in large measure by what the hearer needs or wants to hear.[1]

[5]   Contemporary ecclesiology provides a second and even more fundamental reason for beginning with the assembly rather than with the preacher or the homily. *The Dogmatic Constitution on the Church* describes the church as the mystery of God's saving will, given concrete historical expression in the people with whom he has entered into a covenant. This church is the visible sacrament of the saving unity to which God calls all people. "Established by Christ as a fellowship of life, charity, and truth, the church is also used by Him as an instrument for the redemption of all, and is sent forth into the whole world as the light of the world and the salt of the earth" (#9). The church, therefore, is first and foremost a gathering of those whom the Lord has called into a covenant of peace with himself. In this gathering, as in every other, offices and ministries are necessary, but secondary. The primary reality is Christ in the assembly, the People of God.

[6]   This renewed understanding of the church is gradually becoming con- sciously present in the words and actions of the Catholic people. By means of their involvement in diocesan and parish organizations, their sharing in various forms of ministry, and their active participation in the liturgy, they are beginning to experience what it means to say that the people are the church and the church are people.

[7]   Obviously the development we are speaking of is not uniform. But it is clear that the parish in which the priest acts in an arbitrary manner, in which virtually all active ministry—liturgical, educational, and social—is in the hands of the

clergy and religious, and in which the laity do little more than attend Mass and receive the sacraments, is no longer the norm. Such a drastic change in the practices and self-consciousness of the Catholic congregation is bound to have significant consequences for the content and style of preaching that takes place in the Sunday Eucharistic assembly.

To preach in a way that sounds as if the preacher alone has access to the truth and knows what is best for everyone else, or that gives the impression that there are no unresolved problems or possibility for dialogue, is to preach in a way that may have been acceptable to those who viewed the church primarily in clerical terms. In a church that thinks and speaks of itself as a pilgrim people, gathered together for worship, witness, and work, such preaching will be heard only with great difficulty, if at all.

THE IDENTITY OF THE ASSEMBLY

[8]    The Eucharistic assembly that gathers Sunday after Sunday is a rich and complex phenomenon. Even in parishes that are more or less uniform in ethnic, social, or economic background, there is great diversity: men and women, old and young, the successes and the failures, the joyful and the bereaved, the fervent and the halfhearted, the strong and the weak. Such diversity is a constant challenge to the preacher, for our words can all too easily be heard as excluding one or the other segment of the congregation. We may not mean to ignore the presence of women when we say "Jesus came to save all men," but if exclusion is heard, then exclusion is communicated, whether intended or not.

[9]    While the diversity of every assembly is a factor that needs to be taken seriously by the preacher, and all the more so when the diversity cuts across racial, ethnic, economic, and social lines, this diversity should not blind us to another, even greater reality: the unity of the congregation. This assembly has come together because its members have been baptized into the one body of Christ and share a common faith. This faith, though rooted in a common baptismal identity, is expressed in ways that extend from the highest levels of personal appropriation and intellectual understanding to the most immature forms of ritualism and routine. And yet, to a greater or lesser degree, it is faith in Jesus Christ that is common to all the members of a community gathered for Eucharist.

[10]    To say that a community shares a common faith is to say that its members have a common way of interpreting the world around them. For the Christian community, the world is seen and interpreted as the creation of a loving God. Although this world turned away from God through sin, God reached out again and again to draw the world to himself, finally sending his own Son in human flesh. This Son expressed the fullness of the Father's love by accepting death on the cross. The Father in turn glorified his Son by raising him from the dead and making him the source of eternal life for all who believe. Believers witness to the presence and word of Jesus in the world and are a continuing sign of the Kingdom of God, which is present both in and through Jesus, and still to come to its fullness through the power of the Holy Spirit.

[11]   In very broad outline this is the common faith that binds together the Christian community gathering for worship. No individual in the community would very likely express the faith in quite these words. Some might find it difficult to express their faith in any words at all. They do not possess the background of theology to enable them to do so. We might say, therefore, that one of the principal tasks of the preacher is to provide the congregation of the faithful with words to express their faith, and with words to express the human realities to which this faith responds. Through words drawn from the Scriptures, from the church's theological tradition, and from the personal appropriation of that tradition through study and prayer, the preacher joins himself and the congregation in a common vision. We can say, therefore, that the homily is a unifying moment in the celebration of the liturgy, deepening and giving expression to the unity that is already present through the sacrament of baptism.

## THE PREACHER AS MEDIATOR OF MEANING

[12]   The person who preaches in the context of the liturgical assembly is thus a mediator, representing both the community and the Lord. The assembly gathers for liturgy as a community of faith, believing that God has acted in human history and more particularly, in their own history. The community gathers to respond to this living and active God. They may also gather to question how or whether the God who once acted in human history is still present and acting today. They may wonder how this God, whom the Scriptures present as so powerful and so loving, can be experienced in lives today that seem so broken and meaningless. How can parents believe in a God who raises the dead to life when their daughter has just been killed in a car accident? How can a family hope in a God who leads his people out of slavery into freedom when they are trapped in an inflationary spiral in which costs increase and the buying power of their salaries diminishes? How can young people join with the angels and saints in praise of the glory of God when they are struggling with the challenges of establishing their own identities and their relationship to family and friends?

[13]   The preacher represents this community by voicing its concerns, by naming its demons, and thus enabling it to gain some understanding and control of the evil which afflicts it. He represents the Lord by offering the community another word, a word of healing and pardon, of acceptance and love. Like humans everywhere, the people who make up the liturgical assembly are people hungry, sometimes desperately so, for meaning in their lives. For a time they may find meaning in their jobs, their families and friends, their political or social causes. All these concerns, good and valid as they are, fall short of providing ultimate meaning. Without ultimate meaning, we are ultimately unsatisfied. If we are able to hear a word which gives our lives another level of meaning, which interprets them in relation to God, then our response is to turn to this source of meaning in an attitude of praise and thanksgiving.

[14]   The community that gathers Sunday after Sunday comes together to offer God praise and thanksgiving, or at least to await a word that will give a meaning to their lives and enable them to celebrate Eucharist. What the preacher can do best of all at this time and in this place is to enable this community to celebrate by

offering them a word in which they can recognize their own concerns and God's concern for them.

[15]   The preacher acts as a mediator, making connections between the real lives of people who believe in Jesus Christ but are not always sure what difference faith can make in their lives, and the God who calls us into ever deeper communion with himself and with one another. Especially in the Eucharistic celebration, the sign of God's saving presence among his people, the preacher is called to point to the signs of God's presence in the lives of his people so that, in joyous recognition of that presence, they may join the angels and saints to proclaim God's glory and sing with them their unending hymn of praise.

## II. THE PREACHER

[16]   We began our treatment of the Sunday homily by looking first to the assembly that gathers to celebrate the liturgy of the Eucharist. Such a beginning could be interpreted to mean that the importance of the ordained priesthood is not what it used to be. Nothing could be further from the truth. The priesthood of the faithful and the ordained ministerial priesthood although distinct are not opposed to one another. In fact, they stand or fall together. To the degree that we give full weight to the priesthood of all the baptized, to that degree do we see the full importance and significance of the ordained priesthood. To the degree that we downplay the importance of the priesthood of the faithful, to that degree is the ordained priesthood diminished.

[17]   The community gathered to worship is a priestly people, men and women called to offer God worship. If this community is conscious of its dignity, then those it calls to service in positions of leadership will be able to recognize their dignity as well. We think of the priest as the representative of Christ. This way of thinking is true, as long as we remember that one represents Christ by representing the church, for the church is the fundamental sacrament of Christ. Moreover, it is the church, through its bishops, that calls individuals to presbyteral ministry in the church.

PASTORAL ROLE OF THE PREACHER

[18]   Preachers who are conscious of their representative role strive to preach in a way that indicates they know and identify with the people to whom they are speaking. Their preaching is pastoral, displaying a sensitive and concerned knowledge of the struggles, doubts, concerns, and joys of the members of a local community.

[19]   To be in touch with the cares and concerns, needs and good fortunes of the assembly does not mean that the preacher has to answer questions or solve problems in every homily. There will be occasions when nothing we can say will do anything to change a situation. We cannot raise a dead daughter to life; our words will not stop inflation or lower unemployment. What our words can do is help people make connections between the realities of their lives and the realities

of the Gospel. We can help them see how God in Jesus Christ has entered and identified himself with the human realities of pain and of happiness.

LISTENING AND PRAYING

[20]  In order to make such connections between the lives of the people and the Gospel, the preacher will have to be a listener before he is a speaker. Listening is not an isolated moment. It is a way of life. It means openness to the Lord's voice not only in the Scriptures but in the events of our daily lives and in the experience of our brothers and sisters. It is not just *my* listening but *our* listening together for the Lord's word to the community. We listen to the Scriptures, we listen to the people, and we ask, "What are they saying to one another? What are they asking of one another?" And out of that dialogue between the Word of God in the Scriptures and the Word of God in the lives of his people, the Word of God in preaching begins to take shape.

[21]  Attentive listening to the Scriptures and to the people is, in essence, a form of prayer, perhaps the form of prayer most appropriate to the spirituality of the priest and preacher. There is nothing more essential than prayerful listening for effective preaching, a praying over the texts which seeks the light and fire of the Holy Spirit to kindle the *now* meaning in our hearts. A week of daily meditation on the readings of the following Sunday is not too much time to spend in preparation for the preaching we are called to do on the Lord's Day. Such regular preparation will allow us not only to savor the word in prayer but also to incorporate the experiences of a full week into our preparation.

[22]  Such extended, prayerful preparation is so important for preaching because it helps us reach the moment of inspiration, an inspiration that has affinities to poetic inspiration but is more. We ask for and expect the real movement of the Holy Spirit in us and in the assembly. If the words of Scripture are divinely inspired, as we believe them to be, then divine inspiration must be at work when those words are made alive and contemporary to the believing community in and through our ministry.

[23]  The preacher is thus called, above all, to be prayerful. The prayer we speak of is not prayer alongside of preparation for preaching, or over and above this preparation, but the very heart and center of the preparation itself. Unless the Word of God in the Scriptures is interiorized through prayerful study and reflection, it cannot possibly sustain the life-giving, love-generating words that preachers want to offer their people. Preachers then are called to a prayerful dwelling with their people and to a prayerful dwelling with the texts of Scripture knowing them and allowing themselves to be known by them.

[24]  This dwelling with the Scriptures and with the people which is the necessary prelude to effective preaching points to the necessity for certain pastoral skills and academic knowledge, both of which the modern seminary offers its candidates for priesthood, but which need continual updating and refining. We speak here of the skills of understanding and communicating with people, and of the knowledge required for the accurate and relevant interpretation of Scriptural texts.

[25]  Let us begin with the second requirement first, since that is somewhat easier to describe. The interpretation of texts is the science of hermeneutics, and in order to accomplish its end, hermeneutics relies first of all on exegesis. For exegesis to be done at the highest professional level, the exegete must have knowledge of the original languages, access to the tools of textual criticism, extensive historical and archeological background, a comprehensive knowledge of the development of biblical faith, and a familiarity with the history of the theological interpretation of texts in both the synagogue and the Christian churches. Obviously few preachers have the training or access to the resources for exegesis of this kind.

[26]  Exegesis for preaching need not always be done at the highest professional level. Our seminary training and our continuing education provide us with tools and resources to tap the best of contemporary exegesis in a fruitful way. Even a smattering of Hebrew and Greek is helpful in capturing the flavor or nuances of certain words. An acquaintance with the methods of scriptural scholarship enables us to understand, for example, why the sayings of Jesus can appear in such different contexts, and therefore with such different meanings, in the Gospels. Or again, knowing how the biblical author used a particular passage as a building block in a larger literary context can help us appreciate how the church of succeeding ages found it important to set the passage in contemporary contexts, a task which is ours in the liturgical celebration today.

[27]  It is hard to imagine that a person who has as his primary duty the proclamation of the Gospel to all would be without the basic tools and methods that help to ensure an accurate understanding of this Gospel. Surely every preacher ought to have a basic library to turn to in the preparation of homilies. A good Bible dictionary will help in picturing the background of a passage; a concordance will locate other passages that are related; a "theological" dictionary of Scripture will trace ideas that recur through Old and New Testaments; Gospel parallels will set similar texts that occur in more than one Gospel side by side. Standard commentaries on the major books of the Bible that appear in the lectionary should also be ready at hand, as well as exegetical commentaries based on the lectionary itself.

[28]  The texts of Scripture from which our preaching flows are not locked in antiquity. They are texts which have nourished the church's life throughout all its history, sustaining it in times of trial, calling it back to fidelity in times of weakness and opening up new possibilities when it seemed immobilized by the weight of human traditions.

[29]  The history of the interpretation of the Scriptures is part of the contemporary meaning of the Scriptures. The way they have been preached, the liturgical expressions they have generated, the prayer they have nourished, the magisterial statements they have inspired, the theological systems they have fostered, even the heresies they have occasioned, expand and deepen the way the Scriptures speak to us today.

[30]   It is the faith of the church that the preacher must proclaim, not merely his own. Consequently, the more familiar the preacher is with the history of scriptural interpretation and the development of the church's doctrine, the more capable he is of bringing that word into dialogue with the contemporary situation. Church doctrine is nourished by profound meditation upon the inspired Word, the exegesis of the fathers, conciliar documents and the teaching of the Magisterium. Therefore, the qualified preacher will lead his people to ever greater unity of faith among themselves as well as with prior generations of believers.

[31]   It is somewhat more difficult to speak of what is involved in the understanding of people and how the priest/preacher can prepare himself for this demand of his office. Surely part of the rationale of the requirement that students in theological seminaries have a background in the liberal arts, with an emphasis on philosophy, is that familiarity with the leading ideas, movements, and personalities of human civilization (or at least of Western civilization) will enable preachers to engage in a critical dialogue with contemporary culture, recognizing what is conformable with the Gospel, challenging that which is not. The great artistic and literary achievements of a culture are surely a privileged means of access to the heart and mind of a people.

[32]   Regular and sustained contact with the world's greatest literature or with its painting, sculpture, and musical achievements can rightfully be regarded by preachers not simply as a leisure-time activity but as part of their ongoing professional development. The same can be said of attention to modern entertainment media—television, film, radio—or to the theater. Dramatic presentations that deal sensitively with significant human issues can provide a wealth of material for our reflection and our preaching, both in its content and in its form.

[33]   If preachers are to know and understand their congregations today, some familiarity with popular forms of entertainment may also be necessary. We need not spend whole afternoons watching soap operas, memorizing baseball statistics, or listening to the latest hit albums. Yet if we are totally unaware, or give the impression that we are unaware of the activities and interests to which people devote a good deal of their leisure time, energy, and money, it will be difficult for us to make connections between their lives and the Gospel, or to call them to fuller, richer, and deeper levels of faith response.

[34]   Finally, preachers need to devote some time and energy to understanding the complex social, political, and economic forces that are shaping the contemporary world. Watching the evening news on television or scanning the headlines of the daily paper may be a beginning but it is not enough. Preachers need exposure to more serious and sustained commentary on the contemporary world, the kind of exposure that can be gained through a program of reading or through conversation with people who are professionally involved in such areas as business, politics, or medicine. Without this kind of informed understanding of the complex world we live in, preaching too easily degenerates into platitudes of faith, meaningless broadsides against the wickedness of the modern world, or into an uncritical affirmation of the wonderful advances that have taken place in modern times.

[35] To have a comprehensive knowledge of the social, political and economic forces shaping the contemporary world, while at the same time specializing in scriptural exegesis and theology and being pastorally competent may well appear to be an overwhelming, even impossible, expectation to lay on any one person. The point to be made here, however, is not that preachers must know everything, but rather that there is no limit to the sources of knowledge and insight that a preacher can draw upon. There are many avenues which lead toward a deeper understanding of the human condition. Some will travel more easily down the avenue of the social sciences, others down the avenue of literature and the arts, others down the avenue of popular culture. What ultimately matters is not which avenue we take, but what we take with us as we travel.

[36] As long as we carry the Word of God with us, a word that we have allowed to touch on our own lives in prayer and reflection, and as long as we speak that word in language and images that are familiar to the dwellers of the particular avenue we are traveling, the Word of God will be preached, and the possibility of faith and conversion will be present.

THE LIMITATIONS OF THE PREACHER

[37] It may be good to close this section with a word of caution. While preachers, like other people, cannot be expected to know everything, they are easily tempted to give the impression that they do. As one perceptive critic put it, preachers in their pulpits are people who speak ten feet above contradiction. The Word of God which we are called to proclaim is a divinely inspired Word, and therefore an authoritative and unfailing Word. But we who are limited and fallible possess no guarantee that our understanding of this Word—or of the human situation—is without error and therefore relevant and binding.

[38] Preachers accept their limitations not by making the pulpit a sounding board for their personal doubts, anxieties or problems, but by offering people a Word which has spoken to their lives and inviting these people to think and ponder on that Word so that it might speak to their lives as well. A recent poster says it well: "Jesus came to take away our sins, not our minds." What preachers may need to witness to more than anything else is the conviction that authentic, mature faith demands the hard struggle of thinking and choosing. What the Word of God offers us is a way to interpret our human lives, a way to face the ambiguities and challenges of the human condition, not a pat answer to every problem and question that comes along.

[39] Some years ago a survey was taken among a group of parishioners. They were asked what they hoped to experience during a sermon. When the results were in, the answer was clear. What the majority wanted was simply to hear a person of faith speaking. Ultimately, that's what preaching is all about, not lofty theological speculation, not painstaking biblical exegesis, not oratorical flamboyance. The preacher is a person speaking to people about faith and life.

# III. THE HOMILY

[40] The Sunday Eucharist is a privileged point of encounter between a local Christian community and its priest. Within this Eucharistic celebration the homily is a moment when this encounter can be especially intense and personal. We want now to look at the nature and function of this form of preaching, to relate it to the issues we have already raised in speaking of the assembly and the preacher, and finally to suggest a method for building and preaching the homily.

## THE HOMILY AND FAITH

[41]  Like all preaching, the homily is directed to faith. As Paul writes, "But how shall they call on him in whom they have not believed? And how can they believe unless they have heard of him? And how can they hear unless there is someone to preach?" (Romans 10:14). Some preaching is directed to people who have not heard the Gospel and is meant to lead them to an initial acceptance of Jesus Christ as Savior. Other forms of preaching are directed to a deeper understanding of the faith or to its ethical implications.

[42]  The homily is preaching of another kind. It may well include evangelization, catechesis, and exhortation, but its primary purpose is to be found in the fact that it is, in the words of the Second Vatican Council, "a part of the liturgy itself" (*Constitution on the Sacred Liturgy*, #52). The very meaning and function of the homily is determined by its relation to the liturgical action of which it is a part. It flows from the Scriptures which are read at that liturgical celebration, or, more broadly, from the Scriptures which undergird its prayers and actions, and it enables the congregation to participate in the celebration with faith.

[43]  The fact that the homily is addressed to a congregation of believers who have gathered to worship indicates that its purpose is not conversion from radical unbelief to belief. A homily presupposes faith. Nor does the homily primarily concern itself with a systematic theological understanding of the faith. The liturgical gathering is not primarily an educational assembly. Rather the homily is preached in order that a community of believers who have gathered to celebrate the liturgy may do so more deeply and more fully—more faithfully—and thus be formed for Christian witness in the world.[2]

## FAITH AS INTERPRETATION

[44]  To say that preaching, the homily included, is directed to faith is another way of saying that preaching is involved in the task of interpretation. "Faith" can be defined as a way of seeing or interpreting the world. The way we interpret the world, in turn, determines the way we relate to it. For example, if we believe that a particular race or class of people are our enemies, we will relate to them with suspicion and hostility. A friendly gesture will be interpreted not as a genuine sign of good will but as a ruse to get us to lower our guard. On the other hand, if we believe that a group of people are our friends, we will tend to excuse even a hostile gesture with the explanation that there must have been some mistake: they didn't recognize us or we have misinterpreted their gesture. Our "faith" in the way

things are has led us to live in the world in a way that corresponds to what we believe about it.

[45] The Christian interprets the world not as a hostile and evil place, but as a creation of a loving God who did not allow it to destroy itself, but sent his Son to rescue it. The Christian response to the world, then, is one of acceptance and affirmation—along with the recognition that it is still awaiting its full redemption.

[46] One of the most important, and most specifically human, ways in which faith is communicated to individuals and communities is through language. The way we speak about our world expresses the way we think about it and interpret it. One of the reasons we speak about our world at all is to share our vision of the world with others. The preacher is a Christian specially charged with sharing the Christian vision of the world as the creation of a loving God. Into this world human beings unleashed the powers of sin and death. These powers have been met, however, by God through his Son Jesus Christ, in whom he is at work not only to restore creation, but to transform it into a new heaven and a new earth.

FAITH LEADING TO A RESPONSE

[47] When one hears and accepts this vision of the world, this way of interpreting reality, a response is required. That response can take many forms. Sometimes it will be appropriate to call people to repentance for the way they have helped to spread the destructive powers of sin in the world. At other times the preacher will invite the congregation to devote themselves to some specific action as a way of sharing in the redemptive and creative word of God. However, the response that is most general and appropriate "at all times and in every place" is the response of praise and thanksgiving (Eucharist).

[48] When we accept the good news that the ultimate root and source of our being is not some faceless Prime Mover, not a merciless judge, but a prodigally loving Father who calls us to share in his love and to spread it to others, we sense that it is indeed right to give him thanks and praise.

Although we have received this good news, believed in it, and sealed our belief in the sacrament of baptism, we need to rediscover the truth of it again and again in our lives. Our faith grows weak, we are deceived by appearances, overwhelmed by suffering, plagued by doubt, anguished by the dreadful silence of God. And yet we gather for Eucharist, awaiting a word that will rekindle the spark of faith and enable us to recognize once again the presence of a loving God in our lives. We come to break bread in the hope that we will be able to do so with hearts burning. We come expecting to hear a Word from the Lord that will again help us to see the meaning of our lives in such a way that we will be able to say, with faith and conviction, "It is right to give him thanks and praise."

[49] The preacher then has a formidable task: to speak from the Scriptures (those inspired documents of our tradition that hand down to us the way the first believers interpreted the world) to a gathered congregation in such a way that those assembled will be able to worship God in spirit and truth, and then go forth

to love and serve the Lord. But while the task is formidable, it is not impossible, especially if one goes about it with purpose and method.

## THE HOMILY AND THE LECTIONARY

[50] The homily is not so much *on* the Scriptures as *from* and *through* them. In the Roman Catholic tradition, the selection of texts to be read at the Eucharistic liturgy is normally not left to the preacher, but is determined ahead of time and presented in the form of a lectionary. The basic purpose of a lectionary is twofold: to ensure that the Scripture texts appropriate to a feast or season are read at that time, and to provide for a comprehensive reading of the Scriptures. Thus, we find in the lectionary two principles guiding the selection of texts: the thematic principle (readings chosen to correspond to the "theme" of a feast or season), and the *lectio continua* principle (readings taken in order from a book of the Bible which is being read over a given period of time).

[51] In the section of the lectionary entitled "Masses for Various Occasions," we find the thematic principle at work in a way that corresponds more closely to what some liturgical planners refer to as the theme of a liturgy: e.g., readings appropriate for Christian unity, or for peace and justice. Such thematic liturgies have their place, as the lectionary title indicates, on various or special occasions, rather than at the regular Sunday liturgy.[3]

[52] It is to these given texts that the preacher turns to prepare the homily for a community that will gather for the Sunday liturgy. Since the purpose of the homily is to enable the gathered congregation to celebrate the liturgy with faith, the preacher does not so much attempt to explain the Scriptures as to interpret the human situation through the Scriptures. In other words, the goal of the liturgical preacher is not to interpret a text of the Bible (as would be the case in teaching a Scripture class) as much as to draw on the texts of the Bible as they are presented in the lectionary to interpret peoples' lives. To be even more precise, the preacher's purpose will be to turn to these Scriptures to interpret peoples' lives in such a way that they will be able to celebrate Eucharist—or be reconciled with God and one another, or be baptized into the Body of Christ, depending on the particular liturgy that is being celebrated.[4]

[53] To preach from the Scriptures in this way means that we have to "get behind them," as it were. We have to hear these texts as real words addressed to real people. Scholarly methods of interpreting Scripture can help us do this by putting us in touch with the life situations that originated these texts, or by making us more aware of the different ways language can function as a conveyer of meaning. But scholarly methods are not enough. As we emphasized in the second chapter, the preacher needs to listen to these texts meditatively and prayerfully.

[54] As preachers we go to the Scriptures saying, "What is the human situation to which these texts were originally addressed? To what human concerns and questions might these same texts have spoken through the Church's history? What is the human situation to which they can speak today? How can they help us to understand, to interpret our lives in such a way that we can turn to God with

praise and thanksgiving?" Only when we approach the Scriptures in this way do they have any possibility of becoming a living word for us and for others.

[55]   Such prayerful listening to the text demands time, not just the time of actual reading and praying and studying but, just as importantly, the time of standing back and letting the text dwell in our unconscious mind. This period of "incubation," as it is often called, is essential to all human creative effort. It is especially important for the homilist when reflecting upon texts which have become overly familiar, or which seem inappropriate for a given situation. With the use of a lectionary, the readings assigned for a particular day may seem to have little to say to a specific congregation at a specific time in its life. However, if the text and the actual human situation are allowed to interact with one another, a powerful interpretative word of faith will often emerge. But for this to happen we need to dwell with the text and allow it to dwell with us. Only then will the text reveal new meaning to us, a new and fresh way of interpreting and speaking about our world.[5]

## THE HOMILY, THE CONGREGATION, AND HOMILY SERVICES

[56]   If the homily must be faithful to the Scriptures for it to be the living Word of God, it must also be faithful to the congregation to whom this living Word of God is addressed. The homily will be effective in enabling a community to worship God with praise and thanksgiving only if individuals in that community recognize there a word that responds to the implicit or explicit questions of their lives.

[57]   There are many ways in which priests get to know their congregations and allow themselves to be known by them: involvement with parish organizations, individual and family counseling, social contacts, visits to the sick and the bereaved, planning for weddings and baptisms, the sacrament of reconciliation, and, equally as important, simply being with people as a friend and member of the community. The preacher will be able to draw on all these contacts when he turns to the Scriptures to seek there a Word from the Lord for the lives of his people.

[58]   This pastoral dimension of the homily is the principal reason why some homily services, especially those that do little more than provide ready-to-preach homilies, can actually be a hindrance to effective preaching. Since the homily is integrally related to the liturgy, and since liturgy presupposes a community that gathers to celebrate it, the homily is by definition related to a community. Homily services can be helpful in the interpretation of scriptural texts (though generally not as much as some basic exegetical resources) and give some ideas on how these texts can be related to contemporary human concerns. But they cannot provide individual preachers with specific indications of how these texts can be heard by the particular congregations to whom they will preach.

[59]   Homily services can provide valuable assistance to the preacher when they are concerned to relate the interpretation of the lectionary texts to the liturgical season in which they appear, and when they are attentive to the *lectio continua* principle of the lectionary. They may also be helpful in suggesting some possibilities for the development of a homily, or in providing suitable examples and illustrations. The primary help that a good homily service will offer is to make

available to the preacher recent exegetical work on the specific texts that appear in the lectionary and to indicate some ways in which this biblical word can be heard in the present as God's Word to his people. They can never replace the homilist's own prayer, study, and work.

## THE HOMILY AND THE LITURGY OF THE EUCHARIST

[60] A homily is not a talk given on the occasion of a liturgical celebration. It is "a part of the liturgy itself." In the Eucharistic celebration the homily points to the presence of God in people's lives and then leads a congregation into the Eucharist, providing, as it were, the motive for celebrating the Eucharist in this time and place.[6]

[61] This integral relation of the homily to the liturgy of the Eucharist which follows the liturgy of the word has implications for the way in which the homily is composed and delivered. In the first place, the homily should flow quite naturally out of the readings and into the liturgical action that follows. To set the homily apart by beginning or ending it with a sign of the cross[7], or by delivering it in a style that is totally different from the style used in the rest of the liturgy, might only reinforce the impression that the homily is simply a talk given on the occasion of a liturgical gathering, one that could just as well be given at another time and in another context.

[62] Although the preaching of the homily properly belongs to the presiding minister of the Eucharistic celebration, there may occasionally be times when it is fitting for someone else, priest or deacon, to preach. On these occasions the integral relation of the homily to the rest of the liturgy will be safeguarded if the preacher is present and actively involved in the whole of the liturgical celebration. The practice of having a preacher slip in to read the Gospel and preach the homily, and then slip out again, does not do justice to the liturgical integrity of the homily.

## HOMILETIC STYLE

[63] As regards the structure and style of the homily, we can take a lead from the use of the Greek word *homileo* in the New Testament.[8] While the etymology of the word suggests communicating with a crowd, its actual use in the New Testament implies a more personal and conversational form of address than that used by the classical Greek orator. The word is employed in reference to the conversation the two disciples engaged in on their way to Emmaus (Luke 24:14) and of the conversation Antonius Felix, Procurator of Judea, had with Paul when the latter was held prisoner in Caesarea (Acts 24:26). The New Testament usage suggests that a homily should sound more like a personal conversation, albeit a conversation on matters of utmost importance, than like a speech or a classroom lecture. What we should strive for is a style that is purposeful and personal, avoiding whatever sounds casual and chatty on the one extreme or impersonal and detached on the other.

[64] One of the ways we can move toward a more personal style of address in our homilies is by the way we structure them. Many homilies seem to fall into the same three-part pattern: "In today's readings . . . This reminds us . . . Therefore

let us . . ." The very structure of such homilies gives the impression that the preacher's principal purpose is to interpret scriptural texts rather than communicate with real people, and that he interprets these texts primarily to extract ethical demands to impose on a congregation. Such preachers may offer good advice, but they are rarely heard as preachers of good news, and this very fact tends to distance them from their listeners.

[65]   Another way of structuring the homily, and one that is more in keeping with its function of enabling people to celebrate the liturgy with deepened faith, is to begin with a description of a contemporary human situation which is evoked by the scriptural texts, rather than with an interpretation or reiteration of the text. After the human situation has been addressed, the homilist can turn to the Scriptures to interpret this situation, showing how the God described therein is also present and active in our lives today. The conclusion of the homily can then be an invitation to praise this God who wills to be lovingly and powerfully present in the lives of his people.[9]

[66]   The point of the preceding paragraph is not to substitute a new straight jacket for an old one. There is no one correct form for the homily. On occasion it may be a dramatic and engaging story, on another a well-reasoned exposition of a biblical theme showing its relevance to the contemporary situation, or the liturgical day, feast or season. It might also take the form of a dialogue between two preachers or involve the approved local use of visual or audio media. Ideally, the form and style will be determined by the form and style of the Scriptures from which it flows, by the character of the liturgy of which it is a part, and by the composition and expectations of the congregation to which it is addressed, and not exclusively by the preference of the preacher.

[67]   Whatever its form, the function of the Eucharistic homily is to enable people to lift up their hearts, to praise and thank the Lord for his presence in their lives. It will do this more effectively if the language it uses is specific, graphic, and imaginative. The more we can turn to the picture language of the poet and the storyteller, the more we will be able to preach in a way that invites people to respond from the heart as well as from the mind.

THE LIMITS AND POSSIBILITIES OF LITURGICAL PREACHING

[68]   But isn't all this too limited a view of preaching? Does it really respond to the needs of the people? Doesn't regular Sunday preaching have to take into account the ignorance of the Scriptures on the part of large numbers of Catholics, even those who participate regularly in the Sunday Eucharist, and deal in some systematic way with the fundamentals of the faith? Is there not a crying need for regular and sustained teaching about the moral imperatives that flow from an acceptance of the Good News? What about all those times when people's lives are shattered, when they simply are psychologically incapable of offering God praise and thanks, when it seems they have nothing to be thankful for? How do we speak to all the people in our congregations who have yet to hear the basic Gospel message calling them to faith and conversation, or who may even need a form of preaching that heightens their sensitivity to basic human realities and in this way readies them for the hearing of the Gospel?

[69]  In the last analysis the only proper response to these questions is a pastoral one. Priests will have to decide what form of preaching is most suitable for a particular congregation at a particular time. We would simply like to make two points here. First of all, social science research contends that the oral presentation of a single person is not a particularly effective way to impart new information or to bring about a change in attitude or behavior. It is, however, well suited to make explicit or to reinforce attitudes or knowledge previously held. The homily, therefore, which normally is an oral presentation by a single person, will be less effective as a means of instruction and/or exhortation than of interpretation—that is, as a means of enabling people to recognize the implications, in liturgy and in life, of the faith that is already theirs.

[70]  The second point to be made is that the liturgical homily, which draws on the Scriptures to interpret peoples' lives in such a way that they can recognize the saving presence of God and turn to him with praise and thanksgiving, does not exclude doctrinal instruction and moral exhortation. Such instruction and exhortation, however, are here situated in a broader context, namely, in the recognition of God's active presence in the lives of the people and the praise and thanksgiving that this response elicits.[10]

[71]  It may very well be that what God is doing in the life of a congregation at some particular moment is asking them to change in a way that is demanding and disorienting. The homily can be one way of helping to bring about that change, and it can still lead to a response of praise and thanksgiving by showing that our former way of life, comfortable as it may have been, was a way that led to death, while the new way, with all of its demands and difficulties, is a way that leads to life.

[72]  But even though the liturgical homily can incorporate instruction and exhortation, it will not be able to carry the whole weight of the Church's preaching. There will still need to be special times and occasions for preaching that addresses human values in such a way as to dispose the hearers to be open to the Gospel of Jesus Christ, preaching intended to bring the hearers to an inner conversion of heart, and preaching intended to instruct the faithful in matters of doctrine or morality. These three kinds of preaching—sometimes referred to as pre-evangelization, evangelization, and catechesis—can be found today in evangelistic gatherings, the adult catechumenate, youth ministry programs, spiritual renewal programs, Bible study groups and many forms of religious education.

[73]  The homily can complement all these forms of preaching by attending more specifically to what it is to accomplish. Such would be to show how and where the mystery of our faith, focused upon by that day's Scripture readings, is occurring in our lives. This would bring the hearers to a more explicit and deepened faith, to an expression of that faith in the liturgical celebration and, following the celebration, in their life and work.

[74]  But is it really possible to create this readiness for praise and thanksgiving in congregations as large and diverse as those in which many of us minister? In these congregations some people will be feeling a sense of loss because of a recent

bereavement; some facing marital difficulties; some having problems adjusting emotionally to school, job, home or community; some struggling with a deep sense of guilt stemming from their inability to deal maturely with their sexuality, or because of their addiction to drugs or alcohol. Others in our congregations will be struggling with the relevance of the Gospel to oppressive economic structures, to world peace, or to the many forms of discrimination in our society. Is it really possible to say to these people, "Look at the way in which God is present in your lives and turn to him with praise and thanksgiving?"

[75]   Obviously, it will not always be easy to do this. And we will never be able to do it, at least not with any honesty and integrity, if we have not recognized the active presence of God in our own lives, as broken and shattered as they may be, and out of that brokenness affirm that it is still good to praise him and even to give him thanks. We need to remember in situations like this that our celebration of the Eucharist is done in memory of Jesus Christ who, *on the night before he died*, turned to God and praised and thanked him out of the very depths of his distress. Praise and thanksgiving, therefore, do not automatically imply the presence of euphoria.

[76]   We can and must praise God even when we do not feel like it, for praise and thanksgiving are rooted in and grow out of faith, not feeling, a faith which interprets this world by saying that in spite of appearances often to the contrary, our God is a loving God. It is for this reason that even at the time of death, we celebrate a Eucharist, because we believe that for his faithful ones life is changed, not, as appearances would seem to indicate, taken away.

[77]   The challenge to preachers then is to reflect on human life with the aid of the Word of God and to show by their preaching, as by their lives, that in every place and at every time it is indeed right to praise and thank the Lord.

## IV. HOMILETIC METHOD

[78]   Every art is based on a theory and a method, and preaching is no exception. Some artists, it is true, work solely from inspiration. They do not know why or how they do what they do. Consequently, they are incapable of passing their insight on to others. But they have a method nonetheless, and if their work is lasting, their method will sooner or later be uncovered by interpreters and critics of their work.

[79]   Artists who are conscious of their method are in a much more advantageous position than those who are not. They are able to channel and direct their work more easily, can work more efficiently within time constraints, and can adapt their method to changed circumstances and demands. They know what they are doing and how they go about doing it, and they can pass this information on to others who might like to learn from them.

[80]   Ultimately, individual preachers will have to develop their own method for moving from the Scriptures to the homily, learning from their own successes and failures, as well as from other preachers through whose words they have heard the

Word of God. The description of a method for building the homily that follows is not intended as—nor could it possibly be—a foolproof system for producing outstanding homilies week after week. Rather it provides a model that includes the major components of the creative process (data gathering, incubation, insight, communication) and does so within the framework of a week.

[81] This method also respects the understanding of the homily that is central to this document: a scriptural interpretation of human existence which enables a community to recognize God's active presence, to respond to that presence in faith through liturgical word and gesture, and beyond the liturgical assembly, through a life lived in conformity with the Gospel.

[82] The most important feature of any method is precisely that it be methodical, that is, orderly and regular. In the preparation of the homily, as in other creative endeavors, the total amount of time we spend preparing may be less important than our observance of a regular pattern of activity spread out over a certain period of time. Doing the same thing each day for the same amount of time is often a condition for success, whether this be in study, in prayer, in writing, or in artistic achievement. A regular daily pattern of activity for the preparation of the Sunday homily is likewise often the key factor in effective preaching over the long term.

[83] Each of us called to the regular ministry of preaching needs to determine just what part of each day of the week is going to be devoted to the preparation of the Sunday homily. The time we spend each day need not be lengthy, but it needs to be determined ahead of time and be held sacred. Schedules, of course, are always to be adjusted for emergencies, but unless we determine in advance that a particular time is going to be used for a particular purpose, and stick to it, it is all too easy to have our entire day filled with appointments and meetings which we felt we could not turn down or postpone because "we had nothing special planned."

[84] One final preliminary remark. The method that follows describes a process that extends over a week's time. Some form of "remote preparation" is also in order. Such preparation could take the form of reading a recent work on the theology of the particular Synoptic Gospel that will be the "Gospel of the Year" or spending some time planning a unified sequence of homilies for a particular liturgical season.

[85] One of the reasons our preaching is less effective than it could be is that we have not taken seriously enough the *lectio continua* principle of our lectionary. We preach each Sunday's homily as if it had no connection with what preceded or what will follow. It should be possible, and indeed it would emphasize a sense of continuity and identity in the congregation, if from time to time our homilies would end on a "to be continued" note.

READING, LISTENING, PRAYING

[86] The preparation for a Sunday homily should begin early in the week whenever possible, even on Sunday evening. The first step is to read and reread the texts for the liturgy. Frequently the texts will be familiar, so it is important for us to do everything we can to make this reading as fresh as possible. Read the texts

aloud; read them in several versions; if we read and understand Greek or Hebrew, we might try to read them in the original. Even if our knowledge of these languages is minimal, we may find ourselves becoming aware of nuances and connections that can easily be missed if we rely entirely on translations.

[87]   At this point in the preparation process it is helpful, indeed almost essential, to read the texts in context—that is, to read them from the Bible rather than from the lectionary only. In reading and rereading the texts, continue to read all four of them (Gospel, Old Testament, Psalm, New Testament), even if a decision has been made about which text will become the focus of the homily. It is not necessary for a homily to tie together all the readings. Indeed, for the Sundays throughout the year, when the New Testament lesson is chosen without reference to the Old Testament or the Gospel, attempts to impose some kind of thematic unity can be quite artificial. Nonetheless, the reading of the texts side by side, even if they are unrelated to one another, can often prompt new and rich insights into the "now" meaning of the Scriptures.

[88]   Read the texts with pen in hand, jotting down any and all ideas. Keep in mind that what we are listening for is a Word from the Lord, a Word which can be heard as good news. We will be all the more disposed to hear and receive such a word if our reading is a prayerful, attentive listening to the text of the Scriptures. Try to read the text without asking "What does it mean?" Approach it humbly, dwell with it, and let it speak for itself.

STUDY AND FURTHER REFLECTION

[89]   One of the major temptations of students when they are assigned a paper is immediately to run to the "experts." The same temptation afflicts preachers. All too often our preparation for a homily consists of looking up the lessons, reading them over quickly, and then turning to a commentary or a homily service to find out what they mean and what we might be able to say about them. By so doing we block out the possibility of letting these texts speak to us and to the concerns we share with a congregation.

[90]   Another danger in going to the commentaries too early is that we program ourselves for preaching which, in content and style, is academic rather than existential. We look for information about the texts that we can pass on to our hearers. We think of the text as a container of a hidden meaning that we have to discover and pry loose with the appropriate tools, rather than as a word spoken directly to us by the Lord. This approach to the text leads to preaching that is a word about something rather than a word, God's Word, to someone.

[91]   The process of personal reflection and interpretation, therefore, should go on for a couple of days without the aid of commentaries. We are our own interpreters first of all, and then when we do turn to the professional exegetes, we do so for the purpose of checking out the accuracy of our own interpretation. We will frequently receive new insights and ideas from the professionals, and these will be helpful to us. If we have allowed the texts to speak to us directly, we will be much better prepared to speak a word that is expressive of our own faith and in touch

with the concerns of our people. We will also be able to better recognize and use the insights the professional exegetes give us.

## LETTING GO

[92] Sometime in the middle of the preparation process we should allow ourselves to step back from the work we are doing and give free reign to the subconscious processes of our minds. At times we will find that our preparation has brought us to a roadblock. A passage may make no sense to us. It may even scandalize us. We may want to ignore it, but it will not go away. The more we wrestle with it, the more troublesome it becomes. The words of Jesus about love for enemies fly in the face of our natural inclination for retribution; his words about selling possessions and giving them to the poor contradict our instinctive sense of the necessity for prudent stewardship. Paul's teaching that sin and death entered the world through one man seems to contradict everything we hold about individual, personal freedom and responsibility. We sense a real tension between the Word of God and the human situation.

[93] When this happens we have one of the best signs that we are on to something vital. The Word of God may in fact be challenging our faith, calling us to conversion, to a new vision of the world. This period can be a difficult one, for we can feel that we are being asked to give up a way of looking at and dealing with the world which has served us well and with which we have grown comfortable. At a time like this we need to let go in order to allow the Holy Spirit to work within us and lead us to a deeper and richer faith.

## DRAFTING

[94] A time for writing should be scheduled at least two days before the preaching of the homily in order to provide ample time for alterations. Knowing that there will be opportunity to rework the homily will do much to save us from writer's block. At this stage we need not be concerned with matters of style, or even with making sure that the homily is tightly reasoned and well constructed. The point is simply to begin getting ideas down on paper so that we will have something to work with.

[95] It is quite possible that we will come to this stage of preparation still not having any idea—any new and fresh idea, that is—of what we are going to say. We may simply feel empty and without inspiration. Begin writing anyway, for the very act of writing often unleashes a flow of ideas that will be new, fresh, and exciting. It is often at this point of initial writing that the difficult text suddenly opens up its meaning and provides a new, a richer understanding of how God is present in our lives. At this point, too, the two readings which had seemed so totally unrelated may suddenly come together and illuminate one another. When something like this happens (sometimes referred to as the moment of insight, or the "aha" experience), we may well have the central idea for our homily.

[96] So, at this point, simply write. Jot down words, phrases, unrelated sentences. Think of sketching the homily, or of working on an outline, rather than writing out a text. In fact, it is better not to put the ideas in too fixed a form at this point,

for we may find that it then becomes difficult to alter them. Don't stop to think of the best way to say something; don't go back and cross out words and phrases because they don't sound right. There is time for that later. Let the pen or the typewriter simply go, even though we are sure that we will not use anything we are putting down on paper. The very act of writing is a way of calling to the surface the ideas and the words that will in fact be the stuff of which our homilies are made.

REVISING

[97] The revising stage is one of the most important and the one that is too easily omitted for lack of time. To revise is frequently to cut: the good but extraneous material that surfaced in the jotting down stage of preparation; the technical theological terms and jargony "in" words that creep into our vocabularies; the use of the non-specific "this" or "it" at the beginning of sentences; the moralistic "therefore let us" or "we should" which we so easily resort to in winding up the homily; the references to "he" and "men" when the words are meant to include everyone; the vague generalities that can be replaced with specific incidents or examples.

[98] The time for revising is also the time to arrange the material in the order best suited to gain, and hold, people's attention and to invite them to a response of faith in God's Word. In the sketching stage a story may have occurred to us which exemplified perfectly the human situation being addressed by the Word of God. Bring that story up front. Use it as the opening so that people are able to identify with the situation right from the beginning. Beginning the homily with "in today's Gospel . . ." or words to that effect, risks losing the attention of the congregation right at the beginning for they will not have been given any indication of why they should be interested in what was said in today's Gospel.

[99] The time of revising is also the time to make sure that the homily does in fact have a central, unifying idea, and that this idea is clearly stated and repeated throughout the homily. We need not repeat the idea in the same words all the time, but we need to come back to it several times. People will inevitably drift in and out, no matter how good the preacher is. The restatement of the central idea is a way of inviting people back into the homily again if they happen to have been distracted from what we were saying.

[100] Finally, the time for revising is the time to make sure that the homily is fashioned not simply as a freestanding talk, but as an integral part of the liturgical action. Does the conclusion in any way lead people into the liturgy that follows? Have we spoken the Word of God in such a way that God has become more present in people's lives and they are enabled to be drawn more fully into the act of worship for which they have gathered? Remember that a homily is not a talk given on the occasion of a liturgical celebration, but an integral part of the liturgy. Just as a homily flows out of the Scriptures of the liturgy of the Word, so it should flow into the prayers and actions of the liturgy of the Eucharist which follows.

## PRACTICING

[101] After revising the homily, practice it. Repeat it several times to become familiar with what has to be said and how to say it. Practice it aloud and ask if that is really "me" speaking. Does it sound natural, or have I introduced words and phrases that sounded good when I jotted them down but are not suited to oral communication? It may be helpful to preach the homily to a friend or co-worker or to use an audio/video tape recorder. Can I say to that person without embarrassment what I intend to say to the congregation? Do I really believe what I am saying, or have I hidden behind some conventional expression of piety or theology that I would probably not use in any other situation?

## PREACHING

[102] Our emphasis on the importance of writing in the preparation of a homily does not in any way imply that homilies should normally be read. Writing is a means to arrive at good organization, clarity of expression, and concreteness. Whether or not we actually take a manuscript to the pulpit with us will depend on a number of things: the nature of the gathering (very formal or more informal); how familiar we are with our own material; how apprehensive we feel about forgetting something essential.

[103] Sometimes we know what we are going to say so well, and are so enthused about it that a manuscript would only get in the way or distract us. On the other hand, there may be times when we are sure that our message will be clearer and more forceful if we have the text with us. As long as we have something to say, as long as we are saying it, and as long as we establish and maintain rapport with the congregation, we may be able to preach quite effectively from a text.

[104] In general, it is much better to speak from notes or an outline—or without any written aids at all, for such a way of preaching enables us to enter more fully into direct, personal contact with a congregation. If we feel we must take the text with us, be familiar enough with the material so that instead of reading it, we can simply have it present as an aid to our memory.

[105] In preaching, as in all forms of communication, remember that it is the whole person who communicates. Facial expression, the tone of voice, the posture of the body are all powerful factors in determining whether a congregation will be receptive to what we have to say. If, as we preach, we remember that in carrying out this ministry we are showing our love, and God's, for the people, we will more easily avoid a delivery that sounds affected ("churchy") or impersonal.

## THE HOMILY PREPARATION GROUP

[106] An effective way for preachers to be sure that they are addressing some of the real concerns of the congregation in the homily is to involve members of that congregation in a homily preparation group. One way to begin such a group is for the preachers to invite four or five people they trust and can work with easily to join them for an hour at the beginning of the week. In a parish setting it is advisable to have one of the members drop out after four weeks and invite someone else to take his or her place. Similarly, a second will drop out after the

fifth week, so that after eight weeks or so they will be working with a new group of people.

[107] A homily preparation group can also be formed by gathering the priests in the rectory, the parish staff, priests from the area, priest and ministers, or a priests' support group. The presence of members of the congregation in a group is especially helpful in raising issues that are of concern to them and which the homily may be able to address. Groups that involve only clergy or parish staff members can also be a rich source of insight into the ways in which the Scriptures point to the continuing presence of God in human history.

[108] After the group has gathered and spent a few minutes quieting down, the following steps can be followed:

1. *Read the passages* (15 minutes). Begin with the Gospel, then the Old Testament, Psalm, and New Testament. As one of the participants reads the passages slowly, the others listen and jot down images, words or phrases that strike them.

2. *Share the words* (10 minutes). This is not a time for discussion but simply an opportunity for each person to share the words or phrases which resonated and fired the imagination. As this sharing is going on, the homilist may pick up some recurring words and phrases. He may be surprised to hear what parts of the Scriptures are being highlighted. These responses are already a sign of the concerns, questions and interests that are present in the lives of the congregation.

3. *Exegete the texts* (10 minutes). One of the members of the group presents a short exegesis of the texts. The task is not to bring to the discussion everything that could be said, but to make a special effort to determine what concrete human concerns the author was addressing when the text was written. What questions were there to which these words were at least a partial answer? When dealing with the Gospel passage, one way to answer this question is to show how other evangelists treated the same materials.

4. *Share the good news* (10 minutes). What good news did the first listeners hear in these accounts? What good news does the group hear? Where is God's promise, power and influence in our personal story present in the readings?

5. *Share the challenge these words offer us* (10 minutes). What is the doubt, the sin, the pain, the fracturing in our own lives which the passage touches? To what form of conversion do these words call us? In responding to these questions, the group may resort to generalities. By gentle persuasion and personal example the homilist can encourage the group to speak personally and with examples.

6. *Explore the consequences* (5 minutes). What difference can the good news make in my life? What happens if the scriptural good news is applied to contemporary bad news? Can my life be changed? Can the world be transformed if people believe in the good news and begin acting according to it? These are questions to which final answers cannot be given. They demand prayer and reflection.

7. *Give thanks and praise* (5 minutes). Conclude with a brief prayer of thanksgiving for God 's saving Word .

Working with a homily preparation group will help to ensure two things: that the homilist hears the proclamation of the good news in the Sunday Scripture readings as it is heard by the people in the congregation; and secondly, that the preacher is able to point in concrete and specific ways to the difference that the hearing of this good news can make in the lives of those who hear it. When the preacher spends time with the congregation, struggling with how the Word touches real life, the possibility of this homily striking a listener as "talking to me" increases. The Word of God then achieves that for which it was sent. Preacher and listener, responding together, are nourished by the Word of God and drawn to praise the God who has again given a sign of his presence and power.

## THE NON-NEGOTIABLES OF HOMILY PREPARATION

[109] As we mentioned at the beginning of this chapter, there is no one way to prepare a homily, nor does a particular method work the same way all the time for the same person. But no matter what the method, there are certain elements in the preparation of the homily which cannot be omitted if our preaching over the long term is going to be scripturally sound and pastorally relevant. We may be able to "wing it" on occasion, but to try to sustain a weekly ministry of preaching with little more than a glance at the lectionary and the quick consultation of a homily service is to attempt the impossible.

[110] Effective preaching—that is, preaching that enables people to hear the Word of God as good news for their lives and to respond accordingly—requires time and serious work. Unless we are willing to accept the drudgery that is a part of preaching, as it is of all creative work, we will not know the joy of having the Scriptures come alive for us, nor the profoundly satisfying experience of sharing that discovery with others.

[111] To conclude this chapter on homiletic method we would point to what we consider to be the non-negotiable elements of effective preaching:

1. *Time.* The amount of time will vary from preacher to preacher. However, the importance of the ministry of preaching demands that a significant amount of time be devoted to the homily each week, and ideally, that this time be spread out over the entire week.

2. *Prayer.* All preaching flows from faith to faith. It is only through prayer that faith is nourished.

3. *Study.* Without continuing study, stagnation sets in and preaching becomes insipid. Preachers have a professional responsibility to continue their education in the areas of Scripture, theology, and related disciplines. They might well make a book on preaching part of their regular reading program.

4. *Organization.* Much preaching suffers from lack of direction and the absence of a central, controlling idea. The writing and revising of homilies helps to ensure that there is a point to what we preach.

5. *Concreteness.* Another common fault of preachers is their tendency to speak in vague generalities or to use technical theological language. Once again, writing and revising helps to ensure that homilies are concrete and specific.

6. *Evaluation.* In public discourse we easily fall back on familiar ideas and set patterns of speech. More often than not, we are unaware of such tendencies and need the feedback of others to alert us to them.

## EPILOGUE: THE POWER OF THE WORD

[112] The pulpit of St. Stephen's Cathedral in Vienna displays an elaborate handrail in which are carved a detailed series of ugly, mythical creatures. The open mouths and oversized snouts of the beasts are there to remind the preacher of his inadequacies as he ascends the stairs. At the very top of the handrail, carved into the pillar that separates the stairs from the open, circular pulpit, stands a dog, jaws open, barking down at the ominous figures. The hellish beasts are not to enter the sacred place. The preacher has been enjoined to leave his sinful self behind as he prepares to speak God's Word.

[113] The medieval artisan has captured in stone the inner tension of all of us who dare to preach. We are aware that the words we speak are human words, formed through reflection both on the Scriptures and on our personal experience of the needs of our community. Looking into the faces of the people who sit before us, we see those who are holier, more intelligent, and more creative. And yet they wait for us to speak, to preach, to proclaim and witness to the presence of God among us. Our theology tells us that the words we speak are also God's Word. "What we utter is God's wisdom, a mysterious, a hidden wisdom" (1 Cor 2:7).

[114] We dare to utter that sacred Word because we once heard the voice of Mystery who spoke to Isaiah: "Whom shall I send? Who will go for us?" And we answered with Isaiah, "Here I am; send me" (Is 6:8). With Jeremiah we trust that the Lord will place his words in our mouths, despite our youth or age, our ignorance and our inadequacies (Jer 1:6–9). Even when we fall on our faces, the promise of Ezechiel is there, that a voice will speak to us and a spirit enter into us and set us again on our feet (Ezek 2:1–3). We believe that the Word we speak is the Word God intends to have an effect upon the world in which we live.

> For just as from the heavens the rain and snow come
> And do not return there till they have watered the earth, making it fertile and fruitful,
> Giving seed to him who sows and bread to him who eats,
> So shall my word be that goes forth from my mouth;
> It shall not return to me void, but shall do my will, achieving the end for which I sent it. (Is 55:10–11)

[115] We too stand in sacred space, aware of our personal inadequacy, yet willing to share how the scriptural story has become integrated into our thoughts and actions while we walked among those who turn their faces toward us. The words we speak are human words describing how God's action has become apparent to us this week. Is it any wonder then that excitement and tension fill us in the

moments before we preach? With a final deep breath may we also breathe in the Spirit of God who will animate our human words with divine power.

# APPENDIX

[116] This document on preaching has dealt mainly with what the individual preacher can do to improve the quality of the Sunday homily. In conclusion, we offer some recommendations for steps that can be taken on the national, diocesan, and parish levels to foster more effective preaching.

## NATIONAL

[117] 1. A doctoral program in homiletics to prepare teachers of preaching should be established with diocesan support, perhaps at the Catholic University of America.

2. Seminaries, especially at the theologate level, are urged to emphasize preaching as a priority (cf. *Program of Priestly Formation*, 3rd Edition, Chapter III, Art. 2, Homiletics).

## DIOCESAN

[118] 1. Programs to improve preaching skills should be established at the diocesan or regional level.

2. Programs for the study and deeper understanding of Scripture and preaching theology should also be established.

3. A Center for Preaching Resources should be founded in each diocese by the diocesan office for worship or continuing education, or by the seminary.

4. The Bishop(s) of the diocese should model the nature and purpose of the homily in preaching. They should not accept more preaching engagements per day than allow for preparation.

5. Criteria for the granting of faculties to preach should be clearly formulated and followed.

6. Continuing development of good preaching should be supported by the diocese through the granting of time and funding.

## PARISH

[119] 1. A resource center should be established within each parish to assist preachers and lectors in fulfilling their ministry.

2. Groups to help preachers prepare and evaluate their homilies should be formed.

3. When there are several preachers in a parish, their preparation for preaching should be coordinated.

4. Readers should be trained in the effective proclamation of Scripture and provided opportunities to grow in their understanding of it.

5. Job descriptions for priests should be evaluated in order to highlight the importance and provide adequate time for preparation of the ministry of preaching.

6. Some record should be kept of the themes of each Sunday's homily in order to bring the parish community into contact with the major facets of our faith each year, and to avoid undue emphasis on one truth at the expense of others.

[120] At all levels, national, diocesan and parish, bishops and priests are urged to invite religious and laity to read this document so as to assist, encourage and support priests in efforts toward a renewal of preaching in the church.

# NOTES

1. The material on "audience analysis" is voluminous. Access to the most up-to-date studies can be found by consulting the bibliographies of recent books on speech communication. Such materials frequently describe various methods for determining with some accuracy the interest and abilities of an audience.

2. While the homily is not the same as catechetical instruction, as Pope Paul VI makes clear in his apostolic exhortation *Evangelii nuntiandi* (nos. 43 and 44), the homily can certainly be a means of catechesis for Christian communities. The homilist who preaches from the scriptures as these are arranged in the lectionary over a three-year cycle of Sundays and feasts will certainly deal with all the major truths of the faith. It will still be necessary, however, to provide educational opportunities in and through which the faithful can reflect more deeply on the meaning of these truths and on their concrete contemporary implications for Christian life. In the early church such a systematic presentation of the truths of the faith was given to the newly baptized in the post-baptismal preaching known as mystagogy.

3. A fuller description of the principles guiding the choice of readings can be found in the introduction to the lectionary. These principles should be familiar to all preachers, for a knowledge of how and why passages of scripture are assigned to certain times and feasts provides an important key to the liturgical interpretation of those readings in preaching.

4. Cf. *Lectionary for Mass.* English translation of the Second *Editio-Typica* (1981) no. 24 prepared by International Commission on English in the Liturgy.

5. Ibid. no. 8–10.

6. Ibid. no. 24.

7. With regard to the sign of the cross before and after the homily, the Congregation for the Sacraments and Divine Worship gave the following official *responsum* in 1973:

   Query: Is it advisable to invite the faithful to bless themselves before or after the homily, to address a salutation to them, for example, "Praised be Jesus Christ"? Reply: It all depends on lawful local custom. But generally speaking it is inadvisable to continue such customs because they have their origin in preaching *outside Mass.* The homily is *part* of the liturgy; the people have already blessed themselves and received the greeting at the beginning of Mass. It is better, then, not to have a repetition before or after the homily. Source: *Notitiae 9* (1973) 178.

8. *Keryssein,* "To proclaim," is the word most frequently used for preaching in the New Testament. The word "presupposes that the preachers are heralds who announce simply that which they are commissioned to announce, not in their own name, but by the authority of the one who sends them" (John L. McKenzie, *Dictionary of the Bible,* p. 689). Although the practice of first-century Jewish synagogues may have included explanations and applications of the scriptures as part of the regular service, the New Testament itself does not use a specific technical word to describe the kind of preaching we refer to as a "homily," that is, the exposition of a text of scripture which takes place in and as a part of a liturgical celebration. The word *homileo* does appear in the New Testament, and its usage there can provide a way to understand a homiletic approach to preaching as distinguished from preaching addressed to unbelievers *(kerygma).*

9. The continuing ability of scripture texts to speak to situations that are temporally and culturally distinct from those to which they were originally addressed is one way in which the canonicity of the scriptures continues to be affirmed by the church. The canon is, in fact, composed of those writings which the church considers too important to forget because they address issues which are present in every generation, albeit in different garb and guises.

10. In the Apostolic Exhortation, *On Catechesis in Our Time,* 1979, #48, Pope John Paul II observes, "Respecting the specific

nature and proper cadence of this setting [i.e., liturgy, especially the eucharistic assembly], the homily takes up again the journey of faith put forward by catechesis and brings it to its natural fulfillment. At the same time it encourages the Lord's disciples to begin anew each day their spiritual journey in truth, adoration and thanksgiving. Accordingly, one can say that catechetical teaching, too, finds its source and fulfillment in the eucharist, within the whole circle of the liturgical year.

"Preaching, centered upon the Bible texts, must then in its own way make it possible to familiarize the faithful with the whole of the mysteries of the faith and the norms of Christian living. . . ." Cf. also: *Sharing the Light of Faith*, An Official Commentary on the National Catechetical Directory for Catholics of the United States, 1981, p. 54, Office of Publishing Services, USCC, Washington, D.C.

# AUTHORS

John M. Huels is associate professor of canon law at Catholic Theological Union in Chicago and Prior Provincial, eastern province of the Order of Servites.

Kathleen Hughes, RSCJ, is professor of liturgy at Catholic Theological Union in Chicago.

Mark R. Francis, CSV, is assistant professor of liturgy at Catholic Theological Union in Chicago.

Gerard S. Sloyan, a priest of the Trenton diocese, is visiting professor of theology at St. John's University in Collegeville, Minnesota.

Kevin W. Irwin, a priest of the New York archdiocese, is assistant professor in the department of theology at The Catholic University of America in Washington, D.C.

G. Thomas Ryan is parochial vicar and liturgist at Holy Cross Cathedral in Boston.

Catherine Dooley, OP, is associate professor in the department of religion and religious education at The Catholic University of America in Washington, D.C.

Edward Foley, Capuchin, is associate professor of liturgy and music at Catholic Theological Union in Chicago.

Andrew D. Ciferni, OPRAEM, is assistant professor of liturgy at Washington Theological Union in Silver Spring, Maryland.

Kathleen Cannon, OP, is associate provost at the University of Notre Dame and director of the University's Institute for Pastoral and Social Ministry.

# TOPICAL INDEX

## ABBREVIATIONS

| | |
|---|---|
| CB | Ceremonial of Bishops |
| CSL | Constitution on the Sacred Liturgy |
| DMC | Directory for Masses with Children |
| EAW | Environment and Art in Catholic Worship |
| FYH | Fulfilled in Your Hearing: The Homily in the Sunday Assembly |
| GI | General Instruction of the Roman Missal |
| GIapp | Appendix to the General Instruction for the Dioceses of the United States of America |
| GI Intro | General Instruction of the Roman Missal: Introduction |
| GNLY | General Norms for the Liturgical Year and the Calendar |
| HLS | This Holy and Living Sacrifice: Directory for the Celebration and Reception of Communion under Both Kinds |
| LMIn | Lectionary for Mass: Introduction |
| LMT | Liturgical Music Today |
| MCW | Music in Catholic Worship |

---

## ACCLAMATIONS
between readings, GI 89; LMIn 90–91
element of active participation, CSL 30; GI 14–16
eucharistic prayer, GI 55; MCW 47
in Masses with children, DMC 30
music, MCW 53–59; LMT 15–17

## ACOLYTE
functions at Mass, GI 65, 68, GI 142–147
genuine liturgical function, CSL 29
liturgy of bishops, CB 27–29
*see also* MINISTERS

## ACOUSTICS
EAW 51, 61, 73

## ADAPTATION
children, DMC 3
furnishings, CSL 128
liturgical year, CSL 107
modern conditions, GI Intro 10–15
music, CSL 119
norms, CSL 37–40
role of bishops, CSL 40; GI 6
*see also* CULTURES OF PEOPLES, CUSTOMS

## ADVENT
choice of texts, GI 314–316
description, GNLY 39–42; CB 235
readings, LMIn 93–94
vestment colors, GI 308

## ALB
GI 298–301; CB 65

## ALLELUIA
description, LMIn 23; MCW 55
when sung, GI 37–39; GIapp 36; GNLY 28; CB 371

## ALL SOULS
CB 395

## ALTAR
candles, GI 269
center of every eucharist, GI 49, 259
cloths, GI 49, 268–269; EAW 95
consecrated or blessed, GI 265
cross, GI 270; GIapp 270
decoration, EAW 103; CB 48
design and placement, CSL 128; GI 261–267; GIapp 263; EAW 71–73; CB 48
enclosure of relics, GI 266

facing people, GI 262
place of sacrifice and meal, GI 259
side altars, GI 267
symbol of the Lord, EAW 71
veneration, GI 27, 85, 125, 232;
 CB 72–73
vesture, EAW 95
visibility, EAW 61, 73

## ALTAR SERVERS
see ACOLYTE

## AMBO
design and placement, GI 272;
 LMIn 32–34; CB 51; EAW 74
vesture, EAW 95
visibility, EAW 61

## AMEN (GREAT)
MCW 58

## ANNOUNCEMENTS AT MASS
GI 123, 139; LMIn 27

## ANOINTING OF THE SICK
music, MCW 81
revision of rite, CSL 73–75

## APOSTLES' CREED
DMC 49

## ARCHITECT
EAW 44–47

## ART
and body language of liturgy, EAW 55–62
bishop's concern, CSL 124
commission for, CSL 46
contemporary, CSL 123; GI 254; EAW 33
demands of liturgy, EAW 20–24
different styles of expression, EAW 18
need for criteria, EAW 7–8
need for education, CSL 129; EAW 26
preeminence of music, CSL 112; EAW 6
sacred, CSL 122–127
serves the liturgy, EAW 25

## ARTISTS
bishop's concern, CSL 127
contribution to liturgy, CSL 127
gift, EAW 20
standards, CSL 122; GI 254

## ASH WEDNESDAY
GNLY 16, 28–29; CB 253

## ASSEMBLY
see LITURGICAL ASSEMBLY

## AUDIOVISUALS
potential for enhancing celebrations,
 EAW 106
recorded music, LMT 60–62

## BANNERS
EAW 98, 100
 see also ART

## BAPTISM
gives right and duty to participate in
 liturgy, CSL 14; GI 3
immersion, EAW 76
lenten theme, CB 249
music, MCW 80; LMT 8, 22–26
plunged into paschal mystery, CSL 6
revision of rites, CSL 64–70

## BAPTISTRY
CSL 128; CB 52; EAW 76–77

## BEAUTY
decorations, EAW 103
experience of mystery, EAW 12
of materials, EAW 67
quality of liturgical environment, EAW 34
symbolic role, CSL 122–128

## BELL
GI 109

## BENEFACTORS
EAW 46

## BIBLE
 see SCRIPTURE, WORD OF GOD

## BIBLE READINGS
 see READINGS

## BIBLE SERVICES
principles for celebration, LMIn 1–10
role in children's liturgical formation,
 DMC 13
when encouraged, CSL 35

## BISHOP
adaptations beyond the DMC, DMC 5
and diocesan liturgy, CSL 41–42; CB 1–17
character of episcopal liturgy, CB 1–17
directs all celebrations of eucharist, GI 59
foundation and sign of communion,
 CB 5–10
offices and ministries in episcopal liturgy,
 CB 18–41
pastoral visitation, CB 1177–1184
regulates concelebration, GI 155
regulation of liturgy, CSL 22
reverence, CB 76–83

## BLESSING
at conclusion of Mass, GI 57
of altars, GI 265
of people, GI 124
of sacred vessels, GI 296

BOW
body, GI 84, 234; CB 68
head, GI 234; CB 68

BREAD
consecrated at same celebration, GI 56
eucharistic symbol, EAW 87
experience of mystery, EAW 12
requirements, GI 281–286
*see also* COMMUNION, COMMUNION UNDER
  BOTH KINDS

BREAKING OF BREAD
meaning, GI 56
*see also* COMMUNION RITE, LAMB OF GOD

BURIAL OF DEAD
Masses, GI 335–341; GIapp 340
music, MCW 83; LMT 30–33
revision of rites, CSL 81–82

CALENDAR
and choice of texts, GI 313–325
and evening prayer, GNLY 61
date of Easter, CSL 131
description, GNLY 48–61
diocese, GNLY 51–55
need for unity, GNLY 56
parish, GNLY 59–61
particular, GNLY 48–55
Table of Liturgical Days, GNLY 59
*see also* LITURGICAL YEAR

CANDLES AND CANDLESTICKS
carried in entrance procession, GI 79
placement, GI 269; EAW 89–90
use in all liturgical services, GI 269

CANON
*see* EUCHARISTIC PRAYER

CANTOR
formation, LMIn 56
function, GI 36, 64, 90; MCW 35;
  LMT 68–69
qualities, GI 57
*see also* MINISTERS

CATECHESIS
children, DMC 8–15
first communion, DMC 12
Lent, CSL 109
liturgical, CSL 35

CATECHUMENATE
Lent, CB 249
restoration, CSL 64

CATHEDRA
CB 42, 47

CATHEDRAL
design and furnishings, CB 42–54
marriage, CB 598–620
role in diocesan liturgical life, CSL 41;
  CB 42–46

CELEBRANT
*see* PRIEST

CENSER
EAW 97

CHAIR FOR PRESIDER
cathedra, CB 42, 47
design, placement, meaning, GI 271;
  EAW 70

CHAIRS FOR ASSEMBLY
GI 273, EAW 68–70

CHALICE
on credence table, GI 80
preparation of gifts, GI 100, 103
qualities, EAW 97
use, EAW 96
*see also* VESSELS

CHANTS BETWEEN READINGS
GI 36–40; GIapp 36

CHASUBLE
GI 161, 299; CB 66

CHILDREN
and adults at Mass, DMC 16–19
art work, DMC 36
church's concern, DMC 1–7
liturgical formation, DMC 8–15
mentally and physically handicapped,
  DMC 6

CHOIR
children, DMC 22
development, CSL 14
function, CSL 29; GI 63; MCW 36;
  CB 39–41
funerals, LMT 32
placement, GI 274; EAW 83

CHRISM MASS
GNLY 31; CB 274

CHRIST
and nature of liturgy, CSL 5–7
prayer of, CSL 83–84
presence of, CSL 7; GI 7; HLS 11–16
priesthood of, CSL 7

CHRISTMAS SEASON
description, GNLY 32–38; CB 234
readings, LMIn 95–96
vestment colors, GI 308

CHURCH
activity, CSL 9–10
celebration of Mass is central, GI 1–5;
   HLS 1–7
celebration of paschal mystery, CSL 6
dignity of particular churches, CB 1–4
liturgy manifests, CSL 2, 41; CB 11–14
servant nature, EAW 39
subject of liturgical action, EAW 27–28
word of God, LMIn 7–10

CHURCH YEAR
see CALENDAR, LITURGICAL YEAR

CHURCHES
arrangement for Mass, GI 253–280
dedicated or blessed, GI 255
symbolism, GI 253

CHURCHES, BUILDING OF
diocesan commissions, GI 256
norms, CSL 124
renovations, GI 256; EAW 43
revision of statutes, CSL 128

CHURCHES, DESIGN OF
architect, EAW 44–48
assembly is primary demand, EAW 39–43
cathedral, CB 42–54
furnishings, GI 259–278, 287–312;
   EAW 63–83
general plan, GI 279–280
liturgical-artistic consultant, EAW 44–48
multifunctional, EAW 65
scale, EAW 52
teamwork, EAW 44–48
unity of space, EAW 53–54

CIBORIUM
material, GI 292
on credence table, GI 80
see also VESSELS

CIVIL AUTHORITIES
CSL 32

CLERGY
continuing education of, CSL 18
liturgical formation of, CSL 14–18
training in sacred art, CSL 129

COLLECT (OPENING PRAYER)
GI 32, 88

COLLECTION
GI 101
see also PROCESSIONS

COLLEGIATE CHAPTERS
CSL 95

COLORS
GI 307–310; EAW 93–95

COMMENTATORS
function, CSL 29; GI 68
liturgy of the word, LMIn 57

COMMUNION
at Masses of dead, GI 339
plates and cups, EAW 96
silence after, GI 23
song after, MCW 72
under one kind; minimizing of symbol,
   EAW 96
see also COMMUNION UNDER BOTH FORMS

COMMUNION ANTIPHON
GI 56, 119
see also COMMUNION SUNG

COMMUNION RITE
concelebration, GI 192–206
elements, GI 56
Mass with a congregation, GI 110–122
Mass without a congregation, GI 224–230
Masses with children, DMC 54
music, GI 56, 110, 113, 119, 121; GIapp 56;
   MCW 48, 62, 72; LMT 18

COMMUNION SONG
accompanies rite, GI 17; MCW 48; LMT 18
function, GI 56; MCW 62; LMT 18
seasonal, MCW 62
timing, GI 56
se also COMMUNION RITE

COMMUNION UNDER BOTH
   FORMS
instruction of faithful, GI 240–241;
   GIapp 240–242; HLS 28
in the hand, GIapp 240
ministers, HLS 24–26, 29–38
ministration of the cup, HLS 44–49
more complete form, GI 240;
   GIapp 240, 242; EAW 96
norms, HLS 27–54
option, HLS 48
preparation, GI 43; HLS 39–43
restoration, CSL 55; GI Intro 14;
   HLS 17–19
rite from chalice, GI 244–245
intinction, GI 145, 200, 243, 246–247
using a spoon, GI 251–252
using a tube, GI 248–250
when permitted, GI 242; GIapp 242;
   HLS 20–23; CB 274

COMMUNITY
and liturgical formation, DMC 11
aspect of mass, GI 14

COMPLINE
*see* LITURGY OF THE HOURS

COMPOSERS
create scriptural settings, LMT 26
develop sacred music, CSL 121; MCW 78
*see also* ARTISTS

CONCELEBRATION
bishop with priests, GI 59, 74, 157
communion rite, GI 192–206; HLS 30, 32
concluding rites, GI 207–208
conventual or community Mass, GI 76,
153–154
introductory rites, GI 161–163
liturgy of the eucharist, GI 166–206
new rite, CSL 58
number on same day, GI 158
occasions, CSL 57; GI 153–158; GIapp 153
preeminent expression of the church, GI 74
regulation, GI 154–155
sign of unity, CSL 57; GI 153, 157; GIapp 153
vestments, GI 161

CONCLUDING RITE
concelebration, GI 207–208
elements, GI 57
Mass with a congregation, GI 123–126
Mass without a congregation, GI 231
Masses with children, DMC 54
music, MCW 49

CONCLUSIONS TO PRAYERS
GI 32

CONCOURSE
CB 54; EAW 54

CONFERENCE OF BISHOPS,
ADAPTATIONS BY
altar, GI 263
calendar, GNLY 46
eucharistic celebrations, GI 6, 21, 56
furnishings, GI 288
liturgical books, CSL 39
marriage rites, CSL 77
Masses for various needs, GI 331; GIapp 331
Masses with children, DMC 5
music, CSL 120; GI 26
readings, GI 318, 325; LMIn 20
signs of reverence, GI 232
vernacular, CSL 36
vestments, GI 288, 304, 308

CONFESSION
*see* RECONCILIATION, SACRAMENT OF

CONFIRMATION
music, MCW 82; LMT 8
pastoral visitation, CB 1182
revision of rite, CSL 71

CONGREGATION
*see* LITURGICAL ASSEMBLY

CONSECRATION
of altars, GI 265
of churches, especially cathedral, GI 255
of sacred vessels, GI 296

CONSECRATION OF VIRGINS
CSL 80

CONVENTUAL MASS
GI 76

COPE
GI 303; CB 66

COPYRIGHT
MCW 78; LMT 71–72

CORPORAL
brought to altar, GI 100
on credence table, GI 80

CREDENCE TABLE
candlesticks, GI 84
preparations for Mass with congregation,
GI 80
washing sacred vessels, GI 120, 139, 238

CREED
*see* PROFESSION OF FAITH

CROSS
blessing, CB 1011–1022
entrance procession, GI 82
incensation, GI 236
location, GI 84, 270; EAW 88
multiplication, EAW 86
processional, EAW 88

CRUETS
GI 80; EAW 37

CULTURES OF PEOPLES
adaptation, CSL 37–40
and emphasis on reason, EAW 35
and personal-communal experience,
EAW 16
and tendency to minimize symbols,
EAW 85–87
different styles of artistic expression,
EAW 18, 101
identifying symbols, EAW 101
initiation elements, CSL 65
music, CSL 118–119; GI 19; LMT 54–55

CUSTOMS
popular devotions, CSL 13
rite of funerals, CSL 81
sacred furnishings, CSL 128

sacrifice, HLS 11–14
thanksgiving, CSL 6
*see also* MASS, LITURGICAL CELEBRATIONS

## EUCHARISTIC RESERVATION CHAPEL
*see* RESERVATION OF THE EUCHARIST

## EUCHARISTIC MINISTERS
HLS 24–26, 29–38

## EUCHARISTIC PRAYER
center and summit, GI 54
concelebration, GI 168–191
elements, GI 55
Mass with a congregation, GI 108–109
Mass without a congregation, GI 223
Masses with children, DMC 52
music, MCW 47, 53, 56–58; LMT 15, 17

## EVANGELIZATION
CSL 9

## EVENING PRAYER, EASTER
CB 371

## EXPERIMENTS, LITURGICAL
CSL 40

## EXTRAORDINARY MINISTERS
HLS 24–26, 29–38

## FAITH
expressed in celebration, MCW 4–9
music serves its expression, MCW 23–25
nourished, strengthened and manifested in eucharist, GI 5
tension, EAW 1

## FAMILY
DMC 10

## FAST
Ash Wednesday, GNLY 29
Good Friday, GNLY 20
Holy Saturday, GNLY 20
paschal, CSL 110; GNLY 20; CB 295

## FEASTS
general description, GNLY 8–15, 59–61
of Mary, CSL 103
of saints, CSL 108, 111
of the Lord, CSL 108
vigils, CSL 35

## FILMS
EAW 104–106

## FIRST COMMUNION, CATECHESIS FOR
DMC 12

## FLAGS
EAW 101

## FLOWERS
CB 48; EAW 102

## FONTS
design and placement, CSL 128; EAW 77
immersion, EAW 76
portable, EAW 77

## FOYER
CB 54; EAW 54

## FUNERAL
music, MCW 80, LMT 22–26, 30, 33
revision of rite, CSL 81–82
*see also* MASSES FOR THE DEAD

## FURNISHINGS, SACRED
adaptation, CSL 128
description, CSL 122–128; GI 253–280, 287–288; CB 42–54; EAW 63–83
design and care, CB 37–38; EAW 65
preservation, CSL 126
unity and harmony, EAW 67
use of all arts, GI 287
*see also* individual furnishings under their own headings

## GATHERING PLACE
CB 54; EAW 54

## GENERAL INTERCESSIONS
Mass with a congregation, GI 99
Mass without a congregation, GI 220
Masses with children, DMC 22, 29
meaning, GI 45; GIapp 45; LMIn 30–31
ministers, GI 47
music, LMIn 31; MCW 74
participation, GI 16
restoration, CSL 53–54
sequence, GI 46

## GENUFLECTION
GI 84, 233; CB 69–71

## GESTURES
bows and genuflections, GI 232–234; CB 68–70
concelebration, GI 169–191
contribute to unity of assembly, GI 62; EAW 56
foster participation, CSL 30
homily, FYH 105
Masses with children, DMC 33–34
position of hands, CB 104–109
signs of reverence, CB 68–83

## GIFTS
*see* PREPARATION OF THE GIFTS

**GLORY TO GOD**
  independent rite, GI 17
  Mass with a congregation, GI 87
  Mass without a congregation, GI 215
  Masses with children, DMC 31
  meaning and use, GI 31
  music, MCW 66

**GODPARENTS, DUTIES OF**
CSL 67

**GOOD FRIDAY**
  celebration of Passion, CB 312
  fast, GNLY 20

**GOSPEL BOOK**
  in entrance procession, GI 82, 128, 148
  location at beginning of Mass, GI 84,
    129, 149
  separate book, LMIn 36, 113
  venerated with kiss, GI 232

**GOSPEL READING**
  high point of liturgy of the word, LMIn 13
  incensation, GI 131, 235; CB 74
  Mass with a congregation, GI 93–95
  Mass without a congregation, GI 218
  Ordinary Time, LMIn 105, 109
  procession, GI 131; LMIn 17
  reverence, GI 35; LMIn 17; CB 74–75
  seasons, LMIn 93–102

**GRADUAL**
  *see* RESPONSORIAL PSALM

**GRADUALE ROMANUM**
GI 26, 36, 56

**GRADUALE SIMPLEX**
GI 26, 36, 56; LMT 60, 63

**GREAT AMEN**
MCW 58

**GREETINGS AT MASS**
  introductory rites, GI 28
  Mass with a congregation, GI 86
  Mass without a congregation, GI 1601, 1603

**GREGORIAN CHANT**
CSL 116–117

**HANDICAPPED PERSONS**
DMC 6; EAW 57

**HOLY DAYS**
  *see* CALENDAR, LITURGICAL YEAR

**HOLY, HOLY, HOLY**
  acclamation, GI 55
  concelebration, GI 168
  independent rite, GI 17
  Mass with a congregation, GI 108

Masses with children, DMC 31
music, MCW 56

**HOLY THURSDAY**
  chrism Mass, GNLY 31
  evening Mass of the Lord's Supper,
    GNLY 19, 28; CB 297

**HOLY WATER**
CB 110–114

**HOMILY**
  assembly, FYH 1–15, 56–59, 68–77
  concelebration, GI 165
  dialogue, DMC 48
  faith, FYH 41–49
  integral part of liturgy, CSL 52; GI 41;
    LMIn 24; FYH 40, 60–62, 100
  interpretation, FYH 25–36, 44–46
  lectionary, FYH 50–55
  limits and possibilities, FYH 68–77
  Masses for the dead, GI 338
  Masses with children, LMIn 24–25;
    DMC 17, 24, 47–48
  method of preparation, LMIn 24,
    FYH 78–111
  minister, GI 42, 60–61; LMIn 8, 41;
    DMC 24; FYH 62
  place, GI 97; LMIn 26
  preparation group, FYH 106–108
  presence of Christ, LMIn 24
  purpose, LMIn 24; FYH 40–49, 67, 81
  services, FYH 56–59
  silence after, LMIn 28
  sources, CSL 35; GI 41; LMIn 24;
    FYH 50–55
  steps to more effective preaching,
    FYH 116–120
  study, FYH 55, 89–91, 108, 111
  style, FYH 63–67
  when required, CSL 52; GI 42; LMIn 25
  *see also* LITURGY OF THE WORD, PREACHER

**HOSPITALITY**
EAW 11, 12, 24, 57

**HYMNS**
  in liturgy of the hours, CSL 93; LMT 45
  metrical, LMT 19

**IMAGES**
  art consultant, CSL 126, EAW 98
  criteria for use, CSL 125; GI 278;
    EAW 98–99
  number and placement, GI 278

**INCENSATION**
  experience of mystery, EAW 12
  general use, GI 235–236; CB 84–98
  altar, GI 85, 105

cross, GI 236
offerings, GI 105

## INCULTURATION
see ADAPTATION, CULTURES OF PEOPLES

## INFANT BAPTISM
music, MCW 80
revision of rite, CSL 67–69

## INFANTS
and Mass, DMC 16
baptism, CSL 67, 69
burial, CSL 82

## INITIATION
catechumens prepare during Lent,
GNLY 27; CB 249
music, MCW 80; LMT 22–26
revision of rites, CSL 64–71

## INSTITUTE OF PASTORAL LITURGY
CSL 44

## INSTITUTION NARRATIVE
GI 55

## INSTRUCTION
children, DMC 8–15
clergy, CSL 16, 18
faithful, CSL 14, 25

## INTERCESSIONS
see GENERAL INTERCESSIONS

## INTINCTION
see COMMUNION UNDER BOTH FORMS

## INTRODUCTORY RITES
character, MCW 44
concelebration, GI 161–163
elements, GI 24
Mass with a congregation, GI 82–88
Mass without a congregation, GI 212–216
Masses with children, DMC 40

## INTROIT ANTIPHON
recited when not sung, GI 26; GIapp 26
see also ENTRANCE SONG

## KISS
altar, GI 85, 125
gospel book and altar, GI 232; CB 72–74

## KNEELING
adoration, penitential rites, EAW 57
Eucharistic prayer, GI 21; GIapp 21

## KYRIE ELEISON
see LORD HAVE MERCY

## LAMB OF GOD
accompaniment to another ceremony,
GI 17, 56

concelebration, GI 195
litany, MCW 68, 74; LMT 20
Mass with a congregation, GI 56, 113
Mass without a congregation, GI 226
Masses with children, DMC 31

## LANDSCAPING
EAW 42

## LANGUAGE
homily, FYH 46, 67
music, LMT 49–53
see also VERNACULAR LANGUAGE

## LATIN
songs for international assemblies,
GI 19
see also VERNACULAR LANGUAGE

## LAUDS
see LITURGY OF THE HOURS

## LAVABO
GI 52, 106

## LAYPERSON
as reader, LMIn 51–55
extraordinary ministers of the eucharist,
HLS 24, 29–38
may speak to children after gospel,
DMC 24
may take functions below those reserved to
deacons, GI 70

## LEAFLETS
LMIn 37; EAW 91

## LECTERN
see AMBO

## LECTIONARY FOR MASS
adaptations and translations, LMIn 111–118
arrangement of the first reading on
weekdays of Ordinary Time,
LMIn Table III
arrangement of the second reading on
Sundays of Ordinary Time,
LMIn Table II
format, LMIn 119–125
options, LMIn 78–88
order of readings, LMIn 92–110
Ordinary Time, LMIn 103–110
pastoral aim, LMIn 58–63
principles used to draw up order,
LMIn 64–77
saints, LMIn 70
seasonal table of celebrations,
LMIn Table I
seasons, LMIn 92–102
Sundays and solemnities, LMIn 65–68
weekday, LMIn 65, 69

**LECTOR**
see READER

**LENT**
description, CSL 109–110; GNLY 27–31;
   CB 249
liturgical assemblies, CB 260
liturgical color, GI 308
readings, LMIn 97–98
sacrament of reconciliation, CB 253
see also ASH WEDNESDAY, BAPTISM,
   CATECHUMENATE, INITIATION, PASSION
   (PALM) SUNDAY

**LITANIES**
breaking of bread, LMT 20
more effective when sung, MCW 74
penitential rite, LMT 20

**LITTLE OFFICE**
CSL 98
   see also LITURGY OF THE HOURS

**LITURGICAL APOSTOLATE**
CSL 43–45

**LITURGICAL ARTISTIC CONSULTANT**
EAW 44–48

**LITURGICAL ASSEMBLY**
absence of priest, CSL 35
adults and children, DMC 16–55
diversity, MCW 15–20
is church, EAW 38
ministries, CSL 28; GI 58; CB 19
nature and circumstances to be
   considered, GI 3
norm for designing liturgical space,
   EAW 40–43
order and structure, GI 257
people of God, GI Intro 5
postures, GI 20–21
primary symbol, EAW 28–32
starting point for homily, FYH 1–15
see also PARTICIPATION

**LITURGICAL BOOKS**
cultural adaptation, CSL 38
for liturgy of the word, LMIn 35–37
for Mass, GI 79–80
held by assistant, EAW 92
qualities, treatment, EAW 91; CB 115–118
revision, CSL 25, 31
rubrics for assembly's parts, CSL 31

**LITURGICAL CELEBRATIONS**
actions of entire church, CSL 26, 41;
   EAW 28–32
biblical and ecclesial, EAW 10
bishop and, GIapp 59; CB 1–17

common elements, EAW 55
communal preferred, CSL 27
different functions in, EAW 37
formation of children, DMC 13
ministries, CSL 28; GI 58; LMIn 38–57;
   CB 19; DMC 24; HLS 29–38; MCW 33;
   LMT 63–70; EAW 37; FYH 16–39
music, CSL 112–113; MCW 23–41;
   LMT 6–15
nonrational elements, EAW 35
objects used, EAW 84–106
pedagogical force, DMC 2, 12–13
preeminence, CSL 7
requirements, EAW 9–26
scripture and, CSL 35
theology, MCW 1–9
whole person involved, EAW 5, 35

**LITURGICAL COMMISSIONS**
consultation on art and music, CSL 44, 46
diocesan, CSL 45; GI 256

**LITURGICAL LAW**
CSL 40, 128

**LITURGICAL LIFE**
diocese, CB 11–14
promotion, CSL 41–42

**LITURGICAL SPACE**
   see CHURCHES, DESIGN OF

**LITURGICAL YEAR**
adaptation, CSL 107
contemporary culture opposes, LMT 48
description, GNLY 1–2
in detail, GNLY 17–44
music and, LMT 46–48
Ordinary Time, GNLY 43–44
paschal mystery, CSL 106; GNLY 1, 17
purpose, CSL 102
revision, CSL 107–111
saints, CSL 111
seasons, CSL 107–110; GNLY 18–42
solemnities, feasts and memorials,
   GNLY 8–15
Sunday, CSL 106; GNLY 4–7
Table of Liturgical Days, GNLY 59
weekdays, GNLY 16
see also CALENDAR

**LITURGY**
action of the assembly, EAW 9
action of the whole person, EAW 5, 35
and private prayer, CSL 12
Christ's priesthood, CSL 7
communal nature, CSL 26–32
complexus of signs, LMT 60
didactic character, CSL 33–36
dignity and importance, CSL 5–13
foretaste of heavenly liturgy, CSL 8

formative quality, GNLY 1
hierarchical nature, CSL 26–32
immutable/mutable elements, CSL 21
inherently musical, CSL 112; LMT 5
instruction, CSL 14–19
paschal mystery, CSL 6
pastoral character, CSL 32–36
pedagogical force, DMC 2, 12–13
personal-communal experience,
　EAW 16–17
place in Christian life, EAW 32
promotion, CSL 14–20
radio and TV broadcasts, CSL 20
requirements, EAW 9–26
source of grace, CSL 7, 21
summit and fount, CSL 10
teaching character, CSL 33–36
words and rites, CSL 35

## LITURGY, REFORM OF
continuity with past, CSL 23
norms, CSL 21–40
principles, CSL 5–46

## LITURGY COMMITTEE
GI 73; MCW 10–14; EAW 44

## LITURGY OF THE EUCHARIST
and homily, FYH 60–62
concelebration, GI 166–206
corresponds to words and actions of Christ,
　GI 48
elements, GI 48–56
liturgy of the word and, CSL 56
Mass with a congregation, GI 100–122
Mass without a congregation, GI 221–230
Masses with children, DMC 52–54

## LITURGY OF THE HOURS
hymns, CSL 93
language, CSL 101
liturgical day, GNLY 3
mixing musical idioms, LMT 44–45
parish celebration, CSL 100
personal prayer and, CSL 90
place for celebration, EAW 64
prayer of Christ and church, CSL 83–85, 90
proper hours of day, CSL 88, 94
psalm-singing methods, LMT 34–43
revision, CSL 89–101
sanctification of time, CSL 84, 88
sung celebration preferred, CSL 99

## LITURGY OF THE WORD
books, LMIn 35–37
concelebration, GI 164–165
elements, GI 33, LMIn 11–31, MCW 45
general principles, LMIn 1–10
homily, FYH 40–77
Mass with a congregation, GI 89–99

Mass without a congregation, GI 217–220
Masses with children, DMC 17, 41–49
music, MCW 45, LMT 7
place, LMIn 32–34

## LITURGY PLANNING
GI 69, 73, 313; CB 34–34; DMC 29;
　MCW 10–14, 42; EAW 66

## LORD HAVE MERCY
Mass with a congregation, GI 30, 87
Mass without a congregation, GI 215
music, MCW 65; LMT 21

## LORD'S PRAYER
concelebration, GI 192
Mass with a congregation, GI 56, 110
Mass without a congregation, GI 224
meaning at Mass, GI 56
music, MCW 59, 67
participation, GI 16

## MARRIAGE
bishop, CB 598–620
diocesan music policy, LMT 28
music, MCW 82; LMT 28–29
outside Mass, CB 614–620
revision of rite, CSL 77–78
within Mass, CB 601–613

## MARTYRS
CSL 104; GNLY 8

## MARY
image of church, CSL 103
in liturgical year, GNLY 8, 15

## MASS
action of Christ and the church, GI 1–4
adaptation to modern conditions,
　GI Intro 10–15
arrangement and furnishings for
　celebration, GI 253–280
basic form of celebration, GI 82–126
center of Christian life, GI 1–5; HLS 1–7
communal celebration preferred, CSL 27;
　GI 74–78
concelebration, GI 153–208
conventual, GI 76
fruits, GI 2–4
general rules, GI 232–252
movements and postures, GI 20–22
office and function of the people of God,
　GI 62–64
offices and ministries of holy orders,
　GI 59–61
prayers, choice of, GI 321–323
preparation, GI 79–81
readings, choice of, GI 318–320
requisites for celebration GI 281–312
revision, CSL 47–57; GI Intro 1–9

sacrifice, HLS 11–14
singing, GI 19
special ministries, GI 65–73
texts, choice of, GI 313–325
*see also* MINISTERS, MUSIC, PARTICIPATION

## MASSES FOR THE DEAD
days permitted, GI 336–337
homily, GI 338
liturgical color, GI 308, GIapp 308
music, MCW 83; LMT 30–33
purpose, GI 335

## MASSES FOR VARIOUS NEEDS
days permitted, GI 330–334
liturgical color, GI 310
purpose, GI 326
readings, GI 327–328
types, GI 329

## MASSES WITH CHILDREN
and adults, DMC 24
frequency, DMC 27
gestures and actions, DMC 33–34
great number of children, DMC 28
music, DMC 30–32
offices and ministries, DMC 22–24
parts, DMC 38–54
place, DMC 25
preparation, DMC 29
role of priest, DMC 23
silence, DMC 37
time, DMC 26
visual elements, DMC 35–36

## MASTER OF CEREMONIES
CB 34–36

## MEMORIALS
GI 316, 333–334; GNLY 8–15

## MEMORIAL ACCLAMATION
MCW 53, 57; LMT 17

## MICROPHONE JACKS
EAW 51

## MINISTERS
chairs for, EAW 68–70
consultation in planning, GI 313
diversity should be represented,
   EAW 30, 37
each does only his/her own part, CSL 28;
   GI 58
imbued with spirit of liturgy, CSL 29
lay people may take ministerial roles, GI 70
liturgy of bishops, CB 18–41
one taking several parts, GI 72
several of same rank, GI 71
vesture, GI 297–303

## MISSALETTES
LMIn 37; EAW 91

## MISSIONS
and initiation rites, CSL 65, 68
and liturgy, CSL 38–40, 119
and music, CSL 119

## MUSIC
acclamations, MCW 53–59; LMT 17
adaptation, CSL 119
anointing of the sick, MCW 81
at Mass, MCW 50–74; LMT 16–21
burial rites, MCW 83; LMT 30–33
composers, CSL 121; MCW 50–51, 76–78
copyright, MCW 78; LMT 70–71
cultural heritage, LMT 54–55
diocesan commission, CSL 46
form of song, LMT 11
function of song, LMT 9–10
general principles, LMT 6–15
importance of singing, GI 19
initiation rites, MCW 80, 82; LMT 22–26
instrumental, LMT 56–59
integral part of liturgy, CSL 112
language and musical idioms, LMT 14–15
litanies, MCW 74; LMT 20–21
liturgical judgment, MCW 30–38
liturgical year, LMT 46–48
liturgy of the hours, LMT 34–45
Masses with children, DMC 30–32
ministry, LMT 63–70
musical judgment, MCW 26–29
ordinary chants, MCW 64–69
pastoral judgment, MCW 39–41
pastoral planning, MCW 10–21; LMT 12
penance services, MCW 81; LMT 27
place in liturgical celebration, MCW 23–41
place of song, LMT 8
preeminent art form, CSL 112; EAW 6
processional songs, MCW 60–62;
   LMT 18–19
progressive solemnity, LMT 13
purpose, CSL 112–114
recorded, LMT 60–62
religious music of the people, CSL 118
sacredness, CSL 112
styles approved, CSL 116; LMT 49–53
supplementary songs, MCW 70–74
training in seminaries, CSL 115
union with rite, CSL 112
weddings, MCW 82; LMT 28–29

## MUSICAL INSTRUMENTS
Masses with children, DMC 32
pipe organ and others, CSL 120; GI 275;
   GIapp 275; LMT 56–59
placement, GI 275; MCW 38; EAW 83

## MUSICIANS

challenges, MCW 76
composers, CSL 121; MCW 50–51, 70–78
instrumentalists, EAW 83; MCW 37–38;
    CB 39–41
salary, MCW 77; LMT 65
training, LMT 63–70
*see also* CANTOR, CHOIR

## MYSTERY

experience of, EAW 12
liturgy's climate, CSL 115; LMT 65; EAW 34

## NICENE CREED

Apostles' Creed may be substituted,
    DMC 49
slowly introduced to children, DMC 39

## OFFERTORY

*see* PREPARATION OF GIFTS

## OFFERTORY SONG

accompanies rite, GI 17; MCW 71
functions, MCW 71
metrical hymn may not be appropriate,
    LMT 19
omitted if not sung, GI 50
time, GI 100

## OFFICE, DIVINE

*see* LITURGY OF THE HOURS

## OPENING PRAYER (COLLECT)

GI 32, 88, 216

## ORATIONS

*see* PRESIDENTIAL PRAYERS

## ORDER OF READINGS

*see* LECTIONARY FOR MASS

## ORDERS, HOLY

offices and ministries in Mass, GI 59–61;
    LMIn 41; DMC 23–24
revision of ordination rites, CSL 76

## ORDINARY CHANTS

MCW 64–69

## ORDINARY TIME

GNLY 43 -44; CB 377–380

## ORGAN

placement, GI 275; GIapp 275; MCW 38;
    EAW 83
role, MCW 37
traditional instrument, CSL 120

## OUR FATHER

*see* LORD'S PRAYER

## PALL

GI 80

## PALM SUNDAY

GNLY 30–31; CB 263

## PAMPHLETS

EAW 91

## PARENTS

role in infant baptism, CSL 67
role in liturgical formation, DMC 10

## PARISH

and liturgical formation, DMC 11
liturgical life, CSL 42; EAW 9–10
proper calendar, GNLY 59–61

## PARTICIPATION

act of whole person, EAW 4–5
aim of liturgical reform, CSL 14
and word of God, LMIn 6
arrangement of churches should facilitate,
    GI 253, 257, 273; EAW 39–54
children, DMC 8, 55
communion, CSL 55
communion under both kinds, HLS 17–19
eucharistic celebrations, CSL 48; GI 1–6
liturgy with bishop presiding should be
    example, CB 11–14
manifests church, CSL 41; CB 11–14
means of achieving, CSL 30
promotion, CSL 14–20
qualities, CSL 11
right and duty, GI 3
specific expressions at Mass, GI 15–16,
    20, 101
singing, CSL 114; GI 19

## PASCHAL MYSTERY

CSL 5–9, 106; GNLY 1, 4, 18–21; LMT 46

## PASSION (PALM) SUNDAY

GNLY 30–31; CB 263

## PASTORS

congregational singing, CSL 114
ensure active participation, CSL 11, 19
imbued with spirit of the liturgy, CSL 14
liturgical catechesis, CSL 56
parish celebration of liturgy of the
    hours, CSL 100
planning of funerals, GI 341
represents bishop, CSL 42

## PATEN

on credence table, GI 80
same one used for celebrant and
    faithful, GI 293
*see also* VESSELS

## PENANCE

CSL 110
*see also* RECONCILIATION, SACRAMENT OF

PURIFICATIONS
GI 237–239

PURIFICATOR
brought to altar, GI 100
ministration of the cup, HLS 47
on credence table, GI 180

RADIO
CSL 20

READER
CSL 29
function, GI 34, 66, 148–152; LMIn 49–55
liturgy of bishops, CB 30–32
preparation, LMIn 55
speaking style, LMIn 14
women, GI 66, 89, 91
*see also* MINISTERS

READINGS FOR MASS
*see* LECTIONARY FOR MASS

RECESSIONAL SONG
MCW 49, 73

RECONCILIATION CHAPEL
EAW 81

RECONCILIATION,
SACRAMENT OF
chapel, EAW 81
Lent, CB 253
music, MCW 81; LMT 27
revision of rite, CSL 72

RELICS
CSL 111; GI 266

RELIGIOUS EDUCATION
OF CHILDREN
DMC 8–15

RELIGIOUS PROFESSION
CSL 80

RENEWAL OF VOWS
CSL 80

RESERVATION OF THE
EUCHARIST
separate chapel, GI 276–277; CB 49;
EAW 78–79
tabernacle, GI 277; EAW 80

RESPONSORIAL PSALM
choice, LMIn 89
independent rite, GI 17
integral part of liturgy of the word, GI 36;
GIapp 36
Masses with children, DMC 46
music, MCW 63
response to first reading, MCW 63

should be sung, LMIn 20–22
significance, LMIn 19

RETARDED PERSONS
DMC 6

RITES
equality and dignity, CSL 3–4
need for revision, CSL 21, 62
simplification, CSL 34, 50

RITUAL MASSES
choice of readings, GI 320; LMIn 8
Christian initiation, CSL 67
color of vestments, GI 310
days prohibited, GI 330, 334
meaning, GI 329
readings, LMIn 72

ROGATION DAYS
GNLY 45–47

ROMAN RITE
CSL 3

ROMAN RITUAL
CSL 63

SACRAMENTALS
nature and purpose, CSL 60–63
review, CSL 79
*see also* LITURGICAL CELEBRATIONS

SACRAMENTARY
near priest's chair, GI 80
taken to altar, GI 100

SACRAMENTS
communal celebration preferred, CSL 27
design of liturgical space should
accommodate celebration, EAW 64
music, MCW 79–83; LMT 22–33
other than the eucharist, CSL 59–78
paschal mystery, GI 326
presence of Christ, CSL 7
purpose, CSL 59
vernacular, CSL 36, 63
*see also* individual sacraments under their
own headings

SACRISTAN
CB 37–38

SACRISTY
location, EAW 82; CB 53
preparations for Mass with congregation,
GI 81

SAINTS
and calendar, GNLY 49–61
feasts and date of death, GNLY 56
solemnities, feasts and memorials,
GNLY 8–15

Table of Liturgical Days, GNLY 59
veneration, CSL 8, 111

## SANCTUARY
GI 258; CB 50

## SCHOLA CANTORUM
director also leads people, GI 64
function, GI 63
location, GI 274
see also CANTOR, CHOIR, MUSICIANS

## SCRIPTURE READINGS
see LECTIONARY FOR MASS

## SCRIPTURE
and homily, CSL 35, 53; FYH 50–55
increased use, CSL 35, 51
Masses with children, DMC 43–46
presence of Christ, CSL 7
primacy in liturgy, CSL 24; LMIn 1–10
professors, CSL 16
study, CSL 90
see also HOMILY, LECTIONARY FOR MASS,
LITURGY OF THE WORD, WORD OF GOD

## SEATING ARRANGEMENTS
GI 271; CB 47; EAW 59, 68–70

## SEMINARIES
and sacred art, CSL 129
and sacred music, CSL 115
liturgy, CSL 15–17

## SEQUENCES
GI 40

## SERMON
see HOMILY

## SERVERS
CSL 29; GI 209–231
see ACOLYTE, MINISTERS

## SIGN OF PEACE
concelebration, GI 194
liturgy of bishops, CB 99–103
Mass with a congregation, GI 56, 112;
GIapp 56
Mass without a congregation, GI 225

## SIGNS, SACRAMENTAL
duplication, EAW 86
faithful's understanding, CSL 59
liturgy, CSL 7; GI 5; MCW 4–9
see also SYMBOLS

## SILENCE
after communion, GI 56, 121
after readings, GI 23
and music, LMT 59
form of participation, CSL 30

Masses with children, DMC 37
meaning, times, GI 23

## SINGERS
CSL 29, 114–115

## SINGING
active participation, CSL 30
appropriate texts, CSL 121
celebrant should sing, MCW 22
enhancement of rites, CSL 113
importance, GI 19; GIapp 119
Latin, GI 19
Masses with children, DMC 30–32
purpose, GI 19
recommended on Sundays, GI 77
see also MUSIC

## SITTING
GI 21; EAW 57

## SOLEMN BLESSING
see BLESSING

## SOLEMNITY
description, GI 314; GNLY 8–15
Table of Liturgical Days, GNLY 59

## SONG
form, LMT 11
function, LMT 9
place, LMT 8
processional, MCW 60–62
supplementary, MCW 70–74

## SONG AFTER COMMUNION
MCW 72

## SONG BOOK
placed near priest's chair, GI 80
words approved by conference of bishops,
GI 26

## SPONSORS
CSL 67

## STAINED GLASS
EAW 105

## STANDING
GI 21; EAW 52

## STATUES
CSL 125; GI 278; EAW 98–99

## SUNDAY
civil calendar, CSL 131
first holy day, CSL 106; GNLY 4
nucleus of yearly cycle, CB 228
precedence, CSL 106; GNLY 5
solemnities and feasts of the Lord,
GNLY 6–7
weekly Easter, GNLY 1, 4

## SUNDAY MASS
choice of Mass, GI 315
general intercessions, CSL 53
homily obligatory, CSL 52
obligation, CSL 106
parish Mass, CSL 42; GI 75
participation, CSL 49
pastors, CSL 56
singing, GI 77

## SUPPLEMENTARY SONGS
MCW 70–74

## SYMBOLS
do not capture God, EAW 12–13
duplicated and minimized, EAW 85–89
making up for weak primary, EAW 87
multiplication and diminution,
  EAW 86, 94
must be understood by assembly, CSL 59;
  GI 5; MCW 7–8
opening up of, EAW 15
simplifying and refocusing, EAW 99
see also SACRAMENTS; SACRAMENTALS;
  SIGNS, SACRAMENTAL

## TABERNACLE
CSL 128; EAW 79; CB 49
see also RESERVATION OF EUCHARIST

## TELEVISION
CSL 20

## TRIDUUM
see EASTER TRIDUUM

## USHERS
GI 49, 68

## VERNACULAR LANGUAGE
adaptation to modern conditions,
  GI Intro 13
authorization, CSL 36
lectionary, LMIn 111, 117
liturgy of the hours, CSL 101
Mass, CSL 54
Masses with children, DMC 31
sacraments and sacramentals, CSL 63

## VESPERS
see LITURGY OF THE HOURS

## VESSELS
blessing and consecration, GI 296
dignity, GI 289
materials, GI 290–292, 294; HLS 40–41;
  EAW 97
number and design, GI 295; HLS 40–42;
  EAW 96
one paten for celebrant and faithful, GI 293

## VESTMENTS
alb, GI 298, 301; CB 65
altar and ambo, EAW 95
chasuble, GI 161, 299; CB 66
cope, GI 303; CB 66
dalmatic, GI 300; CB 67
design, CSL 128; GI 304–307; CB 37–38;
  EAW 93–94
liturgical color, GI 307–310; GIapp 308
materials, CSL 128; GI 305; GIapp 305
meaning, GI 297, EAW 93
stole, GI 303
vesting room, CB 53

## VIATICUM
CSL 74

## VIGILS
CSL 35

## VIRGINS, CONSECRATION OF
CSL 80

## VISIBILITY
altar, EAW 73
eye contact, EAW 58
quality, visual flow, EAW 50
requirements, EAW 49, 61

## VISUAL ELEMENTS
DMC 35–36

## VOTIVE MASSES
GI 326–334

## WEDDING
see MARRIAGE

## WEEKDAYS
GNLY 16

## WINE
eucharistic symbol, EAW 87
experience of mystery, EAW 12
not reserved, except for ill, HLS 37, 39
qualities, GI 284
see also COMMUNION, COMMUNION UNDER
  BOTH KINDS

## WOMEN
reader, GI 66
roles in liturgy, GIapp 66
services outside sanctuary, GI 70

## WORD OF GOD
and active participation, LMIn 6
and Holy Spirit, LMIn 9
and plan of salvation, LMIn 5
and the eucharist, LMIn 10
character in liturgical celebration, LMIn 4
church's life, LMIn 7–8

importance in liturgical celebration,
    LMIn 1
principles for liturgical celebration,
    LMIn 1–10
significance in liturgical celebration,
    LMIN 3
*see also* HOMILY, LECTIONARY, LITURGY OF
    THE WORD, SCRIPTURE

# YEAR, LITURGICAL
*see* LITURGICAL YEAR, CALENDAR

# For Further Insight into the Practice of the Liturgy

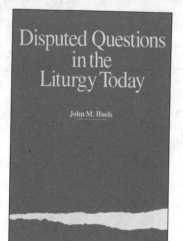

## Disputed Questions in the Liturgy Today
by **John M. Huels**, OSM

A highly readable book that looks at how liturgy and the law come together in the discipline and practice of the church. Includes topics such as lay preaching, Mass intentions, concerts in churches and reducing the number of Sunday Masses. 6 x 9, 125 pages. ISBN 0-930467-95-7.

Order code: DQ **$6.95**

## More Disputed Questions in the Liturgy
by **John M. Huels**, OSM

Huels' second volume tackles issues of contemporary relevance: the reception of sacraments by divorced and remarried Catholics, unauthorized liturgical adapatation, eucharistic reservation, sacramental sharing among Christians and much more. 6 x 9, 200 pages. ISBN 1-56854-171-6.

Order code: MOREDQ **$10**

Servite Father John Huels teaches canon law at Catholic Theological Union in Chicago and in the graduate summer liturgy program at the University of Notre Dame. A specialist in liturgical law, he has written numerous articles, reviews and canonical opinions, as well as eight books.

ORDER FROM YOUR BOOKSTORE OR FROM:

 LITURGY TRAINING PUBLICATIONS
1800 North Hermitage Avenue
Chicago IL 60622-1101

| Phone | 1-800-933-1800 | Fax | 1-800-933-7094 | E-Mail | orders@ltp.org |